MODERN HOUSING

MODERN HOUSING

CATHERINE BAUER

Foreword by Barbara Penner

University of Minnesota Press
Minneapolis
London

Published by the University of Minnesota Press
111 Third Avenue South, Suite 290
Minneapolis, MN 55401-2520
http://www.upress.umn.edu

ISBN 978-1-5179-0906-2
A Cataloging-in-Publication record for this book is available from the Library of Congress.

Printed in the United States of America on acid-free paper

25 24 23 22 21 20 10 9 8 7 6 5 4 3 2 1

CONTENTS

PART FOUR. ELEMENTS OF MODERN HOUSING

APPENDIX TO PART THREE:
NATIONAL HOUSING MEASURES, 1850–1934

FOREWORD

HOUSING IS MORE THAN HOUSES

Barbara Penner

Modern Housing should need no introduction. Nor should its author, Catherine Bauer. Published in 1934, Bauer's *Modern Housing* has been widely acknowledged as one of the most important books on housing of the twentieth century, laying out the recent developments in European modernist housing for an American audience. Bauer would become one of the leading "housers" in the United States, lucidly and passionately arguing for the provision of high-quality planned public housing between the 1930s and 1960s. No one would make the case for housing more powerfully than she did, most memorably in this book.

Yet the reputation of both book and author seems to have faded. One likely reason is that Bauer had many careers, from writer to union activist to public servant to academic, producing a diverse body of work that is not easily accessible or digestible today.[1] She died relatively young, at the age of 59, when many authors still have a few grand projects ahead. Indeed, although written early in her professional life, *Modern Housing* is Bauer's only major book, and, for all its impact, copies are not easy to come by. Perhaps this is why the book is often cited as a milestone in surveys of modern architecture and planning but discussed cursorily, if at all.[2]

Consequently, this book is one we think we know, yet, on reading it, we discover much that is unexpected. *Modern Housing*'s very style is a surprise: from its avant-garde design to its bracing prose, it is a true expression of its time and place. The book emerged from the maelstrom of New York City, where the inequities wrought by the forces of modernization were impossible to ignore, surging skyscrapers throwing airless tenements

Original cover for Catherine Bauer, *Modern Housing*, 1934.

into sharp relief. By 1933, however, the Great Depression had stalled the city's phenomenal growth. Fifteen million Americans were out of work, foreclosure rates soared, and housing starts bottomed. A severe housing shortage loomed. This crisis gave *Modern Housing* its intensity and momentum.

For Bauer, along with other radicals of the day, this crisis represented a once-in-a-lifetime opportunity to correct the worst excesses of capitalism. As Bauer was writing, the government was rolling out a series of emergency housing measures yet still had no comprehensive national housing policy. The election of Franklin D. Roosevelt in 1933 made some kind of permanent policy seem likely, but the form it would take was unknown.[3] *Modern Housing* was infused with the conviction that any future legislation had to be extensive and bold: in reshaping American housing, basic tenets of the existing economic and social order would be reshaped as well. Bauer declared, "Housing is a Major Operation–or Nothing."[4]

"An Aesthete to a Housing Reformer"

What might be surprising to contemporary readers is that Bauer felt she was the person to write this audacious call to

Catherine Bauer, 1930. Lewis Mumford Papers, Kislak Center for Special Collections, Rare Books and Manuscripts, University of Pennsylvania, MS Collection 2, Box 197.

arms. Born in New Jersey in 1905, she had a conventional middle-class upbringing; her father, Jacob, was an innovative highway engineer best known for first deploying the cloverleaf interchange. Bauer had some qualifications: she had taken a year of architecture at Cornell University and received a degree in the arts from Vassar College; she had lived for a stretch in Paris and moved in avant-garde circles there (once dancing the Charleston with Adolf Loos); and she had published several well-received pieces of art criticism, including a *New York Times Magazine* piece on modernist houses in France.[5] By the end of the twenties, she was enjoying a bohemian life in Greenwich Village, mingling with the likes of Alfred Stieglitz and Georgia O'Keeffe. She was vivacious, voracious, and switched on—the quintessential New Woman. But nothing suggested she would soon embark on a game-changing book in the housing field.

Bauer's rapid transformation to housing expert came through her association with cultural critic Lewis Mumford.[6] Bauer met Mumford in 1929 while working as an advertising manager at his publisher, Harcourt Brace. The two began an ardent if turbulent affair lasting nearly five years.[7] In Bauer, Mumford felt he had found a worthy sparring partner, reader, and critic; he soon involved her in his activities around art and architecture and introduced her into his professional circles. He brought her into the Regional Planning Association of America and she became its executive secretary. The RPAA consisted of prominent architects, such as Clarence Stein and Henry Wright, and housing reformers, such as Edith Elmer Wood. Alarmed by metropolitan sprawl and inspired by the Garden City Movement, RPAA members prescribed planned growth along regional lines. They eventually realized their ideas in two communities, Sunnyside Gardens, New York, and Radburn, New Jersey, both of which Mumford helped plan.

In 1930, Bauer set out for Europe and Scandinavia for four months to learn about recent housing developments firsthand. Aided by Mumford's introductions, she visited noteworthy architects and municipal housing estates.[8] In vivid and funny letters to Mumford, Bauer detailed her encounters with a who's who of European architects, from J. J. P. Oud, who toured her around his recent developments in Rotterdam, to Ernst May, about to depart for the Soviet Union, to Mies van der Rohe, newly installed as director at the Bauhaus. She admired the neat brick vernacular housing of Scandinavia and Holland. The Stuttgart *Weissenhof* fully met her expectations and she pronounced Walter Gropius's *Siedlung* in Dessau *"excellent,"* economical, and appreciated by its working-class tenants ("they are really proud of modern architecture as something made *for them* and for a new order which belongs to them").[9] But it was May who most enthused her: she enrolled in a three-day New Construction course and was the sole American of 150 students who toured sites around Frankfurt and heard lectures from Richard Neutra and Mart Stam, among others.

On Bauer's return to the United States, her knowledge of European housing provided rich material for a host of projects, notably a prize-winning essay in 1931 for *Fortune Magazine* on May's Praunheim and Römerstadt developments in the Nidda Valley.[10] Clarence Stein hired her as a research assistant for a book on regionalism. And, despite some misgivings, Mumford and Bauer agreed to contribute to Philip Johnson's

Installation view, housing section, *Modern Architecture—International Exhibition,* MoMA, New York, February 9–March 23, 1932. Gelatin silver print, 7 x 9 inches (17.7 x 22.8 cm). Photographic Archive, The Museum of Modern Art Archives, New York. Catalogue no. IN15.2. New York, Museum of Modern Art (MoMA). Copyright 2019. Digital image, The Museum of Modern Art, New York / Scala, Florence. Text panel that was later reproduced in *Modern Housing* is visible on back wall at left.

Modern Architecture—International Exhibition at the Museum of Modern Art in 1932. While often said to mark the moment at which the Modern Movement was flattened out into an aesthetic movement—a style—architectural historian Barry Bergdoll notes this reading rests on a conflation of Johnson and Henry-Russell Hitchcock Jr.'s publication *The International Style,* also of 1932, with the catalogue for *Modern Architecture,* which, like the exhibit, was more broad-ranging.[11] As proof, Bergdoll points to the exhibit's public housing section and MoMA director Alfred H. Barr Jr.'s statement that "low-rent housing" was the most pressing architectural problem addressed in the show.[12]

Mumford agreed with Barr about the urgency of housing

but in his catalogue essay he did not treat the problem as exclusively architectural and instead gave equal weight to questions of politics, planning, production, and finance. "The new attack upon the housing problem," he stressed, "is distinguished by the fact that it treats the social, the economic, the vital, and the architectural requirements of the modern house on a single plane."[13] Although Mumford was consulted about the show, he kept his distance from it, due to Hitchcock and Johnson's ambivalence toward Frank Lloyd Wright. (From his side, Wright believed the exhibition was a "propaganda-trap" for internationalism and would have withdrawn but for Mumford's intervention.)[14] Mumford's RPAA colleagues worked with Johnson on the housing section: Bauer, Stein, and Henry Wright provided materials on American housing; Johnson organized photographs of European housing and the large Rothenberg *Siedlung* model; and Bauer wrote the text panels.[15] One of these text panels, clearly visible in photographs of the exhibition, is reproduced in *Modern Housing*.[16] This marked the beginning of Bauer's close association with MoMA, where her younger sister, Elizabeth Mock, would also have a notable curatorial career.[17]

In April 1932, Bauer returned to Europe to conduct research for Mumford for a series of articles on housing commissioned by *Fortune*; on this four-month tour, she greatly extended her knowledge of housing developments, revisiting those she had seen previously and familiarizing herself with new ones. (Mumford was also then in Europe working on *Technics and Civilization:* he had accepted the *Fortune* job to pay for Bauer to join him, but it did not go well, the pressure to research housing stifling romance.)[18] After a tense gestation period, the first article was published in November 1932.[19] Mumford appears as sole author yet these articles were obviously collaborations: Bauer conducted the bulk of the research, compiled statistics and notes that Mumford then "boiled down," sourced the illustrations, wrote the long captions, and did the layouts.[20] To Bauer and Mumford's disappointment, *Fortune* pulled the plug after only three of five proposed articles, put off by the authors' promotion of large-scale public assistance for housing. With Mumford's encouragement, Bauer decided to turn her copious research materials into a book. The Carnegie Foundation contributed a grant, and Boston-based publisher Houghton Mifflin offered a contract.[21]

In her work on *Modern Housing,* Bauer would benefit from growing friendships with influential housers and architects from Stein to Wood to Wright (Henry and Frank Lloyd). Yet the book undeniably owes most to Mumford. His connections unlocked doors for her. His heroes, including Patrick Geddes, Thorstein Veblen, and Peter Kropotkin, his historical interest in utopia, and his commitment to regionalism, organicism, and communism all left a deep imprint on her work. But even if theirs was not a relationship of equals, neither was it one-sided. Mumford had a genuine admiration for Bauer's critical abilities and skills as a writer and openly acknowledged her influence.[22] Their lives were deeply intertwined during a defining period of intellectual activity for them both as they raced to complete big books: Mumford compared himself and Bauer to "two bicycle riders, keeping the same pace while we ride around different race-tracks."[23] *Modern Housing* and *Technics and Civilization* would be released close together toward the end of 1934.

"Housing Is More Than Houses"

Certainly, *Modern Housing* is not the work of a disciple. It is an assured, mature, and often brilliantly argued book. Yet it can feel curious in comparison to scholarship today. It is rigorous and well researched, but also selective and idiosyncratic. Like Mumford, Bauer makes no effort at neutrality; rather, she treats past developments as "usable," able to inform the present and future and direct change.[24] The book is more akin to a manifesto, confronting readers, delivering judgments, and demanding action. Its central argument is bluntly stated again and again: modern housing is required for modern cities. While Europe hasn't *solved* the modern housing problem (Bauer is emphatic on this point), it is far ahead of America in terms of addressing it. America needs to learn from Europe's example.

The question of how the housing problem has arisen and

how it can be addressed are then substantially explored in the book's four parts: the former mainly in Part One; the latter in Parts Two through Four. Although not totally original, there is great perceptiveness to many of Bauer's arguments and great exhilaration in watching her make them. What you think is right is usually wrong—and what you think is wrong is usually still wrong. Take Bauer's damning assessment of Victorian social reformers in Part One. Far from improving working-class housing conditions, Bauer depicts their interventions as deeply misguided, entrenching "disastrous" patterns set in an earlier period of uncontrolled Liberal-sanctioned land speculation. "The net result," she concludes, "was that the early reformers—in any case not a very inspiring group—wasted their efforts for the most part within a pattern of things which was quite impossible to begin with."[25]

This harsh sentence—I use the term deliberately—speaks volumes about Bauer's underlying approach. While she admires certain housers, architects, and planners, she generally downplays individual agency, preferring to address patterns and forces (political, cultural, and above all economic) that she views as the key determinants of good housing. Her analysis thus tends toward the macro and the abstract. Even though she personally knew many of the projects featured in the book, she does not go in for long observational passages or tell the stories of the residents who live there, relying instead on the evidence of statistics, comparative charts, and plans. This distinguishes her approach from that of her fellow iconoclast, Jane Jacobs, who would make a specialty of emotive first-person accounts of city life.

In Part One, Bauer identifies laissez-faire economics as the main force behind poor-quality housing. However much her other opinions would change in the future, she never deviated from this view. Quite simply, she says, laissez-faire principles cannot deliver affordable housing because the system dictates that urban land be priced according to the most intensive future use to which it can legally be put. Consequently, Bauer observes, "the price of land is largely determined by the lowest housing standards permissible or acceptable"; extremely high land costs and high-density buildings are the inevitable result.[26] Bauer declares that if a new standard of human environment is to be established for the modern age, land speculation must be stopped and housing transformed into a public utility as it was in Europe following World War I.

The need to remove American housing from private hands is the principal message of *Modern Housing*. Although Bauer does not advocate extreme measures like confiscation, it is easy to see how her prescriptions could be painted as anti-capitalist and anti-American. (And why even a nominal ally like Frank Lloyd Wright would teasingly call her "Communist Catherine.")[27] This does not mean that she neglects design and aesthetics. In her account, however, these can never be isolated from other factors, as she, like Mumford, adheres to Scottish biologist and planner Patrick Geddes's notion of holism, which holds that any community is a total integrated environment that evolves over time. The other reason Bauer does not separate aesthetics from social, political, and economic factors is that the housing projects she hopes Americans will emulate do not do so—as she demonstrates in her analysis of alternative models of housing, beginning in Part Two.

Bauer's picture of the speculative Victorian housing norm in Part One is depressing enough that she issues a wry disclaimer: "if the picture is so unrelievedly black as to lack credibility, it is not the fault of the author" (60). But her account of alternatives to the norm in Part Two also begins in the nineteenth century, surveying the philosophy and projects of well-known radical, socialist, and utopian thinkers from Robert Owen to Charles Fourier to William Morris. She highlights the Rochdale Pioneers as the first successful cooperative organization and considers the cooperative movement more broadly. There is never any doubt where this is all heading: Part Two culminates with a discussion of the RPAA's inspiration, the Garden City Movement, and Mumford's Master, Patrick Geddes, whom Bauer describes in adulatory terms as the "prophet" of "the new science of planning" (113).

Part Three picks up from Part One, considering the housing norm that emerged in the wake of World War I. In place of the blackness of Victorian speculation, Bauer presents us with a dramatically transformed scene: Europe is now taking impressive strides toward meeting its housing shortage. In the countries and districts for which Bauer has figures, she calculates that 4,500,000 new dwellings have been built in the past fifteen years with public assistance, collectively housing 16 percent of the working population (124). With an eye to the American situation, she asks: what induced European governments not only to take action but to take action in such a way that they transformed the standard of housing? She identifies three factors: first, pervasive discontent with existing housing; second, governments assuming responsibility for city development; and third, new forces pressuring governments for action. In Bauer's words, there was *"organized political demand on the part of the people who needed good housing"* (122, italics in original); ineffectual philanthropic reformers gave way to powerful labor organizations and consumers' groups.

Bauer analyzes how this change was practically effected in a chart that indicates the mechanisms used to deliver housing in each country. The key finding, already transmitted in the *Fortune* articles, is that most new dwellings had been removed from the free market: roughly a third were erected by local governments on municipally owned land; another third were put up by public utility housing societies; and the final third were built by private enterprise but with strict building standards and rental and resale restrictions imposed on them to ensure that a stock of decent affordable rentals remained available in the long term. Bauer next elucidates how financial arrangements, from housing funds to subsidized loans, were used to deliver public housing and how governments controlled quality through building standards and in-house architects and planners. She stresses that, in most of these countries, the best designers were "likely to be found in the municipal housing offices," before noting: "(This fact has been recently somewhat modified in Germany)" (131–32).

Bauer's parenthetical remark underscores her awareness of how the National Socialists were changing the direction of Germany politically, not least by neutralizing the left-wing unions behind organized demands for housing. Even as Bauer advocates for European-style housing in America, she can feel the fascists closing in. This creates a distinct tension throughout the book: Bauer's tone is both celebratory and doom-filled as she frets about the future of housing internationally (except in Russia). In one of her most powerful passages, she warns, "There is no 'inevitability of gradualism' about the housing movement," explaining her meaning in a paragraph that we would do well to heed today:

> There is no getting around the fact that "modern housing" and much of the framework of contemporary western society are mutually antipathetic. The premises underlying the most successful and forward-pointing housing developments are not the premises of capitalism, of inviolate private property, of entrenched nationalism, of class distinction, of governments bent on preserving old interests rather than creating new values. [. . .] In a sense, the housing achievement has constituted a world within a world, hampered by all the contradictions and insecurity attendant on such an anomalous position. (136)

And yet, what Europe achieved cannot be denied. Nor can it be ignored if America is to develop a coherent program to meet its own housing crisis. And so Bauer leads us to Part Four, the most explicitly architectural section of *Modern Housing*, which investigates specific European projects and principles. It includes a few star exhibits from MoMA's *Modern Architecture* show, such as Otto Haesler's Rothenberg, May's Römerstadt, and Oud's Kiefhoek, but substantially expands the list. In total, Bauer discusses projects from more than a dozen countries, with a particular focus on England, France, Austria, Germany, and the Netherlands. There are holes in her coverage, including Italy, Poland, and the USSR, which Bauer mostly leaves to one side because she has not visited in person.

The first sections of Part Four deal with minimum standards, the community unit, location, and layout. It is important to emphasize that in none of these does Bauer try to establish an ideal response or solution to housing. Rather, she aims to show and assess what has been done in the context of different countries under variant conditions. Whatever the resolution, she makes clear what the goal of housing should be: it should aspire to deliver "biological standards" and create "a positive synthesis of modern techniques, modern functions, a new standard of living, and a modern aesthetic of design"—a new layer of the human environment, a new *modern* norm (148). Rarely has this synthesis been achieved: of "perfect housing," she states, firmly, "there is most assuredly none at all" (148). She reckons Neubühl near Zurich comes closest in Europe, while only three examples in America even approach the requisite standard, all unsurprisingly by Stein and Wright: Radburn, Sunnyside, and Chatham Village in Pittsburgh.

In her next section, "The Community Unit," Bauer asserts the only way to achieve "vital standards" is to plan and administer housing at the neighborhood scale for the common good, thus realizing economies in land, building, financing, and maintenance costs. Significantly, she insists that an architect must design the entire community right from the start, including communal amenities—at minimum, a primary school, shops, recreation and play spaces, possibly a café, central laundry, and gardens. "Housing is more than houses," Bauer states in the book's catchiest slogan (165). Considering where these new communities should be sited (within or outside city limits), Bauer surveys varying approaches, though she allows her preference for decentralized development to come through. She discusses layouts for new communities, from Raymond Unwin's Super-block to the German *Zeilenbau* (block row). She does not argue for one model or the other; her intent is to show that both improve living standards while delivering decent housing densities.

With equal vigor, Bauer then goes on to present and analyze building types, construction methods, architecture, and economics. Each of these sections is rich in detail, reflecting her minute grasp of on-the-ground developments and a careful attention to the smallest elements—whether or not a rear entrance is provided, a yard is fenced, or gardens are accessed through the kitchen. She considers local customs, appreciatively noting the elevators in one Rotterdam development are big enough to accommodate the delivery hand-carts prevalent in Holland. (It is hard to imagine this detail being admired by Hitchcock and Johnson.) She sorts through the virtues and demerits of one-family houses, multiple dwellings, towers, space standards, plans, and equipment from the perspective of user needs, considering special groups such as children, the elderly, and single women. She approvingly cites—and illustrates—the Frankfurt Kitchen, as far as I am aware one of the first American mentions of the kitchen, apart from her own earlier articles in *Fortune*.[28]

In these sections Bauer touches most directly on architectural matters. With her Geddesian evolutionary views, she insists that the modern epoch requires modern forms and credits the work of the "functionalists" associated with the *Neue Sachlichkeit* as most nearly achieving a new vernacular. Yet she struggles to accept the functionalist insistence that there can be one solution to the problem of dwelling that is derived from "pure engineering" (200). These misgivings, combined with her admiration for the Garden Cities and Frank Lloyd Wright, mean that Bauer comes across as more agnostic about movements and styles than one might expect given her fierce advocacy of modernism elsewhere.[29] But if the aim of "modern housing" is to provide comprehensively planned affordable housing that meets biological standards long-term, then an "honest" brick house in a cul-de-sac can serve as well as a Modern Movement flat in *Zeilenbau* formation. Bauer draws the line at "fakery" or "suburban fancy business," false fronts, cast-iron entablatures, and the like—her critique of ornament here influenced by Veblen (216).

Bauer concludes Part Four by asking, "Modern Housing for America?" Obviously, her answer is "yes." Recently, Bauer notes, housing has been elevated to a front-page concern and a target for action in Roosevelt's Washington. What should the goal of such policy and action be? Considering the high costs of land, Bauer argues that, rather than slum clearance, new communities in cheap areas are the only option. She also takes time to demolish the idea that subsidence homesteads can offer a solution, calling their German equivalent "poor farms." She finishes by stressing again that nothing will happen unless there is organized and well-informed demand on the part of consumers, and she leaves readers with this uncharacteristically wistful note: "If only a small part of the vast energy which was once directed toward individual home-ownership were now organized to demand a realistic program of modern housing [. . .] then there would be an American housing movement indeed. THE END" (255).

Except it isn't the end. Bauer's forty-page appendix with its country-by-country summary of European housing developments follows. Then a twenty-page annotated bibliography of relevant books from around the world, many hot off the presses, representing the latest in modern housing research. And finally, forty-eight plates of photographs and plans: two to four per page, with banner headlines and captions. Like the graphic materials throughout the book, the illustrations represent a massive labor and must have posed a challenge to the book's designer, the influential modernist typographer Robert Josephy, who worked closely with Bauer in laying them out.[30] Bauer's images come from far and wide. They show an extremely diverse range of European housing and related amenities at all scales from aerial photographs of planned communities down to individual interiors.[31]

These images of recently built European developments must have been revelatory. Yet they served a rhetorical purpose as much as a documentary one. Independently of the main text, the plates make the case for planned modern housing. After having laid out the images a half dozen times, Bauer noted, with satisfaction, "They tell the whole story by themselves."[32] Here we might see a link to German modernist book design, which also choreographed image and text to convey an argument; for instance, Sigfried Giedion's 1929 "picture book" on Modern Movement housing, *Befreites Wohnen (Liberated Dwelling),* cited in Bauer's bibliography.[33] But Bauer does not actually seem to have book design in mind at all. Instead, she treats her plates as exhibition panels, deploying the same provocative, comparative techniques as in *Modern Architecture.* Her final plate is typical: "A SIMPLE PLANNING TEST" of rear yards pits the back alleys of American slums against the tidy gardens of planned European communities. The normally voluble Bauer here provides no commentary. If this stark choice does not persuade readers, what more can she say?

"A Standard Work"

Upon its release, *Modern Housing* was well received by the general press, though with some grumbling about its propagandistic tone, its pessimistic representation of the American scene, and its praise of the Russian.[34] A British edition published by Allen & Unwin followed in 1935. The book was expensive at $5.00 and had respectable rather than stellar sales. But a copy got into the hands of everyone in housing who mattered and, as Bauer's peers predicted, it became an instant classic. When, after several years, it sold out its initial run of 1,500 copies, Bauer's publisher, Ferris Greenslet, tried to cajole a revised edition out of her. "Hardly a day goes by that someone doesn't write in for it," he wrote her a tad despairingly in 1939. He would urge her to revise the book throughout the 1940s, but her extensive list of changes combined with her relentless schedule meant that she never had enough time to see the job through.[35]

Evidently the book was a success. Yet where did its real achievement lie? As we have seen, while fortified by Bauer's firsthand research, the book was neither completely novel nor were its examples entirely unknown, as her own bibliography proves. Her allies at the RPAA, such as Charles Harris Whitaker and Edith Elmer Wood, had previously deployed similar arguments with reference to earlier European precedents. And, in their widely read *Fortune* articles and in MoMA's *Modern Architecture* exhibition and catalogue, Bauer and Mumford had already put the case for European-type housing before the American public. Further enshrined by the publication of *Modern Housing,* the projects they identified would come to constitute a canon of good housing. Not only the same projects but also the same images of these projects were reproduced; thus we find the same set of illustrations cropping up in key housing and architecture books and exhibitions throughout the 1930s.[36]

Bauer, then, was far from a lone voice in the wilderness, especially at this juncture when the question of housing was politically front and center. What ultimately seemed to make the book stand out from the crowd was its "usability": it was a masterful yet accessible overview of the housing situation, a systematic discussion of options, and a roadmap for reform. As housing historian Gail Radford concludes, "Bauer's achievement consisted of [. . .] articulating not just a critique but a constructive proposal for basic changes in the American system of housing provision."[37] Most crucial for her personally, Bauer believed she had identified the best "method of attack" to bring these changes about: organized consumer demand and sustained political pressure (121). It explains why, even before the book had been published, she was switching directions: moving to attack.

Based on European precedents, Bauer was convinced that the trade union movement was the most effective lever by which to apply political pressure. On the last page of *Modern Housing,* she mentions a "special" example close to home: the Carl Mackley Apartments in Philadelphia, the first project financed by the Public Works Administration's Housing Division, organized by the American Federation of Hosiery Workers as a limited-dividend corporation.[38] Designed by German émigrés Oskar Stonorov and Alfred Kastner, this was a well-planned affordable housing development along modern lines with generous communal facilities such as a progressive nursery school and pool. The photograph of Carl Mackley's pool became iconic in its own right, appearing, at Bauer's behest, on the cover of MoMA's 1936 *Architecture in Government Housing* catalogue. Although still under construction, Bauer was sure Carl Mackley would seed demands for more such housing among unions.

To help that seed germinate, in spring 1934 Bauer accepted a post as executive secretary of the Labor Housing Conference, a lobby group launched by the Pennsylvania Federation of Labor. Working alongside Stonorov and labor organizer John Edelman, Bauer set about organizing a network of housing committees across the country to fight for a national housing program.[39] To this end, she undertook grueling whistle-stop lecture tours across America, explaining the benefits of European housing programs to local union and consumer organizations. As in *Modern Housing,* rather than pushing for slum clearance housing for the very poor, Bauer argued for

Carl Mackley Houses, Philadelphia. Designed by Kastner & Stonorov, executed under the direction of W. Pope Barney. Cover of exhibition catalogue *Architecture in Government Housing,* New York, The Museum of Modern Art, June 8–July 13, 1936. The Museum of Modern Art Library, catalogue no. 300061901. New York, Museum of Modern Art (MoMA). Copyright 2019. Digital image, The Museum of Modern Art, New York / Scala, Florence.

moderately priced high-quality housing for the working classes; in this way the public sector could provide decent homes for laborers while also stimulating the construction trades—the most appealing message for unions and politicians, who were looking to get people back to work.

Bauer and her confreres in the Labor Housing Conference drafted a federal housing bill, introduced in Congress in 1935, proposing the foundation of a new federal housing agency with the power to make grants and loans to nongovernmental organizations as at Carl Mackley. This bill did not pass, but it led to another, which Bauer also coauthored; this bill, signed into law by Franklin Roosevelt, became the United States Housing Act of 1937. The new legislation had its flaws: under siege from the powerful real estate lobby, lawmakers introduced amendments that promoted slum clearance (never a priority for Bauer), imposed strict unit-cost limits, and denied a role to cooperatives and limited-dividend corporations.[40] Yet by supporting a progressive vision for housing, the act still deserves to be seen as a victory: Bauer called it a triumph "of left over right."[41] She hoped that, as the benefits of public housing became evident, it would garner more popular support and lead to more favorable provisions in future acts.

In order to enlist this popular support, Bauer stressed the need for housers to communicate a convincing argument in favor of housing. Her emphasis on engaging people meant that she rejected the prevailing tendency to frame housing in social workerish or technical terms. She particularly hated what she called the "charity smell" of housing discourse, musing that people need "something to stir up the imagination," but what they get is "the *remedial* (Ugh!)."[42] She elaborated on this view in a later letter to Mumford:

> I don't think there is ever just one theoretically and technically correct solution to a given problem [. . .] There are always several constructive courses possible—and the *right* one among them is the one that can best enlist popular support and understanding and responsible participation. [. . .] And to discover the positive path that *will* strike the spark is a fundamental and vital technique in

> itself—a technique which in my opinion has been almost completely neglected by those very planners and philosophers who are intellectually most advanced.[43]

As her arguments crystallized over time, her language changed, too: "consumers" became "citizens" during the war years with a democratic duty to be active and informed about housing, not only to improve standards but also to counterbalance government paternalism. Her desire to spark participation among those who stood to gain most from public housing would increasingly drive her, resulting in her only other book, the short, rousing *A Citizen's Guide to Public Housing* of 1940.[44] It also ensured her ongoing work on various housing exhibitions and competitions at MoMA and her involvement in curating *The Town of Tomorrow* exhibit for the New York World's Fair in 1939. Although her ambitious plans for a *Weissenhof*-style housing exposition did not materialize, her suggestion that a film be commissioned resulted in *The City,* narrated by Mumford.[45]

For his part, Mumford watched Bauer's swerve into activism with open dismay, convinced she was dissipating her intellectual gifts just when they most needed nurturing. In 1936, in a remarkably patronizing letter, he told her, "the sort of mind that you have potentially is much rarer and more valuable in creative thought than the other sort of mind you have developed is in politics."[46] Mumford's praise of "creative thought" over politics was more than a little self-serving: he was no doubt stung by Bauer's pointed criticisms of "intellectually advanced" philosophers in the housing field.[47] But he was correct in seeing that she was permanently altering course: although she would author many weighty articles and reports over the course of her life, her commitment to practical action meant that she would never write another monumental book like *Modern Housing.*[48]

If anything, Bauer's career in the 1940s and 1950s became even more complex and merits more space than we can give it here. To mention some highlights: in the wake of the Housing Act of 1937, Bauer agreed to head the newly formed United States Housing Authority's Division of Research and Information. Two years later, her career swerved again, this time into academe, when she accepted an invitation to lecture on public housing at the University of California at Berkeley. Here she met the well-respected modernist architect William Wurster; they married the following year. In Wurster, Bauer found a supportive life partner, one whose sense of social purpose, not to mention busyness, complemented hers.[49] Together they were a serious power couple with an extensive and cosmopolitan network across the worlds of architecture, housing, and planning.

Bauer continued to be an influential housing advocate: she served as vice president of the California Housing and Planning Association, served as vice president of the National Public Housing Conference, and cofounded the National Committee on the Housing Emergency, all the while consulting for the U.S. Housing Authority and advising MoMA. In 1943, Bauer and Wurster moved to Cambridge, Massachusetts, where Wurster studied planning at Harvard's Graduate School of Design (GSD) and Bauer audited classes (rather astonishingly, her only formal education in the field). After Wurster became dean of architecture at the Massachusetts Institute of Technology (MIT), and following the birth of their daughter, Sadie, in 1945, Bauer began teaching a ground-breaking cross-disciplinary housing seminar at the GSD for architects, planners, and social scientists. Meanwhile she represented UNESCO at the United Nations meetings that led to the founding of the Center for Human Settlements and campaigned for the Housing Act of 1949.

In 1950, the couple made a final move west, when Wurster took up the deanship of what became the College of Environmental Design (CED) at Berkeley. Bauer took up a position in city and regional planning at Berkeley; campaigned against sprawl, freeways, and pollution; and cofounded the conservation organization California Tomorrow. Her research began to focus less explicitly on housing and more on urban design and developing cities, and she obtained funding for a major study of urbanization in India. While the family thrived overall, there were setbacks, too: in one particularly painful episode, Bauer was investigated by the government for alleged Communist associations, and it would take a year to clear her name.[50] This episode, however, did not prevent

"Judging of the Competition Entries: Two Jurors, Catherine Bauer and Ludwig Mies van der Rohe, discussing an entry. Edgar Kaufmann, Jr., Competition Director standing in background." Publicity photograph released in connection with the exhibition *Prize Design for Modern Furniture,* MoMA, New York, May 16–July 16, 1950. Photographer: William Leftwich (copyright holder and rights status unknown). Gelatin silver print, 7 ½ x 9 ½ inches (19 x 24.1 cm). Photographic Archive, The Museum of Modern Art Archives, New York. Object number IN446.36. New York, Museum of Modern Art (MoMA). Copyright 2019. Digital image, The Museum of Modern Art, New York / Scala, Florence. Photograph taken in December 1948.

President Dwight Eisenhower from appointing Bauer to author the urban environment section for his Commission on National Goals in 1960. Eventually Bauer became an associate dean at the CED. Her career was still in full flow in 1964 when she tragically died in a hiking accident on Mount Tamalpais.[51]

"One of the Staunchest Friends of Decent Housing"

Colleagues and friends of all stripes mourned the loss of this by all counts brilliant, charismatic, and generous woman who had for so long been a guiding light of the housing movement. Given her dizzying array of careers and activities, her contribution overall is hard to sum up neatly. The influential houser Charles Abrams described Bauer as "one of the staunchest friends of decent housing," which possibly is the simplest and best tribute.[52] For his part, Mumford called Bauer "a propagandist for public housing," a description that was more barbed but which Bauer may not have minded.[53] Indeed, in light of the overriding importance she gave to sparking popular support, one wonders how successful she felt her efforts to promote the housing cause had been.

Bauer could not have doubted the long-term impact of *Modern Housing,* which, even unrevised, remained required reading for many years. Although observing that Bauer's success at getting housing policy passed meant her diagnosis of the U.S. scene was soon "obsolete," former Administrator of the Housing Authority Nathan Straus still recommended it for its account of European developments.[54] Ultimately, however, many of the book's most crucial insights about these European examples would never be adopted: embattled and financially restricted, U.S. housing authorities consistently compromised on design quality, communal amenities, maintenance, and management. Most fatally in Bauer's eyes, the government's continued backing of mortgages and home ownership for middle-class suburbanites meant the projects they did build were effectively confined to the very poor. Rather than integrating communities, this two-tiered system reentrenched social and racial discrimination in a way that appalled Bauer, and she fiercely denounced it from the mid-1940s on.

Once the government's preference decisively turned to dense high-rise housing on slum-clearance sites, Bauer foresaw only disaster. There could never be love for housing when what was provided was so mean, isolated, overbearingly administered, and segregated to boot. Twenty years after the first Housing Act, Bauer blasted these developments in her scorching essay for *Architectural Forum,* "The Dreary Deadlock of Public Housing" (1957). The article tried to explain, possibly to its author as much as to others, how it was that "the [housing] program has never called forth the kind of pervasive and persuasive popular support that oils the wheels of change in democratic countries"—support that Bauer had counted on to set right the deficiencies of the 1937 Act. Bauer identified much that was wrong with current housing policy and practice, but most strikingly in light of *Modern Housing,* she charged that housers and architects had "embraced too wholeheartedly functional and collectivist architectural theories."[55]

Just six months before she died, Bauer returned to this theme in "The Social Front of Modern Architecture in the 1930s," a paper delivered at the second biennial Modern Architecture Symposium (MAS) at Columbia University, which reappraised the decade's architecture.[56] She addressed an invited audience including figures such as Hitchcock and Johnson who, like Bauer, had promoted the new architecture, as well as the next generation of historians critically reassessing its impact, such as Colin Rowe and Vincent Scully. Interestingly, there were several other women in the room, including fellow presenter Sibyl Moholy-Nagy, whose lack of reverence for the "primadonnas" matched and sometimes exceeded Bauer's;[57] and Bauer's own sister, Elizabeth, who contributed to the second day's discussion.[58] Bauer's remarks on this occasion showed that, while the hopes she had vested in functionalism as a movement had dimmed, many of the convictions she expressed in *Modern Housing* remained as strong as ever.

Bauer opened her talk by invoking a previous speaker, Vincent Scully, who, she remarked, "is young enough that he is probably not aware of some social and civic contributions that were originally promised by the Internationalists in the late 1920s and early 1930s." (She was evidently intending to needle him here: Scully was then a well-regarded scholar in his forties.) She reminded the audience that *functional* had originally been understood to have a "double meaning," denoting not only an aesthetic but also a scientifically informed approach that sought to improve the human environment. When Bauer first encountered functional developments in 1930, it was their potential for civic improvement that electrified her and, in her pointed words, changed her from "an aesthete into a housing reformer."[59] The unspoken corollary is that this experience confirmed others like Johnson as aesthetes.

Bauer was not there, however, to cross swords with Johnson, who, after more than three decades of collaborations and collisions, was well aware of her views: she simply limited herself to agreeing with Sigfried Giedion that the term "International Style" had not been helpful to understandings of modern architecture.[60] For, she repeated, it allowed people to forget that it was the social that had first driven the functionalist agenda: housing had provided its main proponents with crucial building opportunities and generated their most significant innovations in planning, standards, and construction. In short, workers' housing was not the chief achievement of new architecture; it *was* the new architecture. Or, as she had put it in *Modern Housing,* "One of the most hopeful facts about both modern housing and modern architecture is that *they are not two separate subjects*" (212; emphasis mine).

Nonetheless, due to the weaknesses that Bauer already identified in *Modern Housing*—the tendency to universalize solutions and a fondness for "technocratic symbolism"—functionalism soon ossified. Instead of continuing to experiment and adapt, functionalist architects were content to replicate their designs internationally. In America, this resulted in minimalist housing with an institutional character that stigmatized residents and led them to reject it. In spite of this failure, Bauer felt that strides had been made in the creation of a new human environment. It was simply that the most successful architects had not proved to be the ones predicted decades before; rather, Scandinavian modernists such as Sven Markelius and Alvar Aalto, with their humanized, regionally inspired buildings, had come closest to achieving a truly modern vernacular. In America, Bauer also praised the more flexible, informal Bay Region style, of which Wurster was a leading light.

Given earlier controversies around the Bay Region style, Bauer evidently thought this last assertion might be incendiary.[61] Her takedown of the Internationalists, however, proved very much in keeping with the general mood. Orthodox modernism was out; complexity was in. If anything, the event underscored that *Modern Housing*'s dissident and pluralistic approach had weathered far better than the dogmatic one of *The International Style* and was now in tune with the spirit of the sixties. As we have seen, the book was not overly purist about stylistic issues: it made room for local building traditions and did not disdain romanticism and organicism. It was theoretically informed and overtly political, a heady brew of anarchism, trade unionism, and cooperativism. It was human centered and antimonumental, with few expected modern set pieces (no luxury single-family villas). It did not make architecture "safe for capital."[62]

These features may account for renewed interest in the book. A few months before her MAS talk, Bauer was approached by The MIT Press, which was keen to issue a revised paperback of *Modern Housing*. Bauer warmly welcomed the idea, though noted that the book was now so out of date that it would probably have to stand as "a period piece"; instead she proposed to write a new introduction that would criticize her earlier judgments, insert a brief critique before each chapter, and make cuts to the original text.[63] MIT Press agreed, but Bauer's death meant this plan did not proceed. A reprint, minus the critical self-assessment, would come out only with Arno Press's version in 1974.

More appreciative assessments followed in the wake of Bauer's death, most importantly Suzanne Stephens's celebration of her criticism in the landmark exhibition and publication *Women in American Architecture* (1977). But this spike of interest in both *Modern Housing* and Bauer herself never went mainstream. Bauer continues to be a curiously peripheral figure in histories of modern architecture today—despite having written one of the seminal early texts on modern architecture, co-drafted America's first housing legislation, consulted on major architectural exhibitions of the twentieth century, and influenced generations of students with her interdisciplinary courses on housing and city planning. Indeed, surveying her "prodigious" accomplishments as a public intellectual, writer, curator, activist, and educator over three decades, it seems frankly incredible that she might *not* count as a meaningful figure in the story of modern architecture.[64]

The most plausible explanation for her peripheral status lies with Bauer's primary connection to housing.[65] For all that Bauer tried to unify architecture and housing, they would remain stubbornly separate, certainly in America. (One recalls the separate housing section already in the *Modern Architecture* exhibition.) As a consequence, housing would become further entrenched as a specialist and supposedly lesser field of practice from the mid-1930s on, giving its key protagonists only a limited presence in architectural discourse. This marginality was surely exacerbated by the fact that many of its best-known protagonists were women, for whom housing had historically provided an acceptable sphere of action. Bauer was well aware of the inferior status of housers in architectural circles, not least because Mumford was always reminding her of it, which is perhaps why she so consciously attempted to negate its associations with feminine do-gooding and moralism.

She also continued to try to build bridges with architects, never giving up on what she saw as the basic modernist principle of treating housing as an architectural problem. She addressed architects directly whenever she could, urging them to design innovative housing for social and ethical reasons, though often with little more success than her do-gooding forbears.[66] After seeing her on stage at an Architectural League symposium with Louis Kahn and Josep Lluís Sert in 1960, Sibyl Moholy-Nagy was moved to write Bauer a fan letter, praising her for steadfastly reminding "the great names" of their responsibilities for shelter and planning in spite of being brushed aside.[67] In fact, reading accounts of public events at this time, including the 1964 MAS, one gets the uncomfortable feeling that the few female speakers present were usually fated to play such Cassandra-like parts; and even though Bauer claimed to have never felt professionally disadvantaged by her sex, she must have felt frustration at being called on to act as the social conscience of the great names, who heard her out but carried on as usual.[68]

Architects in this period may have felt more justified than usual in ignoring her advice. Even if Bauer promoted experimentation and aesthetic approaches to housing, this was not what the large-scale national programs tended to support. Historian Richard Pommer fairly lays some blame for this situation on Bauer herself, arguing that the very government programs and standards that she championed bureaucratized housing design and stamped out creativity.[69] By the late 1950s, as the failures of the "projects" became devastatingly clear, the very figure of the houser was being vilified in many architectural circles, attacked for promoting antiurban policies and inhumane environments. Despite also denouncing these developments, it was inevitable that, as one of the nation's most visible housers, Bauer did not escape the backlash.

The harshest and most personal indictment of all would come from Jane Jacobs. In *Death and Life of Great American Cities* (1961), Jacobs specifically skewered Bauer and Mumford as decentrists whose creed of regional development had done much to destroy cities. She deplored their belief that whole communities could be scientifically planned and decried large-scale government interventions to this end. And in one memorably scornful passage, she rejected the very idea of housing as a viable sphere of action requiring expert knowledge, stating, "'housers,' narrowly specializing in 'housing' expertise, are a vocational absurdity. Such a profession makes sense only if it is assumed that 'housing' per se has important generalized effects and qualities. It does not."[70]

That Jacobs and Bauer—both deeply committed activists who vocally condemned the projects—nonetheless found themselves so at odds reveals just how polarizing housing, slum clearance, and urban-renewal programs had become in this period. Bauer's offense in Jacobs's eyes was that, in spite of her sharp criticisms of existing policies and programs, she would not disavow her status as a "houser" or her commitment to government-assisted housing and community planning. But this was because Bauer never backed down from *Modern Housing*'s central contention: as the capitalist economic system on its own could not provide enough livable housing to meet demand, housing had to be treated as a public utility. And was she wrong to hold this view? Her abiding mistrust of free markets was shaped by the Great Depression, but it has been more than justified by events since, not least by the boom in neoliberal speculative development in cities that has fueled today's affordable housing crisis.

Indeed, developments during the past forty years have

reaffirmed many of the precepts laid out in *Modern Housing*. Rather than simply representing a path not taken in modern architecture, might *Modern Housing* not suggest a future path? The power of Bauer's clear-sighted, humane, and equitable conception of housing has surely not faded. For all the tensions in her position, she never doubted what the goal of housing should be: the creation of diverse yet balanced communities that offer tenants of all stripes a chance at a civilized life, whether in cities or in its regions. To realize this vision, Bauer reached out through as many channels and tried to rally as many parties as she could, from politicians to labor organizers to citizens to architects. And while we might wish less of *Modern Housing*'s analysis remains so relevant today, Bauer knew that the battle for forward-pointing housing would be ongoing. Housing design, planning, and policy cannot stand still, because society, politics, and economics do not stand still. In the conflicted and divided environments created by capital, the one certainty is that modern housing will always be needed and will always require champions to spark love for it.

Acknowledgments

Many people have encouraged me in this project and provided much needed insight and support along the way. In particular, I wish to acknowledge Barry Curtis, Hilde Heynen, Nancy Levinson, Michael J. Lewis, Charles Rice, and Gwendolyn Wright, as well as Pieter Martin of the University of Minnesota Press. For generously sharing his unmatched knowledge of Lewis Mumford, I thank Robert Wojtowicz, along with the staff at Kislak Center for Special Collections, Rare Books and Manuscripts, University of Pennsylvania, who look after the Lewis Mumford Papers. Staff at the Bancroft Library, University of California, Berkeley, have also been helpful in dealing with requests related to the Catherine Bauer Wurster Papers. I had the extremely good fortune to be able to present on Bauer at a workshop on Ada Louise Huxtable at the Getty Research Institute in 2019. This foreword has benefited greatly from suggestions received there, especially from Barry Bergdoll, Maristella Casciato, Meredith Clausen, Thomas S. Hines, Mary

McLeod, Peg Rawes, and Suzanne Stephens. Finally, most sincere thanks to Sadie Super for giving her blessing to this reprint and making her mother's valuable work accessible again.

I am grateful to *Places Journal* for first nurturing my interest in Bauer. This essay is an expanded version of one originally published in *Places* as part of its "Future Archive" series. See Barbara Penner, "The (Still) Dreary Deadlock of Public Housing," *Places Journal,* October 2018, https://doi.org/10.22269/181030.

Notes

1. A full bibliography of Bauer's many writings can be found in Bernard J. Frieden and William W. Nash Jr., *Shaping an Urban Future: Essays in Memory of Catherine Bauer Wurster* (Cambridge, Mass.: MIT Press, 1969). This bibliography makes evident that while many of Bauer's articles or transcribed talks appeared in widely circulated mass magazines (*Fortune, New Republic, Nation*) and in architecture and housing journals (*Architectural Record, Architectural Forum, Journal of Housing*), a good number also remain tucked away in specialist conference proceedings, professional bulletins, and government reports.

2. There are exceptions, as feminist architectural historians have particularly explored Bauer's influence. See especially Cynthia Imogen Hammond, "The Interior of Modernism: Catherine Bauer and the American Housing Movement," in Sandry Alfoldy and Janice Helland, eds., *Craft, Space, and Interior Design, 1855–2005* (Abingdon, U.K.: Ashgate Publishers, 2008), 169–88; Hilde Heynen, "Places of the Everyday: Women Critics in Architecture," *Archis* 4 (2000): 58–64; Barbara Penner, "The (Still) Dreary Deadlock of Public Housing," *Places Journal,* October 2018, https://doi.org/10.22269/181030; Tania Marjetta Rikala, "Catherine Bauer and Six Riddles of Modernism," *The Journal of Architecture* 7, no. 2 (2002): 191–203; and Suzanne Stephens, "Voices of Consequence: Four Architectural Critics," in *Women in American Architecture: A Historic and Contemporary Perspective,* ed. Susana Torre, 136–43 (New York: Whitney Library of Design, 1977). Housing historians tend to pay more attention to Bauer. Gwendolyn Wright has cited Bauer consistently across all her works and has written the forthcoming entry on her for the "Pioneering Women of Architecture" website, edited by Mary McLeod and Victoria Rosner, https://pioneeringwomen.bwaf.org/. Also of note for this essay has been Gail Radford, *Modern Housing for America: Policy Struggles in the New Deal Era*

(Chicago: University of Chicago Press, 1996), especially chapters 3 and 7. The most substantial works on Bauer, drawing extensively on her papers and interviews with those who knew her, are Mary Susan Cole, "Catherine Bauer and the Public Housing Movement, 1926–1937," unpublished PhD dissertation (The George Washington University, 1975); and H. Peter Oberlander and Eva Newbrun, *Houser: The Life and Work of Catherine Bauer* (Vancouver: University of British Columbia Press, 1999).

3. For summaries of the rapid developments in government housing programs between 1931 and 1937, see Richard Pommer, "The Architecture of Urban Housing in the United States during the Early 1930s," *Journal of the Society of Architectural Historians* 37, no. 4 (December 1978): 235–64; and Radford.

4. Catherine K. Bauer, "Housing: Paper Plans, or a Workers' Movement," in *America Can't Have Housing*, ed. Carol Aronovici (New York: published for the Committee on the Housing Exhibition by the Museum of Modern Art, 1934), 21.

5. This summary is drawn from Oberlander and Newbrun, 3–48.

6. At this point in his thirties, Mumford (1895–1990) was a well-regarded critic of art, architecture, and literature, and author of four books, including *The Story of Utopias* (1922) and *Sticks and Stones* (1924). He would begin writing "The Sky Line" column for *The New Yorker* in 1931 and contributed reviews to many architectural journals, including the radical Werkbund publication *Die Form*; consequently leading European modern architects, such as Erich Mendelsohn, Ernst May, and Walter Gropius, looked him up on their American tours. For a comprehensive survey of Mumford's life, see Donald L. Miller, *Lewis Mumford: A Life* (New York: Grove Press, 1989); for a focused account of his architectural contributions, see Robert Wojtowicz, *Lewis Mumford and American Modernism: Eutopian Themes for Architecture and Urban Planning* (Cambridge: Cambridge University Press, 1996).

7. Relatively balanced summaries of the affair are provided in Miller, 305–40, and Oberlander and Newbrun, 48–89.

8. Mumford provided her with a "Memo on Introductions" to a lineup of architects and writers including Walter Curt Behrendt, Gropius, and May. On this trip, Bauer visited Norway, Sweden, Denmark, Germany (Berlin, Munich, Stuttgart, Heidelberg, Nuremberg, Frankfurt, Dessau, Weimar, Leipzig), France, and Holland. Oberlander and Newbrun, 54–67.

9. On Stuttgart: Catherine Bauer to Lewis Mumford, July 29, 1930, Lewis Mumford Papers, Kislak Center for Special Collections, Rare Books and Manuscripts, University of Pennsylvania (henceforth, LMP; all materials are from Ms. Coll. 2, III. Correspondence: Personal),

box 87, folder 6338; on Dessau: Catherine Bauer to Lewis Mumford, September 9, 1930, LMP, box 87, folder 6341.

10. Richard Pommer describes the article as "the most perspicacious appraisal of European modernist housing published in the United States in the 1930s" and gives Bauer full credit as one of the first critics in the United States to understand the links between European housing, planning, and architecture (before Mumford). In spite of her enthusiasm about Frankfurt, Bauer did not at this point claim it as a model for American housing, stressing, "This is not a plea for municipal control of housing construction." Catherine Bauer, "Prize Essay: Art in Industry," *Fortune* 3, no. 5 (May 1931): 94–110; and Pommer, 261.

11. Barry Bergdoll, *"Modern Architecture—International Exhibition,"* in *Partners in Design: Alfred H. Barr Jr. and Philip Johnson,* ed. D. Hanks, 136–43 (New York: The Monacelli Press, 2015). The authoritative account of the exhibition is Terence Riley, *The International Style: Exhibition 15 and The Museum of Modern Art,* ed. Stephen Perrella, 9–104 (New York: Rizzoli/Columbia Books of Architecture, 1992).

12. Alfred H. Barr Jr., "Foreword," to *Modern Architecture—International Exhibition* (New York: Museum of Modern Art, 1932), 16–17. The most extensive discussion to date is provided by Suzanne Spencer. She concludes that housing was a significant element of the 1932 show, attracting the most press commentary in New York and on its subsequent tour to cities from Philadelphia to Cleveland; she argues that Johnson and Barr were fully aware of public debates around housing and viewed it, opportunistically, as a means to capture public attention. Along with Bergdoll and Rixt Woudstra, Spencer also highlights MoMA's consistent championing of public housing through numerous shows through the 1930s into the mid-1940s, many involving Bauer or her sister, Elizabeth Mock (later Kassler). Bergdoll, 140–42; Suzanne Spencer, "'Housing on Trial': The Museum of Modern Art and the Campaign for Modern Housing in the United States, 1932–1952," unpublished PhD dissertation (Emory University, 2004); and Rixt Woudstra, "Exhibiting Reform: MoMA and the Display of Public Housing (1932–1939)," *Architectural Histories* 6, no. 1: 1–17; DOI: http://doi.org/10.5334/ah.269.

13. Mumford, "Housing," in *Modern Architecture,* 183.

14. Though publicly supportive, Bauer and Mumford had doubts about the exhibition. After an early meeting, Bauer complained, "one can just feel the superficiality of the eventual staging." Mumford responded that he was sure the show would be "a typical Museum of Modern Art modern exhibition—and that's pretty, pretty bad—Barrbarous *[sic]* in fact." Catherine Bauer to Lewis Mumford, February 9, 1931, LMP, box 88, folder 6345; and Lewis Mumford to Catherine

Bauer, February 9, 1931, LMP, box 88, folder 6345. For Wright and Mumford's exchanges, see Bruce Brooks Pfeiffer and Robert Wojtowicz, eds., *Frank Lloyd Wright and Lewis Mumford: Thirty Years of Correspondence* (New York: Princeton Architectural Press, 2001), 105–7, 123–28, 131–35. The "propaganda-trap"quotation is from page 123.

15. This account of the division of labor comes from Riley, 192. Although they all contributed, Johnson told historian Richard Pommer that Bauer "led" the effort. See Pommer, 261, note 61. Bauer's archive contains several files of visual materials that relate to the exhibition. See Catherine Bauer Wurster photograph collection, BANC PIC 1974.029, The Bancroft Library, University of California, Berkeley, carton 1, folders 3 and 19.

16. As far as I am aware, the reproduction of this panel in *Modern Housing* has not previously been noted. The panels from the housing section are not in the MoMA archives and Riley says only one, "Slum Improvement," is known through a reproduction in *Shelter* magazine. The panel in *Modern Housing,* titled "Good Houses Are Cheaper Than Bad Ones," is different from the one Riley identifies. See Bauer, *Modern Housing,* 278; and Riley, 192–93.

17. Bauer served on MoMA's Committee on Architecture and Industrial Art from 1936 to 1946 and also occasionally as a competition judge in later years. From 1932, she was involved, officially or behind the scenes, in far more housing exhibitions and catalogues than previously appreciated. These include *America Can't Have Housing* (1934; essay); *Art in America in Modern Times* (1934; essay); "Art in Architecture" (1934; consultant); *Architecture in Government Housing* (1936; foreword); *Modern Architecture in England* (1937; essay); "Art in Our Time" (1939; consultant, "Houses and Housing" section); "Wartime Housing" (1942; consultant); "American Housing in War and Peace" (1944; consultant); and "America Builds" (1944; consultant). Bauer's sister Elizabeth Mock worked at MoMA from the late 1930s, first as an assistant curator and then as curator of architecture (1943–46). Mock was author of significant MoMA catalogues and publications on modern architecture in her own right, including *Built in U.S.A.* (1945), *If You Want to Build a House* (1946), and *The Architecture of Bridges* (1949). Spencer's thesis provides a valuable account of Bauer's curatorial activities; she also discusses Mock in chapter 4. Erin E. McKellar explores aspects of both sisters' activities but gives more space to Mock: Erin E. McKellar, "Tomorrow on Display: American and British Housing Exhibitions, 1940–1950," unpublished PhD dissertation (Boston University, 2018). See also Bauer's correspondence files with various MoMA figures from Barr to Edgar Kaufmann Jr. between the 1930s and the 1960s. Catherine Bauer Wurster Papers, BANC MSS 74/163, The Ban-

croft Library, University of California, Berkeley (henceforth, CBWP), Professional Papers: Organizations, carton 2, folders 35–37.

18. Mumford's wife Sophie came for part of the trip, so Bauer and Mumford were together only in Munich, Frankfurt, Vienna, Paris, London, Welwyn, and Letchworth. Bauer's itinerary on this occasion was also shaped by Edith Elmer Wood, to Mumford's annoyance. Lewis Mumford, *Sketches from Life: The Autobiography of Lewis Mumford, the Early Years* (New York: The Dial Press, 1982), 464–68.

19. The first article began in England, the second moved to Germany and Holland, and the third dealt with public assistance for housing. See Lewis Mumford, "England's Two Million Houses, New," *Fortune* 6, no. 5 (November 1932): 32–37, 82–84; Lewis Mumford, "Machines for Living," *Fortune* 7, no. 2 (February 1933): 78–88; and Lewis Mumford, "Taxes into Houses," *Fortune* 7, no. 5 (May 1933): 48–49, 86–89.

20. "Boiling down" was Mumford's term. Lewis Mumford to Catherine Bauer, August 15, 1932, LMP, box 88, folder 6365. See also Mumford, *Sketches from Life,* 465–66. For Bauer's perspective, see Cole, 125–27.

21. The best summary of Bauer's aims and struggles with the book (the publication was delayed by a year and longer than agreed) is found in Cole, 131–37, 167–76. Bauer's correspondence with Houghton Mifflin Company is preserved in her papers: CBWP, Professional Papers: Writing, *Modern Housing,* box 6, folder 3.

22. In one letter after their affair had ended, Mumford told Bauer: "you were the only pupil and collaborator whom I fully respected that I had found in fifteen good years [. . .] by far and away the best raw material, male or female, that I have ever lighted on." Lewis Mumford to Catherine Bauer, March 18, 1936, LMP, box 90, folder 6389.

23. Lewis Mumford to Catherine Bauer, January 27, 1934, LMP, box 89, folder 6381.

24. For a discussion of the "usable past" methodology, see Miller, 250–52; and Wojtowicz, *Lewis Mumford,* 44–45.

25. Bauer, *Modern Housing,* 17–19.

26. In a later section on "Economics," she demonstrates how speculation results in extremely high land costs in America, at least twice that of Europe. See Bauer, 224–36, especially the chart on 235.

27. Wright quoted in Pfeiffer and Wojtowicz, 115. Bauer knew many Communists and was not unsympathetic to Marxist thought, but avoided defining her own position so rigidly. See Cole, 172–76.

28. Bauer, *Modern Housing,* 198; illustration, plate 30 D; Bauer, "Art in Industry," 102; and Mumford, "Machines for Living," 78, 84.

29. Bauer fully appreciated the importance of Frank Lloyd Wright, crediting him with the development of the open plan along with Le Corbusier (but stressing that Wright had done it thirty years earlier)

and noting his strong influence on many European architects. Like Mumford, she was wary of Wright's emphasis on individuality. Bauer, *Modern Housing,* 200. Bauer's sister Elizabeth was a lifelong Wright acolyte, beginning with her apprenticeship at Taliesin in the early 1930s.

30. Josephy has been called "the single most important figure in American trade book design during the crucial decade 1930–40"; he worked on many architectural books, including those by Behrendt, Hitchcock, and Mumford. He knew Bauer well from Harcourt Brace, where he taught her how to select and use types. (Observing her affair with Mumford, he wondered how her "talent for laughter" "fitted with Lewis's total lack of any sense of humor.") Bauer and Josephy were given unusual control in the design process, and Bauer had a say in most decisions, from font selection to jacket design. She reported sparring with Josephy over the best layout for the plates, specifically "on the matter of bleeding at the side": while admitting Josephy's top-bleed was better from an artistic perspective, she felt her side-bleed made the photographs more "readily visible." To settle the matter, she made pasteups of both options for Houghton Mifflin to consider. While Josephy prevailed, such incidents confirm that Bauer had a very clear vision for her book and almost obsessively considered its effects. Letter from Catherine Bauer to Lovell Thompson, April 1, 1934, CBWP, Professional Papers: Writings, *Modern Housing,* box 6, folder 7; Cole, 97, 173, 262; Robert Josephy, *Taking Part: A Twentieth-Century Life* (Iowa City: University of Iowa Press, 1993), 81, 90–91; and Oberlander and Newbrun, 46–47.

31. When Bauer provides image sources, they range from professional architectural photographers such as Frank Yerbury to image agencies such as Soviet Photo Agency; aerial views of cities come from specialist companies such as Aerofilms and Aviatik Basel. Bauer sourced many materials direct from architects and municipal planning bodies; some photographs are reproduced from postcards, periodicals, and publications such as *Das Neue Frankfurt.* A few come via colleagues and friends. Three images of Haesler's, Oud's, and Hans Sharoun's work are from MoMA. On sources of photographs for *Modern Architecture,* see Riley, 79–80; on Bauer's sources, see CBWP, Professional Papers: Writings, *Modern Housing,* 1933–1934, box 6, folder 6.

32. Letter from Catherine Bauer to Lovell Thompson, April 24, 1934, CBWP, Professional Papers: Writings, *Modern Housing,* box 6, folder 7.

33. Sigfried Giedion, *Befreites Wohnen / Liberated Dwelling: Facsimile Edition,* ed. Reto Geiser, trans. Reto Geiser and Rachel Julia Engler (1929; Zurich: Lars Müller Publishers, 2019). On the rise of the picture book, see Reto Geiser, Introduction to *Befreites Wohnen,* 4–36.

34. The important houser Carol Aronovici's assessment was typical:

"Miss Catherine Bauer's *Modern Housing* (1934) will long remain a standard work, both because of its thoroughness and because of the larger implication which she brings into focus regarding the cause of present housing conditions and the necessary remedies." Carol Aronovici, *Housing the Masses* (New York: John Wiley & Sons, Inc., 1939), 280. The book's reception is summarized in Cole, 201–6; Oberlander and Newbrun, 113–15; and Radford, 81–82.

35. Greenslet first raised the possibility of a revised edition in 1937. Copies sold out in October 1938; it seemed that reprinting the original without revisions was not an attractive option due to a combination of cost and the rapid changes in the housing scene. Although Bauer agreed to work on revisions, her schedule kept slipping, not least because she hoped to include an entirely new chapter on Scandinavia. In 1939, Greenslet suggested that it would be better for her to rewrite the entire book and reissue it at a lower price, something they were both keen on. Bauer produced an outline for an intensively revised book in 1942 and signed a contract for it in 1944; in 1947, however, she admitted the outline was "dead as it stands" and, in 1948, proposed an even more radically revised book focusing on the international housing problem. At this point, the trail of letters ends. Bauer's desire to revise her book was sincere, but the more time that passed, the more extensive, time-consuming, and unrealistic her revisions became. This account has been constructed from letters in CBWP, Professional Papers: Writing, *Modern Housing,* box 6, folders 3 and 4; Bauer's "Outline for revised *Modern Housing,*" May 9, 1942, can be found in box 6, folder 4.

36. As photographs were time-consuming and difficult to source, colleagues often lent them to each other; Bauer and Johnson are a case in point. Bauer may have lent Johnson images for the housing section in "Modern Architecture," and she certainly did for the 1934 show *America Can't Have Housing.* In response to a "desperate" phone call from Johnson a month before the show opened, Bauer asked Houghton Mifflin to send the original photographs from *Modern Housing* direct to MoMA once they were finished with them. These exchanges created a sense of déjà vu: the same photograph of Gropius's apartment building in the Berlin Siemensstadt not only appeared in Bauer's *Fortune* article and on the cover of *Modern Housing* but also on the cover of the catalogue for *America Can't Have Housing* and in Gropius's own *The New Architecture and the Bauhaus* (1935). Catherine Bauer to Lovell Thompson, September 12, 1934, CBWP, Professional Papers: Writings, *Modern Housing,* box 6, folder 7. While the reuse of images was pragmatic, it had the effect of reinforcing not only a particular canon of buildings but the machine-age aesthetic, enhanced by

cropping and painting. A pertinent study is George Dodds, *Building Desire: On the Barcelona Pavilion* (London: Routledge, 2005).

37. Radford, 83.

38. See Pommer, 235–64; Radford, 110–44; and Eric J. Sandeen, "The Design of Public Housing in the New Deal: Oskar Stonorov and the Carl Mackley Houses," *American Quarterly* 37, no. 5 (Winter 1985): 645–67.

39. The fullest accounts of Bauer's labor activism and efforts on behalf of various housing bills are Cole, chapter 6; and Oberlander and Newbrun, 115–56. See also Radford, 182–89.

40. For a helpful analysis, see Radford, 189–98.

41. Bauer quoted in Oberlander and Newbrun, 157.

42. Catherine Bauer to Lewis Mumford, September 2, 1931, LMP, box 88, folder 6354.

43. Catherine Bauer to Lewis Mumford, October 26, 1943, LMP, box 87, folder 6335.

44. Hammond gives an insightful discussion of how Bauer promoted a democratic architecture to attract public collaborators to the housing cause. Hammond, 176–81.

45. Oberlander and Newbrun, 151–52; Spencer, 158–60.

46. Lewis Mumford to Catherine Bauer, March 18, 1936, LMP, box 90, folder 6389.

47. Mumford told Cole that he viewed Bauer's increasingly narrow focus on housing as a reaction against his own "broadening" tendency and claimed she had a more "pedestrian" and less interesting career as a result. Cole, 208–14, 267–77.

48. Bauer had planned another big monograph focused on Soviet housing as a follow-up to *Modern Housing,* for which she received a Guggenheim fellowship. A combination of work, a traffic accident, and World War II meant it too was shelved. Oberlander and Newbrun, 146–51, 166–71.

49. Gwendolyn Wright provides a thoughtful account of their partnership, arguing that Bauer sharpened Wurster's politics, as well as his commitment to community planning and experimentation. In turn, Bauer took from Wurster greater respect for preservation, diversification, and architectural aesthetics. Gwendolyn Wright, "A Partnership: Catherine Bauer and William Wurster," in *An Everyday Modernism: The House of William Wurster,* ed. Marc Treib (Berkeley: University of California Press, 1995), 184–203.

50. This episode is fully covered in Oberlander and Newbrun, 251–61.

51. This summary is drawn from Penner.

52. Charles Abrams, *The Future of Housing* (New York: Harper & Brothers, 1946), 257, note 6.

53. Lewis Mumford, *Roots of Contemporary American Architecture* (New York: Reinhold Publishing Corporation, 1952), 421.

54. Nathan Straus, *The Seven Myths of Housing* (New York: Alfred A. Knopf, 1944), 306. As late as 1949, *Modern Housing* was still cited by the Harvard University librarian as having "one of the best housing bibliographies." Letter from Katherine McNamara to Albert Mayer, December 5, 1949. CBWP, Professional Papers: Writings, *Modern Housing*, box 6, folder 8.

55. Catherine Bauer, "The Dreary Deadlock of Public Housing," *Architectural Forum* 106, no.5 (May 1957); reprinted in *Places Journal*, October 2018, https://doi.org/10.22269/181030.

56. Catherine Bauer, "The Social Front of Modern Architecture in the 1930s," *Journal of the Society of Architectural Historians* 24, no. 1 (March 1965): 48–52. Unless otherwise specified, all quotations here are from this source. For a thorough analysis of the Modern Architecture Symposia held in 1962, 1964, and 1966, see Rosemarie Haag Bletter and Joan Ockman, with Nancy Eklund Later, *MAS: The Modern Architecture Symposia, 1962–1966* (The Temple Hoyne Buell Center for the Study of American Architecture, Columbia University in the City of New York; distributed by New Haven, Conn.: Yale University Press, 2014), especially Ockman's "Looking Back at the 1960s Looking Back: History and Historiography at the Modern Architecture Symposia," 17–39.

57. The "primadonnas" quotation is from Sibyl Moholy-Nagy to Catherine Bauer, December 9, 1960, CBWP, Professional Papers: Correspondence, box 23, folder 9. As another powerful but overlooked female voice in modernist debates, Moholy-Nagy is at last receiving her critical due. See Hilde Heynen, *Sibyl Moholy-Nagy: Architecture, Modernism, and Its Discontents* (London: Bloomsbury, 2019), especially the Introduction and chapter 6, for an insightful discussion of the relationship between modernism and feminism.

58. A full transcript of this discussion is in *MAS*. See Haag Bletter and Ockman, with Eklund Later, "Sunday Session: May 10, 1964. General Discussion," 201–24.

59. Bauer, "The Social Front of Modern Architecture in the 1930s," 48.

60. For more on this point, see Ockman, "Looking Back," 22–23, 29.

61. Haag Bletter and Ockman, with Ecklund Later, "Sunday Session," 201–2. The Bay Region controversy had kicked off in 1947 when Lewis Mumford had written an article in *The New Yorker* praising the Bay Region style at the expense of the International Style, drawing a predictably angry response from Johnson, Barr, and Hitchcock. See Introduction to Haag Bletter and Ockman, with Eklund Later, 2–3; and Wojtowicz, *Lewis Mumford*, 109.

62. Colin Rowe stated that "Modern Architecture" made architecture "safe for capitalism," something Bauer had also charged with her remark that Hitchcock and Johnson had made modernism "safe for millionaires." See Ockman, "Looking Back," 23.

63. Letter from Catherine Bauer to Renata B. Pan (MIT Press), May 6, 1964, CBWP, Professional Papers: Writings, *Modern Housing*, box 6, folder 5.

64. The "prodigious" quotation is from Stephens, 138.

65. Hilde Heynen also argues that Bauer's reputation has suffered because of her focus on the social aspects of architecture. Heynen, "Places of the Everyday."

66. Despite these efforts, the "do-gooding" stigma persisted. Philip Johnson, whose return to MoMA in 1945 marked the end of Bauer's and her sister's influence on its agenda, made no bones about his disdain for their position. Of Mock, he said, "She was more interested—as her sister [Bauer] was—in housing and in doing good, which interested me not at all"; quoted in Mark Lamster, *The Man in the Glass House: Philip Johnson, Architect of the Modern Century* (New York: Little, Brown and Company, 2018), 208.

67. Moholy-Nagy told Bauer: "This evening was so revealing and left me with an acute sense of renewed contempt for 'the great names' in architecture, and with an overwhelming sense of pride in the integrity and perceptive intelligence of a woman's mind." She also noted that, afterward, the hundreds of architecture students in the audience carried away "nothing else but a sense of frustration at the shining lights, and a sort of wonder at your meatiness." Sibyl Moholy-Nagy to Catherine Bauer, December 9, 1960.

68. Her sister, Elizabeth, recalls Bauer's genuine surprise at being asked if she had experienced sexual discrimination (Oberlander and Newbrun, 299). While she denied being personally affected, it is fair to say that, in her broader analyses, she was sensitive to the effects of gender—for instance, in drawing attention to the disproportionate impact poor-quality housing had on women and their families.

69. Pommer believes the growing standardization of public housing was well under way by 1935 and "carried housing further and further away from the art of modern architecture." This complicates his positive assessment of Bauer. Pommer, 342–44, 263–64. The "carried" quotation is from page 264.

70. For her critique of Bauer and Mumford, see Jane Jacobs, *The Death and Life of Great American Cities* (1961; New York: Vintage Books, 1992), 16–21. The "housing" quotation is from page 440. The complex relationship between Bauer and Jacobs merits further scrutiny, but a short summary of their dealings in these years can be found in Penner.

MODERN HOUSING

ACKNOWLEDGMENTS

FIRST of all, this book would hardly have been attempted were it not for the encouragement of Mr. Lewis Mumford; it could not have been written without the financial assistance of the Carnegie Corporation; and it might well have never achieved publication without the editorial patience of Mr. Ferris Greenslet. I am further indebted to the New Jersey State Federation of Women's Clubs, whose Fellow I was in the year 1932.

It would be quite impossible adequately to thank all the architects, planners, engineers, students, secretaries, officials, and private individuals who, throughout Europe, gave the author their invaluable time, attention, advice, company, criticism, information, hospitality, photographs, plans, and publications. A traveling student of modern housing comes home as warmly impressed with the international fellowship which exists in these matters as with the houses themselves.

My debt of gratitude to the following, however, must receive particular mention. In Germany: Dr. Walter Curt Behrendt, formerly editor of *Die Form* and Ministerialrat in the Prussian Ministry of Finance; Dr. Martin Wagner, formerly the Stadtbaurat of Berlin; Mr. Adolf Otto, formerly secretary of the German Garden City Association; the late Dr. Hans Kampffmeyer, secretary of the International Housing Association at Frankfurt; Miss Paula Schaefer of the same association; Mr. Ernst Kahn, formerly one of the directors of Frankfurt housing; Mr. Hugo Häring, the Berlin architect; Oberbaurat R. Prell of Nuremberg; Baudirektor Feuchtinger of Ulm; Professor Fritz Schumacher, formerly the chief of housing and planning in Hamburg; Mr. Richard Döcker, the Stuttgart architect; Dr. Robert Schmidt, formerly chief of the Regional Planning Office of the Ruhr; Mr. Lothar Schmitz, of the same; and Oberbaurat W. Arntz of Cologne.

In England: Sir Raymond Unwin, leader of the housing and planning movement; Mr. Barry Parker, architect and planner of Letchworth; Mr. John G. Martin, secretary of the National Housing and Town Planning Council; Mr. H. Chapman, secretary of the International Federation of Housing and Town Planning; Mr. S. Poynton Taylor, of the Ministry of Health; and Mr. F. J. Osborne, one of the managing directors of Welwyn Garden City.

In Holland: Mr. J. J. P. Oud, formerly City Architect of Rotterdam; Dr. Arie Keppler, chief of Amsterdam housing; and Dr. H. E. Suyver, director of the Hague Planning Office.

In France: M. Le Corbusier, architect; and Madame A. Bonnaud, of the Public Housing Office of the Seine Department.

In Switzerland: Mr. Otto Frey, secretary of the Housing Office of Zürich; Mr. Siegfried Giedieon, of the International Congress for Modern Architecture; and Messrs. Moser, Steiger, and their colleagues at Neubühl, Zürich.

In Vienna: various officials of the Municipal Housing Office, particularly Miss Salterer and Dr. Ignatius Musil.

In Stockholm: Mr. Hans Bartning, architect.

Concerning the past, present, and future of housing, particularly in America, I have made liberal use, not always accredited in the text, of the knowledge and ideas of Mr. Lewis Mumford, Mr. Henry Wright, Mr. Clarence Stein, Mr. Albert Mayer, Mr. Frank Vitolo, and Dr. Edith Elmer Wood. Needless to say, no one but the author is responsible for the statements and opinions presented in this book. Some of the material has already appeared, in somewhat different form, in the *Nation*, *Fortune*, and the *American Mercury*.

Catherine Bauer

AN INTRODUCTORY NOTE

'MODERN HOUSING,' let us say, has certain qualities and embodies certain methods and purposes, which distinguish it sharply from the typical residential environment of the past century. For one thing, it is built for efficient use over a period of years: therefore, it is not designed primarily for quick profits. It is 'planned': and so it must be non-speculative. This new housing method recognizes that the integral unit for planning, the economical unit for construction and administration, and the social unit for living, is the complete neighborhood, designed and equipped as such. A modern housing development does not, therefore, constitute a mere mechanical extension of streets and agglomeration of individual, competitive dwellings. It has a beginning and an end, and some sort of visible, organic form. One part is related to another part, and each part serves a particular, predestined use. It can never deteriorate into a slum, or a 'blighted area,' or a case for expensive remedial 'city planning.'

Moreover, modern housing provides certain minimum amenities for every dwelling: cross-ventilation, for one thing; sunlight, quiet, and a pleasant outlook from every window; adequate privacy, space, and sanitary facilities; children's play space adjacent. And finally it will be available at a price which citizens of average income or less can afford.

On such mild premises, how many dwellings are there in the United States which might be termed 'modern housing'? Very nearly none at all. Almost every dwelling put up since the war would have to be eliminated right away on the score of price alone, without even considering the matter of quality. By stretching one point or another, perhaps one could find as many as five or ten thousand, sheltering not more than one out of every three thousand families.

In Europe, however, the figures are quite different. Since the war at least six million dwellings have been put up which do, by and large, really constitute 'modern housing' as the term has here been defined. In England, Germany, Holland, and several other countries, with a combined population only slightly greater than that of the United States, there are four and a half million such dwellings, and about one seventh of all the families live in them. That is the contrast, ten thousand to four and a half million, each serving the same population. 'Modern European housing' would be a tautological phrase: there is practically no modern housing outside of Europe.

How did this happen? During most of this period America enjoyed unparalleled 'prosperity,' while Europe had little but poverty, financial chaos, and political instability. But today, after ten dizzy years of speculative building activity, America has little to show but congested tenements, wooden three- and four-deckers, and jerry-built, jostling bungalows; foreclosures, evictions, worthless mortgages, tax-delinquencies, and municipal bankruptcy; miles of unused pavement, vacant lots and expensive rotting utilities; a vastly increased and rapidly increasing area of blight and decay; and an oversupply of gadgeted millionaires' rookeries; while Europe has millions of low-rental, high-standard, modern dwellings in communities planned carefully to provide a maximum of amenity, pleasantness, efficiency, and long-time economy.

The truth of the matter is that the cities and nations of Europe could no longer support the luxury of speculative, substandard, chaotic house-construction. There was an acute shortage at the end of the war, accompanied by a complete breakdown in the old agencies of house production. And, fortified by half a century of experiment and increasing dissatisfaction, Europe was just realistic enough to supplant the obsolete and wasteful practice of the nineteenth century with an entirely new method. The land, construction, finance, and management of low- and medium-cost dwellings were removed from the speculative market: housing became a public utility.

We also had a housing shortage in 1920, but we were blind to the portents. Instead of setting up a new method, we encouraged, aided, and abetted one of the fanciest periods of speculative housing activity which the world has ever witnessed. With the result that, if the profit and property system were wiped out tomorrow, it would still take half a century to wipe out the bad effect on our environment of the golden era of capitalism.

Pretty soon there will be another shortage, due to the building hiatus of the past four years. Shall we revive the old land-and-dwelling business on the same old terms (if that were indeed possible in its present state of paralysis), or shall we revise upward our standards (at present about the lowest in the western world in all essential matters) of what a dwelling and an environment should be? Shall we put the final touch of ruin on our cities or shall we work out a method of attack at least as broad and realistic as that which Europe developed fifteen years ago? A method, that is, which is not confined to a few futile 'model' projects set up in a vacuum, or to a handful of extravagant and sentimental essays in 'slum-clearance,' but a method which determines that our next five million dwellings shall belong to the twentieth century and not to the nineteenth.

There should be no implication that Europe has actually *solved* the housing problem. Far from it. Of the six million dwellings, not more than half were within reach of the lowest-income groups, even at the time of their construction. And no country has even approached the matter of housing the wageless unemployed (with the exception of Hitler's handful of poor-farms). Indeed, most of those governments whose productive housing policies were their only creative measure in a decade of chaos and contradiction are now quite dead, and the period from 1919 to 1932 is a closed epoch. What even the immediate future holds in store, in housing or in larger matters, no one can say.

But still, there it is for all to see: a new standard of human environment, and a new technique for achieving it. And, although it is not true that any social-economic order which could produce good housing would be *ipso facto* a good system, it is certainly true that any arrangement which cannot do so is a reactionary and anti-social one.

PART ONE

NINETEENTH-CENTURY CITIES

A RECORD OF FAILURE

I. THE PERIOD OF BLACK CONGESTION

The Past, whether cherished with the traditionalists, or scorned with the radicals, or ignored by the 'average sensual man,' yet descends irrevocably upon all of us alike.

— Patrick Geddes and Victor Branford: OUR SOCIAL INHERITANCE

The Old Heritage and the New Deposit

Most European towns are like the nine cities of Troy. Each new layer, whether it lies tranquilly side by side with the earlier deposits or whether it has boldly effaced all but a few obstinate monuments, marks some sort of revolution, some fundamental change in the conception of what environment should offer to the eye, the body, and the mind; to the individual, the family, the class, and the community; to the rich and the poor; to the rulers and the ruled. Whether one reads history by the deaths of kings or by the price of wheat, by battles or by bread or by art, one finds that each succeeding age built a background unmistakably on its own terms.

If there were no written history, one could still deduce a great deal (as indeed a large part of present written history has been deduced) from a ruined Roman bath, a faintly eastern Romanesque cloister, a mediæval cathedral and guild-hall inseparable from the banked-up burgher houses. Moreover, if each authentic layer marks a revolution in purpose and power, it can usually show a development, or at least a change, in means: new techniques — social, economic, structural, æsthetic — for setting up the new pattern.

Each 'Style' marked off neatly in the histories of architecture does not of itself constitute a complete layer. A real stage in the history of environment has its vernacular as well as its monuments, its pattern of streets and open spaces and living habits as well as its ornamental detail and measurable proportions. Most European cities have only three distinct historic deposits, still recognizably intact in some sort of everyday use. Broadly, these layers may be labeled mediæval, neo-classic, and nineteenth century. Or, if one prefers to classify them by their makers — the scale figures which explain them — they are the respective backgrounds of merchant-craftsmen and priests; of princes and armies; of industrialists and wage-earners.

The subject of this book is the promise and possibility, even the concrete beginning, of quite a new layer, as different from any of the others as they were from each other. But let us first recall a few of the general characteristics of the earlier deposits.

First there is the mediæval nucleus: the cobbled market-place with the Guild or Town Hall in immediate focus and the cathedral just outside but still dominant. The steep roofs build up to slender spires and solid towers. And the narrow alleys, with their glass-fronted houses leaning toward each other, converge with less ingenuousness than is at first apparent to our rectilinear eyes. Such a picture, grown a trifle more abstract and four-square toward the end of the period, holds good for most of northern Europe straight through the seventeenth century.

But this nucleus, convincing though it still is for the most part, now stands a trifle off-center except in such towns as Lübeck or Chartres. And if we locate on a map some near-by district with an abundance of 'Squares,' 'Avenues,' parades, and palace parks, we can easily guide ourselves into the next phase of city-development — the neo-classic eighteenth century which built by Rule, but did not always rule by Reason.

Here regularity is a virtue and repetition a means to effect. Here belong the quiet English squares, urbane and dignified. Here also is the dominant symmetrical palace, with windows evenly punched, clipped gardens and military parade-grounds, tree-lined approaches and subtly planned perspective vistas. Above all, here is the radial avenue, straight as the volley which played no small part in its conception. The avenues are flanked by fine trees and imposing façades, impersonal fronts which give little clue to any extremes of luxury or squalor, of spacious gardens or congested alleys, which may exist behind them.

But as we follow the avenue in the direction of traffic, the trees begin to fall away, the impersonal façades have been refurbished in the interests of commercial competition rather than princely perspective. The great bulk of our city — the blanket which fills the gaps between palace and cathedral, which swallowed up the gardens behind the mediæval houses, which turned the palaces into museums for curios or places of business, and which finally carried the city, on a wave of tremendous expansion, far beyond its last outlying set of fortifications — was the work of the nineteenth century.

To see the nineteenth century pure and undefiled we must go to the railroad station. A shade more orderly and prepossessing in Germany than in England or France, a *Bahnhofplatz* is still pretty much the same the world over. A foreground of noise, dirt, beggars, souvenirs and shrill competitive advertising, of tangled street-car lines and tortuous traffic. A middle-ground of warehouses, gilded theaters, competing shop-fronts and commercial hotels with gruesome ornament and unconvincing marble entrances. A background of smokestacks and tall crowded tenements. 'Down by the railroad tracks' or 'Back of the station' means 'slum' in any language.

But perhaps this single vantage-point is unfair. The nineteenth century as it turned the corner into the twentieth built suburbs as well as tenements. It had its reaction toward Romantic escape as well as its orthodox business gods. Any of the radiating trolley-lines will probably take us to one of these residential districts populated by the middle classes in the eighties and nineties.

But alas, what do we find? Of the dim vague hope for a better environment, hardly a trace. But as a witness to the more specific hopes of the land-speculator and the real-estate promoter, there are whole districts, whole towns, squeezed into a gridiron network regardless of geography or any other science, carved up into salable front feet, into twelve- to twenty-foot lots, into solid blocks of tenements, into an ugliness and tastelessness never before produced with such relentless energy on the face of the earth.

In London there are miles and miles of 'By-Law Streets,' with endless bristling rows of narrow houses — Procrustean dwellings which, like the brownstones of New York, were never suited to any of the demands incident to the successive uses to which they were put: upper middle-class residences, boarding-houses, small flats.

On the Continent the five or six or seven or even eight-storied apartment-house, with two or three tiny paved courts one back of the other supplying all the light and air and outlook, and with a grim beetling façade supplying all the architecture, was so perfected that an English doctor writing in 1896 could say that 'the whole town [Berlin] may be characterized as a tableland of bricks and mortar 72 feet high, cut up by intersecting valleys representing the streets.'

A few of the more persistent and adventurous citizens escaped somewhat farther, into straggling 'individual' villas and bungalows on the outskirts. There they could raise a small piece of green lawn and perhaps a few cabbages if they could not, or not for long, contemplate the primeval. But for the most part the inhabitants of the By-Law streets and the respectable suburbs clipped their vague desires to the shape of their condition and concentrated on more pressing matters. The scale figure of the nineteenth century is nothing if not busy. And as for the admitted slum-dwellers, the submerged half or two thirds of the population, they remained exactly where they were, only more so, paying a little more rent for a trifle more dilapidated and congested quarters, and without benefit of even the most fleeting notion of escape.

The nineteenth century did not invent the modern western housing problem. Despite the rigorous land control, house-owning became a speculative trade as far back as the thirteenth century. But the mediæval towns, particularly those which were not too continuously preoccupied with defense, were on the whole remarkably spacious and even hygienic. The same towns in the Renaissance, and later after the expensive and complicated Vauban Bastion fortifications had come in, presented quite a different aspect. Gardens were built over, alleys clogged up, principles of hygiene and sanitation lost, and the 'pestering of many families in one small house' contributed to great waves of disease and sudden death.

That other great period of English commercial prosperity, the age of Elizabeth, was also marked by a housing crisis. Major Barnes quotes the following remarks from a Jacobean tract:

'The desire of Profitte greatly increaseth Buyldinges, and so much the more, for that this great Concurse of all sortes of people draweinge nere unto the Cittie, everie man seeketh out places, highewayes, lanes and coverte corners to buylde upon, yf it be but Sheddes, Cottages and small Tenements for people to lodge inn.... Thes sort of covetous Buylders exact great renntes, and daiely doe increase them in so muche that a poore handie craftesman is not able by his paynefull laboure to paye the rennte of a smale Tenemente and feede his familie. Thes Buylders neither regard the good of the Commonwealthe, the preservacion of the health of the Cittie, the maynetenance of honeste Tradesmen, neither doe they regarde of what base condicion soever their Tenantes are, or what lewde and wycked practizes soever they use so as their exacted renntes be duely payed the which for the moste parte they do receive either weekely or moontheley.'

But still, none of the towns was very large. Nearly everyone had easy access to the open fields, and spent a great part of his time out-of-doors. Factory chimneys had not begun to poison the air, nor industrial refuse to pollute the water.

No, the housing problem as we know it, with its causes and effects reaching into every department of economics, politics, science, and sociology, owes its majestic scale to the developments of the last century. It must always remain one of the great historic ironies that the century which invented the notion of material Progress, which unfolded more scientific possibility than all the preceding years of western civilization put together, was also the century which debased human environment to about its lowest known level. If a civilization is 'the use to which an age puts its resources of wealth, knowledge, and power, in order to create a social life,' then the nineteenth century as a civilization is a record of failure.

But think, the reader may say, think of the great reformers, the great revolutionists, the scientists, the geographers, the countless Utopias (some on paper and some actually constructed). Think of the huge engineering constructions, the household conveniences, the hygienic inventions. Think of bathtubs, running hot and cold water, steam heat, railroads, electric lights, steel skeletons, power, elevators, paved roads, automobiles, steamships, telephone and telegraph, photography, linotype, public education, hospitals, public libraries, museums. Surely there never was an age with so many practical and urgent ideas about civilization.

Which is probably true enough. And yet, looking around at the still visible monuments to a century of building, what can one say but that the constructive energy of Europe and America, from about 1800 onward, was devoted almost exclusively to the production of a definitely low-grade environment — by any standard or from any realistic point of view? The cities grew progressively uglier and more wasteful and less workable. The average dwelling of the average citizen was narrower, darker, dirtier, and more crowded in the prosperous middle decades than it ever had been before. And if it was a trifle more sanitary in some instances by 1900, this advantage was balanced by far less accessibility to work-places and play-places and open country, and by greatly increased rents.

The entering wedges which were beginning to change this state of things, ever so slightly, were all against the dominant currents of the time. They belong to our day rather than their own. Morris and Marx alike, the power engineers and the physicists and the geographers and the sociologists, are all more important to us than they were to their contemporaries. The forces actually dominant in the Industrial Revolution all had their specific influence on city and country, on houses and architecture, and the net effect was almost invariably a bad one. As Morris put it:

'Even if a tree is cut or blown down, a worse one, if any, is planted in its stead, and, in short, our civilization is passing like a blight, daily growing heavier and more poisonous, over the whole face of the country, so that every change is sure to be a change for the worse in its outward aspects.'

Perhaps the classic picture of a high nineteenth-century slum, at its most exuberant and purest stage, is that given by Friedrich

Engels in 1844. He is describing the view from Ducie Bridge on the river Irk in Manchester.

'At the bottom flows, or rather stagnates, the Irk, a narrow coal-black, foul-smelling stream, full of débris and refuse, which it deposits on the shallower right-hand bank.... Beside this, the stream itself is checked every few paces by high weirs, behind which slime and refuse accumulate to rot in thick masses. Above the bridge are tanneries (which fill the whole neighborhood with the stench of animal putrefaction), bonemills and gasworks, from which all drains and refuse find their way into the Irk, which receives further the contents of all the neighboring sewers and privies.... Below the bridge you look upon the piles of débris, the refuse, filth, and offal from the courts on the steep left bank. Here each house is packed close behind its neighbor and a piece of each is visible, all black, smoky, crumbling, ancient, with broken panes and window-frames.... The background is furnished by old barrack-like factory buildings.... and embraces the pauper burial-ground, the station of the Liverpool and Leeds Railway, and, in the rear of this, the workhouse, the "Poor Law Bastille" of Manchester, which, like a citadel, looks threateningly down from its high walls and parapets on the hilltop, upon the working people's quarters below.'

The gasworks, the railroad station, the cemetery, the poorhouse! No realistic painter, no satiric draftsman, could do that typical industrial slum justice: it would require the mystic and infernal palette of a Rouault.

But 1844 is a long time ago, and the science of public health has made great strides in the interim. 'Zoning' has become common practice. Still, there is hardly a single city on either side of the Atlantic which could not today show at least a small area in most ways comparable. And there are literally thousands of mining and mill towns, particularly in America, whose principal features Engels might have been describing. Let us see what Engels himself says, fifty years later, of the improvements:

'Drainage has been introduced or improved, wide avenues have been opened up athwart many of the worst slums I had to describe.... But what of that? Whole districts, which in

1844 I could describe as almost idyllic, have now, with the growth of the towns, fallen into the same state of dilapidation, discomfort, and misery. Only the pigs and the heaps of refuse are no longer tolerated. The bourgeoisie have made further progress in the art of hiding the distress of the working classes. But that, in regard to their dwellings, no substantial improvement has taken place, is amply proved by the "Report of the Royal Commission on the Housing of the Poor," 1885.'

And indeed it was. The essential difference between Engels, the drastic revolutionist, and the plodding, ineffective 'reformers' of this period, whom we shall have occasion to mention later, is principally the fact that Engels really *saw* the world about him, and knew that it was not good.

More People in the Same Space

And these rows of new houses, added to the Wen, are proofs of growing prosperity, are they? These make part of the increased Capital of the country, do they? —William Cobbett: RURAL RIDES

Every major aspect of the Industrial Revolution had its own attendant influence on the form and quality of human background. There were local variations in detail, but it is only remarkable, in a period of such pronounced growth in national spirit, that all the main lines in the environment picture are international and intercontinental in scope. What is true of Philadelphia and Sydney is almost equally true of Berlin and Lyons and Manchester. The same forces were at work, impelled by the same credos and purposes.

That the problem was a large order for any age, no one can deny. In the first place, population increased by leaps and bounds. In spite of emigration, in spite of the beginning of a general knowledge of birth control, in spite of slum diseases and high rates of infant mortality, the population of England increased from less than 9 millions in 1801 to more than 36 millions in 1911. And that of Germany from 24.5 millions in 1800 to 65 millions in 1910. Such facts alone might well account for a certain amount of overcrowding along the way, even if the increase were evenly distributed geographically, real wages high enough to pay an 'economic' rent, and the building industry geared to supply the average demand.

But the additional population was by no means evenly distributed. The Industrial Revolution had, by some means which no science or theory of history has as yet been quite able to explain, called them forth. And to the centers of industry they went, by the hundreds of thousands. By 1891, 72 per cent of the people in England and Wales were living in cities or towns. In Germany the movement came later, but was just as decisive. In 1871, 64 per cent of the population was rural. By 1919, the proportions were reversed, and the rural population made up only 37.5 per cent. The net result, for all practical purposes, is that the large European cities are just as new as the American ones. Indeed, many of them have actually grown much faster. This fact is worth a little emphasis if only to show that, if many European towns have been able of recent years somewhat more effectively to direct and control this growth than have the American cities, it is in no wise because their problem was any less difficult or the emergency less acute.

From 1800 to the present, the people living in the Greater London area increased from about one million to over eight millions. In 1836, Paris had a population density of 11,000 per square kilometer: by 1886 the figure was 29,000. But the most interesting comparisons are between the German and American cities, after the Franco-Prussian and Civil Wars respectively. Between 1871 and 1910, the population of Frankfurt and Düsseldorf quintupled. And in a table prepared in 1913, Mr. Frederick Howe compared various German and American cities of about equal population in 1880, and showed that the former had grown about twice as fast as the latter.

This is not the place to indulge in speculation as to the reasons, or judgment as to the real necessity, for this vast centralizing movement. It happened. And what were the effects on human environment?

Overcrowding, of course. Overcrowding in every department of the housing operation. Congestion of people in rooms; 'extra' families in dwellings; contraction of room areas and of the number of rooms per dwelling; overstuffing of both rooms and dwellings into tall honeycomb rookeries and tenements; overcoverage of land by buildings; and the endless multiplication of packed residential blocks, without benefit of even the slenderest intervening slice of open area — whether country, park, playground, grass-plot, or mere breathing-space. Overcrowding, moreover, of every family's budget with a newly exorbitant rent item.

But how could this be? According to the most respectable nineteenth-century economic theories (or, at least, according to that section of the theories which was taken to heart by the most respectable people), the increased demand should have fostered tremendous competition; and the competition should have resulted in large-scale production and greater efficiency; and that should have produced in turn a better and cheaper product, profits for the most efficient, and general satisfaction all around. But alas, if there is any commodity to which that little equation applies less than to any other commodity, it is land — land and buildings. Large-scale production of a kind there was, and even, in a sense, there was greater 'efficiency': less land and less building per person. And profits there certainly were. But the satisfaction, however intense, was limited to a few, and the dwellings themselves got steadily worse and more expensive.

This is about the way it worked. The people came down on the towns like the proverbial Assyrians, except that as it turned out they were rather the sheep than the wolves of the story. And the thin tradition of Mediæval and Renaissance city-building, which constituted all the ideas there were as to the nature and form of urban environment, was totally inadequate to the emergency. On the one hand there was the remnant of a conception, very vague, that a city is a sort of static picture, surrounded by walls and containing a more or less constant population. But, while the walls remained in many cases well on into the nineteenth, and even the twentieth, century, there was no longer any control, either exterior by authority or interior by conviction or desire, over the influx of new residents. And on the other hand the population increased by leaps and bounds, finally bursting all the old barriers, and there was no *new* idolum, no re-formulation of ideas as to the æsthetic, economic, or social nature of a city, to create a new organic form. Many an old town with a designed nucleus and an air of leisurely 'artificial' dignity was, as Professor Abercrombie has said, 'suddenly overwhelmed by a rush of prosperity: the lava streams of irrupting urbanism seem to flow blindly in natural devastating confusion. The whole of the nineteenth century outburst of town-building was likened by Cobbett, who was living in the midst of it, to an epidemic of wens, with London as the GREAT WEN. And the wen, though it depends upon human sustenance, is beyond human control.'

For convenience, one can distinguish three periods in this process. The first was that of chaotic concentration, when alleys and gardens were covered over with flimsy, disreputable shacks of the kind described in the forties by Engels. The second is that of legalized congestion, when the standardized built-in slum appeared for the first time. And the third is that of unregulated speculative expansion, when the new slum types were extended outward over miles of surrounding open country. Obviously, this is a somewhat arbitrary distinction, varying greatly from city to city. But there is hardly a town which cannot show one aspect or another of all three.

The early period of wild disorder was the natural first result of increasing population density in the city-centers. Cottage industries and scattered self-sufficient workshops were being replaced by large centralized factory-plants. The network of coach and canal routes was superseded by the single main-line railroad. And the people perforce clustered around the factory and the junction station and the warehouse. It is the period when all the small gaps and remaining open spaces, which had tended somewhat to mitigate the lack of sanitary appliances or hygienic regulation, were covered over. The reports of later sanitary inspectors in every country describe block after block, mile upon mile, where rear gardens and service roads had been converted into noisome courts and alleys, unpaved, unventilated, and without even the benefits of a neighborhood pump. (Those in Washington, D.C., are still among the worst of these.) Thousands of families had to beg water day by day. There were few sanitary regulations, little inspection, and no building codes. Any sort of building could be, and was, used for a dwelling.

But still there were not enough places for the people to live. And still, it was not possible in most cases for them to live at any great distance from the center. In many cities there were actual walls, often with gate-tolls and customs inspection. Cheap and convenient transportation means were still lacking. Often outlying land was kept from development through being in large estates, or in the hands of speculators who did not desire to build as yet. Moreover, particularly in the Continental cities, the ancient traditions of a close town life and urban culture, centering around the market-place and the inns and the public halls, made life in a *vorort* or *banlieu* seem hardly worth living, even to the poorest denizens of the alleys. (And who can say, looking at some of the later Anglo-Saxon suburbs, that they were not right?)

A great international wave of cholera and typhus began to result in a few timid and very mild sanitary measures. And about the same time the demand for dwellings brought about a degree of standardization and considerable large-scale construction in the building industry. And thus, still for the most part within the old limits of the city, we come to the second period in the archæology of the nineteenth-century dwelling.

The Built-in Slum: A New Standard

Land-values in the central districts had sky-rocketed. The average family had to be content with a smaller and smaller share of his dwelling-site. And presently two people were living where one had lived before. But the chaotic alley shanties were not sufficient to the requirements of this more systematic land-sweating. New forms had to be found.

This is the period when the modern built-in slum was really invented. There had, of course, been plenty of slums before, but not until the prosperous middle decades of the nineteenth century did buildings appear which were slums from the moment the plans were conceived or set on paper, slums duly legalized and codified and accepted in general practice. In some localities, it is true, they came in earlier: notably in the early periods of commercial prosperity in London and Glasgow. And it was not the industrialism but the military barracks of Frederick the Great which introduced them to Prussia. But the results, in any case, were quite internationally comparable. It is the heyday of the back-to-back house, of the railroad flat, of the worst Continental tenements.

In America it was largely the Negroes and 'foreigners' who had found lodging in the alleys and early tenements. In England, it was the Irish workers. Nassau Senior described the homes of the Irish in Manchester in 1837:

'These towns, for in extent and number of inhabitants they are towns, have been erected with the utmost disregard of everything except the immediate advantage of the speculative builder. A carpenter and builder unite to buy a series of building sites and cover them with so-called houses. In one place we found a whole street following the course of a ditch, because in this way deeper cellars could be secured without the cost of digging, cellars not for storing wares or rubbish, but for dwellings of human beings. Not one house in this street escaped the cholera. In general the streets of these suburbs are unpaved, with a dungheap or ditch in the middle; the houses are built back to back, without ventilation or drainage, and whole families are limited to a corner of a cellar or a garret.'

By the end of the century some of the more striking sanitary defects in such houses may have been somewhat remedied, but unless they had fallen down or been removed to make way for a railroad or a chance commercial extension, they were still standing, and still overcrowded.

But a mere back-to-back house, two stories high, would have been an unheard-of luxury for the immigrants to America. The first New York tenements (and, incidentally, one of them was a 'model' philanthropic enterprise) were erected in the thirties, thus inaugurating four decades of 'railroad flats,' an utterly incredible type of construction which breaks all known records (short of ancient Rome) for environmental insalubrity. The buildings are twenty-five feet wide and about ninety feet deep on a twenty-five by one-hundred-foot lot. They are five to seven stories high and there are four dwellings per floor, containing all together two rooms looking on the street, two on a ten-foot rear court, and ten to twelve interior rooms, sometimes with tiny air-shafts, but often without windows of any sort. Privies or 'school sinks' were in the yard, and there might be as much as one faucet per floor.

In Continental cities during this mid-century period, the poorer citizens were still likely to inhabit the basements, garrets, and back-buildings of apartment-houses whose only livable quarters were occupied by the middle class. Old buildings were cut up into tiny rooms, stories were added, wings were built on. The gauge of housing standards can be judged all too adequately from the quality of the 'model' tenements which began to appear, and which will be duly described in a later chapter. Between 1853 and 1887 in Berlin, the building code permitted apartment-buildings six and a half stories high (although many were higher), sixty-five feet wide and one hundred and seventy-five feet deep, covering all of the plot except three inner shafts, each about seventeen feet square. Strictly speaking, however, this ordinance belongs to the next period, when public authorities were endeavoring to bring 'order' into the chaos.

But why describe these paleolithic conditions? Many of the buildings are no longer in existence, and they never did cover a very large area by comparison with the present extent of our cities. Now we have paved streets, sewers, and whole volumes of building and sanitary codes. The back-to-back house and the railroad flat are alike outmoded. There is nothing like the density of population living in the city-centers today that there was in the mid-nineteenth century. Why bring up the old horrors which, even if they were never solved satisfactorily, are still no longer with us in the same form?

Which is all quite true, or at least almost quite true. For plenty of the buildings which horrified the hardy investigators of the fifties and sixties, and were officially 'condemned' in the nineties, are still inhabited and still in much the same state. But that is not the point here. The real reason for describing the first results of centralization and for analyzing the various influences which made them the way they were is a much more direct and positive one than mere historical muck-raking. For during that comparatively short period, *the basic standard for a whole era of construction was established.* The standard of demand was completely broken down. There was an entirely new housing 'norm,' and for generations thereafter any movement away from it was merely a matter of degree, of slow and expensive and frustrated 'reform.' The fundamental pattern could not be changed until a completely new set of purposes and methods could be set in motion, not to reform, but to supersede the old ones. A machine had been set up to grind out a new environment for a new age, and there was no way to change the product in any basic respect without scrapping the whole apparatus and inventing a new one.

This housing machine had two major elements: the land speculator and the small builder, both almost entirely uncontrolled in accordance with the economic credo of the time. And, however the Liberal principle may have worked out in other departments of production, its effect on housing and city-building was little short of disastrous. Land is a very peculiar commodity, and 'real estate' is in some ways the most unreal and purely relative notion in our psyche.

Space is probably the most important single factor, short of a certain minimum of firmness, in the quality of a dwelling, particularly an urban dwelling. The amount of space per house, both inside and out, plays a determining part not only in the convenience and adequacy of the interior arrangements, but also in light, air, ventilation, outlook, health, cleanliness, quiet, privacy, and recreational facilities. It is not true *ad infinitum*, that the more space there is, the better is the dwelling (as many of our mathematically quite open mid-western American cities can prove). But there is a definite point in urban housing below which it is true, that the less space the worse dwelling.

And what determines the amount of space per dwelling or per person, whether in terms of site, block, neighborhood, or city? Obviously, although there are other factors, the most important and immediate one is the price of land. But what determines the price of land? And here is where we get into one of those intricate little equations which, because they were not neat and arithmetical, were so utterly disregarded by the Manchester Liberals. For the price of urban land is almost never the result of anything even faintly resembling the orthodox conception of a free market deal. It is almost never achieved by agreement between willing competitive sellers, and buyers who know and desire the best for the least possible money, and who do not have to buy. On the contrary, it would present a much more nearly accurate picture of the process to say that the price of urban land is determined by the most intensive future use to which a speculator estimates that the plot can be put. And this 'most intensive use' is unfortunately determined by a great many factors other than mere realistic considerations of residential quality or long-run economy. A thousand purely psychological and circumstantial variables arise, and perhaps the most important of these is the current evidence as to what *is* the lowest standard of space which people are putting up with at any given moment. In short, the price of land is largely determined by the lowest housing standards permissible or acceptable.

It was not, therefore, the high price of land which produced the tenement. It was the possibility of high density, crystallized in building-codes, street-plans, development-costs, and eventually in taxes, which pushed up the land-prices.

And this is why that short period of utter chaos and unregulated congestion was so disastrously important. The whole standard of space, and the amenities which depend on space, was lowered to a point nearly approximating zero. And there it was to remain, with minor variations, for seventy-five years. Theoretically, and if the 'public' were ever in economic actuality the conscious and canny defender of its own long-time welfare which the classic economists liked to believe it was, the outcome would have been quite otherwise. This hypothetical united 'public' would have constantly realized that the bad conditions of the forties were only a temporary emergency. It would have prevented the expansion and infinite multiplication of those conditions by collectively and individually refusing to move to the newer districts unless they offered something fundamentally better. But how could this 'public' have acted that way? The pressure was becoming greater all the time, instead of less. To refuse to move into bad dwellings would have been to refuse to have any shelter at all.

The net result was that the early reformers — in any case not a very inspiring group — wasted their efforts for the most part within a pattern of things which was quite impossible to begin with. Horrified sanitary inspectors, irate clergymen, conscience-salving philanthropists, nationalists worried over the death and debility rate, earnest ladies bent on 'improving' the lower classes, occasionally a few honest doctors — they succeeded merely in spreading and crystallizing the very things which they seemed to be fighting. At most they invented new, and always more expensive, kinds of slums to supersede the old ones. Do not misunderstand me: I am not 'blaming' them. Perhaps the whole cycle was quite inevitable, or at least entirely beyond any easily imaginable contemporary control. But on the evidence one must admit that their achievements were remarkable only for their insufficiency.

'Progress' by Compulsion: the Anatomy of Fear

It must not be thought that this failure was merely a relative one, that our eyes were bigger than our resources, the standard of living rising faster than the means of satisfying it. It is quite true that one of the largest factors in increased costs was the gradually increasing provision, by legal enforcement, of various services and utilities: water, sanitary plumbing, sewers, refuse collection, paved and lighted streets, transportation. And if they had been used creatively, to set up that really new and better form of environment which they so obviously made possible, they would most certainly represent unqualified progress in standards of living.

But there was very little either creative or progressive about either the purpose or the immediate results of the early sanitary regulations. They arose out of stark necessity, and in that spirit they were administered.

A very real and significant distinction must be made, particularly in the field of restrictive building legislation, between *convenience* (which may be taken to mean something positive to be worked *for*) and *necessity*, which implies something negative, to be fought against at any cost or by any means. As far as convenience is concerned, plumbing and hot and cold running water and flush toilets are just exactly as desirable and valuable to a rural housewife as they are to an urban tenant. But when it comes down to simple vital necessity, the situation is quite different. A well-laid-out five-acre farm with merely a pump and an outhouse by way of utility, can be just exactly as healthy although by no means as convenient, as an urban flat provided with every latest hygienic gadget, from air-conditioning to glassed-in showers. But a crowded tenement centrally located in a high-density area, without ample running water, without flush toilets, and fronting on an unpaved and unserviced street, will probably have double the death- and disease-rate of the simple farmhouse — not to mention its wider effect as a likely breeding-place for city-wide epidemic.

In the same way, a town of the usual early mediæval type, small and definitely limited in extent and closely surrounded by open country, a town in which almost every house has a garden behind it, and whose air is not polluted by smoke or gasoline, has infinitely less of sanitary requirements than the same city when its area has been multiplied by ten, its population density quadrupled, and most of its workers spend their days in offices and factories. The modern metropolis has to start with an enormous burden of expensive equipment and services, merely to keep life going at all.

And this was the form that the problem took, about the middle of the past century. Here and there a few doctors and inspectors began to connect disease and epidemic with smells, and smells with filth, and filth with miserable living conditions. There was a trickle, and then a deluge, of surveys and threatening statistics. In every large city, it began to appear that if you had the bad luck to be born in a working-class district, your expectancy of life was just about half what it would have been had you had the foresight to select middle-class parents. In slum districts, anywhere from thirty to seventy-five per cent of all babies born alive died within their first year. The prevalence of cholera, typhus, tuberculosis, rickets, pneumonia was shown to mount with beautiful geometrical regularity as the density of population and the lack of sanitary conveniences increased. Inadequate food was of course one factor, but food had grown somewhat cheaper around the middle of the century, with little appreciable effect on vital statistics. Given a 'back-to-back' house and a 'through' house comparable in every other respect including rent, and the death-rate was twenty per cent higher in the former. And so on.

Such facts, when combined with the cholera epidemics (fifty thousand people died of it in England in 1850) which hit rich and poor alike, and when duly seasoned with the ever-increasing signs of desperation and revolt on the part of the under-classes, were not designed to let even the smuggest Malthusians rest easily forever on their ruffled Victorian beds. If the French Revolution, as the Hammonds pointed out in *The Town Labourer*, served to make the class lines clearer and to strengthen the upper classes in their conviction that the proletariat was something to be kept down at all costs, then Chartism, 1848 and 1870, had a somewhat different effect. People looked down the Iron Age pit which they had created, and, reluctantly, were disposed to feel that a certain minimum of compromise might be advisable.

But the anatomy of nineteenth-century fear included still another bogey. The tremendous growth of commercial imperialism, plus the attendant and ever-present threat of international warfare, resulted in great concern for the defenses of the National State. The birth-rate, the death-rate, and the general stamina of the nation became objects of serious internal *Realpolitik*. When health statistics resolved themselves into the necessity, on two occasions before 1900, of reducing the standard of height of men entering the British army, even generals and bankers began to take an interest in sanitary conditions. Much publicity and discussion were raised by the fact that, in 1899, of eleven thousand Manchester men who tried to enlist, only three thousand were accepted — and of them only one thousand could be sent into the regular army. The fact that Germany had an excessively high death-rate (26.2 per thousand in 1886) and a relatively even higher rate of infant mortality was surely not an unimportant factor in Bismarck's social insurance legislation of the late eighties. In France, the major political emphasis in all matters of sanitary and housing legislation straight through to the present day has been the desire to increase the birth-rate, and thereby the number of potential defenders of the country. There was much thought throughout Europe in the eighties on the actual cost to governments of premature deaths, notably at an International Conference on the Value of Human Life, held at The Hague in 1884.

It was such considerations, then, and not any very positive desire for material progress or convenience for its own sake, which from mid-century onward resulted in a steady stream of regulations, restrictions, and sanitary provisions, in every country of the Western world. The stimulus was almost entirely a negative one, and the measurable immediate results can perhaps most adequately be described as a series of emergency compromises, rarely designed for either real economy or amenity. In the course of meeting these emergencies, great technological and scientific progress was undeniably made, but the application was in almost every case of a remedial or ameliorative nature. The real nature of either problem or possibility was rarely looked into. The reformers, earnest and industrious though they very often were, merely for the most part trailed after the ills of the day, in a complaining but respectful queue. Not all of them, to be sure: for the seeds of every sort of fundamental change were also sown during this period. But their visible results at the time were negligible, and cannot enter into a picture of the average nineteenth-century environment.

The net results were at first hardly even as 'progressive' as the reformers themselves had intended. The utter chaos of the first period was replaced in the new mushroom districts, to be sure, but merely by legalized and standardized dreariness. After the great English Public Health Act of 1875, it was no longer possible to stuff flimsy shanties into noisome courtyards or to build rows of houses over an open sewer. But it was eminently respectable to cover whole square miles with a gridiron of 'By-Law' streets and nasty little houses twelve to fifteen feet wide, four or five rooms deep, and fifty or sixty to the acre. In Germany and France every dwelling had now to be supplied with running water, but entire new districts were laid out in a pattern expressly designed to accommodate deep six- or seven-story tenements, with two or three tiny courtyards, one behind the other. In New York the Old Law or 'dumbbell' tenement may have been an improvement, considered abstractly, over the railroad flat; but when one remembers that there was never more than a comparatively small area covered by the latter, and that there are today miles and miles of dumbbells in Brooklyn, the Bronx, and all over Manhattan, it would be difficult to prove that the housing standard had really been raised even by a fraction of an inch.

Much the same can be said for the next wave of remedial and restrictive legislation, which swept through Europe and America around 1900. The gains in sanitary convenience within the dwelling were real this time, but they were quite overbalanced by two other gains, one in the inconvenience and loss of exterior amenity due to the greater spread of the city, and the other in the actual cost of the dwelling in relation to income.

II. THE ERA OF WASTEFUL EXPANSION

Speculative Chaos

Which brings us well into the third period, the great age of speculative expansion. The outlying land is 'ripe' at last: it can be built on at a density justifying the hopes of the waiting dealers. The city bursts all the walls and spreads out like a spring flood over the meadows. The last vestige of a conception of the city as either a simple framed picture or an organism with natural inherent limitations on size and extent vanishes completely. The ideal of abstract Metropolis is born in a gridiron maze of new roads, roads without beginning and without end, squared off on paper in the city engineer's office sometimes years ahead of any idea as to what they may be used for. (In some mid-western cities in America, this operation was so mechanical that even the curvature of the earth's surface was not allowed for, and every so often one comes on a sharp right-angle jog, where the irritated developers were forced to bring their ruled paper line back to the proper degree of longitude.)

The primary result of such superficial 'mass-production' planning was that no street was ever quite right for anything that might happen to be located on it. If it turned out to be a residential road, it was noisy, dirty, too wide, too expensive to pave, and unsafe to cross. Every street was potentially a through traffic street, but if traffic did happen to come that way, it usually turned out to be quite inadequate and had to undergo successive and very expensive widenings, with accompanying blight for any residential district which had happened, equally fortuitously, to get there before the traffic. The only thing for which the mechanical undifferentiated gridiron-layout was ever really good for (with its hills leveled off and its valleys filled in), indeed, the only thing for which it was expressly designed, was facility in the sale and resale of front-foot lots.

And this is the period of land-speculation *par excellence.* If perhaps its most feverish heights were reached in America, Germany (whose era of industrial expansion tallies quite closely with our own) was no mean second. The total value of land in Berlin doubled between 1865 and 1880. The market price of the land under Charlottenburg, a Berlin residential suburb, was more than quintupled from 1886 to 1897. Each incoming family of six during this decade, according to Dr. Jaeger, brought an average profit of fifteen thousand Marks to the Charlottenburg property-owners.

Following is the history of a typical city plot in a South German city:

1887 Sold to an investor at $.03 a square foot.
1896 Reckoned in wife's legacy at $.20 a square foot.
1900 Sold to a syndicate at $.50 a square foot.
1902 After spending $.20 a square foot for streets, sold to a speculator G at $1.10 a square foot.
1903 Sold by G to another speculator H at $1.60 a square foot.
1904 H to J, the builder, at $1.75 a square foot.

Such figures make the Fabians' complaint, in 1892, that 'the princely gift of the London worker to the London landlord' in net unearned increment had increased the value of London by one third in twenty years, seem rather captious and tame. Very large land-companies dominated the situation around most of the German cities. They were closely allied with the banks and controlled the middlemen, the lot-developers, and finally also the builders. The fact that both speculative prices and speculation itself have been greatly reduced, in some cases practically eliminated, in post-war Germany is due almost entirely to the development of municipal land-purchase and housing policies.

But the speculation in the eighties and nineties was, of course, not confined to land. After all, the fun of raising the ante on a bare piece of pasture could not continue forever. Buildings were built, ingeniously squeezing by the latest set of half-hearted restrictions, and that familiar cycle was set in motion: building expansion, overproduction, crash, period of inactivity and fear, shortage, higher rents, expansion — and so on. This was true from Copenhagen to Rome, and from Paris to San Francisco. In Stockholm early in this century apartment-buildings to half the total value of apartments in the city changed hands at least once within less than four years.

For a classic description of the results of all this tremendous bustle, we must again go to England — even though she was still building two-story cottages almost exclusively, and her habitual standards of new construction were somewhat higher, on the whole, than those prevailing on the Continent and in America. On the other hand, however, the chaotic spread of her towns was very like that over here, and much worse than the partially zoned German towns. The following paragraphs are from H. G. Wells's *The New Machiavelli*, and refer to a thriving London suburb in the sixties and seventies:

'Roper's meadows... were now to be slashed out into parallelograms of untidy road, and built upon with rows of working-class cottages. The roads came, — horribly; the houses followed. They seemed to arise in the night. People moved into them as soon as the roofs were on, mostly workmen and their young wives, and already in a year most of these raw houses stood empty again from defaulting tenants, with windows broken and woodwork warping and rotting. The Ravensbrook became a dump for old iron, rusty cans, abandoned boots and the like....'

'I realized that building was the enemy. I began to understand why in every direction out of Bromstead one walked past scaffold poles into litter, why fragments of broken brick and cinder mingled in every path, and the significance of the universal notice-boards, either white and new or a year old and torn and battered, promising sites, proffering houses to be sold or let, abusing and intimidating passers-by for fancied trespass, and protecting rights of way.'

'The outskirts of Bromstead were a maze of exploitation roads that led nowhere, that ended in tarred fences studded with nails (I don't remember barbed wire in those days; I think the Zeitgeist did not produce that until later), and in trespass boards that used vehement language. Broken glass, tin cans, and ashes and paper abounded. Cheap glass, cheap tin, abundant fuel, and a free untaxed Press had rushed upon a world quite unprepared to dispose of these blessings when the fulness of enjoyment was past.'

'The whole of Bromstead as I remember it, and as I saw it last — it is a year ago now — is a dull useless boiling-up of human activities, an immense clustering of utilities. It is as unfinished as ever; the builders' roads are still run out and end in mid-field in their old fashion; the various enterprises jumble in the same hopeless contradiction, if anything intensified. Pretentious villas jostle slums, and public-house and tin tabernacle glower at one another across the cat-haunted lot that intervenes. Roper's meadows are now quite frankly a slum; back doors and sculleries gape toward the railway, their yards are hung with tattered washing unashamed; and there seem to be more boards by the railway every time I pass, advertising pills and pickles, tonics and condiments, and suchlike solicitudes of a people with no natural health or appetite left in them....'

Of this same process, which was fast turning all industrial regions into sharply divided Black Countries and Green Countries, Verhaeren wrote in *Les Villes Tentaculaires:*

'La plaine est morne et morte — et la ville la mange.'

Increasing Costs

In the field of purely factory-made goods, there is no question but that the century succeeded in providing more and more people with more and more things. Clothing, and to a certain extent food as well, tended to become cheaper (although often at the expense of quality) in relation to average incomes. (This is true, of course, only if the basis of real wages is put at its lowest known point, in the early decades of the nineteenth century: if it were put several centuries earlier, it would be difficult to prove much of any real rise at all.) But there is no such trend in the house-cost and rental curves.

Instead of cheapening it, everything tended to make the dwelling more expensive. Some of this increase was quite legitimate and necessary and represented a gain in quality; but most of it merely reflected and crystallized the wastes incurred in aimless and unregulated urban expansion. Here are some of the cost-factors and what was happening to them:

LAND. There is one very important little rule to be drawn from the experience of this period: namely, that no degree of architectural ingenuity or human suffrance directed toward reducing the unit-cost of expensive land by increasing the coverage and density has *ever* resulted in lower land-costs per dwelling. On the contrary, every time it has become apparent that the land could be used more intensively, the speculative value of such land immediately increased — sometimes more than proportionately. For if people will stand for this today, what may they not put up with tomorrow? New York, of course, with its miles of four- to six-storied flats on land still rated at skyscraper expectancy figures, is the classic — or perhaps the romantic — example. There is no exterior economic abracadabra of 'absolute' value about it. If the people of New York either individually by choice or collectively by law decided that they would not live and work in crowded skyscrapers, the price of land would have to fall.

American suburbs provide another example. Not seldom, in districts identical in convenience, social desirability, and cost and type of residence, but where in one case custom or accident has dictated twenty-five foot lots and in another case fifty-foot lots, it will be found that the price of the lots is just about the same. Moreover, as the fifty-foot lot costs much more to develop than the twenty-five-foot one, it would not be difficult to show in many cases that the accepted price of raw land for the former was actually less than the price for half as much land in the latter.

Dr. Pribram, in his analysis of European housing, claimed that the speculative price of land in an expanding city tended to increase during periods of depression as well as in prosperous years. In a rising market, it goes up along with everything else; but in depressed seasons, the cost of building always falls faster than rentals, thus leaving a larger spread of possibility for land-cost. Whether or not it always works out quite as neatly as that, it is certainly more than less true, under our present economic system, that if real standards of new construction are not raised *during* a depression, they probably never will be.

In any case, the cost of a unit dwelling's share in the site increased steadily from the middle of the century onward, quite irrespective of its area or adequacy. Indeed, in spite of the degree of competition among numberless small and large speculators, it is hard to see how the situation would have been changed very much if all the potential building-land around each city had been in the hands of a single uncontrolled monopolist. Perhaps some of the more open American towns would have had tenements instead of strings of little frame bungalows and two-deckers, but perhaps, on the other hand, in places where exorbitant land-prices have enforced the most wasteful and expensive type of apartment construction, some of the figures might have been actually added up and the resulting situation thereby improved.

UTILITIES. Here, to a certain extent, was a factor of increased cost in the dwelling which represented a real gain. Bathrooms, water, sewers, gas, pavement, furnaces — these are all of real 'utility.' But this does not mean that they do not add tremendously to the cost of a dwelling, nor that they are necessarily provided in accord with any long-time economical plan of housing improvement.

Land development, the structural dwelling, equipment, and taxes were all substantially raised in cost by the added utilities. Where a house was once little more than a shell, now around forty per cent of its total cost, direct and indirect, was buried in the ground, strung up in wires and sunk in services and equipment.

But the gain in cost is not a clear gain in amenity. In many cities, the new utilities were administered in such a way as to promote *further* speculation and land-sweating. Paved streets and water-pipes were laid out well in advance of use, to tempt lot speculators (the theory being, of course, that with a rising price of land and 'improvements' would come a greater tax-income). Trolley and subway lines were laid down, almost always radiating from the center, whose long-run effect was merely to increase the average amount of time spent going to and from work or place, instead of reducing it. Real comforts and gadgets alike were installed in new dwellings, principally to offset the disadvantages of land-crowding and the lack of exterior amenity. And the net result in many instances is not very impressive, unless one subscribes to the psychology which grew out of the condition, and measures dwelling-standards purely by bathtubs and elevators. To take the extreme example — which is fair enough as it has also been something of a general ideal — in New York we probably have the highest general standard of mechanical convenience that exists in the world, and at the same time we have the lowest standard of light, air, outlook, and convenience to work. But this does not mean that the advantages and the disadvantages cancel out, even in a purely economic sense. For we pay, not an average rent, but the highest rents in the world, both absolutely and in proportion to our income.

PURE CONSTRUCTION COSTS. Utilities and equipment increased the cost of the structural dwelling unit, but there were changes in the shell itself which tended to make it even more expensive. The increased height and density necessitated tortuous remedial building codes and restrictive legislation of all sorts. These resulted in a complexity of plan and construction which greatly magnified the cost of building while having an almost negligible effect on amenity. Endless winding corridors, stair-halls, and inefficiently shaped rooms contributed greatly to this waste. Fire regulations had to be more rigid and the accompanying equipment more complicated.

And, curiously enough, it was not until very recently that those twin vertebræ of the nineteenth-century industrial economy — standardization and mass-production — had even the slightest cheapening effect on the production of dwellings. The very forces which were promoting centralization and creating the housing problem were the last ones to have any positive effect on the method of housing itself. Even unto the present time, the effect can hardly be said to have been very remarkable. Superficial 'standardization' came as the result of building codes, not of real economies.

FINANCIAL COSTS. The transition of the shelter business from a matter of individual production for individual use, or large-scale production (often 'planned,' as in the English squares) for a safe long-time investment, to an almost purely speculative enterprise had, of course, a direct effect on the financial set-up. The cost of money is the most important single factor in the determination of rentals. A variation of one per cent can alone raise or lower rentals anywhere from eight to twenty per cent, depending on the rest of the set-up. And the cost of money for housing has increased much faster, by and large over the past hundred years, than the general interest-rate. The chronic housing shortage in the low-rental groups on the one hand, and the highly speculative nature of the business on the other — with no possible clue as to what might happen to a neighborhood almost overnight — raised both the expected immediate profits and the cost of loans. One result of this tendency to discount probable blight was the high-pressure sale, to individual owners, of small houses put up by speculative builders. The possibility of unloading the houses as soon as they were built increased the temptation to flimsy construction, and the necessity to get rid of them as soon as possible introduced a very considerable new item of first cost: namely, sales and promotion. Finally, the prevalence of small-scale enterprise with limited capital, and of individual owners with almost no capital, favored the development of a very intricate and expensive credit system.

Who Could Pay?

The sum of all these factors of increasing cost naturally brought about a very decided rise in rental scales. In Berlin in 1870, in the then working-class quarter a dwelling of one small room and kitchen cost 108 to 120 Marks a year. By 1919 in a corresponding section, but of course much farther out, the equivalent accommodation cost around 300 Marks. (Meanwhile, it might be noted, the cost of wheat had declined ten per cent.) But rental scales can be judged only in relation to wage and income scales. If the two had increased at the same rate, and if the average worker had been able to afford an average decent dwelling at the beginning of the century, one might suppose that at the end of it he would be able to pay at least for the better plumbing if not for those newly unattainable luxuries, light and air and pleasant surroundings.

But such was not the case. Wages did rise somewhat toward the end of the century, in much the same slow and tortuous manner in which the houses were being 'improved.' But, like the houses again, they rose, not from a norm of decency, but from absolute scratch. Up to around 1850 (later in many countries) real wages — that is, the actual standard of living and working — had on the whole been growing worse ever since the end of the Middle Ages. In England just after the Napoleonic Wars, and again in the 'hungry forties,' what was probably an all-time bottom for 'free white' workers was reached, and few slaves or serfs could ever have sunk much lower. The rich got richer, but the poor got steadily poorer.

In the cities and industrial towns a large new class of people was growing steadily larger, people without power and without hope living at the barest subsistence level or lower, housed worse than the average pig, and forced to send their children into factories at the age of six or seven, whole families working fourteen or sixteen hours a day for a pittance. It was not possible in England to enforce even such a monstrously ineffective act as a thirteen-and-a-half-hour day for children under sixteen years, until the late thirties. In the rhetoric of an English preacher of the early fifties:

'A change has come over us. The rich have room, have air, have houses endeared to them by every comfort civilization can minister, the poor still remain sad heralds of the past, alone bearing the iniquities and inheriting the curse of their fathers. Worse paid, do they breathe a purer air? Worse fed, are they better housed than their ancestors? Regent Street attracts the eye! Rookeries still remain! Westminster, at once the seat of a palace and a plague spot; senators declaim, where sewers poison; theology holds her councils, where thieves earn their trade; and Europe's grandest hall is flanked by England's foulest grave-yard.'

No, even in the fifties, when new houses were still relatively cheap, the proletariat could not afford them. The problem of housing the 'lowest third income group' was already in full swing. In the eighties, Charles Booth, in his exhaustive survey of 'Life and Labour' in London, estimated that there were one million completely impoverished people, none of them 'housed as well as a prudent man provides for his horse.' In 1890 in Brussels, more than half of the working class was in receipt of charity.

The rise in wages after the seventies has not yet, at any time, caught up with the rising rentals. In the first place, the wage-increases were by no means evenly spread. The period saw the emergence of a large new lower-middle class, and also the growth of an aristocracy of labor. The accident that the building workers, who were early rather well organized in most countries, managed to raise their own wages very much faster than did most of their co-workers merely emphasized the spread. And everywhere, in old buildings as well as in new, rent has taken an increasingly larger share of income straight up to the present time. (It may be worth noting that the usual rent share of income has always been much higher in Germany and in America, the two countries where land-speculation reached its most extravagant proportions, than in the other countries. In Holland, where speculation has been reasonably well controlled, rentals still amount to only one seventh of income on the average.)

The worse-paid half or two thirds of the population was left to rot in the older districts, now definitely run down, although commanding higher rents than ever. A system of absentee ownership, with management in the hands of speculative middlemen, saw to that. Indeed the slums were ordinarily the most profitable branch of real estate. Twelve to fifteen per cent net return was the regular thing in all the metropolitan capitals of the western world.

Circles of Incipient Blight

But I must not give the impression that there was anything static or remotely formal in the physical layout of these cities. In very few towns was there a definite recognizable line between the upper-class districts and the working-class quarters. And as the century took its course, any line which there may have been widened out to a vague fuzzy belt taking in the greater part of the city's extent. The central nucleus of very bad and usually quite ancient slums remained in the same place. But the fringe of newest and for the moment most respectable dwellings was pushed farther and farther out: each year it moved, like an army, to new encampments. And in between the fringe and the nucleus all was chaos. The image, if a somewhat romantic one, is of people striving desperately to get out of a slough. Some climb a little way up, then others climb out over their heads and push them back in again; then still others scramble beyond the first victors, and so it continues with the net result merely a much larger slough surrounded by a large area of trampled mud.

Of course, it was not nearly as simple as all that. Sometimes the wealthiest groups rebelled against the growing distance from the center to open land, and sacrificing amenity for convenience, tore down old central slums and replaced them with somewhat more luxurious tenements. Occasionally also (particularly in those small closed eighteenth-century squares which still remained) there were islands which somehow avoided the blight of changing use. And very often on the outskirts there were new developments which were built-in slums from the moment they were erected. But the general rule — and this is particularly true of the English and American cities, where every effort was made to extend the fringe as far as possible — has been one of ever-widening circles of blight and decay.

Very few of the neighborhoods were properly designed, either as to streets, open space, or dwellings, even for the specific uses of their original inhabitants. And as the more privileged moved away and the next lowest income group took possession, and as this process went on over and over, the result was mile after mile of dreary waste and hopeless makeshift. Large private houses were cut down into flats or transformed into rooming-houses; large rooms were cut up into smaller rooms and alcoves. Utilities and services which had once kept new tenements fairly livable were neglected when lower rentals became necessary. One house allowed to run to ruin could blight a whole block in a few years. The accidental coming of heavy traffic to a street could make it a mixed shambles of decayed residences and clamorous marginal shops within a year.

H. G. Wells described just such a shabby-genteel London slum through the eyes of the hero of *Tono-Bungay*. The young man concludes as follows:

'I had thought of London as a large, free, welcoming, adventurous place, and I saw it slovenly and harsh and irresponsive. I did not realize... what weakness that whole forbidding façade might presently confess. It is the constant error of youth to over-estimate the Will in things. I did not see that the dirt, the discouragement, the discomfort of London could be due simply to the fact that London was a witless old giantess of a town, too slack and stupid to keep herself clean and maintain a brave face to the world.'

Wells is right. The nasty, inconvenient, crowded houses — the ugly, formless cities — were not, at least in any direct or simple sense, the result of cunning design, of any malevolently conceived purpose on the part of the upper classes to keep the under classes 'down.' The mere fact that the dwellings of the privileged were so little better, when all is said and done, than those of the masses would tend to prove it. It is true, as Engels pointed out, that the new avenues with their glittering commercial facades tended to 'conceal from the eyes of the wealthy men and women of strong stomachs and weak nerves the misery and grime which form the complement of their wealth.' But it is not true that the bourgeoisie lived in 'fine, comfortable homes.' There is no dramatic picture, with all the rich and powerful living in splendid palaces and all the others living in clay huts. I should hesitate to ascribe to any but the most hypocritical and unpleasant Tory and Junker reformers a *conscious* purpose, however secret, that would fit perfectly into the Marxist equation.

No, the broad history of the environment of the nineteenth century is in simplest terms a history of failure. A vast army of new problems and possibilities descended on the western world, and there was absolutely nothing ready to take care of them, or even understand them. On the contrary, every dominant psychological influence of the times mitigated against the possibility of creating a new and coherent outward form for a new civilization. It may well have been quite inevitable. Perhaps we should never have developed modern science and technology and the possibilities of power had it not been for the very qualities which made it impossible for so long to use them directly in the general welfare. The circular movement between interchangeable cause and effect is just as evident here as in most other sociological equations. But it may be worth while briefly to consider some of these dominant factors in the nineteenth-century psyche, and how they worked out with such inevitable unsuccess in the matter of physical environment. For, if they are no longer young and triumphant, these credos and habits of mind are still in the saddle throughout most of the western world.

III. VICTORIAN MIND AND MATTER

Even their discovery of evolution conveyed no warning to them about the fate of every species in the past that has failed to adapt itself to changed conditions. They pinned their faith to change, or, as they called it, Progress, and left adaptation for chance or Providence to provide. — E. Wingfield-Stratford: THE VICTORIAN SUNSET

Laissez-faire

The splendid abstractions of the eighteenth century were converted, in the nineteenth, into concrete but strictly limited realities. The Rights of Man and the Freedom of the Individual were codified to mean the right of a smart man to acquire, own, and dispose of property in any way which might benefit him. The Social Contract became largely a code of non-interference with these property rights. Social upheavals as different in character as the French Revolution of 1789 and the English Reform Bill of 1832 furthered the same cause: the triumph of the commercial middle class over not only the hereditary aristocracy, now on the wane or in process of 'modernization,' but also the workers, just appearing on the horizon as a disinherited proletarian class whose interests were essentially different from those of either of the other two groups.

Theoretically, the religion of every individual responsible only to himself, but entirely responsible *for* himself, would seem to imply a sort of grand heroic anarchism. The States disappear and the pure Free Trade Utopia recognizes only the battling individual, with no privilege other than his own acumen, and the world of limitless supply and insistent selective demand.

But the pure teachings of the dismal science were never really tried. And how could they have been? The success of England, which served to spread the doctrines of the Manchester

School all over Europe and America, was after all due not to philosophical abstractions but to her head-start, first in industries, and later in Imperialism. To preserve her advantage, thus gained, the Free Trade Utopia was the first thing to be thrown overboard.

Nor was the ideal of the free economic individual realized any more successfully within the countries. On the contrary, it hardly even received lip-service. Manufacturers regularly agreed among themselves on prices and wages, and just as regularly, with the entire weight of law and effective public opinion behind them, put down strikes by force, prohibited unions, transported labor leaders, and generally kept the workers in a state of helpless slavery.

Nevertheless, in the convenient form in which the doctrine of *laissez-faire* was assimilated by the prosperous middle classes, it served to clothe them in well-nigh unpuncturable righteousness and romantic self-satisfaction. As the Hammonds have said, 'When the landowner looked in the glass he saw a public benefactor, who incidentally received sums of money in the form of rent; when the employer looked in the glass he saw a public benefactor, who incidentally received sums of money in the form of profits.... The dominant conceptions of the time made it an act of public virtue in itself to own land or to employ labour.' And it was this fact, coupled with that curious lack of simple physical sensibility which we shall later discuss, that did most perhaps to impede the development of any new concrete idea of what a good environment is and how it can be achieved.

But the smugness went farther than mere inarticulate acquiescence. With Malthus and Ricardo for text, a whole system of common ideology was evolved, to rationalize the existence of a large class condemned to live in perpetuity at a bare subsistence level — which implied, of course, living in a slum. A period of relative comfort or prosperity, it was held, would induce the workers to have more babies, which would result eventually in unemployment and a tax on the means of subsistence, which would lower wages and the birth-rate, and so on around and around the cycle. The theory of social betterment which went with this is perhaps nowhere phrased with more striking brevity than in the words which Miss Martineau put into the mouth of her beau idéal of a wise and benevolent manufacturer: 'We [the manufacturers] do what we can for you in increasing the capital on which you are to subsist; and you must do the rest, by proportioning your numbers to the means of subsistence.' (This, of course, in an era when people were put in jail for mentioning birth-control.)

The early notions of 'reform' and popular education had almost invariably this unctuous twist. A Society for the Diffusion of Useful Knowledge was formed in 1831, which included some of England's most eminent statesmen (including Lord Ashley, who was later the first English housing reformer). This earnest organization was immortalized as the Steam Intellect Society in Peacock's contemporary *Crotchet Castle*. Such worthy efforts are well summed up by Wingfield-Stratford:

'Popular treatises of an offensive lucidity were turned out, to drive into the stupid heads of workmen the absolute, scientific impossibility of improving their conditions by interfering with the free play of capital. Only put your trust in Mr. Gradgrind and Mr. Bounderby, and something will eventuate that will no doubt be highly satisfactory to these gentlemen.'

And yet it would be entirely wrong to paint a picture of deep-dyed villainous hypocrisy to fit them: rather were they the most sincere romantics, all the more dangerous because of their pride in 'science' and statistical hard-headedness. Even the brutal honesty, according to her lights, of a Miss Martineau is rather refreshing by comparison with the soft cold tears and condescending Christianity of the Tory reformers. Moreover, there really was a faintly heroic aspect to the picture, before the capitalists became a privileged caste. The early Victorian manufacturer had much the same hardiness and gambling courage as the frontier pioneer of the same era. He took his chances, which were tremendous both ways, and to do him justice, if he lost out he claimed no right to anything better than the workhouse which he prescribed for his employees.

But such virtues, whether in wilderness adventurers or textile manufacturers or speculative builders, are not those which go to make a concrete civilization. As one Tory preacher put it, the dwellings of the poor are 'swelling the gains of some middleman, whose heart is seared by the recollection of his own poverty, and who learns to grind as he was once ground by others.' And all the ingenious new slums were the handiwork of 'practical, hard-headed, common-sense, blunt men of business.'

It must always remain one of the great historic ironies that, in a period when centralized power and machine-production were daily creating ever more and newer situations over which the individual alone had no control whatever, the doctrine of complete economic individualism should have attained a fever-heat not known before or since. Every ordinary Liberal middle-class citizen, whether he lived in Chicago or Manchester or Essen or Lyons, and whether he believed vaguely in 'progress' and some future Great Society or merely in the necessity of keeping the workers in their place, was the born enemy of any concrete effort to investigate the nature of cities, of houses, of architecture, of land-use, or of a healthy environment. In Paris in 1885, a judge declared that for a landlord to be compelled to lay on water in his house for the use of the tenants was an interference with the liberty of the subject, and held that a water-supply was not an indispensable necessity for maintaining the healthiness of a dwelling. Such examples could, of course, be multiplied *ad infinitum.*

The immediate result was that for several generations every direct reform was in the hands of the Tories or the Junkers, who were at once more cynical and more realistic than their Liberal or Democratic brethren. They it was who were terrified by cholera into putting in sewers and water-supplies. And they again who were frightened by the uprisings of 1848 and 1870 into embarking on a few weak factory measures and a handful of ineffective if ostentatious housing experiments. As philanthropists, they instituted the era of 'model tenements.' And as landed proprietors, quite a few of them still had either keen enough sensibilities or 'enlightened' enough self-interest to keep their tenants' cottages in fairly good condition.

But the real ideas were not produced either by orthodox Liberals or by frightened Tories. And in the long run it will probably be the great apologia for the rampant individualism of the nineteenth century that out of it sprang great *individuals* who saw and comprehended the world around them, criticized it creatively, and offered what are still in essence the soundest solutions. Owen and Marx and Morris and Ebenezer Howard and Fourier and Patrick Geddes were just as representative Victorians in their own way as were Cobden and Bright.

A Peculiar Lack of Sensibility

Over and above any economic credo (and yet in and around and through it) there was a quality much harder to analyze. Whether it was more cause, result, or mere attendant accident would fill a whole volume of conjecture. But the fact remains that the citizens of the nineteenth century, taken as a whole from one end of the western world to the other, were extraordinarily lacking in what may be called direct physical sensibility. From the visual fine arts to simple bodily comfort, they seemed to have either no standards at all or false ones, and a marked incapacity for qualitative judgment. Even where one can perceive that real imaginative effort and pleasure went into making some object, there seldom seems to be any broad underlying comprehension of materials or functions or the nature of the craft, and the result is likely to be quaint or pathetic rather than beautiful or satisfactory. Looking at a jig-saw Gothic villa, one is astounded at the fertility of 'design,' one even rather admires the boldness and energy of execution, but one wonders what had happened to the architect's eyesight, and what the owner really thought he wanted.

The real expression of the age was in words: in poetry, in novels, in history, in criticism, even astute criticism of ugliness and disorder, and in philosophy, even the philosophy of art. But when this same spirit came to be translated into paint or stone or wood, architecture or cities, the results were not so happy. Materials had lost their meaning. Forms and purposes were forgotten. Old crafts were lost, and new techniques were not assimilated. New requirements were not analyzed and new possibilities were not understood. Tradition was cut off, and experiment was for the most part aimless and inhibited.

Of course, any such broad generalization must bring to mind

a hundred exceptions. Some of the greatest painters of modern times lived and worked in the latter part of the century. But do they not, like the other revolutionaries, belong to our day rather than their own? Some of the finest London and Edinburgh squares were built in the early years, but what part have they in the nineteenth century? Were they not, like the half-modern, half-Baroque buildings of Schinkel in Germany, late survivals of an art which, because fewer and fewer people knew how either to practice or appreciate it, was running itself into the ground?

On the other hand, it is merely remarkable that we take the low state of the visual and useful arts in the past hundred and fifty years as much for granted as we do. Utility was God, and the smoking factories were largely engaged in turning out streams of keepsakes, mottoes, and ornamental novelties. Comfort was the aim of the age, and you could probably not have purchased a well-designed chair had you been singular enough to desire one. Materialism was the dominant philosophy, and wood was painted to look like marble, and steel contorted to look like wood. Science and technology were the prophets, and great engineering works hid themselves behind Greek temples. Chaste respectability was the law, and women's clothes were of an obscenity to make a lusty eighteenth-century courtesan hide her face. Hygiene was mistress of the rites, and hardly a single really sanitary dwelling was constructed. Great cities were the pride and boast of their inhabitants, yet their form and function troubled no one. The practical man was king, and waste lay on every hand.

One is reminded of the opposite historic irony, the Middle Ages, when a completely mystic and anti-material religion produced not only some of the most splendid engineering architecture that the world can show, but a cosmopolitan culture and hygienic, functional cities.

What was the difference? Partly, I suppose (and it is not an answer which leads very far), the simple fact that in the one period physical sensibilities were sharp and well grounded in the materials of solid reality, while in the other they were dull and confused and degraded. Kropotkin, writing of the Middle Ages, suggests another: 'The very fact that of all arts architecture — a social art above all — had attained the highest development, is significant in itself. To be what it was, it must have originated from an eminently social life.' And the life of the nineteenth century was certainly not that.

But the superficial contradiction still remains. 'In even the smallest things,' said Theodor Fritsch, the German precursor of Ebenezer Howard, 'the human spirit works restlessly for improvement. From pants-buttons to stick-pins, from billiard-cues to pen-holders, every possible object is pursued toward inventive perfection. There is only one thing toward the improving and reshaping of which no thought has been given, and that is the most important of all, our environment.'

Havelock Ellis offers an apology if not an explanation. 'The nineteenth century,' he has his Utopian remark, 'was satisfied in architecture with the cold, bald, artificial reproductions of styles that died hundred of years before; and these were of course wholly unsuited for their purpose and no one ever took any delight in them. We have to remember, however, that it would be unreasonable to expect architecture from an age which had been inevitably rendered indifferent to the human body, except when its architectonic mechanism was unrecognizably swathed in hideous coats and petticoats.'

Ruskin and Morris thought the failure was at least in part due to the machine, to the triumph of mass-production and cheap standardization over individuality and the hand crafts. Yet the machine was quite able to create a beauty of its own: it was merely that every obstruction was put in the way of its doing so.

Perhaps the most remarkable thing about this ugliness and disorder was the fact that it extended from bottom to top of society, even in an age of great extremes of wealth and poverty. What the poor had to put up with because they had no choice, the rich on a different scale very often chose for their own environment.

There was a photograph in the *New York Times* not long ago, of an old private house on Fifty-Fourth Street, taken at the time it was built in the fifties. It was bought later by the Rockefellers. The house stands all alone in the picture, with a surrounding vista of mud, refuse heaps, half-developed lots, and a few distant tenements. It is five stories high, very narrow and very deep. Its façade is faced in brownstone, but the other three sides (which were at that time equally exposed) are covered with cheap brick. It was in fact a very Forward House for its time, a pioneer among upper-class built-in slums. And it was the chosen environment of a man who could have had anything that an individual could buy.

The hideous tenements of Belleville and St. Pancras are not one whit more ugly than the apartment-houses of Charlottenburg or Boulogne. In a way, the typical mid-nineteenth-century dwellings were all barracks, solidly built though they often were (for the real age of jerry-building did not appear until 'Art' was revived in a cloudburst of gim-crackery in the sixties and later). Their inhabitants were engaged in battle. And even later on, when the business man and the industrialist began to consolidate his gains into a system of privilege; when they lost their early Victorian honesty and directness and the term 'middle class' became one of opprobrium; when the sturdy Philistine, or his wife, began to ape the manners and trappings, alas long decayed, of the aristocratic Barbarian; when Art reappeared as a certificate of Success — it cannot be said that either the form or the living quality of their dwellings was greatly improved.

'Slums, semi-slums, and super-slums,' said Patrick Geddes. It was used for a caption over two large air photographs in an exhibition at the Museum of Modern Art. One view showed several blocks of tenements on the Lower East Side — the grimmest type of construction to be found anywhere. The other was taken over Park Avenue in one of the most expensive residential districts in the world. But they were not shown for any simple moral contrast: they were shown because they were essentially so alike. Tiny paved courts; ugly, contorted, formless buildings surrounded by noisy traffic streets; deep apartments betokening interior windowless rooms; these were true of both upper- and under-class residence.

As for interiors, it would be hard to prove that there was any fundamental æsthetic difference between some chromo-calendar cherished by a miner's wife and the most expensive *fin-de-*

siècle Japonaiserie. If the factory workers were forced by circumstances beyond their command to drag out miserable lives in dark cellars and filthy hovels, miles from a breath of fresh air or a direct ray of sun, the privileged classes, when they happened to have more spacious quarters in pleasanter surroundings, exercised their privilege largely in the direction of wiping out their advantage. Windows were permanently sealed against air or, as it was commonly called, 'draughts': and whatever outlook they chanced to offer was carefully covered by three or four pairs of heavy curtains. Practically every Victorian invention in the field of interior decoration was something almost purposefully designed to catch dust, make work, prevent free movement, or transform something once useful into a useless atavism. And the net result was that many a potentially fine apartment was turned into a 'den' which, for either beauty, comfort, convenience, or health, was not greatly better than a mean tenement.

Of course, one can carry the parallel too far. If the working-class woman did not have as much dusting to do as her betters, she did have to forego the satisfaction of obviously possessing a tremendous number of objects. And there is no group in history to which Veblen's *Theory of the Leisure Class* — the practice of conspicuous waste — applies more concretely than to the late Victorian upper bourgeoisie and their peers in all of Europe and America.

But the practice of conspicuous waste has occasionally in past ages produced quite handsome monuments. Perhaps it would not have failed to do so in the past century if it had been possible to satisfy the will-to-waste by the *direct* and sensitive use of materials to that end. But the genius of the time happened to be one which understood words better than materials, which could recognize symbols but could not see forms. And this gave all objects, whether dog-paintings or churches, pottery or houses, a certain literary one-dimensional quality. Everything always *meant* something. Sentiment, archæology, and art were practically indistinguishable. And whether the sentiment happened to be patriotism or a lofty yearning after the romance of Gothic, or a moral precept about the sanctity of the Home, the real clue to the resulting art was almost always to be found in the words with which one might describe it. Movements which had some reality in literature were ridiculous travesties in stone and brick. *Wuthering Heights* is still a fairly good book, but the Gothick Fabricks were never even remotely good buildings. (Indeed, they never achieved any reality at all except at one remove from the concrete: for the engravings of them, duly surrounded by impregnable virgin forests and stormy twilight, are much more impressive than the buildings themselves.) It is no accident that the one realized visual art which achieved popular success was that of the social or political cartoonist. Daumier and Cruikshank presented pictorial art in the only form assimilable by any large number of persons.

The great battle of the century between Classic and Romantic, although it had a sound emotional basis in the psychology and events of the times, took place, when it came to the visual arts, in a sort of stratosphere of dead literary 'culture.' Revival succeeded revival, whole libraries were filled with heated arguments, entire æsthetic philosophies were concocted to substantiate one side or the other, there were even occasional riots. But so far as the actual physical aspect of things was concerned, the effects were almost entirely negligible. The net result for architecture amounted to little more than whether a building whose site and location were predetermined by a gridiron street-layout, whose dimensions and plan were established by a narrow building-lot, whose use would necessarily be an office-building, and the material of whose façade would be cast-iron, should have near-Corinthian pilasters or ogive windows. And cast-iron Classic versus cast-iron Gothic is not a major choice.

Two much more important nineteenth-century movements must be mentioned, however, which, although they played little part in the literary squabbles of the day, still had their source in the classic and the romantic tradition respectively. One was the thin tradition of Renaissance city-planning, and the other was the ideal of the Country House. Both of them struck much deeper than any mere matter of façade ornament and both of them left monuments and attitudes of mind which, for better or worse, are still to be reckoned with.

The Classic Panacea: Squares and Avenues

The only major element in the classic art of city-planning which had survived was the Avenue, with its due punctuation in the form of squares, *rond-points*, and public monuments. And even this was almost completely forgotten during the first fifty years of the century. The last major effort had been L'Enfant's plan for Washington, and that, as it worked out, was itself no complete job of planning. For the admirable network of diagonal boulevards and circles was merely superimposed, quite artificially, over a rigid mechanical scheme of ordinary gridiron blocks.

It was not until the ambitious Napoleon III and his architect Haussmann set out to open up and beautify Paris that the nineteenth century began even superficially to consider the purposes and possibilities of 'city-planning.' The sort of planning practiced by Haussmann and his followers, from Chicago to Mexico City, was a matter almost entirely of streets, usually only main thoroughfares, and as a rule only in the center of the city. Now there are obviously great advantages in a well-placed boulevard, broad and straight and tree-planted, as against a congeries of twisting, murky alleys. Circulation, both of air and of traffic, is facilitated, at least temporarily. Sites for public monuments, shops and restaurants are provided. An opportunity for architecture in the grand manner is furnished. A few blocks of insanitary dwellings may be torn down in the process of cutting it through. And finally, remembering the garish and glittering Second Empire which Haussmann was serving, both imperial pomp and imperial defense are better served. Indeed, in a capitalist country it is likely to require an imperial will in order to be accomplished at all.

Nor should such activities be belittled. Without question, the diagonals and radials of Paris, which do at least have 'vistas' and monumental punctuation of a suitable if not always beautiful design, give that city the nearest approach to clarity and form achieved by any modern metropolis. Joseph Chamberlain's work in Birmingham in the seventies, which involved a complete reconstruction of some ninety-three acres in the center of the city, was of the same order.

But still, cutting a boulevard through the old section of a town is only one small department of city-planning, and, unless even that is properly related to a thousand other activities and considerations, its benefits can be eclipsed by new evils. The professional city-planners of the nineteenth century were for the most part far too easily satisfied. Or perhaps they merely presumed too much for their very limited art. The question of whether or not radial avenues, converging on the old city-center, are the best way to solve the problem of metropolitan circulation cannot be entered into here. But the matter of highway-cutting as a slum-clearance measure must be given brief mention, for this express purpose played no small part in many such operations.

In Paris, in Birmingham, in Brussels, in London, they cleared out many insanitary districts in putting through their new avenues, and virtuously believed that the gods of Art, Commerce, and Hygiene were being served at one throw. But what really happened? No new provision was made for the residents of the cleared areas, and they could not, unfortunately, be swept away as easily as were their rookeries. The perfectly natural result was that they adjourned to neighboring slums (whose rents had meanwhile been greatly increased by land-speculation, always an accompaniment to old-fashioned city-planning, and by the shortage of dwellings resulting from demolition) and helped their neighbors to make both ends meet by huddling in with them, whole families to a room. This was markedly true in Paris, where conditions created by Haussmann's activities are yet to be remedied. And in London, where St. Giles, one of the worst slum districts, was pulled down to make way for New Oxford Street, a survey made some time afterward in a neighboring area showed that the density there had been very nearly doubled, until in whole blocks there were sometimes only one hundred and seventy-five cubic feet of interior air per person.

In this respect the new boulevards had much the same effect as the railroads, which destroyed hundreds of thousands of dwellings without providing new ones, and rendered millions of others unwholesome. Like the railroad cuts also, the avenues, as traffic grew heavier and noisier and more dangerous to pedestrians, and as the automobile came in, became less and less desirable frontage for residence, and tended to divide, rather than bind together, the districts which they chanced to cross. Verhaeren's line,

> 'Et trains coupant soudain les villages en deux,'

applies equally to a modern highway. And unlike the railroads, which often served to make uncomfortably visible some ancient slum which it chanced to cross, the avenue, with its imposing new façades, sometimes only helped the city fathers to forget all about the bad conditions which existed behind those fronts.

The Renaissance Avenue, used as it has been used in the past century, contributes exactly nothing to the solution of the housing and city-living problem. And in so far as it has promoted further excessive concentration, raised the speculative price of land, and lulled people into thinking that it comprised the whole of city-planning, it has been positively detrimental. The later developments of the Haussmannizing zeal may be held to include the pompous emptiness of the Great White City at the World's Fair of 1893, and also the resulting City-Beautiful Movement in America, which did perhaps awaken a certain amount of vague civic consciousness, if it did not turn out any beautiful cities.

But there is one positive movement for which the classic city-planners and the city-beautiful promoters are to be thanked. And that was the public park, probably the only unqualifiedly happy contribution of the nineteenth century to urban environment. It was, of course, not a new idea in itself, having gradually evolved in Europe in part out of the old commons, and in part out of the princely private garden and hunting preserve. But the late nineteenth century was re-awakened to the necessity of preserving such chance open green spaces, of planting and equipping them for various forms of recreation, and of acquiring land for new ones. In the American cities, Central Park, Fairmount Park, and the work of Olmsted and his followers in hundreds of other towns, constitute the most valuable legacy of the last century.

Romantic Escape: the Isolated Villa

So much for the classic heritage. But the effect on human environment of the Romantic Movement, in its several ramifications, was of quite another order, and much more profound and complex. On the surface, it brought in the new excitement of 'Art,' partaken of as a somewhat unhealthy luxury. As early as 1853, *Punch* records an 'æsthetic tea,' at which 'the atmosphere was one of architecture, painting, stained glass, brasses, heraldry, wood-carving, madrigals, chants, motets, mysticism, and theology.' And long before the Pre-Raphaelite Brotherhood, Peacock satirized an ardent mediævalist in the person of Mr. Chainmail, who had 'a large hall, adorned with rusty pikes, shields, helmets, swords and tattered banners.'

It was the same anæmic pseudo-mediæval frame into which the fundamentally healthy emotions of the Arts and Crafts Movement were cramped. In its own day this movement, although undeniably the first link in a long international chain which finally resulted in authentic modern architecture and industrial design, must be accounted a failure. Contrary to the purpose and spirit of Morris, and, at his best, of Ruskin as well, the immediate results of their efforts constituted hardly more than a kind of 'arty' snobbery. The new knowledge of the past which they made public only served, in their own time, to provide new styles for mass-produced gadgets, the very thing which they most detested. It is not difficult to sympathize with their hatred of the Iron Age, but in so far as they endeavored to escape backward into a literary vision of the Middle Ages, they failed by just so much to face the real problems — in the design of pots and buildings as well as in the ordering of society. Of William Morris the social revolutionist, who is far more important than the entire output of Batiks, stained glass and wood-carving for which he may be held partly responsible, mention will be made in a later section.

But there is quite another aspect to the Romantic Revolt, one with much deeper social roots in its own time and with a far more complex network of effect on environment. Rousseau and the new feeling for romantic Nature were one side of it, and the self-sufficiency of the pioneer adventurer was another.

The economic doctrine of the individual battling for his property against all other individuals, and the scientific one of the survival of the fittest, were both related to it. It produced that exceedingly powerful modern idolum, the Country House. If a more or less mythical thirteenth century provided the background of the Pre-Raphaelites, then the great abstractions of the eighteenth century would have made quite suitable, if sometimes ironic, mottoes for a very large number of nineteenth-century homes.

What sort of homes were they? The very rich had, of course, ever since the Renaissance, tended to maintain large estates in the country to which they escaped at intervals to enjoy the private luxury and sporting pursuits which were the due reward for power and success.

But soon the prosperous new upper middle classes began likewise to seek castles for themselves, apart from the hurly-burly. Privacy was the great desideratum, and the impregnable Family, jealously guarded from exterior influences, became the most important social institution. In spite of many recent modifications, this idolum is still so strong and so much taken for granted that it is difficult to remember that it is quite a new idea. Until well into the nineteenth century the burghers had almost universally lived in the very center of the cities. Their houses, although of course 'private' in a sense, were closely banked around the public squares and family life was more or less subordinated to civic life. For better or worse, the bourgeoisie provided active participating leadership, and were the social hub of their communities.

If it was considered a misfortune to have to live outside the walls of a city, this feeling was equally true of even the smallest and poorest villages. Mr. Terpenning has shown, in his *Village and Open Country Neighborhoods*, that even today most of the Continental villages maintain their integral form and character. The French or German or Italian or Russian peasant does not want to live in an isolated farmhouse, even if it might bring him personal advantage or comfort. And as a matter of fact, it is only in England and above all in America, that the ideal of secluded privacy and the self-sufficiency of the family has ever been overwhelmingly strong. In Germany and France, where the closely integrated town and its culture had reached a very high state of development, the new forces were not able to vanquish the old ones quite so easily. Indeed, particularly in Germany, the ancient urbanity survived to combine forces with that of the latest and most 'radical' developments in communal housing technique, so that it is sometimes difficult to say just where the tradition leaves off and the modernity begins.

But in the English-speaking countries, the triumph of the Country House ideal was almost complete. The working purpose of every family, as it rose from lower to upper middle class, was to secure for itself as large a piece of land as possible, and to set down in the middle of it a private house, as commodious as means and site would permit and as 'individual' as the current canons of taste would allow — therein to carry on its normal functions, far from a vulgar or curious world.

On the whole, this was quite an understandable reaction. Every English or American town which has been touched by the early brutalities of industrial prosperity was a ravaged place. Sensitive people were beginning to recognize two distinct countries in England, the Black and the Green, and anyone who endeavored to escape from the one into the other was merely exercising his instinct for self-preservation. It was quite natural that the half-world of Coketown should, as Lewis Mumford showed in *The Story of Utopias*, produce its antithesis in kind, the half-world of the Country House.

And the newer American cities, whose only tradition for the most part was pioneering individualism, were from the beginning very loosely put together agglomerations whose central chaos, even if it was not often quite as impenetrably black as that of Manchester or New York, offered no reason other than necessity for living in the middle of it. Moreover, the psychology of the frontier was by no means lacking in the children and grandchildren of the pioneers. Everybody wanted elbow-room. And if the cities were felt to be great achievements in the abstract, to be boasted about when away from home, nobody really liked them. The man who felt crowded and had to move on when there was another cabin within two miles of him is reflected not only in the scattered, isolated farmhouses, but in the spreading suburbs.

That such a psychology, being one of individual escape rather than collective construction, would not tend to produce handsome cities, cleanly and harmoniously designed and functioning organically from the center outward, must be perfectly obvious. And that it would condemn the poorest third or half of the population, whatever their desires or aspirations, to the worst sort of slum environment, is equally patent. But it did not succeed in the single task which it had undertaken; it did not even provide good, comfortable, individual dwellings in pleasant surroundings for the middle classes.

To say what they believed in, or what they thought they were getting, is in no way to describe what they got. For almost a century, for instance, it has been an American theory that any honest, hard-working man could save a little money, go out and find the site of his dreams, and erect thereon his personal ideal of what a home should be. This idea, embodying very accurately the abstract sentiments of the nineteenth century, was documented and promulgated in tons of books, pamphlets, and magazines. But alas, it has practically no basis in reality. In all the countries of the world, only a very negligible portion of the city working population, and that almost exclusively of the very highest income-group, actually resides in a dwelling which it had the smallest hand in designing.

Perhaps there was a time when the individual dwelling, in a strictly physical sense, was more or less self-contained, when a man was quite free to consider his house his castle and, if he had a mind to, build a moat around it. Curiously, however, this ideal never made any sort of general headway until after the technical developments of the nineteenth century had rendered it thoroughly impracticable. Today, physically speaking again, a dwelling is little more than a ganglion on a network of interlacing wires and pipes, pavements, school districts, fire districts, shopping districts, transportation lines, mail delivery lines. If a man were to put a moat around his house today, he would find himself cut off from every comfort and convenience and economy that the past hundred years has produced.

What actually did happen to the small individual builder?

First of all, the high cost of a piece of land which had provided a juicy profit to five or six intervening speculators before it finally reached him meant that he could never buy very much of it. Then, the unavoidable waste and extravagance incurred in building a custom-made house, usually of archæological style, with Machine Age standards of equipment, meant that either the design or the equipment or the space had to suffer, usually all three. And even where, by exceptional resources or ingenuity, the middle-class family was able actually to construct its own house according to its own plans, the result, squeezed into a narrow lot between other equally compelling symbols of romantic individualism, did not bear much resemblance to the hazy magazine-clipped ideal which had inspired it. As for those other attributes of a dwelling, which the magazine probably forgot to mention, the schools, paved roads, utilities, and trolley-cars, they came as God saw fit to send them.

But as a matter of statistical fact, almost the entire output of urban dwellings, up to the war in Europe, and until this moment in America, has come from the speculative builder. And here is where the romantic ideal suffered its final degradation. '*L'haleine de l'homme est mortelle à ses semblables*,' said Rousseau. And so the contractor built his houses thirty to forty feet deep, but kept them carefully separated by a two- to twelve-foot alley, neatly proving the axiom by having most of the windows face each other directly across the crack. 'My house must express my individuality,' said the buyer. So alternate gables or fake fronts were painted red or green. 'Culture and Art,' sighed his wife. So half-timbers, carefully rotted in advance, were tacked onto the façade and asbestos shingles were laid in careful confusion. 'We must preserve the sanctity of our home,' said the whole family. And presently, when the street outside got intolerably noisy and dirty, when the neighbors began to take in boarders and the house on the corner was turned into a saloon, they sold their home at a considerable loss and moved out into a more expensive and newer development. 'To invest in Your Own Home is to be secure and respectable,' said the whole world. And so finally, when a depression came and they could not meet their exorbitant monthly installments, they were turned out of their latest house and lost all the savings they had put into it. Moreover, all the best-intended efforts of the most progressive cities were spent in promoting just such chaos.

And still, with all the effort and expense, with all the agitation for 'cheap trains,' with all the tons of little books on How to Own Your Own Home, with all the building and loan associations, with all the cut-throat competition among speculative builders, with all the fifteen-foot lots, there remained at least half of the population which could not afford a new home of any kind whatsoever. Half the population, and as the cost of new dwellings mounted, two thirds finally, who lived in ancient tenements, in cast-offs, in hand-me-downs, in single rooms, in 'remodeled' houses, or (millions and millions of them) who had no separate dwelling at all and were classed in the census as 'surplus families.' For every shiny, gadgeted new district that was opened up, there was an older one that was 'blighted,' cut up or merely allowed to decay, to accommodate the lesser 'effective demand' of the lower economic orders.

There is even a whole theory to rationalize this. If the richer people move into the new dwellings, it has been held, then everyone along the line moves up a peg. And a very nice evolutionary idea it is, which shows nineteenth-century optimism at its best. Just allow Nature to take her course, and soon all the slum-dwellers will be living in those fine apartments on Park Avenue. But alas, when a luxurious apartment or a large private house is converted into a cheap tenement, it becomes just that, another cheap tenement. And rather worse, on the whole, than the buildings which were actually constructed for that purpose.

Moreover, the worst sort of tenement went right on being constructed. Indeed, they soon spread even to those late green meadows which had been opened up so hopefully for 'cottages' or 'bungalows.' During the entire period in which the conscious idolum, the only admitted 'decent' dwelling-form, was purely and simply the private house (which in America had to be surrounded on all four sides by a lawn) in most cities on both sides of the Atlantic the proportion of flats to single houses increased with enormous rapidity. And, largely because no one paid much attention to them and few even acknowledged their existence, they were for the most part very bad flats. In all the large housing literature of the period, I personally know of only two books which seriously consider the form of the low-rent apartment-house. And both of these are mere apologies for exorbitant land-speculation and its resulting congestion. Not until Wijdeveld and Le Corbusier and other post-war architects, did anyone really analyze the multiple dwelling to see what its potential virtues and real economies, if any, might be.

The Megalopolitan Ideal

The old concrete conception of the city as a working organism, with a definite form and inherent limitations to growth, was dead. But there was a new idolum to take its place. The greatest abstraction of all, which includes and explains many of the separate failures and unrealities, was the ideal of Megalopolis. There is nothing which so surely indicates that the bias of the times was quantitative rather than qualitative. Bigger was always Better, and a mere increase in population, extent, land-prices, transit mileage, building heights, or number of Owned Homes, was taken as an absolute index of progress and prosperity.

If this faith had gained currency only in those cities which, by virtue of one accident or another, really were metropolitan centers, it might give evidence merely to the powers of defensive rationalization of the inhabitants. They *had* cities whose principal attributes were statistical, they did not know how one could do very much otherwise about it, and so why not put the best face on the matter and act as if that was what they had wanted all along.

But the Megalopolitan ideal was not confined to the biggest cities. Every little town with any industrial success whatever had metropolitan aspirations, and laid out its paper streets and extended its paper population-curve accordingly. If Boosterism has been pre-eminently an American phenomenon, signs of it have not been lacking abroad. In *The New Machiavelli*, Wells marks the final emergence of his rural village as a full-fledged industrial suburb at the point when the local papers began to use the epithet 'Bromsteadian' as one expressing peculiar virtues.

A recent *New Yorker* provides as good a summary as any of the typical pre-depression aspirations of an American civic body, not too burlesque to be recognizable. 'The only Chamber of Commerce we ever had much truck with,' they remark editorially, 'was one in Seattle. As we recall it, their ideal of a planned society was to increase the population of Seattle by 100,000,000, wipe San Francisco off the map, extend the continent one hundred miles westward toward the spices of the Orient, simonize Mount Rainier, and establish a chain of doily factories in Snoqualmie Pass.'

If the biggest cities found themselves enmeshed in a spiral of congestion, high land-prices, skyscrapers, worse congestion, higher land-prices and higher skyscrapers, the smaller towns hastened to follow suit. Some of them hopefully put up tall buildings when not even the most superficial speculation economics would have justified them. Tenement-house laws, which marked in some ways an improvement over conditions in New York, were copied by cities whose ordinary practice was not as bad as the new 'reform' standard.

Long before the editors of *The New Yorker*, two eloquent Englishmen pointed squarely at the weak spot, with a luxuriance of venom which few present-day orators could achieve.

'Have I not, for twenty long years,' cried William Cobbett in 1821, 'been regretting the existence of these unnatural embossments, these white swellings, these odious wens, produced by Corruption and engendering crime and misery and slavery? We shall see the whole of them abandoned by the inhabitants, and, at long last, the cannons of the fortifications may be of some use in battering down the buildings.' But, as if the overcrowding evil were not already enough and too much in 'that greatest wen of all, the monster, called, by the silly coxcombs of the press, "the metropolis of the empire"... our pretty gentlemen must resort to positive institutions to augment the population of the Wen.'

William Morris said much the same thing, three quarters of a century later:

'Not only are London and our other great commercial cities mere masses of sordidness, filth, and squalor, embroidered with patches of pompous and vulgar hideousness, no less revolting to the eye and the mind when one knows what it means: not only have whole counties of England, and the heaven that hangs over them, disappeared beneath a crust of unutterable grime, but the disease, which, to a visitor coming from the times of art, reason, and order, would seem to be a love of dirt for its own sake, spreads all over the country, and every little market town seizes the opportunity to imitate, as far as it can, the majesty of the hell of London and Manchester.'

But the cities continued to spread, nevertheless. And their inhabitants, if they were not themselves able to move to the biggest city, continued to treat them all as potential Chicagos or incipient Londons. Metropolis flourished as the great romantic symbol for a restless people in a railroad age: it was the end of the line.

And so it has remained, long after the material and economic forces which brought it into being have either ceased to operate or been modified by newer forces. Coal and steam-power, the huge centralized plant, made Megalopolis at least understandable if not inevitable. But today there is a whole series of new forces operating in the other direction. The transmission of electric power instead of the carrying of coal, the automobile instead of the train, the network of highways instead of the single main-line railway, the small automatic plant instead of the huge paleotechnic monster, the radio, the telephone, the movies, all tend to negate whatever virtues the biggest city ever had. But the abstract idolum continues, for radicals as well as conservatives, and the only real signs of revolt come still from those who merely desire to escape the machine altogether — to the Country House reborn at a lower level as a 'subsistence homestead.'

Is the Picture too Black?

Perhaps I have overdone the horrors. Was there really nothing but ugliness, petty reform, frustrated romanticism, smug exploitation, darkness, filth, overcrowding, waste, indiffer-

HERITAGE OF THE 19th CENTURY

Representative dwellings from the age which glorified the 'home'

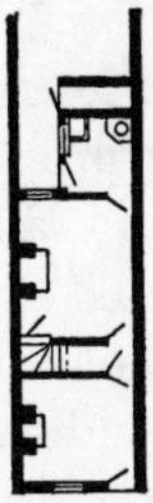

An English row house, 12 feet wide. Gas-light for the living-room at high noon.

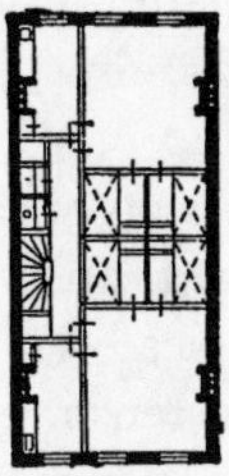

Dutch flats, two to the floor, with all the beds in interior closets.

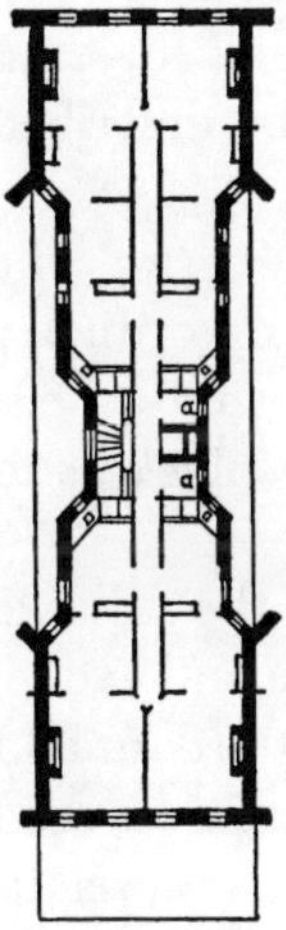

The New York Old Law tenement (the result of 'reform'), probably the worst legalized building form in the world.

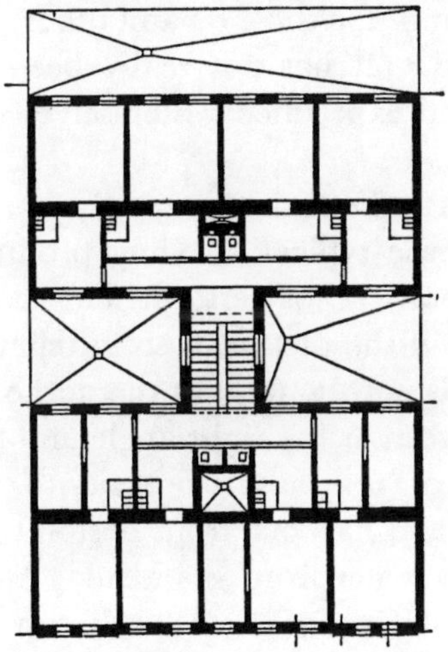

Typical flats from Imperial Vienna. One of the two rooms often opened only on a corridor.

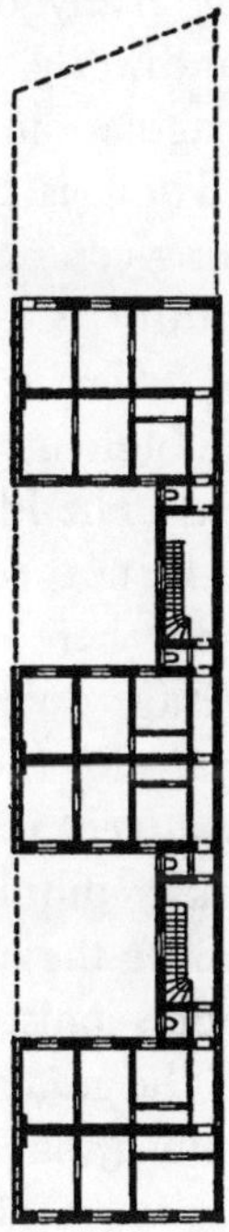

This is from Cologne, but is typical of prewar Germany. Middle-class in the front, proletariat in the rear.

ence, chaos, and despair? After inventing the whole notion of material progress, was the only contribution of the Victorians to human shelter a mere list of emergency sanitary regulations, a string of misused utilities and a handful of gadgets?

Not quite. Or perhaps, indeed no. For, if they did invent a great many of the evils which make up the housing problem as we confront it today, they also suggested practically all of the means by which it may be solved, and actually tried out a great many of them on a small scale. If as a whole they were remarkably unresponsive to sensory stimuli, individually many of them were able to criticize the results of their handiwork with eloquence, sensitivity, and revolutionary imagination.

There is hardly a single currently offered remedy for the living-conditions which we have inherited from the nineteenth century which was not itself a product of that century. But the 'effective demand' for these or any other remedies had not yet been mobilized. (It has not really been mobilized, even yet.) The ideas and experiments themselves will be described in the next section.

But here we have been looking only at the 'norm,' the average quality of the typical dwelling produced by ordinary means for the general run of persons. For that is what an environment is. And if the picture is so unrelievedly black as to lack credibility, it is not the fault of the author.

Even the chaos, seen at the right angle and from the suitable impressionist point of view, has its capacity to startle and excite. All the great ports and harbors, from Boston to Rotterdam and Bremen, have their water-front grandeur. And readily would I admit that the skyline of New York can be a marvelous spectacle. The conflux of smoke, steam, and gleaming rails in an industrial junction town like Chicago has likewise its occasional magnificence. Even the tall stone barrack slums of Glasgow possess a kind of dignity, at least by comparison with the later frippery.

But at best such spectacles and isolated phenomena provide only a fleeting sort of present comfort or a dim intimation of some possible future. At worst the emotions they inspire are mere passing snobbisms of sentimental 'appreciation,' which

THE CHAOTIC SLUM

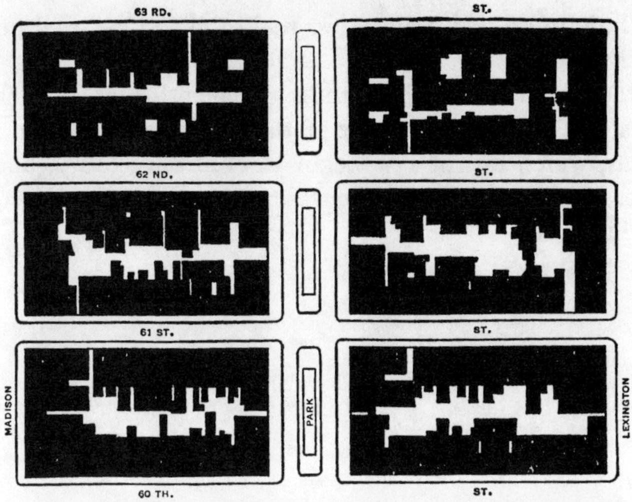

This is not, as one might suppose, the plan of some ancient shambles, long torn down. It is the present layout of a wealthy residential section of New York City; Park Avenue in the East Sixties. Patrick Geddes would have called it a Super-Slum.

THE MECHANICAL SLUM

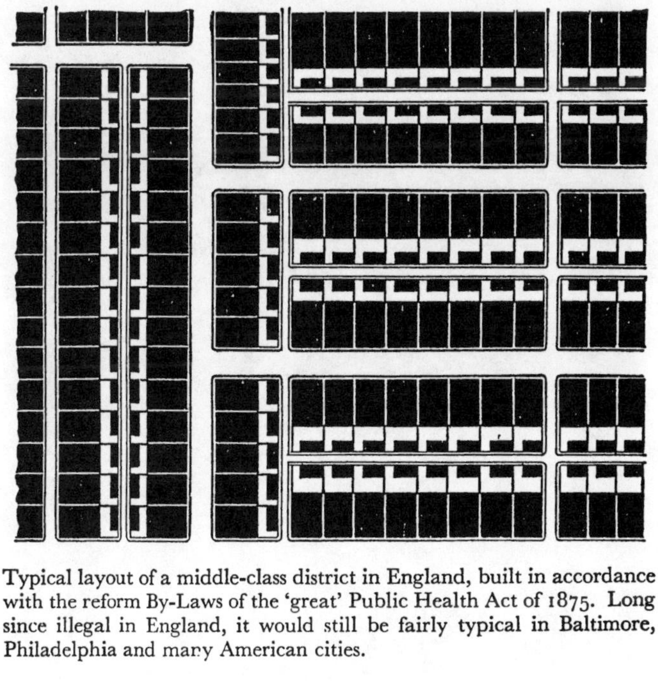

Typical layout of a middle-class district in England, built in accordance with the reform By-Laws of the 'great' Public Health Act of 1875. Long since illegal in England, it would still be fairly typical in Baltimore, Philadelphia and many American cities.

have little to do with real cities, real architecture, real houses, real civilization.

But let us consider some of those nineteenth-century ideas, all against the current, and some of those separate difficult experiments, which did at last begin to confront reality, and endeavor to channel the flow of Things into a navigable stream of civilization.

PART TWO

GATHERING FORCES

I. AN ADVANCE GUARD OF IDEAS

The Stage is Set

So much for the average nineteenth-century environment, as it was created, is now in America, and ever shall be until new machinery is set going to supersede the old. But even before the first real tenement was constructed in New York or London, there was a whole literature of revolt, protest, proffered remedies, and revolutionary Utopias. The Victorians were an extraordinary race, and it is sometimes forgotten that, along with the fatuities and hypocrisies which can be laid at their door, they must also be credited with criticism of themselves and their works as pungent, as satirical, even as creative, as any that their twentieth-century deriders have offered.

Moreover, it was the commercial middle class itself, directly responsible though it was for most of the new horrors, which in scattered individuals provided all the best early ideas as to what could be done about it. The aristocrats, although they were more alert to the threat of cholera and revolution, confined their activities for the most part to paternal philanthropy and condescending reform. The clergy and the professions, although their closer contact with conditions occasionally drove them to indignant eloquence, did not on the whole show much inclination to embarrass their betters. (One must except a few doctors and sanitary inspectors, especially in London.) And the workers, the new proletariat, were too disorganized in the beginning, and too desperately busy with the acquisition of such immediate necessities as food and work and wages, to play an active part. Later, of course, this was considerably changed: without the impulse and ideology of revolutionary socialism, without the co-operative movement and the trade unions, there would have been no constructive move toward housing at all.

The energetic middle classes were the people of destiny in

the nineteenth century, and out of their numbers came not only the inventors, the Free Trade economists, and the new industrial millionaires, but almost every propagator of important new ideas working *against* the current, every radical leader from Robert Owen to Marx and Engels, from Fourier to William Morris and Patrick Geddes.

Perhaps it will seem, both in this section and the preceding one, that a disproportionate amount of space and emphasis has been given to the situation and the counter-developments in England. However, the typical nineteenth-century *milieu* was first developed there, and there attained perhaps its 'purest' distillation short of America. On the Continent there was never quite such a complete break with the past, and certain modifications and controls were present almost from the start. England provided an initial battle ground for all the significant emergent ideas: socialism as well as Manchester liberalism, the cult of Nature as well as the cult of Megalopolis. What Robert Owen is to modern communist ideology, William Morris is to modern architecture. The Chartist Movement marks the first conscious uprising of the urban proletariat; and the modern science of regional planning and community housing had its greatest impetus from Ebenezer Howard and Patrick Geddes and Raymond Unwin. The Rochdale Pioneers were the first successful consumers' co-operative organization. In the opposite field of official 'reform,' from the top down, it is not too much of a stretch of the imagination to suggest that the *Realpolitik* of the Tory Disraeli was merely carried through to its logical conclusions in the social legislation of the Junker Bismarck. And Prince Albert's model cottages at the Great Exhibition of 1851 inspired similar worried activities on the part of half a dozen Continental royalties.

By 1830 in England there were already clear examples of all those different colored threads of purpose and 'interest' which still distinguish protagonists of social change in every country. The revolutionary agitator, the reformer, and the Utopian were all in full swing.

First there was William Cobbett, that eloquent hater, who saw the pregnant evils of the capitalist city and fought them all his life long. And at the same time there was also Thomas

Spence, the prototype of all land-reformers and Single-Taxers. 'Something to the Purpose, a receipt to make a Millennium,' was the title of one of his broadsides on the communal ownership of land, and his Utopia, Spensonia, although it looked backward to merrie England along with Cobbett, is not without contemporary significance.

Then there was a group of conscientious, hard-working gentlemen who, although never large in number and seldom popular, were perhaps more typical of their age than any others. Let me introduce you to the Philanthropic Reformers. (If you would like to know what they looked like, see Daumier's *Les Philanthropes du Jour*). Already in 1797 the first association for housing reform had been organized, the Society for Bettering the Condition of the Poor, with Wilberforce as one of its promoters. And thus was set in motion a long line of individuals, associations, and foundations, whose efforts extend into our own time. In the early years of the nineteenth century, however, they were more inclined to emphasize the soul than the body of the objects of their attentions. Bad living conditions and slums were supposed to be the unequivocal result of either laziness or low morals, and there was an endless flow of uplift. Model tenements did not appear until the forties.

But a book of rather decently designed model cottages for rural workers was got out in 1816, directly after Waterloo, called *Hints for Improving the Condition of the Peasantry.* This is worth noting if only for the fact that its author, Richard Elsam, was an architect, one of the very few who betrayed an interest in housing matters before 1900. There is a certain quaint but up-to-date quality about his introductory sentences:

'Now the blessings of peace are restored to these happy isles by the united efforts of our countrymen, who have bled in the field of battle to protect our civil rights and independence, it is the happy moment when we should turn our eyes towards the condition of the poor, and in particular to our interesting peasantry, whose comfort in every part of the United Kingdom at the present period either more or less calls for attention: and, as monarchs, statesmen, and philosophers of all ages have concurred in opinion, that the riches of a nation are the people, and as the peasantry constitute so considerable a portion of our wealth, it is doubtless the duty of those in whose hands Providence has placed the means, to assist in promoting their welfare. The comforts and advantages derived in Society by their laborious exertions, make it absolutely necessary that the greatest pains should be taken to improve their condition. It is therefore a subject of deep concern that the miserable state of their habitations in many parts of these countries have never been seriously taken into consideration.'

Almost exactly a hundred years later, England was conducting another post-war housing campaign, in much the same sort of fulsome and slightly nervous spirit. 'Homes for Heroes' was the slogan!

The Plan of Robert Owen

Of much greater significance, however, was a man who combined in one remarkable person all the characteristics of a moral reformer, a doctrinary socialist, a romantic Utopian experimenter, a practical sociologist, an earnest statesman, a labor organizer, an enlightened employer and a successful self-made business man.

Owen looked upon the same world which Cobbett and Elsam saw — England after Waterloo, suffering an economic depression, and with both the promise and the threats of the Industrial Revolution already clearly apparent. Nothing can serve so well to bring Owen's problem up to date as his words concerning the crisis of 1816:

'The want of hands and materials (during the war), with this lavish expenditure, created a demand for and gave great encouragement to new mechanical inventions and chemical discoveries, to supersede manual labour.... The war was a great and extravagant customer.... And on the day on which peace was signed, this great customer of the producers died, and prices fell as the demand diminished.... The barns and farmyards were full, warehouses loaded, and such was our artificial state of society, that this very superabundance of wealth was the sole cause of the existing distress.'

How little of novelty there is in the capitalist world, in spite of a century of progress! The impulse of all of Owen's activi-

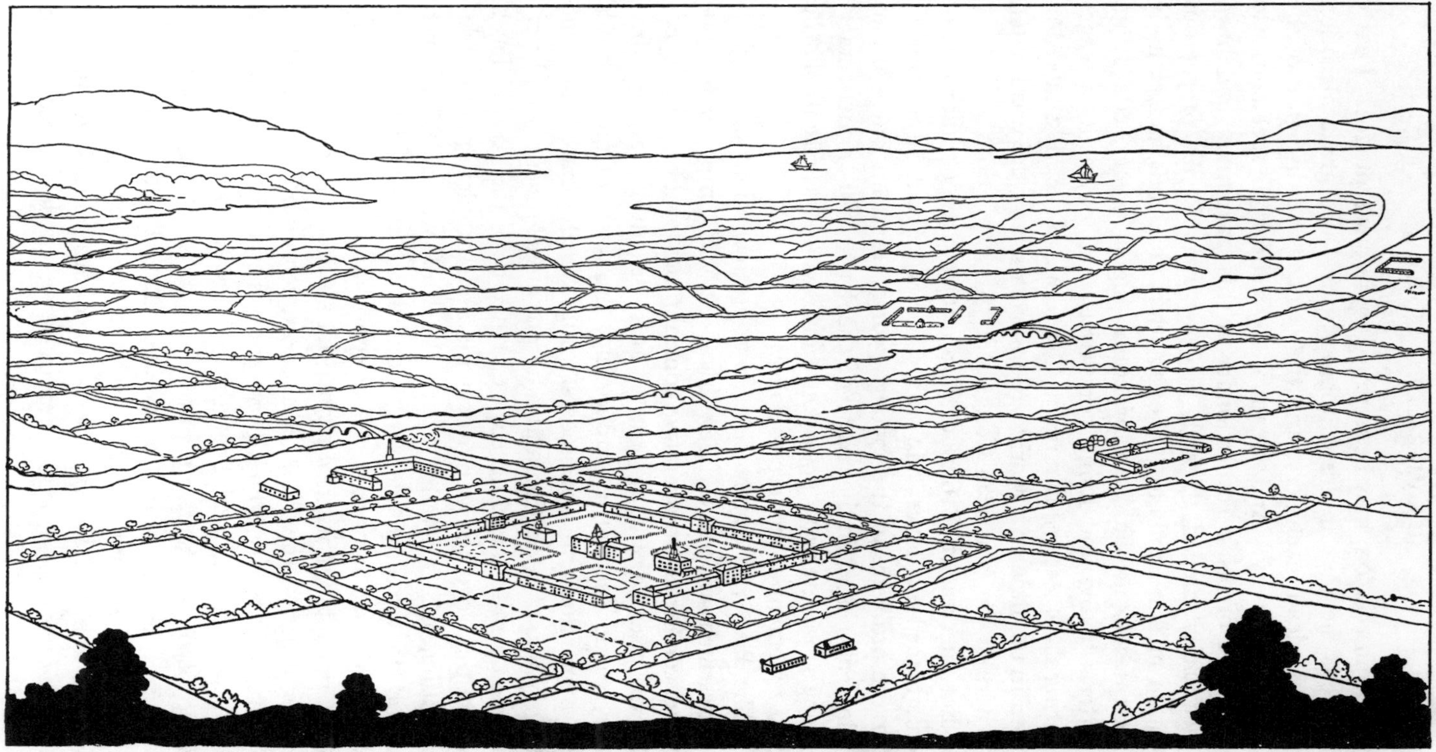

'The above Plan exhibits, in the Foreground, an establishment, with its Appendages and appropriate Quantity of Land; and at due distances, other Villages of a similar description.' Thus did Robert Owen caption this drawing, which accompanied his famous Plan of 1816.

ties, from 1800 on, may be summed up in one sentence. 'I early noticed,' he says in his autobiography, 'the great attention given to dead machinery, and the neglect and disregard of the living machinery.' And already many reforms, all spectacular to the point of being revolutionary in his own time, had been successfully carried through at New Lanark, his prosperous cotton mill in Scotland. The fact that dividends had actually increased along with shorter hours, higher wages, education, better working and living conditions, and payment of wages during slack seasons, had made Owen one of the most talked-of men in the industrial world. (Some years later, he was invited to address the American Congress.)

But the crisis of 1816 made him outgrow the popular rôle of enlightened employer. He wanted a larger and surer solution for the problems of the modern world. And his once-famous 'Plan' developed in the course of the battle from a mere emergency substitute for a poor-house into what was essentially the first statement of modern socialism.

The Plan was simple enough at its inception, although it represented an entirely new idea. It was proposed to construct completely co-operative communities for the unemployed, for the practice of both industry and agriculture. After a time they would become self-supporting, the waste of public funds on poor relief and workhouses would be eliminated, and the advantages of education and a decent environment would permanently raise the children, at least, above the pauper level. All of this, together with a drawing and complete physical description, and a detailed financial set-up, was presented in a report to the Parliamentary Committee on the Poor Law, during the session of 1817. The report had indeed been specifically requested of its then influential author.

For a period the Plan received immense and on the whole favorable publicity. The *Times* and other newspapers printed his report in full, and Ricardo and several other economists were disposed in its favor, just so long as they understood it to be merely a new form of charitable relief. But the Committee itself seems never to have considered the project at all. And Owen, who had hitherto been ingenuous enough to believe that the world was peopled entirely with little Owens, began to sense something 'strange' and calculatedly obstructive in his treatment. His arguments forthwith grew more militant, and his theories more comprehensive. Not merely the paupers and the unemployed, but the whole world, would sooner or later have to adopt his way of thinking if the machine were to be really used for the benefit of mankind. Collective ownership of land and the whole means of production, and equalized consumption, *plus* a careful scientific analysis of the social and economic nature and function of a community organism, were to be the axioms of civilized progress.

Curiously enough, it was not so much the socialism (which was probably incomprehensible to them) that stirred the wrath of all respectable citizens, but Owen's insistence on religious toleration. The whole matter was hushed up in the press, and Owen was left thenceforward to work out his ideas on social revolution in solitude.

But the design for a sample community which accompanied his report will repay a glance. 'Squares of buildings,' he writes, 'are here represented sufficient to accommodate about 1200 persons each: and surrounded by a quantity of land, from 1000 to 1500 acres.' The rectangle is bordered by two-story houses, occupied on three sides by apartments for married couples and their smaller children and on the fourth by dormitories for children over the age of three. In the centers of each of these four sides are three-story buildings which provide apartments for superintendents, teachers, doctors, clergymen, and the like. At one end of the dormitory unit is an infirmary and at the other a guest-house for visitors. In the middle of the rectangle there are three buildings, the central one for a public kitchen and dining-hall. The other two provide a nursery and other schools, a library, a lecture-room, a place of worship and several social and committee rooms for adults. The open space within the square is to be planted and laid out for exercise and recreation. The whole rectangle is surrounded by gardens and it is noteworthy that the entering roads do not permit of straight through traffic, which would tend to cut the neighborhood in two.

Beyond the circle of gardens on one side lie the factories and not far away the slaughter-house, stables, etc. On the opposite side is a public laundry. 'And at a still greater distance from the squares are some of the farming establishments, with conveniences for malting, brewing, and corn-mills, etc.: around these are cultivated enclosures, pasture-land, etc., the hedgerows of which are planted with fruit trees.'

Women are to rotate as aids in the public kitchen and dormitories, and, if employed in the factories, are not to work more than four or five hours. Apparently all the men are to be engaged in both manufacturing and agricultural pursuits.

Perhaps the only fundamental criticism which the best modern housing practice could offer would be in the matter of space and privacy per person. In Owen's community each couple, together with the smallest children, were to be allowed only one large sleeping-room for themselves. In most cases, however, it was cross-ventilated.

No public action resulted, of course. And, ironically enough, the work of the Poor Law Committee finally took shape in the repeal of the fairly generous if chaotic relief measures then in operation, and the enactment of the notorious Poor Law of 1834. This act established the policy (endorsed by all the Liberals of the time) of solving the problem of unemployment relief by making the lot of the recipient of charity somewhat less preferable than death by starvation. The workhouse described in *Oliver Twist* was one of these 'Poor Law Bastilles.'

Perhaps the only justification for reviving Owen's ill-fated Plan is that in some respects it has greater significance today than it had in 1818. Certainly its central idea must seem more valid than it could have during most of the intervening period. The notion of setting up pre-planned communities, limited in size and extent, providing a variety of productive occupations and many centralized services, was not a Utopia of 'escape' from the industrial and economic realities of Owen's time, and it is not today. For the coal-steam-railroad era, together with the tremendous urban centralization, regional specialization and huge production plants which it brought in its wake, had hardly appeared over the horizon in 1818... and now is already on the down grade. Neotechnic industry, with electric transmission and small automatic plants and its network of highways has more in common with the water-power and pre-railroad economy than it has with the paleotechnic paradise of Manchester or Pittsburgh.

Several Utopians and One Successful Experiment

Of the other early Utopians little need be said here. Few of them had Owen's essential realism, and almost none of them, even in the act of founding ideal communities, made so much as a diagram. Such positive or constructive ideas as they had belong rather to the history of economic and administrative theory than to that of housing or community-planning technique.

Perhaps one should except Fourier, if only for the sake of the *Familistère* at Guise. In many respects, with his abstract rationalism and his tight little philosophical system, Fourier is more a son of the eighteenth century than of the nineteenth. And although he was a disciple of Owen's and had gained both his living and his sociological insight as a commercial traveler, he paid no attention whatsoever to the developments of the machine or to the current political situation. His 'scientific' community, for exactly 1620 people, was designed largely to accord with a metaphysical synthesis of the 'passions.' Each phalanx was to live, work, and play in a single and imposing group of buildings, or 'social palace,' the various wings being connected with each other by a continuous covered gallery at the second-floor level. There were to be variations in income and social position, but eating and cooking and other functions were to be largely collective, and everyone was expected to do productive work.

The Brook Farm experiment among the New England intellectuals was guided by Fourier's ideas, but the work of Charles Godin at Guise was the most lasting result of his inspiration. It is also one of the earliest and one of the most successful experiments in productive co-operation. Godin, a self-made and prosperous maker of heating apparatus, began to reorganize his plant in the fifties, for complete co-operation both in production and in manner of living. Three large blocks of living-quarters for the workers and their families (including himself, it might be added) were put up, closely following Fourier's conception of a Phalanx. Each building is a hollow rectangle two rooms deep, and with galleries (like the modern exterior corridors in Germany) extending all around the courts at each floor, connecting the apartments with the corner stairs and the buildings in each group with each other. There were toilets and baths at each floor. Perhaps the most singular mark of 'progressiveness,' however, is the fact that in the older blocks the interior courts are entirely covered with a glass roof, like the shopping 'galleries' of the same period. Each group of buildings had its own co-operative store, day nursery, restaurant, dispensary, hospital, social rooms, etc. A theater, large school, café, laundry, bathing establishment in the river, stable, and finally the factory itself, complete the community. A similar unit was established in connection with the branch factory in Belgium. Additions made after the death of Godin have all followed the original idea, and the company is still fully co-operative, with the largest output of ovens and enamel vessels in France. What other experiment in Utopia has such a record? If the English garden cities fulfilled (only partially, however) some of the aspects of Owen's plan, in Guise may be found the physical prototype of modern Viennese housing.

Etienne Cabet, whose *Journey to Icaria* was a best-seller among workers in 1845, was really the elder blood-brother of Bellamy in his Utopian rationalization of the Metropolis and the State. Icaria, with all its standardized and force-imposed splendors, is modern to the extent that it represents with great accuracy a 'social-fascist' Utopia.

Buckingham's Bourgeois Utopia

But here we must turn to a gentleman of quite a different order. James Silk Buckingham, as Mumford wrote, 'was one of those erratic men of affairs which the fertile soil of British individualism produces, and which hard British common sense persistently ignores.' A successful business man and courtier who had traveled widely and had much practical contact with the colonies, he was completely untouched by any intoxicating abstractions or by any fundamental impulse against the Victorian order of things. He desired neither escape nor revolution: and his suggestions are solidly compounded of middle-class ideology, with a touch of the inspired real-estate developer. His book, published in 1848, *National Evils and Practical Remedies, with a Plan for a Model Town,* puts Utopia on a sound, respectable business basis. Some intimation of Buckingham's cosmopolitan progressiveness may be derived from the title of an address which he gave in Paris in the same year: 'Concerning certain Social Reforms which remain still to be accomplished, before Civilization has achieved its final perfection.' [1]

And yet, if even a small fraction of the contemporary hustlers had been possessed of anything akin to Buckingham's largeness of vision and concrete practicality of mind, the world would be a much better place for most of us to live in. Particularly the New World, for it was the spectacle of chaos and dreary waste in the new cities of Australia and America which drove him to think up a better way of doing things.

It is not without significance that even Buckingham could not conceive of any way to build a decent, economical, and attractive town without (1) laying down a clear and functional plan at the start, (2) constructing most of the town at once, (3) keeping all the land and buildings in single ownership, and (4) permanently limiting the size and extent. And these are the premises on which Victoria, 'An Associated Temperance Community,' was to be founded. A limited liability stock company was to be formed, and every inhabitant of the town must be a *bona-fide* shareholder to the sum of twenty pounds at least, one share entitling the member to one vote. Dividends of ten per cent to resident and seven per cent to non-resident members were to be declared, and additional profits would be divided by class (on the pattern of the distribution of prize-money in the British navy). Buckingham estimated that profits would be large.

The layout of the town is also on clearly defined class lines. The richest live in the biggest houses with the widest gardens around the central square. The next richest reside in the next belt with slightly smaller gardens, and so on, until finally the

[1] This may have been ironic. Victorian bombast is sometimes difficult to distinguish from Victorian satire.

poorest workers are established in the outer ring, along with a row of workshops. Each row of dwellings is completed with a flat-roofed colonnade (suitable for promenading in good and bad weather alike) whose architecture is perhaps the most perfect expression to date of Liberal eclecticism in a bourgeois social order. For the outer colonnades are 'Gothic,' and then, in ascending scale of wealth and social position, there is one Doric, one Ionic, one Corinthian, and finally one magnificent Composite colonnade for the plutocrats at the center! On common land at regular intervals between these rows is located every conceivable sort of building and equipment for education, recreation, sanitation, religion, culture, and moral uplift. The entire town, colonnades and all, is to be constructed of *iron.* And the *pièce de résistance* is a tremendous electric light surmounting a thirty-foot tower in the center, which will serve to illuminate all the streets.

The town is about a mile square, with a population not to exceed ten thousand. The whole is surrounded by ten thousand acres of farm land, to be worked on the latest scientific principles. Heavy industries, abattoirs, a cemetery, a hospital, a botanic garden, playing-fields, and a sewage farm are to be located outside the town proper. Provisions are to be made for colonizing daughter towns.

The administrative set-up is dominated by blue laws, and seems to be a sort of composite glorification of all the Associations for the Advancement or Prohibition of this, that, and the other thing, which were then springing into existence. No alcohol, no tobacco, no divorce, but religious freedom is allowed. On the other hand, there are interesting examples of those national minima which were later to be the backbone of Fabian policy. Minimum wages, light, air, and sanitary equipment, maximum hours of work according to age and sex, free administration of justice by arbitration, free education, free medicine. One person is entitled to one room. The final touch of progressiveness, which should have touched the heart of every Englishman with a grain of sensibility left in him, was the installation of smoke-consuming apparatus.

Here is Buckingham's explanation of his purpose:

'We have the government of the country itself, passing Acts of

Parliament for the better drainage of towns and a more ample supply of water and air for ventilation.... Hence, too, arise associations of noblemen and others for building model lodging houses for the labouring classes; associations for improving the conditions of the poor; societies for providing baths and bath-houses... associations for establishing suburban villages for the working-classes.... They are, after all, mere palliatives, and do not reach to the seat of the disease.... This can only be done by uniting the disjointed efforts of all these well-meaning but partially curative bodies into one, in order to achieve, by their union of means, influence and example.'

Not particularly inspiring, you say? And yet, what a shame that not a single one of the new towns in Australia or America adopted it for a model. It was not entirely wasted, however. Most of the best features of Victoria were later incorporated by Ebenezer Howard in his plan for a Garden City, the most influential and productive Utopia yet devised.

Perhaps I have devoted too much space to separate theories and paper plans. Still, as far as the early background of modern housing is concerned, it is quite useless to distinguish too closely between unrealized ideas and concrete experiments. One had quite as much influence as the other and, in a literary age, who knows but that the extravagant or romantic words may have been more effective in the long run than the timid constructions in stone or brick — or iron?

Sombard's objection to the Utopians, that 'they forget... that in a long process of reconstruction men and things must first be created in order to make a new social order possible,' seems to me really to be an argument in their favor. For they *did* recognize, often better than the later 'scientific' revolutionaries, that human nature itself had to be changed, and that one of the best ways to accomplish this is to change the forms and symbols of man's desires — his 'standard of demand,' in short.

II. THE HEYDAY OF PATERNAL REFORM

Do not aim too high. Be thankful to make any reasonable progress. It is far better to prove that you can provide a tolerable tenement which will pay than a perfect one which will not.... Be thankful if you can secure for the same rent even one room in a new, clean, pure house. Do not insist on a supply of water on every floor, a separate wash-house for each family....

— Octavia Hill: HOMES OF THE LONDON POOR, 1874

An Illuminating Chronology

Many things in social history cannot be dogmatically classified into cause and effect without losing some essential validity. Most historians of the housing movement used to imply that the reforms of the latter half of the nineteenth century were entirely the result of benevolent Christianity, good-will, prosperous generosity, and the progress of science. Today quite the opposite belief is generally accepted; that any betterment in living and working conditions was more in the nature of a concession, 'for fear of getting something worse.' This latter definition is not quite three-dimensional enough adequately to explain all the early experiments in housing reform. (It does not, for instance, account for the fact that the problem was not merely housing 'the poor,' but housing everybody.) And yet, if one considers only the typical works of the Tory reformers and philanthropists from 1840 to 1900, together with their offspring today, there is very little which does not seem readily explicable in terms of fear and class politics. The paleotechnic slum had played its part, along with starvation wages, child labor, and general exploitation of the under by the upper classes, in driving the former at last to some sort of desperate consciousness, and developing in the latter that halting, compromising new 'conscience' whose major element by weight was fear. The bogeys were revolution, epidemic, and the weakening of national defenses.

The chronology of the 'hungry forties' and the fifties is very illuminating on this score. The high point of the Chartist Movement in England was in the late thirties. And from then on there was a stream of warning reports on slum conditions and public health, which resulted in the first Royal Commission on Health and Housing in 1844. By 1844, Lord Shaftesbury's Society for Improving the Condition of the Labouring Classes had opened its first model dwellings. In 1845, Disraeli published, in *Sybil*, his memorable awareness of England's 'two nations, between whom there is no intercourse and no sympathy: who are as ignorant of each other's habits, thoughts and feelings as if they were dwellers in different zones, or inhabitants of different planets: who are formed by a different breeding, and fed by a different food, are ordered by different manners, and are not governed by the same laws.' In short, 'the Rich and the Poor.' In 1844, Friedrich Engels had published his book on the condition of the working classes in England.

Then came 1848, the year of Continental revolution, and of the Communist Manifesto. In the same year in England there was the beginning of a cholera epidemic (which carried off fifty thousand people in 1850), the first Public Health Act was passed, and Lord Shaftesbury introduced the first piece of positive housing legislation of modern history, which became law three years later. In 1851, Prince Albert sponsored two model workers' houses at the Great Exhibition, which inspired Napoleon III to construct forty-one 'model' buildings in Paris and influenced several other princely Continental experiments. At the same period, the arch-conservative Victor Aimé Huber started the Berlin Building Society under the protectorate of Prince Wilhelm, who had taken counsel with Prince Albert during his enforced stay in England. (Only loyal subjects were admitted to these houses.) In 1852 there was cholera in France and in 1853 the first French housing society started operations at Mulhouse, under the paternal eye of the Emperor. Almost every country in Europe can show a similar situation and an equivalent outburst of activity.

The following paragraphs are excerpts from a Memorandum of the Earl of Shaftesbury in the memorable year of 1848:

'The Queen sent for me to Osborne.... The Queen was greatly alarmed, and so was the Prince, by the Revolution in France and the exile of Louis Philippe. They feared the continuance of the commotions in England, and were desirous to know how they could exercise their influence to soothe the people.

'The Queen, on my arrival, expressed this sentiment very warmly, and added at dinner, "The Prince will talk to you tomorrow. We have sent for you to have your opinion on what we should do in view of the state of affairs to show our interest in the working-classes, and you are the only man who can advise us in the matter."

'On the following morning, during a long walk in the gardens, lasting for an hour and a half, I discussed with the Prince the condition of affairs and the state of the nation. He asked me my advice, and how he could best assist towards the common weal.

' "Now, sir," I said to him, "I have to ask your Royal Highness whether I am to speak out freely, or to observe Court Form?"

' "For God's sake," he answered, "speak out freely."

' "Then, sir, I would say that at this juncture you hold a position in which you can render to the country far greater assistance than if you were its King.... My earnest advice to you is, that you should put yourself at the head of all social movements in art and science, and especially of those movements as they bear upon the poor, and thus show the interest felt by Royalty in the happiness of the kingdom."

' "What can I do?" the Prince asked eagerly.

' "On the 18th of May next, the anniversary of the Labourers' Friendly Society will be held, and if your Royal Highness will accompany me, first to see some of the dwellings of the poor, and afterwards to preside at the Meeting, I am satisfied it will have a good effect. You should come in three carriages, and have the footmen in red liveries — even these things are not without their influence."

'The Prince at once fell in with the suggestion, and arrangements for carrying it out were discussed....

'The result was very happy.'

Alas for 'disinterested scientific progress'! There can be little surprise that the immediate results of such efforts tended to be either trivial or unpleasant, contributing little or nothing toward solving the problem of urban environment.

'Model' Housing

There is nothing which shows the depths to which standards of environment had sunk better than a typical model tenement put up under the auspices of some earnest group of reformers. For after all, the ordinary slum types, even the standardized built-in ones, were hardly more than the result of an accumulation of accidents, and the owners themselves would seldom have claimed any 'model' virtues for them. But the new tenements put up by improving societies were born of months of care and calculation. With what result? Almost without exception they were merely new types of slum which, after the first freshness had worn off, were just exactly as bad as the old ones. And often worse, when one considers their influence on standards of restrictive legislation and on the critical judgment of the public at large.

In London, for instance, although there were of course thousands of tall private houses which had decayed into flats and rookeries of the foulest kind, there were no actual built-in five- or six-story tenements before those erected in 1864 by the Peabody Foundation. In Paris a seven-story walk-up complex, consisting of three buildings built one behind the other on one interior lot, and put up by a philanthropic housing society, received first prize in a competition in 1901. In Berlin, Huber's society erected a flat-building which, although it was only five stories high and two rooms deep, had its toilets in the yard. As for New York, I defy anyone unacquainted with the history of model tenements before the war to distinguish them from any average speculative slum. And even the community development at Mulhouse, most renowned model housing of the early period, included rows of back-to-back houses.

From the beginning there were two distinct branches of paternal housing effort. One group advocated minor 'practical' reforms within the congested central districts, embodying little more than a modicum of sanitation and a degree of structural safety to be superimposed on already existing habits and forms. They would have been more than satisfied had they been able to see the entire lower-income half of the population housed in six- or seven-story tenements covering, say, seventy-five per cent of their plots, provided each room had some sort of window and each family had some sort of water-supply and every inmate was loyal to the government and had signed a temperance pledge.

The other group was more ambitious. Romantically, it desired to see every worker happily ensconced in his own little cottage surrounded by his own little garden. Politically, its purpose was perhaps best stated in the legend inscribed on the corner-stone of a house erected on the outskirts of Berlin by one of Huber's societies: 'Die Verwandlung eigentumsloser Arbeiter in arbeitende Eigentümer... eine der dringendsten Aufgaben der verhängnisvollen stürmischen Gegenwart.' (To change property-less workers into working-men of property... one of the most urgent necessities of this fateful and stormy day.') These were the people who believed that everything would be solved if outlying land were opened up, cheap transportation provided, and long-time methods of financing small own-homes devised.

But they both failed, in their ulterior as well as in their immediate purposes. True, restrictive legislation tended to crystallize into general practice the forms of the early model tenements. But the new forms, since they involved no fundamental changes, became speedily just as insanitary as the old ones — which still continued to house the worst-paid groups in any case. And since such reforms as were effected usually increased the cost of the new buildings, they often tended to be even more overcrowded. The villa promoters also failed, for their cottages were from the start too expensive for all but such workers as were already safely middle-class, and too far from the factories in a day when an average unskilled worker labored for twelve or more hours. Moreover, the current bourgeois ideals were so strong that in most of these early cottage developments there was no attempt to set up safeguards against future speculation, and time after time the houses were resold at a handsome profit and ended up as mere upper middle-class suburbs.

The Premises of Reform

Why did they fail? Just simply because it was an absolutely impossible job on their premises. They wanted to provide good dwellings, on an 'economic' basis, at a price which everyone could pay, and without disturbing or even questioning any part of the current social-economic system.

The most important principle was that the buildings should pay. And in this solitary respect these model developments were remarkably successful. Mr. E. R. L. Gould made a report to the Commissioner of Labor in Washington in 1895 which included financial data on some forty-eight 'improved' dwelling companies, located in America and in several European countries. About one third of them were limited-dividend companies. Twenty paid dividends of five per cent or more, and only eleven paid less than four per cent. Not one paid less than two per cent. This in a day when three per cent was considered a good return on a safe investment!

But alas, in almost every case either the rents were much higher than those in the current commercial product, or the buildings were little if any better, or there were exceptional conditions in favor of the model enterprise.

There were four factors in building economics which the reformers, almost to the last man, accepted as acts of God which it would be immoral and subversive even to question. One was the price of land, however fantastic the level to which speculation and previous unregulated congestion might have brought it. It never seems to have occurred to them that a few fairly simple public measures could have punctured most of the slum-expectant land-prices. Throughout those two monumental volumes on the Tenement House Problem in New York edited by Messrs. De Forest and Veiller in 1903, the price of land is taken completely for granted. Mr. Veiller remarks without surprise or indignation that 'the value of an ordinary 25-foot interior lot on the lower East Side is about $18,000 to $20,000,' and that the cost of a tenement building on such a lot is also 'about $18,000 to $20,000.' That is, half and half. Or, to put it another way, it is quite just and proper and to be expected that the poorest people in the city should pay eight dollars a square foot for the land under their dwellings, while the rich, who have houses and gardens, probably cannot afford more than one dollar!

The next item which they did not question was the return to be expected on a money investment. For, even though their model tenements did bring in a somewhat lower immediate profit than that made by the average speculator, they were constructed to last longer with less need of repairs, and in many respects they were more profitable investments than the ordinary run of building.

The third item was the sovereignty of uncontrolled private initiative. If good houses could not be supplied by the ordinary workings of the laws of supply and demand, with a minimum of public interference, then it would be better to have bad houses or no houses at all than to interrupt those laws.

But the most important item in capitalist housing economy is the relation between what people can afford to pay and the 'economic' rent of a minimum decent dwelling. And here we come up against the strongest article of general faith of all of them. The Poor were as God or their own bad habits had made them, and no power on earth could be evoked for the purpose of increasing their ability to pay. Any suggestion of subsidy as an indirect means of raising real wages, or a direct means of building decent and livable cities, was sure to raise a furor of horror and consternation. The reformers would rise in a body to protect the 'under-privileged' from the loss of Self-Respect which such a thing would bring to them. The co-operative apartments for Negroes erected in Harlem in 1927, under the auspices of Mr. John D. Rockefeller, Jr., provide an extreme example of this credo. The co-operators refuse to take advantage of the provision for tax-exemption on such housing possible under the law of the State of New York, and make the following statement in one of their pamphlets: 'The Dunbar co-operative community rejoices that it has not been called upon to sacrifice its own civic self-respect by foisting upon others its due proportion of the burden of taxation.'

As Dr. Wood puts it, 'one may be pardoned for a certain amount of scepticism as to the extent of the rejoicing.'

Often among the early reformers one comes on a certain air of unbelief in this matter of poverty. Or at least a deep feeling that really people are only poor because they are lazy, dishonest, intemperate, or improvident. The English Poor Law of 1835 crystallized this conviction, and even today in America there are people who firmly believe that anyone who really wants a job can find one. In 1903, by way of acknowledging that the latest reform dwelling, the New Law Tenement, was somewhat more expensive than the old dumbbell type, Mr. De Forest makes the following curious statement: 'It would be a sorrowful comment on the intelligence of the working people if they were not willing to pay a little more for vastly improved living accommodations.'

Ruskin himself, that Toriest of Tories, put his erratic finger very neatly on this spot:

'Nothing appears to me at once more ludicrous and more melancholy than the way people of the present age usually talk about the morals of labourers. You hardly ever address a labouring man upon his prospects in life, without quietly assuming that he is to possess, at starting, as a small moral capital to begin with, the virtue of Socrates, the philosophy of Plato, and the heroism of Epaminondas. "Be assured, my good man," — you say to him, — "that if you work steadily for ten hours a day all your life long, and if you drink nothing but water, or the very mildest beer, and live on very plain food, and never lose your temper, and go to church every Sunday, and always remain content in the position in which Providence has placed you, and never grumble or swear; and always keep your clothes decent, and rise early, and use every opportunity of improving yourself, you will get on very well, and never come to the parish." '

John Ruskin and Octavia Hill

In his often maddening and contradictory way, Ruskin did at least have a clearer notion as to what a paternal aristocracy might be than had all the Alberts, Wilhelms, and Louis Napoleons put together. He had no use for the petty abstractions of orthodox Liberal economics, which he called 'nothing more than the investigation of some accidental phenomena of modern commercial operations.' And his private Utopia, as embodied in the unrealized Saint George Experiment, is a sort of Bourbonized version of Robert Owen. Everyone is to work with his hands and have his own house and garden. There are to be strong class divisions; the Master is to be absolute dictator, and even reading matter is to be censored, no newspapers being permitted at all.

However, in his actual experiments in social reform, through his friend Octavia Hill, he was not quite so ruthless. And the movement initiated by him and developed by her was perhaps the most realistic, if in some ways the most irritating, of all the paternal efforts. They built no model tenements, cleared no slums, and created no proletarian *Eigentümers*. Their idea was really a very simple one: merely that competent disinterested people should take over the management of tenement buildings in behalf of the owners and that, though keeping them on a strictly paying basis, they should by example and education gradually introduce a modicum of co-operative order and cleanliness and decency. They proposed to prove that it made for greater economy and efficiency all around to keep the tenements in as good condition as possible than to let them drop to pieces through negligence. And, in so far as a whitewashed wall is better than a dark and mouldy one, or a clean corridor better than one infested with vermin, or an open courtyard better than one littered with garbage, the work of Octavia Hill and her female confederates may be said to have been effective. If such activities seem today rather like an attempt to rescue society (as Marx once said) 'behind its back,' still they were in their own time rather refreshingly direct. Her influence was widespread: in several German cities companies were formed to buy up old houses and put them in order. It is probable that the later 'Elberfeld system,' whereby every well-to-do citizen was required by law to accept a certain amount of responsibility with respect to the living conditions of five or ten poor families, was an indirect result. And in addition to the social workers, perhaps even those highly trained and professionally efficient women who manage the multifarious threads of community house-keeping in the modern Dutch and German housing developments are Octavia Hill's direct descendants.

The New Line of Action

What was the net result of all this activity? In so far as the actual dwellings erected are concerned, it would be safe to put it not far above zero. (Although numerically the reform houses were by no means few: by 1906 in London more than eighteen thousand tenement dwellings and six thousand cottages had been put up by one sort of improvement society or another.)

However, the fact that a line of action has been inaugurated under negative and unimaginative auspices does not by any means prove that it will end that way. And if the history of the housing movement has very little of positive value to show before 1900, and not very much before 1918, this does not mean that its early history is unimportant. Quite the contrary. For, almost inadvertently, the reformers managed to give an initial impetus to every one of the major elements in the technique of modern housing as it has been practiced in Europe since the war.

For one thing, they brought many of the facts to light for the first time — facts about overcrowding, slum diseases, exploitation. For another, they introduced the idea of the housing society — that is, on broadest terms, an organization equipped for large-scale building enterprise and not dominated by a desire for the maximum of financial profit. The original societies were for the most part highly paternal affairs which, if they admitted tenants to membership or participation at all, did so merely in order to insure themselves of 'deserving' beneficiaries. But as soon as the first fruits of the consumers' co-operative movement began to make themselves felt, housing societies were formed from the bottom up and not from the top down. Moreover, the cities themselves took over the form and set up semi-official societies for non-profit house construction. And legislation appeared which favored the various kinds of 'public utility,' 'limited-dividend,' or 'co-operative' society.

Another housing principle developed by the reformers was the notion of large-scale construction *per se.* Introduced at first purely as a matter of economic policy in competition with wasteful small builders, it soon became apparent that the orderly planning and building of large tracts at one time was not merely the cheapest method, but also the only way by which permanent amenity and adequate neighborhood equipment could be provided.

The last step in housing policy which must be credited to the philanthropists was probably the least intentional of all. But there it stands: for the first piece of constructive housing legislation in all Europe was passed in England in 1851 through the efforts of the Earl of Shaftesbury, a law which permitted governments themselves to undertake the responsibility for building and renting low-cost dwellings.

Enlightened Employers

There is one chapter in the history of private reform which deserves a brief separate mention. From the time of Robert Owen on, there was an increasing stream of new factory villages, the best of which are definitely superior to the work of those philanthropists who merely directed their activities toward that vague quantity, the Poor. I am not, of course, speaking of average 'company housing,' which is still one of the worst branches of the nineteenth-century heritage. And obviously, there are extremely real social disadvantages connected with even the best employer-owned housing, so real that a worker might quite reasonably prefer to live in a bad urban slum rather than an admirable company cottage.

However, from the point of view of purely physical standards and the technique of planning, there is a solid advance visible in such experiments as the Krupp housing at Essen, the Lever Brothers' Port Sunlight, and the colliery villages designed by Percy Houfton.

The reasons are not far to seek. In the first place, such housing was ordinarily constructed in connection with a new factory outside of a town, and therefore on cheap land. Furthermore, an employer, whether he was intelligent enough to see it or not, had a perfectly direct, concrete interest in the living conditions of his workers — far more realistic than the nebulous relation of the metropolitan reformer to the 'lower classes.' Owen himself was the first man to show that better living and working conditions could actually be measured in greater efficiency and more profits. And, whether or not one approves the acknowledged side-purpose of much later company housing, built largely to keep the workers 'quiet' and duly appreciative, one must admit that Owen's discovery does mark a positive degree of enlightenment in the matter of understanding the importance of human environment.

One of the first attempts to build a 'model' town was undertaken in 1852 by Sir Titus Salt in connection with his large textile mill near Bradford. Saltaire is supposed to have been inspired by Disraeli's *Coningsby* (1844), and, although its plan is not remarkable and the rows of houses seem now somewhat crowded and grim, the town included a vast array of communal equipment, including a very modern recreation park and a 'Literary and Philosophical Institute.' Various developments in France, Denmark, and Holland followed within the next decade or so.

In 1865, Frederick Krupp initiated a very ambitious housing policy in connection with his works at Essen. And from that moment until the war, there is little housing in all Europe which is physically better than that of the Krupps. They had three acknowledged purposes: to attract the best workers and keep them efficient, to inspire 'filial loyalty,' and to insure that Essen itself should be a wholesome, attractive, and modern city. As for the last purpose, they succeeded quite remarkably. Their own large-scale construction served to heighten competition, lower speculative land-prices, and raise the standards of purely commercial building. Their favorable attitude toward city and regional planning makes the Ruhr district today one of the most advanced and orderly regions in the world in this respect. Anyone who will compare Essen with its American counterpart, Pittsburgh, cannot sneer too hastily at the paternal 'enlightenment' of the Krupps.

In England from the nineties onward, the work of Percy Houfton in designing various new colliery villages was noteworthy. The town for the Creswell branch of the Bolsover Colliery, built in 1895, is still one of the best pieces of community planning in

England. The houses are grouped around a hexagonal common and, about thirty years before Radburn, they face inward on the gardens and the footpath is separated from the street. At the Ashington colliery, there are oriented row-houses put up around 1900 which provide a foretaste of modern German *Zeilenbau* layout.

More renowned than the coal towns are two other English developments: Bournville, started in 1879 by the Cadburys, and Port Sunlight about 1886 by Lever Brothers, manufacturers of cocoa and soap respectively. Bournville is not company housing: it has been an autonomous Village Trust since 1900, open to people other than Cadbury employees. It now has about two thousand houses, and has been developed largely by various public utility societies, some of them with government assistance. The land remains in single ownership and all the buildings must conform with standards of form and amenity laid down by the village administration. Bournville has not the forcibly uplifting atmosphere of many other experiments of the time, and is in many respects comparable to the later Garden Cities of Letchworth and Welwyn.

Port Sunlight, on the other hand, is highly paternal. No financial return on the capital is expected, and its literature is a remarkable compound of high-pressure advertising for 'Sunlight Soap' and chatty statistics on the extraordinary health, happiness, loyalty, and cultural advantages of the inhabitants. Yet the physical plan is rather an impressive one. From the beginning very large blocks were used, with interior space devoted to extra gardens and common recreation fields, an idea which was not formulated into a planning theory until much later, in Raymond Unwin's *Nothing Gained by Overcrowding*. Moreover, the large amount of park and open space 'flows' in the best modern manner, a formal plaza connecting with a stretch of rough wooded common, and that in turn joined to other parks by belts of green space, the whole forming a net around the houses and community buildings.

Earswick, near York, is a community trust on the pattern of Bournville, established by Sir Joseph Rowntree, also a cocoa manufacturer. It was laid out in 1905 by Barry Parker and Raymond Unwin, architects and planners of Letchworth.

In Germany, the pre-war housing for the Siemens plant, just outside of Berlin, was of a very high standard, both architecturally and in plan. Post-war housing at Siemensstadt has been carried out on a large scale through public utility societies, without intervention of the employers.

III. CHANGES IN THE SOCIAL STRUCTURE

If Individualism, in the property sense, was the dominant force of the nineteenth century, Socialism was its great idea. Its forms were as manifold and as mutually contradictory as those of Liberalism itself, but through all of its mutations — from the ideal of aristocratic responsibility to the conception of a revolutionary proletariat — runs a belief in some social order more fundamental than a mere market equilibrium and some human right more important than the right to buy and sell without interference. And it is curious, when one comes to think of it, how very few important social critics there have been since the middle of the century, who supported whole-heartedly an uncontrolled profit-system, or even a constitutional democracy based on private property. Indeed, probably the most thorough-going apologists for Capitalism were those theorists of the Second International who, like Kautsky, had such implicit faith in the historic necessity for a big business prelude to Socialism that they refused to believe in the Russian Revolution for many years after it had occurred.

What was true in the larger field was equally true in the matter of housing. The vast bulk of construction was of a purely profit nature. But every real advance in both planning technique, housing standards, and architectural design came from that small body of experiment which was removed from the speculative field. Underneath the impressive structure of capitalism, a vast number of more or less separate movements, some of them conscious crystallizations of socialist theory and others developing unconsciously toward some sort of collective action out of the very nature of the situation, were beginning to gather strength. And every one of them — the co-operative movement, trade-unionism, workers' parties, revolutionary sects, and the increase in municipal services and State protection, mutually unsympathetic though they often were — had its own particular influence on the development of modern housing.

Co-operative Association and Housing

Co-operative housing and the eventual establishment of self-sufficient productive communities was part of the original program of the Rochdale Pioneers in 1844, who were still greatly influenced by Owen and Fourier. However, although the members of consumers' co-operatives represented very nearly half the population in Great Britain in 1925, they had not themselves undertaken many large-scale housing experiments. This was left to separate co-operative societies, organized specifically for housing purposes, who had by 1907 put up about twenty-five thousand houses in England alone. Before 1900 these houses were usually sold off to members once they were constructed, but the Garden City Movement — itself an outgrowth of the idea of co-operative association — served to emphasize the virtues of permanent single ownership, particularly of the land, as an essential safeguard against speculation and deterioration by change of use. The first co-partnership 'garden suburb' was built at Ealing in 1901, and was shortly followed by Hampstead, which is still one of the best housing developments in England. The consumers' co-operative organizations, although rarely building themselves, invested large sums in such co-operative schemes.

In Germany the co-operative movement had at the start a much more paternal flavor than it had in England. Herr Huber himself was one of its most ardent promoters, and one feels implicit in the arguments of these gentlemen the notion that, if workers were going to 'associate' anyway, it would be best to see that they had conservative and respectable leadership. After 1889, however, favorable legislation changed this and there was an immense growth in co-operative workers' housing on the workers' initiative. The garden city idea spread from England around 1900, and the most advanced architects and planners of the day worked with the trade unions and labor organizations to produce some of the best housing built on the Continent before the war. This machinery was so well established that after the war a very large section of the national housing program was carried out through co-operative agencies (including actual construction as well as supervision), the societies supplying only a very tiny part of the necessary capital.

The Belgian co-operative movement, allied from the start with the unions and the workers' party, was theoretically socialist. The *Maisons du Peuple* (some of them among the most interesting examples of Art Nouveau architecture) provided many facilities for education and recreation, and are admirable early examples of 'community equipment.' The housing movement proper, however, does not seem to have had any very direct connection with these co-operatives.

In Denmark, aside from the rural producers' co-operatives which have changed the whole economic and social pattern of the country since the sixties, there was considerable co-operative housing in the towns. Much of it was on a large scale and included day nurseries, laundries, churches, and other common facilities. Systematic and orderly planning standards were early developed, and probably had some influence on post-war German practice.

The Russian co-operative movement, non-existent before the unsuccessful revolution of 1905, had attained a tremendous growth by the beginning of the war. Within a few years of its inception, there were eight million members, largely among the peasantry, who published thirty weekly newspapers and undertook every sort of producers' and consumers' enterprise. Housing, however, received a relatively small emphasis. During the Revolution, the Communists found it necessary to liquidate most of these societies, and this fact is often used by radicals as an argument against any possible revolutionary virtues in the co-operative movement. However, it seems to this writer entirely unimportant that the *organizations* had to be reconstituted. But the fact that eight million peasant families had become habituated to collective, non-competitive enterprise may well, on the other hand, have played no small part in the eventual success of the revolution.

The reorganized co-operative societies are a highly important item in the present Russian economic set-up. Housing, for instance, at first constructed largely by the State, has become more and more a group or co-operative activity, due to the greater degree of economy and general satisfaction made possible thereby.

Engels versus the Housing Reformers

In Germany social movements early took on a more political character than those in other countries. Class distinctions were immensely sharpened by the revolution of 1848, and have always remained the outstanding element in German politics. To belong to the 'Mittelstand' or to be a 'Kleinbürger' or an 'Arbeiter' is part of the everyday consciousness of a German citizen, and regulates many of his activities. The bourgeois Liberals never had any illusion nor made any public pretensions about the class to be benefited by the development of capitalist commerce, and the class which was to be kept down at all costs. Every measure to alleviate the condition of workers was put through by the ruling aristocracy for their own devious purposes, against the united opposition of the middle class, and also against the Marxist workers.

The result was a strong workers' party, able to poll more than one third of all the votes cast in a national election in 1912. But from the beginning the contradictions arising from a workers' party organized solely for parliamentary agitation in a capitalist state, and yet imbued with the doctrine that nothing whatsoever could be done to better their lot until a complete revolutionary overturn had been effected, were apparent. And nowhere more obviously than in the matter of housing. Indeed, it was this point as much as any other which finally split the party, around 1900, into the two wings which were to become after the war the Social Democrats and the Communists respectively. And already in 1872, when Engels published his articles against 'housing reform' and against the Prudhon ideal of home-ownership, the issue was a clear one.

Zur Wohnungsfrage is an exceedingly interesting document, embodying the best Marxist virtues and at the same time betraying certain typical dogmatic weaknesses. As a biting and eloquent criticism of the aristocratic reformers and their works, and as a devastating analysis of the home-ownership ideal, no better piece of work has ever been done. Engels showed how, by the very nature of the situation, upper-class reforms either accomplished exactly nothing or reached only the middle classes. He demonstrated once and for all that the average employers' housing, good or bad, must inevitably be paid for by a lowering of workers' wages and by limitations on their freedom. As for Prudhon, who had advocated the 'abolition of rent' and who was in some measure the father of petit-bourgeois anarchism and also of the land-reformers, Engels disposed adequately of his thesis that 'the tenant is to the home-owner as the wage-worker is to the capitalist.' The small home-owner in an industrialized society, he showed in an argument which still has great significance, can never be a capitalist, because a house is not strictly a piece of capital goods. No matter what land-reforms might be introduced, the small home-owner must still surrender a large part of his one advantage as a worker, namely, freedom. The ideal of Prudhon, and with him one could well put those modern homestead-promoters in America and elsewhere, could only be put into effect if society turned its back squarely on the machine and its possible benefits, and relapsed into a state of peasant handicraft. The overcrowded slums and the miserable great cities were alike necessary conditions of capitalist expansion.

This much of Engels' argument is admirable, and a glance at any company town or any model tenement or any district sprinkled with foreclosed small homes, or at the feeble and frustrated efforts toward slum-clearance, will bear him out. But all of these things, no matter when they were built, are still strictly of that nineteenth century which produced Marxism as its logical antithesis. Strictly of the nineteenth century, too, was Engels' conviction that all the more pressing aspects of the housing problem could readily be taken care of merely by redistributing the existing dwelling-space on the morrow of a revolution. Beyond this (so strong was the reaction of 'scientific socialism' against the Utopianism of Owen and Fourier) he offers not the slightest notion as to what new sort of environment the social revolutionists might be fighting for... other than the abstract axiom that the 'contradiction' between the city and the country must eventually disappear.

However, there are a large number of elements in the new technique of housing for which one can find no adequate explanation or criticism in Engels. The enormous increase in State and municipal responsibility, for instance, and the method of providing large-scale rental housing on a non-profit basis, under working-class leadership and with little if any equity. Such developments, springing directly from the failure of speculative enterprise rather than from politics bourgeois or otherwise, have considerably increased the complexity of the housing problem for the modern radical.

In Engels' day, however, to promote housing or any related measure was to accept middle-class ideology. And the radicals had many a bitter argument on the subject. In general, before about 1900, they were pretty well united in their opposition to every sort of 'reform.' But the Future State, momentarily expected, did not put in its appearance, and the Second International had taken on a much milder and more evolutionary tone. Therefore, whether or not it was a mistake from their point of view, they began to promote trade-union and other co-operative housing, and to urge municipal land-control policies and municipal house-construction. Indeed, they swung over so far that from about 1900 onward the majority Social Democrats were hardly more than the left wing of the burgher reformers.

Municipal and State Responsibility in Germany

Pure Liberal individualism has never played a very important rôle in Germany. On the one hand there was the authoritarian Imperial State whose interests were to be served above all others and which, to safeguard those interests, guaranteed a minimum of physical security to its underlings in the form of social insurance. And on the other hand there was the much older and even more deeply embedded tradition of the city as a working organism in which every citizen, no matter what his class, took an active pride. The welfare and orderliness of a German city was something to be promoted for its own sake, over and above any individual 'interests.'

There was therefore nothing essentially new about the growth of city-services and city-planning which began to take place toward the end of the century: rather were they a revival of the habits of mind which had built the Free Cities of mediæval Europe. This municipal enterprise took two general forms, one the provision of all sorts of productive services (not limited to the field of necessities or 'natural monopolies') and the other the wide purchase of land and other resources and the control of land-development. A remark made to me in 1932 by the city-planner of Cologne was already substantially true in 1900. The difference between a German and an American city, he said, is the fact that the American town only does what it is expressly permitted to do, while a German city does everything except what it is expressly forbidden to do. And there is very little which it cannot undertake. Outside of the ordinary utilities, many towns operate markets, warehouses, slaughter-houses, sewage-farms, mortgage banks, insurance companies, and port facilities. They often maintain forest preserves, mines, recreation parks, public baths, opera houses, museums and concert halls.

It is a mistake to call such activities 'socialism.' Rather do they represent a form of municipal capitalism, in the fact that 'economic' prices for these services were usually charged, making them not equally available to all citizens, and in so far as the profits, when they were successful, were likely to go toward lowering income taxes. Indeed, there was little or no social idealism in the attitude of the ruling burgher toward his city's enterprises. He merely felt himself, together with all the other present and possible residents, as a shareholder in the town, and desired that the quality should be improved continually and that it should be managed in as efficient and business-like way as possible. The result was that, though the budget of many German cities even before the war was many times that of an American town of equal population, its per capita taxes were not likely to be any higher. This is not socialism, most certainly, but it goes far to show how easy it was for the German cities, when the time came, to assume responsibility for housing and land-development.

By 1900 the stream of travelers who had once gone to England to behold the industrial marvels was beginning to turn in the other direction. One of them, T. C. Horsfall, wrote a book called *The Improvement of the Dwellings and Surroundings of the People: the Example of Germany.* The meanest citizen of a German city, he said, had pleasanter places near their homes for fresh air and recreation than the wealthiest people of Manchester. This was true in spite of the fact that the dwellings themselves in Germany, almost entirely tall crowded tenements in the cities, were much worse than the two-story houses of England. The difference lay in the broad tree-lined streets, in the parks and schools and public buildings, in the orderly differentiation between residential and industrial zones, in water-fronts carefully preserved for amenity and recreation, and in the greater accessibility of unspoiled open country.

Why was it? Horsfall thought that a good part of the reason lay in the fact that governing cities was a full-sized professional job in Germany, entailing long special training, ostensibly removed from politics, and bringing with it honor and a substantial salary. None of which was true of England. In 1900 about half of the Council of a large German city was made up of paid experts. This was not due in any degree to political socialism: there was even still a property qualification on the municipal vote. The only real explanation, it seems to me, is that those substantial, pompous, eminently 'class-conscious' burghers did nevertheless have a real heritage of pride and responsibility, at least in so far as the outward appearance of their cities was concerned. They saw no reason why a city should not be at least as carefully planned, and managed as professionally, as a big private business. And scandals were almost unknown.

The post-war housing in Germany would not be as good as it is if the cities themselves had not already owned a very large proportion of the surrounding land, and if they had not been exercising stringent control over the use of unbuilt areas for some years. Land-purchase policies go back to the Middle Ages, and there are many small towns and villages which own so much property that their inhabitants pay no taxes. From about 1890 onward, stimulated by a desire to offset the evils of speculation, most of the cities rapidly increased their domain. In 1902, eighteen out of thirty-one representative large towns owned more than sixty square yards of unbuilt land per capita of population.

'City-planning,' as we know it, was already in full swing in Germany in 1900. But in addition to careful zoning as to use and height, most cities had also detailed development plans, to which every builder had to conform. Only certain sites were considered 'ripe' at any one time, and no building could be done in other areas. (Most of these plans had to be considerably revised after the war, however, to suit the advances in housing standards and layout technique.) Frankfurt, under Mayor Addickes, had adopted a law in 1902 which permitted the compulsory pooling, rearrangement, and redistribution of privately owned plots, in the interests of more efficient planning. The city was allowed to keep forty per cent of any such area, without payment, for streets and parks. A system of graduated 'increment-value' taxation of land was also instituted in Frankfurt and became a Prussian law in 1911. Speculative land-prices, if they were not to be really curbed until after the war, were recognized to be the root of the housing evil. A Saxon Building Law of 1898 had officially stated that the price of land is determined by the amount of building which is allowed on it, and that 'every increase in the amount allowed causes considerable increase in the price of land, not only in the same building district but also in the adjoining districts.'

All of this was in the nature of preparation for a direct attack on the housing problem, which was just as urgent in Germany as anywhere else. But housing is not merely a matter of land: it is also a matter of money. Where were housing credits to come from?

And here we come to perhaps the neatest dovetailing in the German system of paternal security and municipal services. Bismarck had put through the social insurance measures in the eighties, and there was a clause in this legislation permitting the funds to be loaned for housing purposes. No great use was made of it until after 1900, but by 1914 insurance funds had been loaned for housing by the various regional agencies up to more than $114,000,000. Almost all of this sum went to either co-operative or trade union societies or directly for municipal housing. It was loaned at rates varying from two and one-half to four and one-half per cent, and probably assisted in the erection of at least 100,000 dwellings. Funds from other public and semi-public sources were also made available for public-utility housing.

Much of this new activity may be traced to the movement against Liberal individualism which, springing from middle-class intellectuals and officials, was known as 'Kathedersocialism.' The Society for Social Politics had made a vast housing survey in 1886. And the work of carrying forward and putting through national legislation to promote land-purchase, land-use control, adequate housing standards, official credits, and direct public construction was carried on by the German Society for Housing Reform, whose activities have continued until this day.

Along with such movements as these, the co-operative housing movement was taking on a different color. The desire to make over every worker into a harmless bourgeois property-owner was subsiding, for the simple reason that it could not be done. The new societies did not sell off their houses and, as more and more public funds became available, they required less and less initial capital on the part of their members. Rents and profits were regulated, and any surplus went into more housing or into communal equipment of one sort or another. By 1914 there were 1400 co-operative housing societies in Germany, many of them controlled directly by trade unions or other workers' organizations. This machinery for house-production was to be of major importance in post-war German housing.

Fabians, Labour and Housing: England

The British Labour Party, a product of that long depression which began in 1889, has never been either revolutionary or Marxist, and was therefore not faced with the necessity of making tremendous decisions as to policy in the here and now. 'The inevitability of gradualism' amiably sheltered any sort of immediate reform or small concession, from social insurance and better factory conditions to housing and town-planning. The Fabian Society, under the leadership of Shaw and Sydney Webb, were influential in setting up this policy for English Labour.

Now it might be supposed that such a workers' movement, practical, realistic, would play a considerable rôle in furthering such matters as housing, at least in so far as anything *could* be done about it within the capitalist framework. Certainly the Labour Party and the Fabians were always in favor of 'housing.' Also, the National Housing Reform Council (now the National Housing and Town Planning Council) was organized in 1893 largely through the efforts of the miners and other labor groups. And from that time on, leadership in housing and planning matters began to swing across from the Conservatives to Labour, undergoing a considerable change of atmosphere in the process.

Nevertheless it would be very difficult, looking through a file of Fabian Tracts, to discover many new or positive ideas on the housing question. Perhaps the best one could find would be this, 'That a life-interest in the Land and Capital of the nation is the birth-right of every individual born within its confines,' which was part of an early Manifesto, later withdrawn ostensibly because it was too radical.

The Fabians had a very bad habit of making all possible compromises before they presented their plan. They did this, of course, quite consciously in order to avoid any appearance of romanticism or 'impracticality' and with the idea of disarming their enemies. But the inevitable result was that their projects never had any dash, any capacity to inspire either fear *or* desire, and very often they were so tame and dull as to be a good two steps behind even the average progressive thought of the moment. And, as even their successful ideas would necessarily be further compromised in execution, the results were seldom exciting. Much of the dryness, and a great deal of the undercurrent of solid good sense, is attributable to the Webbs, who were efficient administrators rather than socialists, and in many ways might have been just as valuable to Mussolini as to the labor movement.

The contribution of the Webbs and their co-workers to housing education was to bring out the undeniable fact that houses are merely the next step in that increasing line of public services and utilities which now includes water-supply, street-paving, transportation, and such matters. Every individual is just as much entitled to a minimum of shelter as he is to a minimum of clean water, and the conditions of a complex industrial society make it unavoidable that governments should themselves assume the responsibility for providing both.

The Fabians had a curious way (the exact opposite of German abstractionism) of reducing all theories to a convenient, even a cozy, scale. Communism and Anarchism, they suggest in 1886 under the title 'What Socialism Is,' will probably provide the new social order with a handy balancing device, much like the Whigs and the Tories! And in the same way the Webbs have tended to reduce the entire philosophy of socialism, particularly in its relation to environment, to the doctrine of National Minima, a notion which could be safely promoted even by Mr. Asquith. Minimum standards for all citizens, that is, of sanitation, of education, of leisure, of wages, of housing, and so on. And in so far as this is almost exactly what England attempted during the past generation (albeit at considerably lower 'Minima' than the Webbs would probably have desired), credit may well be allotted to the Fabians and the Labour Party.

In order to achieve such standards, they advocated more efficient State and municipal governments providing ever more and better services. And here again there has been considerable success. Once excessively weak and amateurish, the English local governments extended their powers and abilities so far that they were able after the war themselves to carry through the major part of the housing program. Nevertheless, even the Fabians hardly went as far in these matters as the progressive burghers who ruled the German cities in 1900.

Minimum standards, however high and although they are of primary importance in any social-economic system, are not enough all by themselves. And in no field are they less adequate than in the matter of housing and physical planning. Assuredly there must be working standards, but even before these are established one must also have a clear picture of what one would really like to achieve, whether it be practical or impractical. When a Fabian Society devotes all its energies to the 'next step,' its best function as an unofficial educational and propaganda organization is weakened, and that step itself may not be taken in the right direction.

And, at least in so far as housing and planning are concerned, the Fabian Tracts are almost invariably backward, and often ridiculous in their timidity. They criticize the Local Government Board for recommending a higher standard of space than usual, because of the horrible possibility that this might make the house a 'charge on the rates.' And in a 'Workers' Political Program' for 1891 they do not mention housing at all, even though the Housing Act of 1890 was a remarkably complete piece of enabling legislation for its day.

Moreover, they fell heir to that ancient delusion that all that need be done is to break up the big estates by taxation, without realizing that competitive speculation in the ensuing small parcels might well prove worse for the housing situation than the former condition.

What Engels was to the German 'socialists of the chair,' William Morris, curiously enough, was to the Fabians. He despised them for somewhat different reasons, no doubt. But he saw very clearly that the Fabians and the Labour Party were setting up nothing worth fighting for, call it socialism or anything else, and that what they were talking about was for the most part little more than 'machinery,' which could be used quite as well against the real interests of society as in its favor. Romantic mediævalist though he was, his Utopian *News From Nowhere* and a handful of essays have more direct bearing on the problem of what can be done with this modern chaos than have the whole stack of Fabian Tracts. (Perhaps one should except two of them, both a little outside the general line: Raymond Unwin's *Cottage Plans and Common Sense*, and Clutton-Brock's *Socialism and the Arts of Use*.)

However, there were during this period considerable parliamentary developments in English housing policy, with or without the assistance of the Labourites. A Fabian pamphlet of 1893 begins as follows: 'There are three stages through which every new notion in England has to pass: It is impossible: It is against the Bible: We knew it before. Socialism is rapidly reaching the third of these stages.' Now if this is by no means accurate with regard to socialism, it does sum up quite neatly the public attitude toward housing.

Between 1851 and 1890 a large number of laws were passed which, when finally consolidated in the latter year, gave to the State and the local governments practically every necessary power and means for dealing with the immediate housing problem. They could buy land or expropriate it for housing purposes; they could build and let dwellings without an intermediary; they could borrow money cheaply from the Public Works Loan Fund; they could take subsidies out of taxes; they could take over condemned areas and rebuild them. And by 1914 they had made considerable experiment in the exercise of these powers.

For the actual data as to laws and achievements before the war in the other countries as well as in England and Germany, the reader is referred to the Appendix. This section has been designed merely to show some of those background forces and elements which went into the shaping of national housing policies.

IV. TOWARD A NEW PHYSICAL WORLD

The 'Public'

By 1900 any fairly acute person might have realized that this matter of housing, in its largest sense as average human environment, was bound to be one of the pivotal questions of the twentieth century. It was not merely that the doctors and the sanitary inspectors, the reformers and the revolutionists, the progressive bureaucrats and the sentimental philanthropists, managed to agree at least that housing conditions were bad. Certain elementary but nevertheless fundamental changes in the general standard of demand were becoming apparent. After a full century, during which even the houses of the rich had been inconvenient, ugly and uncomfortable, there were vague stirrings of revolt. The 'elements' — sun, air, cleanliness, order — were just beginning to come back over the threshold of consciousness.

Perhaps the best symbols of this new realism (and they were often hardly more than symbols) can be found in the typical suburban house of a 'progressive' and fairly wealthy American of the period. A century had passed without any important changes in plan or equipment, and then quite suddenly what do we find? A white tiled bathroom, for one thing; a sleeping-porch for another; and finally, a 'sun-parlor.' The notion of 'labor-saving' was also coming in: kitchens were to be 'planned' to fit their functions. Moreover, there was a vague sort of idea, just gaining foothold, that 'good taste' had something to do with simplicity. Some of the bric-a-brac and perhaps one set of curtains and one layer of carpet were dispensed with. I do not mean to imply that any of these things were achieved very *directly*, because people consciously and suddenly wanted sun and air and order in their lives. They have all been snobbisms to greater or less degree: and yet there *is* a qualitative difference between a snobbism about sunlight and a snobbism about useless objects.

In Europe there were not so many tiled bathrooms, perhaps, but the new desires and demands were just as apparent, and often rather wider in scope. Outdoor recreation, sports, 'physical culture,' and what a German sociologist called the 'Back-to-the-land-Bewegung' were making large numbers of people dissatisfied with crowded tenements and dark, dirty cities. Perhaps no one has described this new attitude more accurately than Horsfall, when he was commenting on the changes which were going on in Germany at the turn of the century:

'Whatever improves the physical condition of a population, by causing its boys and girls, its men and women, to be taller, better-looking, and broader muscularly and nervously stronger and more vigorous, than they would otherwise be, and at the same time develops in them a healthy appreciation of health and strength and good looks, and a wholesome pride in possessing these advantages, necessarily does much towards giving desire for the conditions which are most favorable for the maintenance of health, strength and good looks, and distaste for the conditions which are unfavorable to their maintenance.'

The proof of this, in so far as the 'housing movement' in Europe is concerned, is that within fifty years it had developed from a simple little matter of providing a few philanthropic tenements for paupers to the problem of providing a decent living environment for everybody. There is nothing which shows the extent of public interest better than the growing number of associations, congresses, exhibitions, and publications which by 1910 is already too long to chronicle. From 1851 onward, every international exposition had its quota of 'model' houses. The Paris Exhibition of 1900 had a complete block, including exhibits from Belgium, Switzerland, England, Germany, Holland, and France, just as 'modern' for their time as the Stuttgart exhibition housing of 1927. Most important of all, these activities were no longer confined to social theorists: architects, engineers, and technicians were beginning to take part, however fruitlessly for the time being.

The Engineer and the Architect

As early as 1850 there were forerunners of the modern promoters of 'pre-fabrication,' who saw the whole problem as a challenge to industrial and structural ingenuity alone. At the 1867 Paris Exposition a small house with an iron skeleton was given a medal. Shortly afterward, much attention was bestowed on a patent cement slab process invented by Mr. W. H. Lascelles, who received an award for designing an exhibition house in 1878 consisting of one large living-room and three rather constricted but nevertheless highly ingenious sleeping-alcoves which collapsed in the daytime. From the eighties onward, there is a whole series of standardized folding wooden houses, particularly from Scandinavia, usually complete with a diagram showing how neatly they could be fitted onto a horse-cart, jig-saw trimmings and all.

But it cannot be said that the really significant engineering-architecture of the time, of which Paxton's Crystal Palace of 1851 was the first important example and in some ways one of the masterpieces of the century, had any direct influence on the form and technique of housing until after the war. The tower of M. Eiffel looked down on the First International Housing Congress, and it may well have been the same sort of inspiration which led M. Cacheux, the engineer who was responsible for the model house exhibit, to betray such obvious pride in the dimensions and modernity of his 'model' sewers and in the steam-laundry and drying equipment provided at Mulhouse. But there is no outward reflection in early housing of the structural audacity evident in the new iron and glass department stores, and in the remarkable experiments in reinforced concrete being conducted by M. Hennebique. M. Godin had covered his interior courts with glass roofs in the fifties, but actual window-areas in small dwellings underwent no particular change. (Indeed, the Tudor cottage designs submitted by Mr. Elsam in 1816 were probably more generous of light and air than almost any model housing of the century.) Albeit 'ventilation' as a point of departure for ingenuity rather than sound planning was already well established. When 'model' houses were still being built back-to-back, as they were at

Mulhouse, there was often some complicated system of air-ducts, and the plans usually show such a whirlwind of breezy arrows that one instinctively turns to shut the window.

On the side of architectural form, there has been a fairly close relationship between the innovators and the housing movement almost from the beginning, although few very striking or ambitious experiments were made until after the war. Through Morris and some of his followers, above all through Raymond Unwin, the English Arts and Crafts Movement revived the decent tradition of brick craftsmanship and the simple cottage vernacular, which still mark the better part of English housing. (It should not be forgotten that even while the rage for degraded and pastiche 'Queen Anne' was at its height, William Morris himself was lecturing eloquently against all forms of exterior ornament, and declaiming that even the ugly 'brick box with a slate lid' of the utilitarian fifties was better than the jerry-built frippery of the nineties.)

But it was in Holland that the Romantic Movement left its most enduring mark. Berlage and his followers, influenced on the one hand by the mediævalism of Morris and on the other by the freer and more original genius of the American, Frank Lloyd Wright, achieved the first real *vernacular* of modern architecture. That is, a 'style' whose monuments were not merely to be found in isolated villas or public buildings, but in whole blocks and streets of 'housing' and shops and offices, in plotting and planning, and within the dwelling of *l'homme moyen sensuel* as well as in those of the more advanced or Bohemian literati. This was particularly true in Amsterdam, where entire districts, including many low-cost workers' apartments put up with official assistance, and also palatial hotels and schools and bath-houses and bridges, bear witness to a fresh approach to a modern world, for the most part quite unified. Much of this was accomplished before the war, and largely determined the form of post-war housing in Holland. The same sort of rejuvenation (for there was no complete or revolutionary break with the past until much later) was going on in the Scandinavian countries, where the early co-operative housing has a sort of decent dignity difficult to discover in the model tenements of London or Paris or New York.

The Art Nouveau of Paris and Vienna had little direct effect at the time on housing forms, except in so far as it encouraged the use of new materials and a fresh approach in general. In Germany by 1900 there was already a pretty thorough break, at least among the younger architects, with that pompous and dreary neo-Baroque which had dominated the nineteenth-century cities. And the bristling Romanesque which one is led to call the Bismarck style, because so many of that gentleman's monuments are clothed in it, was fortunately short-lived. Hundreds of experiments followed: almost every city has its own assortment of pre-war 'modern' buildings. And almost all of the innovators, among them many who were to guide the current of modern architecture into a more rational and unified stream after the war, were identified with the co-operative housing movement. Indeed, it was the modern architects themselves who took the lead in organizing most of those small suburban communities which were the best examples of pre-war German housing.

A Modern Utopia: The Garden City

The Garden City Movement might well have been described in the section devoted to Utopias but for one thing. Namely, that Ebenezer Howard's idea has the remarkable distinction of having been concretely realized in two complete experiments and in many other partial ones.

Howard was neither a revolutionist, a millionaire suffering pangs of conscience, nor a modern architect. He was a shorthand writer. In Chicago in his youth he had seen the effects of the fire and had been led to think about the possibility of creating entirely new cities, whole and fresh from the bottom up and built according to a rational plan. In 1898 he published a little book called *Tomorrow* (later reissued as *Garden Cities of Tomorrow*) which outlined just such a project.

His idea was a simple one, not essentially very different from that of Buckingham and not nearly as radical in its social framework as that of Owen or Fourier. But the physical details were both original and eminently practical, and the convinced enthusiasm of Howard was equaled only by his common sense.

The easiest way to outline the principle involved is to quote the later definition of a Garden City. It is 'a town designed for healthy living and industry; of a size that makes possible a full measure of social life, but not larger; surrounded by a rural belt; the whole of the land being in public ownership or held in trust for the community.' No tiny isolated colony, then, but a complete working city whose estimated population was to be around thirty thousand. The diagrammatic scheme is circular, with a large central park containing also the principal public buildings and skirted by a main shopping street, with an outer circle of factories and the permanent green belt beyond. The city itself was to occupy one thousand acres and the agricultural belt five thousand. The railroad by-passes the town, meeting the circle at a tangent. By keeping the land in single ownership the possibility of speculation and overcrowding would be eliminated, and the increment of value created by the community in industrial and shop sites would be preserved for itself. Essentially, a thorough-going experiment in middle-class consumers' co-operation.[1]

In 1899 the Garden City Association was formed, and in 1901 it had thirteen hundred members. A site was procured in Hertfordshire, about forty minutes from London, and in 1903 the First Garden City, Limited, a limited dividend society, was organized and the building of Letchworth commenced. Today Letchworth has fifteen thousand inhabitants, pays the permitted five per cent on its stock, has one hundred and eleven factories and workshops, and is in every way a going concern. Its post-war successor, Welwyn Garden City, was started in 1920, has now about ten thousand population and something over fifty industries. Both towns have profited by the southward move of manufacturing in England, and have been able to draw relatively more new plants than have the neighboring cities. Howard's general principles, including the communal ownership of the land and the permanent green belt, have been carried through in both cases, and the garden cities have

[1] Theodor Fritsch, in *Die Stadt der Zukunft*, had expressed many of the same ideas a decade earlier. And the Archbishop of Canterbury at an official housing conference in 1884 had advocated a belt of common land to surround every town, beyond which all new development must take place.

been a trying-ground for technical and planning improvements which influenced all of English post-war housing.

Both towns were fortunate in their makers. Letchworth was entirely planned by Barry Parker and Raymond Unwin, leaders and foremost practitioners of European town-planning in the past generation. Welwyn was planned by Louis de Soissons and various other architects. If the latter is at present the more attractive, due to a firmer architectural control of individual buildings and also to a somewhat more urbane central arrangement, the improvements in Welwyn grew naturally out of the experience at Letchworth and the better knowledge thus achieved. They are both disappointing if one is looking for architecture as modern as the plan conception. Only some of the Welwyn factories are really modern, the houses being for the most part various modifications, ordinarily simple and decent enough, of the traditional English cottage. They are built of brick, plain or stuccoed, and are usually grouped together.

Two important street-and-block planning principles, which have been largely followed in post-war English housing, were there developed. One was the idea, given wide circulation in Raymond Unwin's early pamphlet, *Nothing Gained by Overcrowding*, that very large blocks with a central common are actually more economical if the land is reasonable in price than the usual narrow By-Law block, due to the savings in street-pavement and utilities. The other was a further development of this, the super-block with indented dead-end streets, which insulates its residents from the traffic nuisance and also involves a maximum of economy in utilities and paving. One more feature of post-war English housing would hardly have been adopted if it had not been for the standards set up in the Garden Cities. Namely, the law which limits the number of houses to twelve per acre.

Letchworth and Welwyn remain the only Garden Cities, strictly speaking. However, their influence has been responsible for many partial suburban experiments. Here there can be no clear definition, as the phrase Garden Suburb or even Garden City has been applied, in any number of languages, to anything from a unit-planned strictly co-operative or public undertaking, with the land remaining in single ownership and at least a partial protective green belt, to a perfectly ordinary commercial front-foot-for-sale development. But such communities as Hampstead and Earswick, both largely designed by Unwin, and Hellerau near Dresden or Grünewald near Cologne — all built before the war — and also Radburn, New Jersey, and several post-war municipal developments in England, have a character and control unified enough to make their relation to the original idea a positive one. Almost every country has its Garden City Association, and the general principles and standards involved have exercised a very wide influence on all post-war housing policies, from the *Cité-Jardins* of the Seine to the more radically planned German communities.

The New Science of Planning, and its Prophet Patrick Geddes

The nineteenth century was a mining age. 'Exploit and get out' was its slogan, and the methods of mining were applied, not merely to coal and iron, but, far more significantly, to forests and soils, to real estate and international markets, to wage labor and to consumers. The cities were built by the combined efforts of speculators, small and large, to mine congestion land-values. A whole system and ideology of house-production arose, which enabled the builder to 'unload' as quickly as possible and escape with his profits.

But mining, by its very definition, is not a process which can be continued forever. Presently the end of the vein is in sight; the last frontier reached; the untended soil worked out; the exploited worker-consumer cannot buy any more; the jerry-built house and the inflated skyscraper no longer pay their taxes; the burden of palliatives and remedies — subways, policing, health measures, relief — becomes unbearable; the congested metropolis is bankrupt. And the whole paper scheme collapses — to be revived for another cycle of 'prosperity' only by the ever more difficult discovery of new veins to work.

This state of things may or may not have been inevitable during the first century of the Industrial Revolution. In any case, it is fair to assume that the same psyche which accomplished the enormous changes in the productive pattern could not easily have set up the new system of values necessary to turn it to useful human purpose. The best revolutionaries are not ordinarily the best people to be entrusted with setting up a new order after the revolution has been accomplished.

But even from the beginning there were scientists who saw and protested against the waste and injustice and irrationality implicit in this scheme of things. The early Utopians; Marx and Engels; the anarchist geographers Kropotkin and Réclus; the sociologists Taine and Comte and Le Play; Ruskin and William Morris and Ebenezer Howard — they were all, in greater or less degree, scientific critics of an exploitive mining civilization. They saw the earth as a sum of resources, abundant but nevertheless limited in supply and location. And they saw human beings with certain needs and also with certain techniques for adapting resources to their needs. And most of them saw that mere restriction or even 'conservation' would not be enough to transform a paper-and-profit economy of exploitation into a productive system based on permanent concrete values.

Indeed, everyone who confronted the housing problem squarely, even if he saw only one side of it, was forced into habits of thought which were not merely foreign to the current scheme of things, but were even subversive to it. This is why no judgment of the nineteenth century is complete unless it includes the houses and cities which that century created. For a social-economic system which in ordinary practice and on its own terms cannot provide a decent living environment is not a great civilization no matter what other things it can do; and conversely, a system which could provide good houses and workable cities would have something to be said for it no matter how outlandish its abstract deities might appear.

There was one scientist who gave a wholly new interpretation to this matter of human environment. Patrick Geddes, between the founding of Outlook Tower in Edinburgh in 1892 and his death in 1932, did work which entitles him to profound respect as a biologist, an economist, a sociologist, a geographer, a city-planner, and a philosopher. His great importance lies, not in any one narrow piece of specialization, but rather in the broad and consistent point of view with which he attacked any problem, from the plan of a city in India to the making of a metaphysical diagram. Probably not one piece of his thought could be made to fit neatly into any of the orthodox categories. 'Simultaneous thinking' was one of his phrases, and it was his own method.

The importance of Geddes in the history of housing lies in the fact that he was the first person who really *placed* the housing problem within the larger physical and social framework of society. He saw a dwelling, not as a 'model' something existing in a paper vacuum or at an International Exposition or set down in any available hold in the old pattern, nor yet as part of an idyllic and isolated community. He saw that people who live in a house require not merely private shelter but food and work and recreation and social life, and that this makes the house an inseparable part of the neighborhood, the city, the surrounding open country and the region. Folk, Work, Place — Organism, Function, Environment — these were the three poles of his 'simultaneous thinking.' 'For the biologist,' he said, 'life is process; life is reaction; and this two-fold, of environment in action upon organism, and of organism in reaction upon environment.'

Geddes introduced the technique and purpose of the Regional Survey, that thorough understanding of resources and possibilities and needs which must precede any plan or action. A British planner wrote of him:

'It is safe to say that the modern practice of town-planning in this country would have been a much simpler thing if it had not been for Geddes. There was a time when it seemed only necessary to shake up into a bottle the German town-extension plan, the Parisian Boulevard and Vista, and the English Garden Village, to produce a mechanical mixture which might be applied indiscriminately and beneficently to every town in this country; thus would it be "town-planned" according to the most up-to-date notions. Pleasing dream! First shattered by Geddes, emerging from his Outlook Tower in the frozen north, to produce that nightmare of complexity, the Edinburgh Room at the great Town-Planning Exhibition of 1910.

'It was a torture-chamber to those simple souls that had been ravished by the glorious perspectives or heartened by the healthy villages shown in the ampler galleries. Within this den sat Geddes, a most unsettling person, talking, talking, talking... about anything and everything. The visitors could criticize the show — the merest hotch-potch — picture postcards — newspaper cuttings — crude old wood-cuts — strange diagrams — archæological reconstructions: these things, they said, were unworthy of the Royal Academy — many of them not even framed — shocking want of respect; but if they chanced within the range of Geddes' talk, henceforth nothing could medicine them to that sweet sleep which yesterday they owned. There was something more in Town-Planning than met the eye.'

And it would have been a great deal more unsettling if his ideas had actually been put into practice. For if Geddes recognized and allowed for all the scientific physical and biological and social realities, he paid little heed to those abstractions which were almost the only realities of the paleotechnic world: paper 'interests.' Not because he was impractical or visionary; on the contrary, he saw that the old age was dead; that if the credits and debits were really added up, Megalopolis would not exist. That, granted the will and the desire, we have all the tools at hand ready to consolidate our scientific and technical gains into a civilization founded on real values; a 'neotechnic' age as different from the paleotechnic nineteenth century as an automatic electrically driven plant is different from a cotton-mill of the sixties, or as the best modern housing developments are different from a speculative tenement district of the eighties. But, although Geddes comes at the end of the background section of this book, it must not be supposed that we will find his ideas realized in the second half.

PART THREE

POST-WAR HOUSING: FACTS AND FIGURES

A detailed analysis of the housing policies and accomplishment of a dozen European countries is presented in the *Appendix* to this book. Only the general lines pursued, and the broader aspects of the achievement, will be dealt with in the present section.

I. THE SITUATION

Shortage

The fact that most European governments after the war adopted vigorous official policies toward the housing problem is not in itself remarkable. The nature of the emergency, in quantitative terms alone, plus the pre-war precedents for public responsibility in housing matters, made it inevitable.

In all countries, the ratio of rents and building costs to incomes had been steadily rising for fifty years or more, and the proportion of population able to pay an 'economic' rent for a new dwelling of minimum decency had as steadily declined. Everything contributed to this increase in the relative cost of a dwelling: both the higher standard of equipment, *and* the lower standard of space, light, air, and accessibility. This latter point will not seem paradoxical if one considers that the lower average dwelling-amenity of 1900, as compared with 1800, was largely due to land-crowding, which was itself both cause and effect of exorbitant land-prices, and that the latter, while reducing the quality of the dwelling, materially increased the costs of both location and construction. Moreover, the greater extent and congestion of cities necessitated a large number of very expensive remedial services, transportation-lines, utilities, and restrictive regulations, which increased the tax-rates and the costs of building and upkeep without providing any proportionate increase in real convenience or amenity. Or, to put it another way, a dwelling of 'minimum decency' in 1920 was very much more expensive relative to income than a dwelling of 'minimum decency' in 1800, without necessarily involving any appreciable net increase in *real* living standards.

This state of things had resulted in various official measures and tentative experiments in all European countries long before the war. But in 1918, the cumulative shortage of a century *plus* the complete building hiatus of the war years created a dire emergency which could not be evaded or postponed.

There are two ways of measuring a housing shortage: one by the number of overcrowded rooms, and the other by the number of 'extra' families with no separate dwelling. And on both counts the need was very great. In England by the 1921 Census there were only 91.9 separate dwellings for every one hundred families, and about ten per cent of the population was living more than two persons to a room. In Germany in 1927 there were still a million 'surplus' families sharing a dwelling with another family, and room-overcrowding, due to the smaller average size of the pre-war German dwelling, was greater than in England. In France in 1921, one eighth of the population lived more than two per room, and almost half of the residents of the Seine Department had less than one room per person. In Vienna just before the war, seventy-five per cent of the dwellings had only one or two rooms plus kitchen, and ninety per cent were without separate water-supplies; of the people living in these smaller dwellings, twenty-five per cent lived more than two per room and twenty per cent sublet parts of their dwellings to strangers. In the Scandinavian cities in 1920, half of the dwellings had no more than two rooms, and at least a quarter of the smaller dwellings housed more than two persons per room, in spite of the very low birth-rate and small number of children. (It might be noted in passing that, in spite of their large activities, none of these countries, with the possible exception of Holland, has yet made up the mere quantitative shortage which existed in 1918.)

The first measure necessitated by these conditions was rent restriction, first applied in most European countries during the war, and continued in many of them, in modified form, up to the present moment. The actual figures are not important, but rents were kept down as closely as possible to the pre-war scale, while the index of building costs, of food and other materials, rose to double or even treble the 1914 figure, and wages hovered somewhere between. Unaided private enterprise, therefore, which had supplied very few new dwellings to the lowest-income half for fifty years, was now equally unable to take care of the middle-income groups, and had to confine its activities to those better-off people to whom the rent restriction did not apply.

Method of Attack

Some form of public aid was obviously necessary, if any low-cost houses were to be constructed at all. The only question was, what form should it take? It must not be forgotten that we in America after the war had the same emergency shortage, the same increasing spread between costs and incomes, and even in many localities the same rent restrictions. And in New York, from 1921 to about 1925, we had public subsidies for housing, in the shape of unregulated tax-exemption, just as heavy to the taxpayers as the official aid provided in the same period in England or in Germany; the only difference being that the London and Berlin dwellings were of quite high quality and were let at relatively low rentals, while the New York houses were uniformly bad in standard and could not be afforded by any but the top-third income group. One kind of aid, therefore, was a subsidy to the consumer while the other was a subsidy to the speculative building trade.

What made the difference? Why did all the European governments, to a greater or less degree, face the housing crisis, not merely as an expensive emergency, but as an opportunity both to raise the general dwelling standard and to demonstrate a more effective and economical building method? How was it possible to make such a sudden revolutionary change in the method of producing dwellings, in countries which had no matching political-economic revolutions?

There were essentially three reasons, all of which have been suggested in earlier sections of this book. The first, and the hardest to define concretely, was a very general dissatisfaction with the old kind of residential environment, as produced by the old private-profit, individual agencies. This had been evidenced in countless difficult experiments and in a vast and popular Utopian literature. It touched rich and poor, and cut across political factions. The 'housing problem,' as popularly understood in Europe in 1919, was no longer confined to the provision of shelter for paupers or clearing out a few particularly noisome slums. It was quite the opposite of 'saving' the real estate business. It was a problem of finding *a new way to house everybody.* The modern architects and the early planning engineers were all groping toward some solution larger than mere palliative and reform.

The second factor, which applies more particularly to Germany than to any other country, was the tradition of public responsibility in matters of city development. Inherited from the Middle Ages, it had never quite died out even during the most rampant period of *Manchestertum.* German towns had been run by professionally trained people for several decades. And even the English cities were able to take land-use control and housing more or less within their stride, and without any very devastating legal complications.

But all the Utopians, modern architects and enterprising city fathers in Europe are not enough to explain either the quantity of post-war housing or the method by which it was constructed. *If there had been no organized political demand on the part of the people who needed good housing, there would have been no such achievement.* Housing was not bestowed from the top down in Europe any more than it ever will be in America. It had to be acquired by people who knew what they wanted, and how to get it. For good, planned, community housing available to the average citizen is not a 'normal' product of a capitalist society. It can be achieved, even partially, only when there is an active demand on the part of workers and consumers which is strong enough to over-balance the weight of real estate and allied interests on the other side.

The various post-war governments of a 'Labor' or 'Social Democrat' flavor had, as subsequent events have proved, little greater desire or power to 'socialize' anything as a theoretical objective than had the Liberals or the Conservatives. But they did represent a large and powerful body of voters who needed housing, who demanded good housing, and who realized that private enterprise would never do the job. The critical turn in the history of the European housing movement had come as a matter of fact in the early years of the century, when the initiative in promoting housing and planning passed from upper-class reformers into the hands of labor organizations and consumers' groups. It was then, and only then, that the long line of experiment and legislation which had been accumulating since 1850 began to bear real fruit.

The result was that when the post-war governments began to consider their method of attack on the housing problem, they found not only a whole machinery all ready to hand, but a demand so clearly formulated and well organized that it could not be turned aside. The English municipalities had been constructing houses and clearing slums, on a small scale, for twenty-five years or more. The various German governments, State and local, had been housing their own employees for years. Co-operative limited-dividend housing societies had been operating, often with official loans, in every European country. Trade unions and other workers' organizations were all prepared with concrete programs and the power to make them effective. And the public as a whole was able to distinguish a good house from a bad one, and a pleasant environment from an unpleasant one. The importance of this matter of education and of the standard of demand cannot be overestimated when one comes to consider the flabbiness and frustration of the current housing measures in Washington. If people are still perfectly satisfied with Old or New Law tenements, or with wooden three-deckers four feet apart, then it is foolish to expect any fundamental changes from the Federal Government.

II. THE HOUSES BUILT

On pages 126–27 will be found a chart which summarizes the post-war State-aided construction of dwellings in five countries and various urban districts of six other countries. The total population of these regions, it will be observed, is only slightly more than the population of the United States, or about 132 millions.

The number of new dwellings built with public assistance and under public control as to quality, which serve this population, is now about four and a half millions. In the countries for which figures on the total residential construction, unassisted as well as assisted, are available, the State-aided dwellings amount to about seventy per cent of all new dwellings.

At a fair estimate of four and a half persons on the average per dwelling, this means that almost sixteen per cent of the population in these countries lives in modern, new houses which could not have been erected if there had not been an active public housing policy. It would be safe to say that almost all of these twenty million people belong to the lower-half income group: which means that very few of them could have afforded to live in a new dwelling of any standard of decency at any time since the middle of the past century or earlier. On the other hand, it must be admitted that not more than half of the new dwellings are actually available to the lowest-income group, that is, to unskilled wage-workers. Moreover, even this vast construction does not in most cases yet meet the mere quantitative shortage of low-rental dwellings. Overcrowding still continues, and very few countries have been able to start on any large program of slum-clearance.

The simple fact that four and a half million dwellings have been put up with public aid is not in itself of primary importance. Houses *had* to be built, and they could not have been built without such assistance. The significant thing about it is that almost every one of the new houses is not only better, but completely different, from the general run of dwellings put up in the past century. For the technique of modern housing implies a wholly new conception of environment, beginning with land and sun and air, and extending — in purpose at least — to include the daily routine of the last working-class housewife. Various elements in this new housing standard will be described and illustrated in the rest of this volume: at present we must confine ourselves to the more statistical aspect of the achievement.

The vast majority of these four and a half million dwellings, in addition to being regulated as to form and quality at the moment of construction, have been permanently removed from the speculative market. In the first place, almost thirty per cent of them were directly put up by local governments on municipally owned land. In general, these are the dwellings with the very lowest rental scales or those which involve slum-clearance. They either remain in public ownership or are turned over to a semi-official organization for administration. Then another thirty-eight per cent were erected by co-operative or other forms of public-utility society. No speculative profits can ever be made by such companies, and even in those rare instances where small houses are eventually sold off to members, there are usually adequate safeguards against later speculation or change of use. Of the remaining thirty-two per cent, put up nominally by private enterprise, the majority were probably rural or semi-rural dwellings erected for themselves by small farmers. And very little of it was private enterprise in the sense that we know it, for, in addition to compulsory supervision of standards of layout and design, there are usually rental regulations and restrictions as to resale.

It should be remarked as well that the effect of such competition in standards and rental scales has meant that the vast majority of even the unassisted private-enterprise construction since the war (probably amounting to almost two million dwellings in these same regions) has shown much the same complete break with the past, at least in the matter of layout.

The dwellings summarized in the chart are not by any means all of the public-utility construction in Europe. Almost every nation has an active housing policy similar to those here under

POST-WAR HOUSING IN EUROPE

COUNTRY (*or* CITY)	POPULATION 1930 (*or nearest census*)	PERIOD COVERED BY FIGURES (*incl.*)	TOTAL DWELLINGS CONSTRUCTED	TOTAL BUILT WITH OFFICIAL AID
ENGLAND AND WALES	39,948,000	1919–1933	2,112,000	1,180,000
SCOTLAND	4,843,000	1919–1933	*not available*	176,000
GERMANY	62,430,000	1919–1933	†3,000,000	†2,500,000
HOLLAND	7,527,000	1919–1928	450,000	†250,000
BELGIUM (except war reconstruction)	7,466,000	1919–1933	†250,000	†200,000
FRANCE: PARIS AND ENVIRONS	†4,800,000	1922–1933	*not available*	†100,000
AUSTRIA: VIENNA	1,839,000	1920–1933	†65,000	62,000
DENMARK: COPENHAGEN	772,000	1920–1929	45,800	†35,000
SWEDEN: 280 TOWNS	†2,000,000	1917–1929	129,800	57,400
NORWAY: 5 BIG TOWNS	478,000	1914–1928	16,600	14,900
SWITZERLAND: ZÜRICH	251,000	1910–1931	*not available*	12,100
TOTAL	132,354,000			4,587,000 (70% of total built, in countries where latter can be estimated.)

† *Figures are approximate, due to conflicting or inadequate source material, or to the difficulties of statistical classification. Final totals and percentages are therefore estimates only.*

A SUMMARY CHART

TOTAL BUILT BY PUBLIC AUTHORITIES	TOTAL BUILT BY PUBLIC UTILITY SOCIETIES	* % OF POPULATION LIVING IN STATE-AIDED DWELLINGS	TYPICAL FORM OF PUBLIC AID
758,000	22,000	13½%	Loans at cost. Subsidy from State and local government at around $50 per house per year (at present discontinued). More for slum clearance.
133,000	600	16½%	Same as above, approximately.
†250,000	†1,500,000	18%	First mortgage at cost from semi-official funds. Second mortgage at 1% out of State tax fund. Municipal land on lease, low rent.
40,000	†110,000	15%	Loan from public funds at cost. Annual subsidy from State and town (now only for slum clearance.) Municipal land on lease.
none	†70,000	12%	Loan from public funds at 2%. Occasional additional subsidies.
†50,000	*not available*	10%	Loan from public funds at less than cost. Additional subsidies for large families.
59,000	3,000	15%	Capital cost written off, funds come out of current taxes. Rent pays only for upkeep.
9,300	18,700	20%	Loan from public funds at cost. Occasional subsidy.
12,200	16,000	13%	Loan from public funds at cost. Occasional subsidy.
7,800	4,800	14%	Loan from public funds at cost. Occasional subsidy.
2,100	10,000	22%	Loan from public funds at cost. Occasional subsidy.
1,321,400	1,755,100	15.7%	
(29% of all aided dwellings)	(38% of all aided dwellings)	*At 4½ persons on average per dwelling.	

discussion, and producing similar results. The total number of new State-aided dwellings throughout Europe is probably in the neighborhood of seven millions, and the only reason that this book does not discuss the housing of Russia, Hungary, and Italy, for instance, is either that figures are not available or that the author has not seen their work. Only in the case of Russia, however, is there any essential difference in either methods or results. And even here they are not as different as one might expect. State funds, co-operative housing societies, and the technique of community-planning and large-scale construction are as true of Russian housing as of German or Dutch: and indeed, much of it has been done by planners and architects who received their training in Germany. The author regrets that she has not been to Russia, and therefore cannot describe what they are doing in any detail or with personal authority. In any case, housing and city-building in the Union of Socialist Soviet Republics is only just beginning to be achieved on any ambitious scale, while the 'post-war housing movement' in the capitalist countries is already seemingly on the decline, temporarily at least. They are therefore two quite separate subjects, historically as well as politically; and perhaps in another ten years a book on 'modern housing' will have to be a book almost entirely devoted to Russia.

III. THE MEANS

Housing Becomes a Public Utility

Politically, there was nothing very radical about those vacillating Labour and Social-Democratic governments which were generally in evidence after the war. Except in Russia and possibly upon occasion in Vienna, it has never been the conscious vocal purpose of either the city fathers or the State officials to 'socialize' housing. Very often the officials and technicians and average citizens, even the labor leaders, who are responsible for modern European housing could be heard uttering old phrases and shibboleths which no more applied to what they were producing than they did to a Hopi Mesa.

Nevertheless, the fundamental premise about housing has undergone a tremendous change. It has become a Public Utility, in accepted theory at least, if not as yet in any complete sense of accomplishment. The right to live in a decent dwelling has taken its place among the 'national minima' — the right to good and abundant water, to sanitation, to adequate fire and police protection, to the use of paved and lighted roads, to education, to a certain amount of medical care, and, in most European countries, to various forms of social insurance.

It was no conscious politics which worked this change, but rather a degree of realism as to the houses themselves. Houses had to be built. Public funds had to be used in any case. The only question was, who should build them and how?

And here was where that long training in concrete experiment came to the fore. One and all, they agreed that the old methods had failed to provide a decent environment; that bad houses made bad cities, that wasteful houses made cities bankrupt. The individual builder and the speculative builder had both failed, not so much from their personal wickedness or stupidity, as because of the very nature of a modern dwelling. The modern problem is so complicated, the necessary controls and planning techniques so integral in the whole social pattern, that individual efforts cannot be expected to solve it. The entire future of our urban environment depends on the method which we now set up to deal with housing and its related problems. Why should the old methods, proven to be inadequate, be artificially and expensively resuscitated? New methods must be found, for — and this was the real stroke of collective genius in this process of subconscious reasoning — *bad dwellings are not an unavoidable necessity.* Properly directed, it should be cheaper to build good houses than bad ones.

Housing as a Public Utility, therefore, includes three major features of policy: one, the investment of public funds; two, subsidies where they are necessary; and three, control over the form, quality, rental-scale, and financial set-up of the resulting houses.

'Investment' and 'Subsidy'

It is worth while to make a careful distinction between these terms. The investment of public funds in low-cost housing is a permanent policy in most European countries, as a means not only of reducing financial costs to a minimum, but also of insuring adequate powers over the quality. It does not in itself imply any outright cost to the government. Subsidy, on the other hand, is a variable item, involving non-returnable outlay, and resorted to in order to make rentals low enough for those who need the houses.

Most countries have long-established housing funds, used to finance either municipal or public-utility society construction. Money from such funds is ordinarily loaned at cost; that is, at the price which the government has to pay for money plus a small service charge. Many semi-official agencies are tapped to provide cheap capital for housing: social insurance funds and savings banks above all. Modern co-operative housing in Germany got its start long before the war because it was promoted by the public insurance foundations. The same is true in many other countries with respect to official savings banks.

In France and Belgium the investment of State funds in

housing also involves subsidy, as the money is loaned at less than cost (usually around two per cent plus a long-term sinking fund). The government, of course, must make up the difference.

In Germany the State loans money on second mortgages at such a low rate (one per cent interest plus one per cent amortization) that the funds must come out of a special tax rather than by government borrowing. First mortgages must then be found in the open market or else from semi-official sources. In Vienna the entire official housing investment is in the nature of a subsidy, as costs are written off and rentals cover only upkeep and administration. Here also a special tax is levied to provide the housing funds.

Many other forms of subsidy, in addition to that implied in a low interest rate, were provided. Lump-sum grants were occasionally made, and England and Holland allotted a fixed annual payment per house over a period of years. Any further subsidy necessary is borne by the local governments. Complete tax-exemption is seldom granted in any country, and never in England.

How Quality is Insured

All countries have national agencies for establishing standards, for supplying information, education, plans and technical advice, and for conducting experiments in materials and methods. In England the Ministry of Health has to pass on every plan eligible for government aid, and issues manuals of design and procedure. In Germany the State Society for Housing and Building Research has erected several complete experimental housing developments, and publishes innumerable reports and investigations.

Outside of England, however, actual control over permits and the investment of public funds is not centralized, but in the hands of local or regional authorities. The cities themselves in Holland and usually in Germany are responsible for all housing in receipt of public aid, that of co-operative societies as well as their own construction. The best architects and planners in the country were likely to be found in the municipal housing offices. (This fact has been recently somewhat modified in Germany.)

In France the Public Housing Offices, semi-official autonomous bodies established locally, are responsible for almost all the public-aided housing. As in England, they are answerable to the Ministry of Health. In Vienna the municipal government itself does the whole job; investment, regulation, experiment, and construction.

Agencies: Direct Governmental Construction

In England, Vienna, and a few other places (notably Oslo and Zürich) most of the government-assisted housing is directly constructed and administered by the municipal government itself. In almost all countries the very cheapest houses are thus erected, and also those involving slum-clearance. The possible disadvantages due to 'politics' do not seem to have been very great. The advantage, outside of the better control over location and form, lies in the greater facility for maintaining rentals in some sort of relation to income instead of to the financial set-up. In Vienna there is no relation between costs and rents at all. And in English municipal housing there have been experiments in charging lower rentals in proportion to the number of small children. In Germany and Holland a large number of dwellings have been put up by the towns, but of recent years these have been more often turned over to separate although still official organizations for both construction and administration. The French Public Housing Offices are official corporations, but responsible to the State rather than to the city governments.

In Vienna the actual job of construction is ordinarily done by municipal employees, and the city maintains a material supply agency as well. In England a certain number of municipal housing developments are usually put up by 'direct labor,' thus maintaining an indirect control over the prices and methods of contract jobs. (A system employed, it might be noted, by Henry Ford, who buys many of his parts from other companies, but always makes up a small number of each kind himself to insure that he is not being cheated.)

Agencies: the Housing Society

The official definition of a public-utility housing society varies from country to country, and can include everything from a strictly co-operative tenants' society (as is usual in Holland) to a municipal corporation or even a company set up by a builder or an architect (as occasionally in Germany). However, it is always subject to official supervision of its finances, dividends are always strictly limited, and the members are never allowed to recover more than their original investment in the event of liquidation.

The disadvantage of a housing society within the present economic system is that its rentals are rigidly determined by its original financial set-up, which is, however, equally true of much municipal housing. The advantage, of course, lies in the fact that the tenants, either directly or indirectly, may have some voice in its design and administration, and are somewhat more likely to form a natural social group. (It is very interesting that the trend in Russia of recent years has been away from straight official housing construction and toward group responsibility of the tenants themselves: in short, co-operative housing societies.)

In Germany and Holland the greater part of State-aided housing has been done by public-utility societies. The required equity is very small, and prospective members invest hardly more than a few cents a week. In Holland they are likely to be strictly co-operative undertakings in rather small separate groups allied by some religious, political, or trade interest. In Germany there are (or were) huge trade-union housing societies with branches all over the country whose individual members had no direct vote and were not necessarily affiliated with the union. Alongside these, also in Germany, was a strong movement among the building workers toward co-operative building guilds. The two types of organization worked together to a considerable extent — one of the few examples of an amiable relationship between producers' and consumers' co-operation. Both of them have, needless to say, been completely disrupted by the present régime, although it is unlikely that the houses already put up will be allowed to drop into the speculative market.

Position of Private Enterprise

In the central European countries there has not been any very great amount of private building enterprise since the war, except that which received government aid and was therefore subject to some sort of public control. This was due to abnormal conditions in the money-market as much as anything else. But in countries where the cost of money returned to something like a normal level — that is, in England and the Scandinavian countries and Switzerland — ordinary private construction went ahead at much the same rate as it had before the war. Indeed, it seems actually to have increased in some cases, stimulated no doubt by the higher standard of demand set up by assisted housing. No better proof could be found, it seems to me, not of the eternal virtues of private enterprise, but of the fact that the government-aided housing was almost entirely in a field not touched by speculative building activity throughout the past generation. Dr. Wood and several other authorities have found that in America almost no new housing is built for any but the upper-third income group. This would have been equally true of post-war Europe if there had been no official intervention, and if the new housing methods had not been set going.

IV. THE OUTLOOK

Europe did not Solve the Problem

There should be no suggestion that any country has even approached a final solution of the housing problem. Perhaps thirty million people throughout Europe have been housed in a much better sort of environment than any but a very few of them could have hoped to find before the war. But there are probably a hundred million more who are still badly housed. The slums still stand, many of them more crowded now than they were five years ago. Only a comparatively small portion of the new dwellings actually reaches the lowest income-group, and the matter of housing the unemployed has hardly been approached. In every country, moreover, there has been the difficulty that houses which average workers could pay for in 1930 are entirely beyond their means at present. The housing problem can never be solved all by itself: in final analysis it depends on the distribution of purchasing power.

A member of the International Labour Office estimates that some ten to fifteen million dwellings would have to be built in Europe during the next decade if satisfactory housing conditions were to be provided for everyone. Without even considering such broader matters as regional planning and the re-location of industrial centers (which would have to be taken into account if any such program were attempted) I should put the figure considerably higher.

Nor should anyone assume that the machinery set up during the past fifteen years will just go on functioning until everyone is decently housed. There is no 'inevitability of gradualism' about the housing movement. Much of this machinery was of a purely emergency nature, and most of it depended on a particular set of conditions which has already shifted considerably in many countries. Very little housing would have been done, and what was done would not have been of nearly as high quality, if there had not been an organized, effective, political demand on the part of the people who needed the houses. This demand made itself felt, in general, through the various left-wing parties, the trade-unions and the co-operatives. Today, in Germany and Austria, there are no more left-wing parties, and no free workers' organizations of any kind.

There is no getting around the fact that 'modern housing' and much of the framework of contemporary western society are mutually antipathetic. The premises underlying the most successful and forward-pointing housing developments are not the premises of capitalism, of inviolate private property, of entrenched nationalism, of class distinction, of governments bent on preserving old interests rather than creating new values. And the full implications have as a rule been better understood by the jealous guardians of the old order of things than by the advocates and direct beneficiaries of housing. In a sense, the housing achievement has constituted a world within a world, hampered by all the contradictions and insecurity attendant on such an anomalous position.

And for the moment at least, the trend of housing in most European countries is downward. Laws which were designed to be permanent measures have suddenly been repealed. In spite of numerous pamphlets purporting to show that it is more 'economic' to build houses than to give doles to unemployed workers, building has been greatly cut down in the past few years. The supposedly long-time English program was brought to an abrupt close last year by the Conservatives, although if a Labour government comes in the old policies will probably be renewed to a certain extent. In Germany no aid is now given except for a few miserable 'subsistence homesteads' of a quality and significance immensely inferior to the earlier work. The workers' societies which built and administered much of the best modern housing no longer exist. In Vienna, a large section of the Socialists' housing achievement has actually been destroyed. Only Russia is embarking on an ambitious program of new dwelling construction, designed to raise the standard of living of a very great number of people.

The Next Decade of Housing

A book about 'modern housing' today is necessarily a book largely devoted to the achievements of the past fifteen years in western and central Europe. Ten years from now, where shall we have to go in order to see housing and city-building and resource-planning which carries this achievement forward? Will the housing book of 1945 be entirely about Russia? Or will there perhaps be evidence of real accomplishment in the United States?

M. Méquet, the gentleman from the International Labour Office who was quoted above, makes a concrete if somewhat optimistic suggestion with regard to the next decade of European housing. He proposes, in view of the obvious correlation between unemployment and the housing shortage, an international housing bank. He points out that all European countries have elaborate and fairly adequate machinery all set up for building and supervising low-cost housing. All they need is funds. Moreover, innovations in planning and structural technique as well as in architectural form have come already to have an international significance, and a pooling of ideas as to the nature and possibilities of houses and cities would be highly desirable. M. Méquet also thinks that an international labor exchange might be able to solve some of the seasonal difficulties in the building trades, building labor being in any case quite mobile. This amiable vision of a sort of neo-mediæval age of international construction, with houses and engineers substituted for cathedrals and traveling craftsmen, is just another one of those things, I am afraid, which is too practical to be possible in a world of abstractions.

What the next ten years will bring forth, in Europe or elsewhere, in housing or in other matters, is impossible to predict. There is one realistic if partial test, however, with which to judge whatever does happen. If the implications of the past fifteen years of activity and ideas in housing and land-planning and architecture are carried *ahead*, toward an effective realization of a modern environment, then surely there will be some element of health and promise in society. But if, on the other hand, there is only retrogression and frustration in these matters, that must serve as a final condemnation of a sinister and moribund social-economic system and of a people who lacked the will to change it.

The fact that the 'post-war' chapter of the housing movement is in many respects now a matter of history merely doubles the necessity for inquiring into it more closely. For, whatever the future, the achievement of the past fifteen years has been a positive one. New standards were established; new methods were evolved; new techniques developed; new and creative ideas given some sort of concrete form. These millions of new dwellings constitute both a starting-point and a gauge for future activity — whether in the United States, in Russia, or in Europe itself. American housing must, of course, develop its own technique to meet its own requirements. But there are certain broad elements in the European experience of which America cannot afford to be ignorant. Some of these elements will be discussed in the following chapters. A summary of the laws and quantitative accomplishment of various European countries will be found in the Appendix.

PART FOUR

ELEMENTS OF MODERN HOUSING

I. MINIMUM STANDARDS IN PRACTICE

The New Norm

'The modern house is a biological institution,' writes Lewis Mumford. 'It is a shelter devoted primarily to the functions of reproduction, nutrition, and recreation. To expand the definition a little, the house is a building arranged in such a fashion that meals may be easily prepared and served, that rest and sleep may be enjoyed, that sexual intercourse may take place in privacy, and that the early care of the young may be opportunely carried on. None of these functions, needless to say, is restricted to the house; but the house is peculiarly adapted to facilitate all of them together. Add to these primarily physiological requirements, the provision of space for social companionship and play and study and the definition of the house is complete.'

The basic premises underlying modern European housing method are grounded in just such biological and social realities. Certain first principles, which we may call *vital standards*, are common to almost all the new dwellings, from Stockholm to Liverpool. Over and above these there are, of course, innumerable variations, affecting both method and form, which are due to local requirements, habits, limitations or desires. But the irreducible minimum in various categories is remarkably the same. What these minima are, and how they tend to affect physical form and planning, are shown in the accompanying chart. Obviously, the categories themselves are somewhat arbitrary and overlap in many instances. It should be borne in mind that *each* minimum standard is an essential, and that an excess of luxury in one department does not make up for a lack in another.

REQUIREMENT	MINIMUM STANDARDS
	DECENCY
Shelter unit suited to population groupings.	One structurally separate dwelling for each family or other natural unit.
Subdivision of unit for carrying on ordinary functions.	Enough bedrooms so that parents, boys, girls can sleep separately. In addition, a living-room and a kitchen, or a living-kitchen.
Possibility of privacy.	Relatively sound-proof walls.
	No windows looking directly into windows of other dwellings.
	HEALTH
Facilities for cleanliness and sanitation.	Running water and flush toilet within each dwelling. Toilet ventilated.
	Bath or shower either in the dwelling, in the building, or in the neighborhood (depends as much on local habits as on absolute standards).
Adequate air and cross-ventilation.	No dwelling more than two rooms deep in any part, which in apartment-buildings ordinarily means no more than two dwellings per landing, if the stair-halls are also to be adequately ventilated.
	As large a glass area as climate and heating provisions make practical.
Purity of air.	No noxious industrial or other fumes near-by.
	No heavy-traffic streets immediately adjacent.
Maximum light and adequate sun in all rooms and public corridors.	No small courts. Definite proportion between height of buildings and open space between them.

Facilities for outdoor recreation.	Play-spaces for small and larger children. Walks, parks, athletic provisions, gardens conveniently located for adults.
	AMENITY
Attractive outlook.	Lawn and gardens visible from all windows. Preservation of natural features of site in the plan. No paved inner courts. No blighted or rundown areas adjacent.
Moderately prepossessing architecture (note that these are minima).	Buildings which more or less obviously fulfill their purpose, of good materials, and simple and direct design. Grouped harmoniously. Plan clear and simple to follow, both physically and with the eye.
Quiet.	Adequately insulated walls. No major traffic street immediately adjacent. No noise-amplifying courtyards or side alleys.
	COMFORT AND CONVENIENCE
Domestic.	Rooms designed to accommodate furniture and living habits and to facilitate circulation and cleanliness. Closets, cupboards, kitchen equipment (especially apparatus for cooking and hot water). Laundry and drying facilities, either within the dwelling, within the building, or, if with additional labor-saving devices, centralized within the community.

	Electricity.
	Not too many stairs to climb. Say, no more than four stories or three flights.
	In cold climates, adequate heating provision.
	In hot climates, high enough ceilings.
Communal.	Immediate or easy access to schools, necessary shops, cafés, and social centers.
	Work, let us say, not more than thirty minutes away at a maximum.
	Some facilities for choice of dwelling and location on part of tenant and therefore possibility of natural population groupings.
	SAFETY
Firmness of construction.	Adequate and workable building codes.
Play-space for small children without crossing a through street.	Use of super-block, dead-end street, or large open block-interior.
Passably fireproof.	Regulations against predominantly wood construction except for isolated low dwellings.
	Stairs and corridors wide and directly accessible to outside.
Permanent immunity from partial or total neighborhood 'blight.'	Communities planned, constructed, and administered continuously as a functional unit.

Here, then, are minimum standards which would be accepted in principle by almost any architect, public official, or housing authority in Europe. Let us see how well the new houses live up to them.

Out of the four and a half million dwellings put up since the war with official aid and regulation in the eleven localities we have listed, I think it would be quite safe to say that *not less than four million — or about ninety per cent — come quite adequately within these bounds.* A few of the major exceptions are listed herewith.

Deficiencies in outlook, sun, and recreation facilities: many of the Paris city apartments and also some of the central slum-clearance flats in Great Britain and Holland.

Too few rooms per dwelling: some of the Scandinavian and Scotch city flats.

Rooms too small: possibly some of the Dutch flats.

Lack of some of the sanitary conveniences and also of convenient location: many of the recent emergency semi-rural dwellings for the unemployed in Germany.

Lack of direct cross-ventilation within the dwelling: a few of the Viennese and Stockholm flats.

More than three flights up: occasional urban flats, particularly in Vienna.

Definite lack of architectural amenity: many of the French and Belgian dwellings, particularly among those constructed before about 1928.

Location on major traffic street: some dwellings in all countries, but very few.

More than thirty minutes from work: some of the London, Paris, and Berlin small houses.

Taken all together, however, I do not believe that these exceptions amount to more than ten per cent of the total new domestic construction. But in almost every country there are what one might call *extra-standards* in certain departments, sometimes due to local traditions and habits, sometimes to conscious new effort. For instance:

Scientific orientation for sunlight: to secure to all rooms, especially living-rooms, a maximum of sun at the most desirable times most German and many Scandinavian and English dwellings.

Extra standards of light and sun by means of wider glass areas: many German, some in all countries.

Extra space-standards: on the interior, particularly in English small houses and in the earlier German dwelling; in the community as a whole, also England (where the legal maximum is twelve houses per acre) and often Germany (where apartment-blocks rarely cover more than twenty-five per cent of the site).

Interior equipment: occasional central heating and hot water in all countries. In England and Switzerland, occasional electric stoves and heat.

Private balconies or public roof-terraces: most German apartments, many in other countries.

Dwellings not fronting on a through road of any kind: very many English and German culs-de-sac and all German and Scandinavian *Zeilenbau* super-blocks.

Built-in communal facilities as an integral social and architectural part of the development (modern schools, nurseries, kindergartens; social rooms, cafés, mechanically equipped laundries, clinics, gymnasia, etc.): almost all Viennese housing, and many separate developments in Germany, Holland, France, Switzerland.

Really positive and creative effort toward modern architecture: many separate communities in Germany, Holland, Scandinavia, and Switzerland.

Place of work planned in the residential community: notably the two English Garden Cities, Letchworth and Welwyn, but some few others (mostly only partial) in Germany and elsewhere.

These are the average working principles of ordinary everyday legislators, inspectors, bureaucratic officials, and contractors. And they do not in any sense constitute a sliding scale, an 'ideal' which must be modified in practice. The whole point of view behind such minimum standards precludes the possibility of modifying them in deference to class or income distinctions. If you start with sun and air and biological requirements, you cannot say that because this family has only half the income of that family, they should have only half as good an outlook or half as big a playground or half as much water or half a toilet.

Another deduction from these biological working standards is the fact that no partial or mechanical measures are sufficient for a critique of housing quality. 'Coverage' and 'density' have only a very relative significance, and mean nothing when separated from other facts. On paper, therefore, many of our American suburbs show a low density of population, and are often therefore considered to be high in amenity. But the figures do not show that a wasteful layout has more often than not canceled out the possible advantages of spaciousness, and that lack of co-ordination and control may already have turned the neighborhood into a partially blighted semi-slum. Likewise the gross floor area per family in many New York apartments, even in the Old Law tenements, is often rather high, but unless the figures also show waste in corridors and the number of windows opening on air-shafts or dark courts, not even a partial judgment is possible. Also, there are a few of the newer apartment-houses, though not often in New York, which have a site-coverage of under fifty per cent. But to keep the argument merely to numbers, a twelve-story building covering fifty per cent of its plot is just under four times as bad, from the point of view of light, ventilation, and open space per tenant, as a three-story building with the same 'coverage.'

Not Reform but New Form

It is not merely that the housing standard of one class of people has been hauled up a few notches nearer the next most privileged group, and the bill grudgingly underwritten by the taxpayers. (Although it is undoubtedly true that never in history has so large a proportion of the current output of dwellings been available to the lower-income groups.) But far more important than any mere scaling-up within the old pattern, which could after all be told quite adequately by a simple page of charts and statistics, is the fact that the average low-rental cottage or flat of the past ten years has certain built-in qualities which even the upper-middle-class residence of before the war rarely achieved. And the community of which this average new dwelling is a part offers a permanent amenity — biological and social — which the richest house-builder would hardly have known how to command. Compact planning and rational construction lessen the burden of house-keeping and house-maintaining. Adequate neighborhood layout and public control prevent blight — and boom — from descending on one section at the expense of the other sections. And new building forms grow, on the one hand, out of the new standards and materials and methods and functions, and are related just as clearly on the other to that quickening and renewal of æsthetic sensibility which we call 'modern' in the best twentieth-century painting and sculpture and photography. In short, a new layer of human environment.

Perhaps on the face of it this may seem an extravagant claim. Even people who have seen some of the new housing may feel that no such broad implication was intended, and no such revolutionary progress achieved. It is quite true that the developments which really do stand by themselves — which represent a positive synthesis of modern techniques, modern functions, a new standard of living, and a modern æsthetic of design — might easily be counted on one's fingers. While of really 'perfect' housing there is most assuredly none at all. It would also be quite false to suggest that the movement has been undertaken in any mood of joyous, extravagant, creative *élan.* Every step has been difficult, and often enough the conscious purposes of the leaders themselves have been vague and narrow by comparison with the importance which I am here attaching to the results.

Nevertheless, the fundamental ideas behind practically all of the work have been very much the same all over Europe — and entirely different from any set of motives which produced the mass of nineteenth-century dwellings. The experiments, whether successful or unsuccessful, complete or partial, have all pointed in the same direction. The best developments are not exceptions or 'Parade-Horses' — they are all fulfillments in one way or another of earlier efforts and generally accepted principles. Römerstadt, its handsome curved white rows silhouetted against the Taunus Mountains, and facing Frankfurt across the wide permanent 'green belt' of the Nidda Valley, is in many respects the partial fruit of experiments at Letchworth and Welwyn in England, at Breslau, at Stuttgart, and on the

Hook of Holland. Siemensstadt in Berlin and Rothenburg in Kassel, with their free-standing oriented apartment-blocks, cap countless experiments in functional street-planning, orientation, utilization of open space, and interior layout. Neubühl near Zürich is probably the most thoroughly successful and attractive modern community in Europe — but it could never have been done if numberless ideas, arguments, and experiments in England, Germany, Holland, and France had not preceded it. The Karl Marxhof in Vienna, with its kindergartens and libraries and clinics, its laundries and baths, its playgrounds and wading-pools and post-office and shops and restaurants, is not an exception, but merely the fullest realization to date of the working idea behind all Viennese housing.

To return once more to the new European 'norm.' There has been practically no crowding of the land — and therefore none of the large number of evils which result from this practice as it is habitually resorted to in America. Almost none of our wasteful and distorted 'T'-, 'H'-, and 'U'-shaped units which, no matter how ingenious, never have any result except to increase construction costs and decrease amenity. No building, whether of one, two, three, or four stories, is ever more than two rooms deep, practically all dwellings have cross-ventilation and direct sun throughout most of the day, and nearly every single one looks out onto a sizable and *usable* stretch of lawn or garden. There is probably not a single spot in western Europe in which it would have been legally possible at any time since 1919 to erect a New York New Law tenement, or a Boston or Chicago three-decker, or one of the mill-town flats, or deep houses with two- to twelve-foot side alleys, for any income group whatsoever.

Post-War Standards in America

How many American dwellings put up since the war (and that means as a rule only dwellings for the upper-third income group) would actually measure up to this minimum standard? How many are as good as the European four million, serving a population about the same as that of the United States, which do measure up to it?

Almost all the city apartments, for rich and less rich alike, would have to be thrown out immediately due to their fundamental deficiencies in light, sun, ventilation, outlook, and recreational facilities for children. True, more of them had central heating, tiled bathrooms, elevators, and electric refrigerators — and I do not intend to belittle these virtues — but even if they tend to distract our attention from the deficiencies in more elementary matters, they do not in any case really make up for them.

Then almost every one of the two- and three-decker flats would have to go — for the same reasons, plus, in many cases, the extreme fire-hazard of their frame construction. And finally, a very large proportion of even the one-family houses and bungalows would be below standard, because of the long narrow side alleys onto which most of their windows look, or because of rear projections cutting off light and air from many rooms, or because the yard is merely a paved service-court with a garage on it. Not to mention the little matter of architecture in all three categories, which is less easy of statistical proof.

Even among the most luxurious, ample, and well-designed suburban houses, there are not many which are as well secured against neighboring blight as, for instance, the ten-dollar-a-month houses in Frankfurt.

But there are a few exceptions. Some of the Government war-workers' housing, particularly that at York and Bridgeport, came up to all the minimum requirements. But this was abruptly stopped at the end of the war, and the houses were sold off to private individuals without strings of any kind. Here and there are a very few middle- and upper-class suburbs which were planned and constructed as units and which, by various 'restrictions,' manage to maintain some sort of integral order. Almost all the 'model apartments' put up by limited-dividend companies in New York and elsewhere would have to be eliminated, because their light and outlook and recreation facilities are usually not even as good as the London slum-clearance tenements which we have already excepted. The only really significant work which measures up to our tabulated standards are the two developments of the City Housing Corpo-

MAXIMUM DENSITY IN BERLIN: 3 STAGES

or, How to Reduce the Price of Land

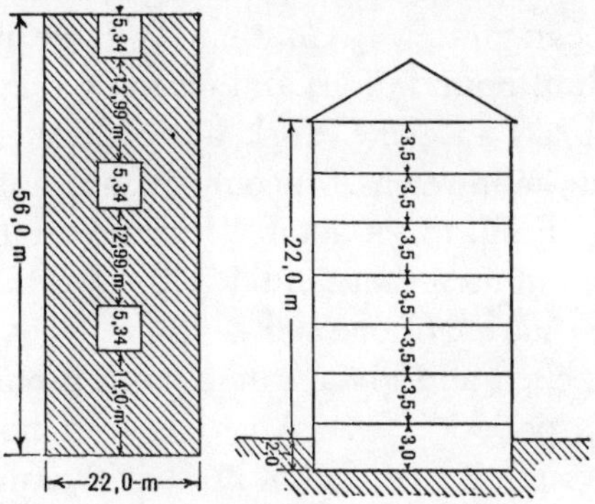

Legal coverage from 1853 to 1887: why Berlin was the *Mietskasernen* city and the Mecca of land speculators.

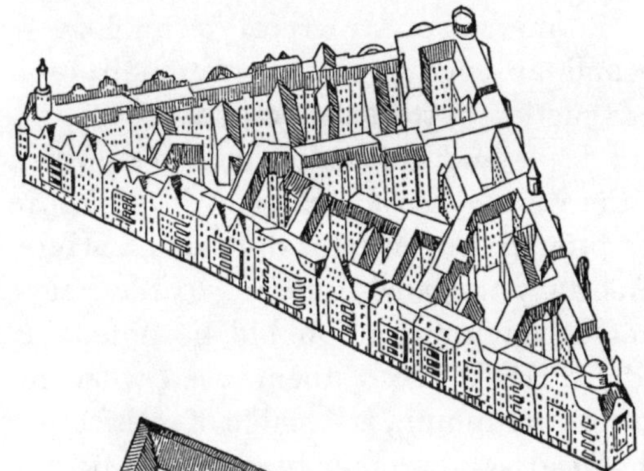

The result of a reform law of 1897. (The lower-paid half live in the rear-buildings.)

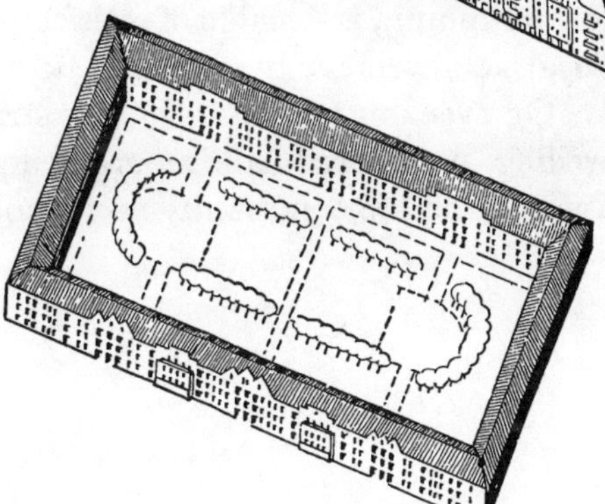

The legal maximum after 1925, for all outlying districts. This law, plus an effective policy of municipal land-ownership, has reduced the price of land for new housing to less than one fifth of what it used to be.

Drawings from 'Das Steinerne Berlin,' by Werner Hegemann

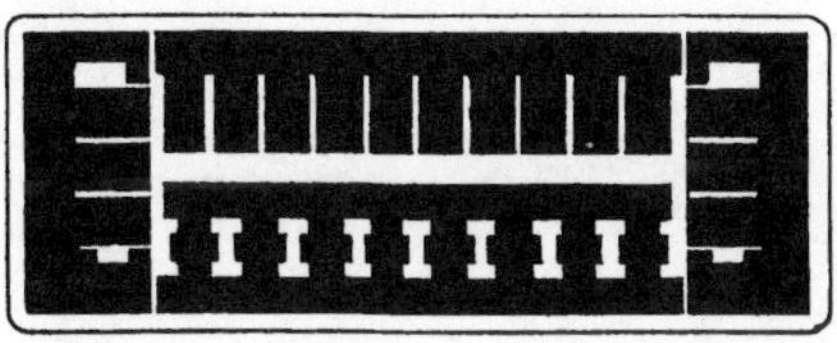

. . . but this is what we were building in the suburban boroughs of New York City in 1925, five or six stories high.

ration, Sunnyside in Queens, and Radburn, New Jersey, both of which include sound and progressive planning features quite comparable to European practice; Chatham Village in Pittsburgh, erected by the Buhl Foundation; and perhaps a few smaller limited-dividend blocks in New York and Chicago. None of these is available to the lower-half income-group. But how many would that make in all, to set against Europe's four million? Certainly not more than ten thousand dwellings at the very outside. Or about one quarter of one per cent.

This contrast is only sharpened and given ironic point if one remembers that during this period it was America, and not Europe, which was going through a New Era of Prosperity; and that it was to America alone that all Europe turned for knowledge and inspiration in matter of structural technology — from central heating and air-conditioning to rationalization in method and the construction of steel skyscrapers.

The more important legal and restrictive measures which have been adopted in the various European countries to insure these standards will be brought out in later discussions. Here, however, one very important thing with regard to these new first principles of domestic environment should be noted. It will be seen that hardly a single one of them, even when reduced to the barest possible minimum, is capable of satisfactory or permanent or economical achievement by attention to the individual dwelling *alone*. Or even by regulation and restriction of the individual dwelling, considered as a separate unit. The real unit in every case must be the community as a whole.

II. A NEW METHOD: THE COMMUNITY UNIT

Economical Use versus Speculative Profit

The standards are established. The next step, therefore, is how to set about embodying them adequately in houses, with the utmost possible speed and economy.

Leadership, fortunately, backed up by a fairly large and well-educated body of public opinion, happened to be for the most part in the hands of men who believed that:

1. The primary problem is to provide as many good new houses at as low rentals as possible, and with a minimum of long-time real cost to the government.

2. This problem has nothing whatsoever to do with 'reviving the real-estate industry' as it had formerly been practiced. On the contrary, as the old practices are largely responsible for the bad condition of the cities and the existence of a 'housing problem' of major proportions, the old methods must be considered outmoded, and new ones set up in their place.

3. The new dwellings, in order to maintain the new standards in *time*, must be permanently removed from the speculative market.

4. The new standard and new method must be set up, not merely on an emergency basis, but in such a workable, efficient form that it will tend to replace old standards and methods entirely, even in fields unaided by the government. That is, a *new standard of demand* must be established.

5. It should be entirely possible to build good new houses that are, actually and in the long run, cheaper than the bad and wasteful old ones.

With such a point of view, and with the body of pre-war experiment for example, there could be only one answer in so far as the vast majority of post-war dwellings was concerned. And that was that the complete neighborhood, and not the individual house or apartment-building, must be the unit of planning, of finance, of construction, and of administration.

Quite outside of any social considerations, the economic basis alone would have justified such a decision. There are five main departments in housing economy, and every one of them stands to be materially benefited by the use of the complete neighborhood unit.

The cost of raw *land*, when backed up by an efficient policy of municipal purchase, expropriation, or control of land for housing use, would obviously be lowered through not undergoing the expensive process of subdivision into small parcels and the speculative sale and resale of 'lots.' Moreover, by continued application of the community-unit principle, it should be possible to prevent future speculative excesses in raw land and also to reduce the inflated market-prices caused by past speculation.

The cost of *land-development* is also lowered by comprehensive planning. Streets and utilities designed only for specific permanent purposes and for full immediate use, would clearly cut out most of the extravagant waste hitherto largely borne by municipal governments. The economies of large-scale operation go into lower rents and not, as in the past, into promoting speculation.

The next item in housing economy is the cost of *construction*. Here the possibilities of rationalization, of mass-production of parts, and of efficient large-scale operations, would be utilized in a way quite impossible to small private enterprise. Structural experiments could be conducted, scientific tests made in new materials and methods, which might revolutionize the whole industry.

Then comes the cost of *money*, probably the most vital single element in any system of house-production, but particularly so in post-war Europe. All money was expensive, and a large part of the housing funds must come from the various governments in any case. Therefore, anything which would keep interest and amortization charges down would make for enormously greater economy. The best way to lower money costs is by guaranteeing a safe long-time investment. And the only way to build houses as a safe investment proposition is to make sure that they will be continuously sound and useful and desirable for a long time. That they will not be subject to blight, either in themselves or in their surroundings; that they will be conveniently located for the present and for the future; and that they will not soon undergo any predictable obsolescence. Again, the neighborhood unit in single ownership and designed to be permanently administered as such is the only way out. Moreover, in addition to ordinary financial charges, the governments had another interest in promoting the life-expectancy of a housing development. Subsidies, due either to inflated post-war prices or to low wages and therefore necessarily low rents, could be strung out in annual payments and need not be given outright.

And finally, there is the cost of *upkeep*, which, by the use of standardized parts and the provision of centralized services and management, would also be considerably reduced.

Financial and rental set-ups in typical new European developments will be presented in another section. (See Chapter VIII.) Here it must suffice to say that for the same unit of original cost (that is, without allowing for substantial economies in land, land development, and construction), and without allowing for subsidies, the 'economic' rent on most European housing would be less than half as high as it would be in America.

Nevertheless, the real significance of this modern housing method is not the economic saving. It is rather the fundamentally higher quality of the achievement. Even if it cost twice as much, I am not sure but that it would have to be done that way sooner or later.

As soon as the neighborhood is accepted as the unit of growth, a multitude of old conceptions and habits become quite meaningless. Standardized streets without beginning or end, automatically drawn up in the city engineering office, have no place in an organic plan whose use and form and limits have been established in advance. With the streets disappear the old-fashioned block and the standardized lots and also the 'front feet.' For the latter is a marketing and not a consumers' unit of measure. Building-sites are no longer a commodity existing chiefly on a piece of paper. They become areas of land, each with its distinct topography, to be systematically planned to fit a thousand specific functions.

The change is essentially one from a mechanical standardization for profit to functional standards for use. And it is only by the latter method that the real *technological* benefits of standardization may be realized.

Instead of standardized streets and lots which result only in wasted land and pavement and possible amenity, we must have planning standards which reduce the cost of streets to a minimum. Instead of separate houses whose design has been standardized after an obsolete pattern, and which are therefore both wasteful and monotonous and ugly, we can have truly standardized *parts* which will lend themselves to harmonious arrangements as various as human requirements demand. The former merely degrades and travesties old forms. The latter creates at least the possibility of new forms.

Such words as 'unit,' 'standard,' and 'large-scale production' are, I realize, very likely to grate ungently on the average American ear when they are applied to the matter of dwellings. The traditional idea still prevails that everyone who works hard and saves his money can eventually buy a piece of ground and put up on it a house designed after his heart's desire. But, whether or not it would be nice to have it so, this idolum happens to belong to the realm of mythology. And anyone who entertains it must never have looked around as he entered an American city. In seventeen cities recently surveyed in detail, eighty to ninety per cent of the dwellings had been built by mass-production methods, most of them, of course, by small or large contractors without benefit of either architect or planner. We have plenty of 'standardization,' only we happen to have it in an excessively wasteful and ugly and unproductive form. And what of the other ten to twenty per cent, who do presumably build a house after their heart's desire? Even most of these are erected from 'standard' plans, and the result can never be anything more than a house and a lot, both of them far more expensive than they are worth. But a house and a lot are not all of a residential environment, and a single house in the city or in a suburb can hardly be said to have any independent existence at all. One house may be good in itself, but three houses of the same general kind, when set down without relation to each other on three adjoining narrow lots, may constitute a slum. Physically, a modern house is a knot in a network of utilities. Æsthetically, it is just as dependent on its neighbors. Socially, it is not a complete or successful dwelling without a close and convenient relationship to schools, shops, clubs, recreation fields, transportation lines, work-places. If it is so related in any of our cities, it is only by a happy accident; and in any case there will be none of that more comprehensive and fundamental relationship which can be achieved only by unified architectural planning from the start.

What is a Community Unit?

How big should a housing development be? What functions must it provide for? Should the measure be by area or by population or by some special condition? And above all, where should it be located? There are probably as many good answers to these questions as occasions on which they might arise. The new European developments range in size all the way from a hundred families or less up to Becontree, London, with provisions for more than one hundred thousand people. Plessis-Robinson, built near Paris by the Housing Office of the Department of the Seine, will have a population of twenty-five thousand, and a great many German and Austrian developments house five thousand or more. Certainly there is no simple formula to be derived from such figures.

The *ideal* has undoubtedly been the self-contained regional town, complete with assorted industries, and agricultural belt, and full facilities for social life. This is the one way to carry the premises underlying modern housing and planning through to a really satisfactory conclusion. The building of completely new cities, of a size and extent limited in advance and located scientifically with respect to natural resources, manufacture, and distribution, is the only way in which the use-standards embodied on a small scale in the best modern housing can be enlarged to include all of modern human environment. It is the only way by which the waste and confusion of the nineteenth century can be really canceled out. To do this, however, is apparently quite impossible within the present class-property-profit economic system, itself a heritage from the nineteenth century and earlier. And it is probably even more impossible within a Fascist State, which is essentially nothing more than a forcible crystallization of that system. The all-important problem of how and when real three-dimensional planning can be achieved is unfortunately not a subject into which this book, which deals with the actual housing accomplishment of a dozen capitalist countries, can fruitfully enter.

It is not surprising, therefore, that the ideal of self-contained regionally planned new towns has not so far been achieved, outside of the separate private experiments at Letchworth and Welwyn, and outside of various plans in Russia which must inevitably provide significant material for later judgments. A few important and highly interesting first steps in the regional planning of resources and distribution and the location of new industries were attempted in the Ruhr district in western Germany. But they were in the main adapted only to an expanding industrialization, and it is very unlikely that they will be carried forward under the present régime. The regional surveys in England are gathering up a vast store of scientific knowledge which must be of immense value if and when comprehensive land-economic planning becomes possible. In the distribution of giant power electric lines — the backbone of neotechnic planning — several countries, above all Norway and Switzerland and now England, have shown real foresight. In no country short of Russia, however, can it be said that the actual post-war housing construction has been particularly influenced by such larger emergent factors.

But there are many steps between the barrack-metropolis of the nineteenth century, with its more recent sprawling dormitory suburbs, and the complete regional city, newly planned from the center out in relation to all the resources of a continent. Even such a city would not be a single unit, but made up of smaller integrated groups. And it is in the technique of planning and constructing and administering this smaller and simpler unit, for which 'neighborhood' is probably the most accurate

THE PLANNED COMMUNITY UNIT

1. ENGLAND

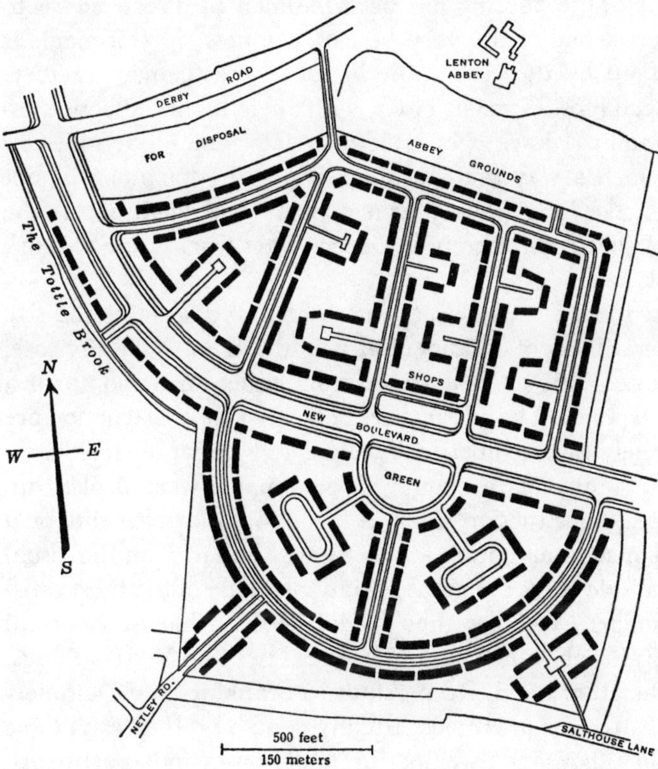

Lenton Abbey, municipal housing estate in Nottingham, consisting of about 880 small houses. This type of informal layout, with large blocks and indented culs-de-sac, and without specific attention to orientation, is typical of post-war housing in England.

term, that modern housing in Germany and England and the other western countries has made its real progress.

Few of these, as I have said, do actually include work-places — except perhaps the German agricultural villages which are more or less 'self-contained,' though at a simple peasant level. But much of the housing has been planned in direct *relation* to work-places: one of the very best of the new developments is that put up by the city of Berlin near the Siemens factory. And indeed most German cities, with their highly effective industrial zoning, have been able to locate new residential colonies in such a way that the majority of the tenants will not have to make long daily journeys, back and forth across the center of the town, merely in order to get from home to work and back again.

But are there any principles with which to determine the size and general form of a residential neighborhood? In any case, there are certainly no exact rules, from either an economic or a social viewpoint. The advantages of large-scale construction are not infinitely and geometrically increased by larger-scale construction. Many of the larger developments were broken up into several construction units, a few rows of apartments or a hundred or so small houses at one time. Similarly, on the visual and social side there are great variations. One of the most satisfactory modern colonies that I have seen is that at Neubühl outside of Zürich, which has only around two hundred dwellings. But on the other hand, Römerstadt in Frankfurt and Dammerstock in Karlsruhe are almost equally good, and they each have more than a thousand dwellings in small houses and apartments. Watergraafsmeer outside of Amsterdam has about the same number (although this is unusually large for Dutch developments), while several Berlin suburbs and some of the Viennese complexes, also designed as single neighborhood units, have almost two thousand dwellings each.

However, a few general statements can be made from the European experience. No housing project can be adequately planned and lived in as a social unit unless it includes a school for at least the younger children, the shops which are necessary for everyday purchases, and some sort of public open space for outdoor recreation for all ages, although not necessarily the

THE PLANNED COMMUNITY UNIT

2. HOLLAND

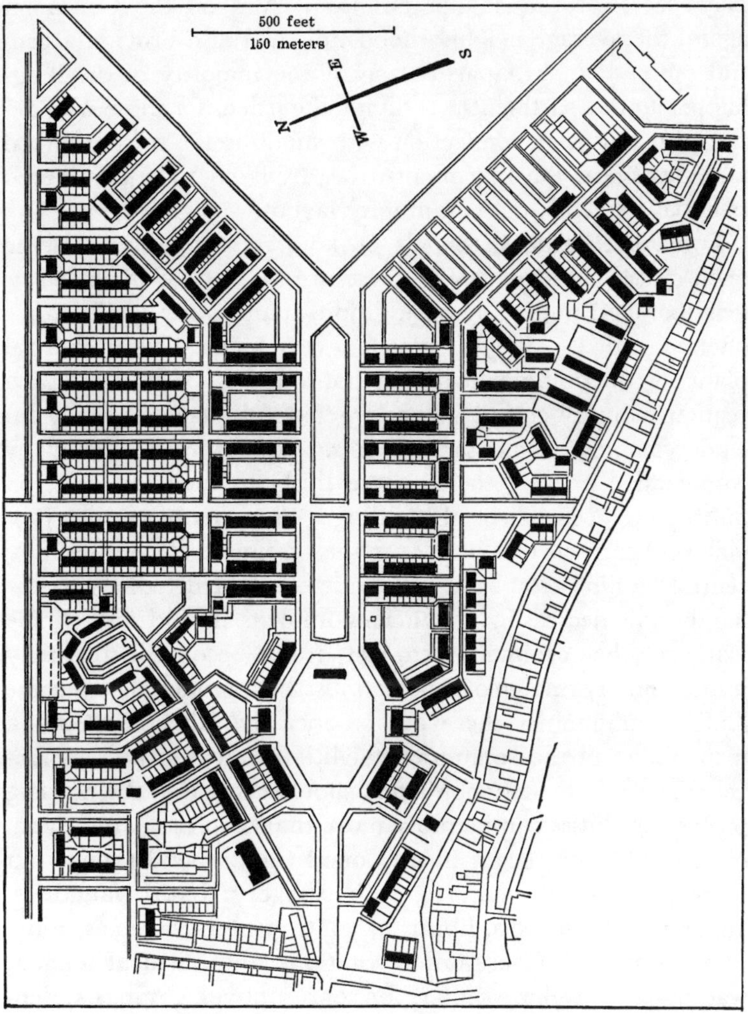

Nieuwendam, partly municipal and partly co-operative housing, in Amsterdam. It contains a thousand one-family houses, a school, a special section designed for old couples, an administration building, shops and other community equipment. The density is much greater than in the English communities, and there is nothing novel about the street-plan except the broad central parkway and the large interior play-spaces. The greater formality, however, makes possible a degree of urbanity not found in the more scattered English developments.

more formal types of playing-field. On the Continent, I think one should also include a café or some other form of public meeting-place. In such a community, there will ordinarily be several play-spaces for the smaller children. And on the Continent again, the average neighborhood unit will also provide a central power laundry,[1] particularly if the majority of dwellings happen to be apartments. Individual gardens for those who desire them, either in connection with small houses or in grouped allotments near the apartment-rows, are likely to be considered essential elements in a community layout.

Dwellings, gardens, schools or kindergarten, shops, usable open space, laundry, café — these are all part of the *minimum* neighborhood unit. But in addition, many other facilities are often provided. Many German developments have a central plant for distributing heat and hot water to all tenants at a regular monthly charge. The larger developments usually include complete elementary schools. Communities erected by co-operative housing societies are likely to plan, at least, on putting up a central social building. Where baths are not provided either in the dwellings or in the basements of the buildings, central bathing establishments must be constructed. With the family unit decreasingly sufficient unto itself, and with single workers to be accommodated, restaurants become increasingly important. Formal sports-fields must be considered. In some Dutch communities there are co-operative kitchens. And a mere listing of the communal facilities built into housing developments by the city of Vienna should show that the housing problem includes considerably more than houses. All of them, of course, do not occur in any one neighborhood group, but there are a great many in each category: baths, laundries, kindergartens, schools, libraries, youth centers, cinemas, nurseries, Maternal Consultation Stations and medical clinics, wading-pools, welfare centers for consumptives, gymnasia, dental clinics, post-offices, playgrounds and allotment gardens.

Plessis-Robinson, near Paris, which will house about twenty-five thousand people, is a complete urban entity with the single

[1] The seriousness with which Germany undertakes this problem of communal equipment may be judged from the fact that the German Engineering Association has a 'Scientific Institute on Clothes-Washing.'

THE PLANNED COMMUNITY UNIT

3. GERMANY

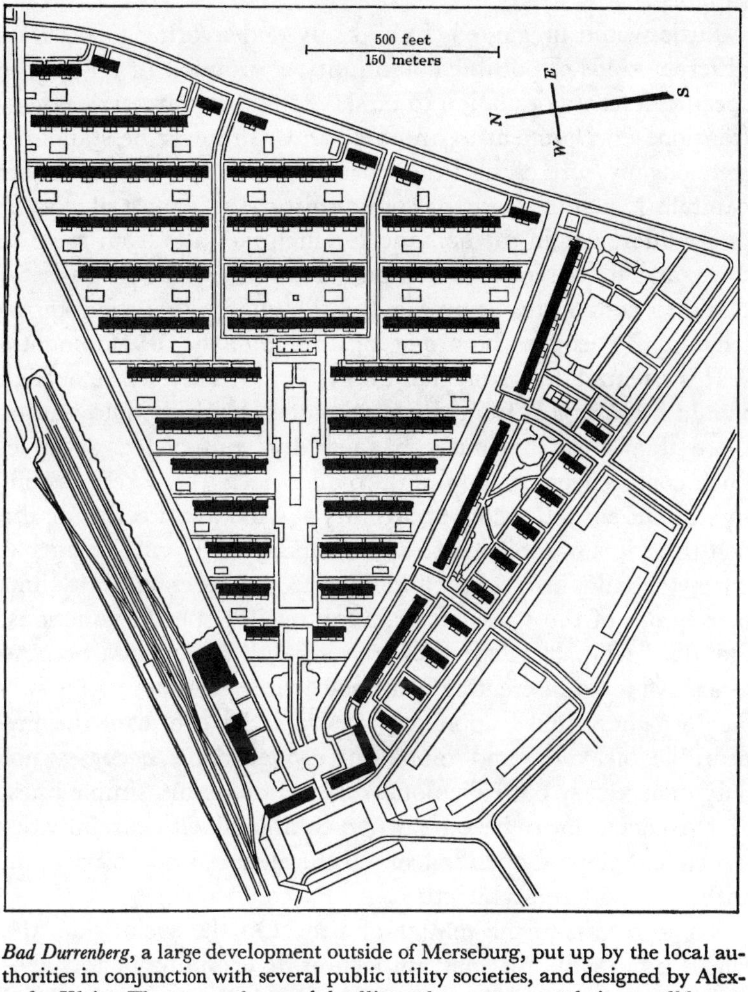

Bad Durrenberg, a large development outside of Merseburg, put up by the local authorities in conjunction with several public utility societies, and designed by Alexander Klein. There are a thousand dwellings, the western part being small houses and the eastern section, with wider spacing between the rows, 3-story apartments. Heat and hot water are supplied from a central plant, and there is a communal power-laundry and other equipment. The major part consists of one huge superblock, with every dwelling oriented for maximum sunlight, no dwelling fronting on a street, and a large central park. This is one of the most complete examples of German *Zeilenbau* planning.

exception of work-places. It includes a *mairie*, a social center, an open-air theater, a public market, a church, large sports-fields, and a concert-hall. Heat and hot water are also centrally supplied.

Little would be gained, I think, by endeavoring to tabulate different kinds of possible community equipment in relation to specific units of population to be served. They vary enormously from one development to another, and can never be standardized on any sort of statistical basis. And, whether society is capitalistic, nationalistic, or communistic, there must always be great differences in the demand for such facilities from town to town and from region to region. The only realistic basis for planning community equipment is to have quite a solid knowledge of the people who are going to live in the development.

It is essential, however, that everything which may be needed should be *planned in* from the start. Sites should be allowed for those things which cannot be actually constructed at once. Such comprehensive planning provides both a new responsibility and an entirely new opportunity for the architect. For the first time, it is possible to use a great many different elements at once, to build up groups and balanced masses and rhythms merely out of the varied forms required for specific functions. Standardized parts, instead of creating dull uniformity, become a positive force in creating a unified whole. Meaningless surface ornament, once applied to distract the eye from the unbearable bleakness and monotony underneath, becomes not only unnecessary but ridiculous. Good materials, simple lines, and geometric forms become, when combined with carefully designed and planted open spaces, all the elements necessary to an authentic modern architecture.

But to return to the matter of size. On the social side, the school is probably the most important determining factor. Together with its recreation space, it is likely to supply the focal point of a planned neighborhood. Whether this school is merely a kindergarten and a nursery, as it often is in Swiss communities, or whether it is a complete elementary school, as is usual in Germany and Holland and England, is a matter which obviously cannot be decided out of hand. Physically, there are vital factors limiting the size in both directions. A unit must be

HOUSING IS MORE THAN HOUSES

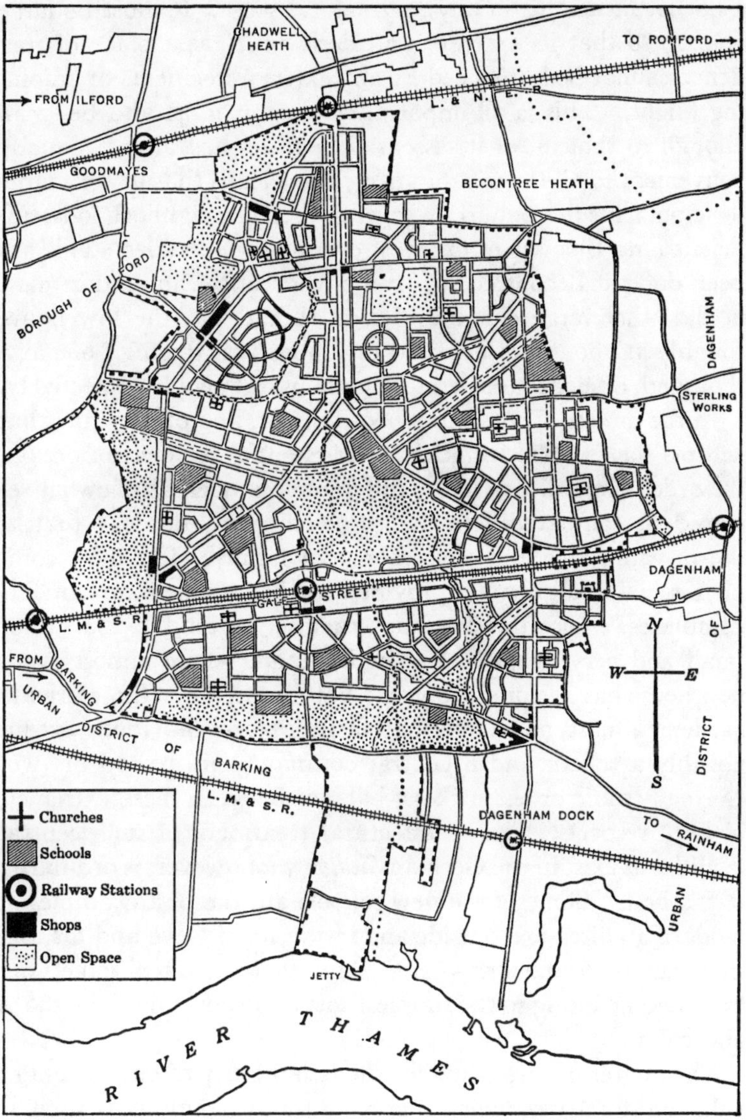

Becontree, outside of London, put up and administered by the London County Council. Its 25,000 dwellings, almost all of them small one-family houses laid out in rows or groups, make it one of the largest public authority housing developments in the world. The partial green belt, and the variety of community equipment provided, may be seen on the plan.

at least large enough to create a neighborhood atmosphere. And I do not mean this in any sentimental sense. It must be large enough so that its amenity and desirability as a place of residence cannot be influenced by any exterior accidents or adjoining blight. This is all-important. And it must also be small enough so that all of its essential facilities are almost equally convenient to all the inhabitants. This means that in very large developments there must be several distinct neighborhoods, sufficient unto themselves for most everyday necessities. This has been done at Becontree, at Britz outside of Berlin, and in most of the other large communities. I should put the low figure roughly at about two hundred dwellings and the high one at a thousand, or eight hundred to five thousand people respectively.

In the matter of community equipment, and of planning that accepts such public facilities as an essential element of design, the order of excellence in the different countries is somewhat reversed, as compared with the *net* dwelling standards — that is, the private space and equipment per family. The most complete social equipment is provided in the Viennese apartment-complexes, where the dwellings themselves tend to be rather small and very simple. And in England, where almost every new house has five or six rooms, a bathroom, and a large private garden, almost no communal facilities are provided, except possibly a school and a central common and a shop or two. Germany more or less strikes a balance between these extremes, in both respects. The architectural treatment of such central facilities as exist in the German *Siedlungen*, however, is ordinarily of the best. Some of the new schools are the best examples of modern architecture, outside and inside, for the eye and for use, that can be found anywhere. And there is often something fresh and arresting in the simplest sort of disposition of the shops and cafés.

The matter of preserving for the community the increment of value on store-sites, which is created by the community itself, is automatically taken care of in most of the larger developments merely because the shops are built in from the start and all the land and buildings remain in single ownership. And, particularly in Scandinavia, Austria, and Germany, the store which supplies daily necessities to the new houses is likely to be a consumers' co-operative in any case. Letchworth Garden City, by giving long leases at too early a stage, lost a very considerable part of its possible store-value increment. But Welwyn profited by its example and started with a large co-operative building, in which various departments were let out on short concessions. Long leases will be given only after the maximum of population has been reached.

III. LOCATION: HOUSING AND CITIES

CLOSELY related to the matter of size and degree of self-sufficiency is the question of location. Indeed, the first step must be the decision between a central reconstruction — 'slum-clearance' — and an entirely fresh development on new land, which must ordinarily lie somewhere toward the outskirts of the town, if not entirely beyond its corporate limits. Obviously, this is a much more important and complex question for the large cities, where central land-prices are high and large areas of open land relatively distant, than it is for the smaller ones. Perhaps the best way to show some of the aspects of this problem will be to describe briefly the policy and experience of various representative cities.

London

There is no city where the question of location is more acutely complex than in London. There are still, even after half a century of effort, a large number of definitely insanitary districts in the old central parts of the town. Moreover, the fantastic extent of nineteenth-and early twentieth-century London makes unbuilt land very far from most of the work-places. But in spite of the fact that England has expropriation laws which would be considered fearfully 'radical' over here; and also in spite of the fact that, due to the predominance of low buildings, central land-prices have never been anything like what they are on the Continent and in America; London has still been forced to do almost all of her new housing on new land. And every single one of the central slum-clearance projects has not only cost a tremendous sum of money outright, but is greatly inferior in quality, both of the dwellings themselves and of surrounding environment, to the outlying developments. The present cost of re-housing a family on the site of a central slum is about three thousand dollars. The cost of re-housing the same family on new land is only half as much. And in the first case, the family has only a small flat in a high and rather crowded building; while in the second it has a whole house and a garden. It is part of the law in England and Holland that, in clearing a slum, the identical people must be re-housed. Ordinarily this also means that at least part of them must be re-housed on the same site. The latter stipulation is probably a more important condition in these two countries than it would be in America. The slum neighborhoods of London and Amsterdam and Liverpool, have often, like the old East Side in New York, a definite social character. Most of the families have lived there for generations and would rather stay in their rookeries than move to a new district among strange people.

But the complexities of the problem of housing location in London only mount when we turn to the new developments outside of the center, particularly to Becontree, the largest and most pretentious of them. Around 1920 the London County Council began to acquire, by compulsory purchase where necessary, a tract of nearly three thousand acres lying outside its own corporate limits. This tract was laid out in several distinct neighborhoods, with ample community equipment to be provided. All the benefits of large-scale comprehensive planning were realized in the pooling of open space to make a partial green belt and large commons. The total number of dwellings will eventually reach twenty-five thousand. It is therefore a complete residential satellite town. But work-places are far away, and transportation is relatively expensive. And, although the rents are very low, not many former slum-dwellers can afford to live there even if they want to. If they do live there, they may be forced to scrape their living-standard in other matters to a bare minimum or lower. But there is a new ironic twist to the situation. Recently a Ford plant was opened almost adjacent to Becontree, and indeed the industrial outlook in this district is a very good one in general. *But the people who live in Becontree cannot work there* (or not, at least, without paying much higher rents than those scheduled). Why not? Because all the dwellings in Becontree are a charge on the taxes of London County, and therefore only London workers can live there. Of all the situations which call for revolutionary regional planning, this is certainly one of the more obvious. But there is still another side to it. Eventually, without doubt, Becontree will become a civic entity by itself and, regional planning or not, Becontree tenants will be able to work in the Ford factory. But unless something drastic happens in the mean time, Becontree will be a town inhabited only by poor people. There will not be enough taxable wealth in the place to support the utilities and services absolutely necessary for a city of more than one hundred thousand persons.

Now I do not bring up such gloomy examples (and Becontree does happen to be the most extreme one) in order to dampen the enthusiasm of housing promoters. Housing can be done. And housing must be done, if only to bring into clear relief the larger things which *cannot* be done. But no one should blind himself with any fond illusion that the really fundamental problems of Megalopolis can be solved within the present scheme of things.

Berlin

No slum-clearance has been attempted, but several facts tended to make the location problem on outlying unbuilt land less difficult in Berlin than it has been in London. In the first place, the city has always been relatively decentralized — not in the sprawling chaotic manner of Chicago, but rather because it consisted of four or five distinct towns from the start. Moreover, the city fathers of 1900 were just enough more enlightened than their contemporaries in New York and elsewhere, to build their first subway, not in a radiating pattern, but in a ring around the outside, with only a spur to the center. The old towns, therefore, maintained their identity, and factories and even offices grew up in several outer sections. And, due to the strict building and zoning codes, large areas of unspoiled land were still accessible when the city began to purchase enormous tracts after the war. Therefore, although the workers who live in the new colonies at Neukölln or Britz or Siemensstadt are a good half-hour or more by train from the center of the city, they can often walk to work, to social centers, and also to open country.

Vienna

This city also bought up a great deal of land at a time when inflation and rent restrictions made the price very cheap. And a few thousand dwellings have been located in compact new garden villages on the outskirts. But most of the Viennese housing is within the city, not on cleared sites, but on any sizable unbuilt plot which the city was able to pick up. The principle involved was largely one of economy, as all Viennese housing represented outright expense in any case, and any saving in streets or utilities meant just that many more new dwellings with which to meet an extreme shortage. This accounts for the fact that almost all the new housing is in large apartment-blocks, sometimes five or six stories high and ordinarily covering rather more ground than the post-war average European standard. On the larger sites, however, even where the apartments are surrounded by nineteenth-century slums, careful unit planning and admirable built-in communal facilities make for a degree of integration rarely achieved in even the entirely fresh neighborhoods of England, which are often surrounded by at least a partial belt of open green space or common.

Paris

The work of the Public Housing Office of the city of Paris is almost all below standard, and does not enter into either the figures or the discussion of this book. One can at least give them credit for not following the post-war advice (seriously discussed at the time) of one eminent authority, who proposed that the housing problem be solved by adding two stories to some fifty thousand buildings in Paris. However, the achievements of the Housing Office of the Seine Department, which operates in a strip of land a few miles wide encircling the city, are of another order. Through the energetic foresight of M. Henri Sellier they bought up enough land as early as 1916 to fill out their whole immediate program, including several estates large enough for complete villages. The fact that Paris has sprawled less than almost any modern metropolis (due more probably to the psychological aversion of the population to a *banlieue* than to any planning regulation) was undoubtedly of great assistance. But this same desire for social urbanity made it necessary for the housing authorities to provide something more than a mere dormitory suburb. Which undoubtedly accounts for the remarkable equipment of Plessis-Robinson, described some pages before, and of many of the other new villages. However, one must admit that they are far out, and that work is in most cases not very easy of access.

Frankfurt

The problem of location has been more successfully met in this city than in any other town of its size. Frankfurt has a long tradition of prestige in planning matters. Two of its nineteenth-century Mayors, Miquel and Adickes, introduced important reforms to prevent land speculation and to facilitate better layout of residential districts. Its pre-war housing societies did some of the best work of the time. And in 1914, Patrick Geddes described the admirable comprehensive planning of its new port district. It is not remarkable that a large proportion of the fruitful experiments in planning and layout and construction in Germany after the war took place in Frankfurt. Under the leadership of Stadtbaurat Ernst May, who later supervised the building of new cities in Russia, a positive and scientific principle of city-development was put into practice in Frankfurt's housing. The tendency of all cities to expand indefinitely in concentric circles was to be stopped once and for all, the new residential construction was to be located in so far as possible in the new planned units, permanently separated from each other and from the main part of the city by open green space. In short, a satellite plan of growth instead of mere inorganic accretion. The city (if one may be forgiven a somewhat fancy metaphor) becomes a higher organism, producing new residential districts by separate and carefully 'planned' birth rather than by spawning thousands in order that ten may survive. As a principle, this has of course been accepted in almost all European cities, but nowhere has it been put more effectively into practice than in Frankfurt. The first thing done was to purchase (by expropriation at actual and not at

HOW TO AVOID 'BLIGHTED DISTRICTS':

PRINCIPLE AND PRACTICE

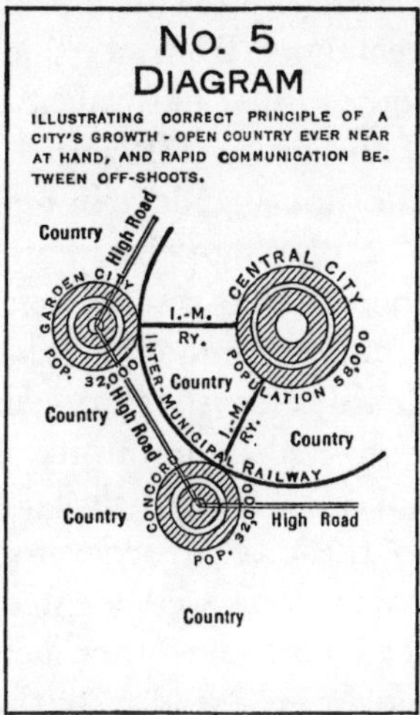

Howard's original diagram, showing how to build new, planned cities instead of straggling megalopolitan suburbs. Welwyn and Letchworth, the two English Garden Cities, resulted. (From 'To-morrow,' by Ebenezer Howard, 1898.)

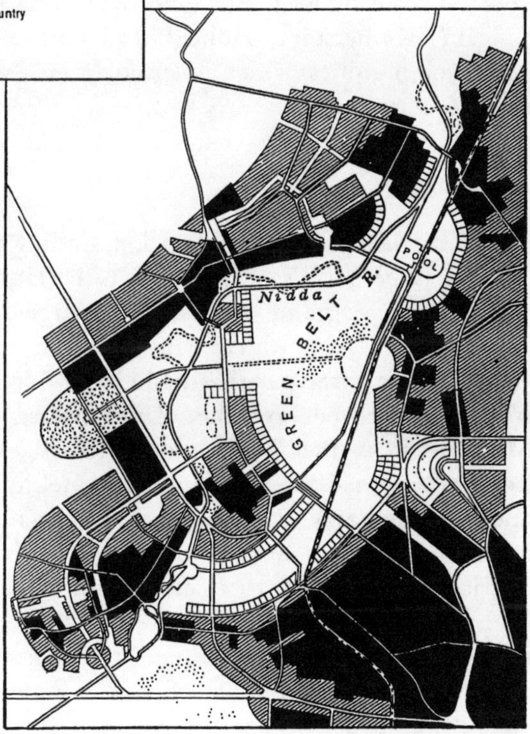

Frankfurt on the Main modified the Garden City principle, but insulated the new developments at Römerstadt, Praunheim and Westhausen from the old city with a strip of permanent green space. Black areas are already developed, cross-hatched are projected for building, dotted areas are permanent park and open space, small squares are allotment gardens.

speculative value) almost the entire valley of the Nidda River, which winds around the city on two sides at a distance of from two to five miles from the center. Reclaimed from marshland, its undulating meadows make a region of great natural beauty — and provide both a large part of the green belt and ideal areas on the other side for large-scale housing developments. Some of the open space is utilized for playing-fields, bathing establishments, and allotment gardens; the rest is left as open pasture for a flock of presumably municipal sheep. There are direct transportation facilities to the city-center (not more than twenty minutes) from each community, but the neighboring industrial zone makes it unnecessary for a large part of the tenants to go into the city in order to get to work. Not all of Frankfurt's housing is as well located as Praunheim, Römerstadt, Höhenblick, and the other neighborhood communities which overlook the Nidda, but the average is very high.

Manchester

In 1926 the Manchester Corporation, finding that there were not enough large parcels of land within the city limits to carry out the housing program, purchased the larger part of an area outside its boundaries which will eventually comprise some 5600 acres. The three parishes included, which are separated from the city proper by the River Mersey, were added to Manchester as the Wythenshawe Ward, and the whole is being developed as a complete satellite town. The planner is Mr. Barry Parker, who, together with Sir Raymond Unwin, laid out the original Garden City, Letchworth. An agricultural belt of 1000 acres and a whole string of parks have been provided for, together with the sites for every sort of community equipment which will eventually be needed by the inhabitants of 25,000 houses. There are two industrial zones.

Most of the houses will be erected by the Council, but sites have been left for middle and upper-class private construction. There are already almost 5000 houses, 4600 of them low-rental dwellings built by the Council.

Other Towns

Many of the smaller towns, particularly in Germany, have also concentrated their new housing in definite neighborhood units, set apart from the old center. Henry Wright, the American planner, has advised special attention to 'hillside housing' because such desirable sites were often left unused hitherto, not being well suited to the mechanical subdividing practice of speculators. And by placing their new developments on neighboring hilltops overlooking the town, Stuttgart and Kassel and Zürich have produced, not merely fine places to live in, but examples of modern architecture which have a distinct educational value even to unsuspecting visitors. The modern suburbs of Dessau and Karlsruhe are also given a separate identity through being located in the midst of open meadows.

The tying-in of new housing with the general park and recreation system is another important aspect of urban responsibility. In those fortunate cities, particularly Cologne, where a ring of old fortifications has made it possible to have a continuous park system almost accidentally, this problem tends to be easily if by no means completely solved. That much more difficult job, the introduction of connecting green spaces within an old city and extending into new districts, has probably been best accomplished in Essen and Nuremberg, where the map of green spots makes a visible network through most of the residential districts. The extensive city forests in Germany, often stopping just short of the town proper, have also been of great assistance. Zehlendorf, a new suburb of Berlin, is surrounded by the municipal forest on two sides. And every German city with any sort of water near-by has a public bathing establishment, usually set in a park, and often not far from new housing developments.

IV. LAYOUT AND BUILDING ARRANGEMENT

'Nothing Gained by Overcrowding'

Long before the war, Sir Raymond Unwin wrote a pamphlet under that title, which showed very neatly that it was actually no more economical, even from an ordinary profit standpoint, to jam thirty-four houses onto an acre than to limit the number to fifteen houses. By using a much larger block with semi-detached or grouped houses around all the sides (instead of the close rows then customary) and by eliminating rear alleys, the savings in street-cost and street-area provided larger individual plots and also a common park in the center of the block. This principle had as a matter of fact been put into practice at Port Sunlight in the eighties, and was largely adopted in other pre-war English experiments.

Sir Raymond has recently brought it up to date, in response to a certain amount of pressure to raise the present minimum from twelve to twenty houses per acre. His new diagram makes use of a typical device of the best English post-war planning, the cul-de-sac street. The more important figures in his comparison are reproduced with the plans herewith. It will be seen that, at twenty houses per acre, there is little choice but to lay out standardized parallel roads with the wide expensive paving required by through streets. At twelve houses per acre, on the other hand, it is possible not merely to provide differentiated 'living-streets,' safe from the noise and danger of traffic, but also to vary them to suit the topography, which would in many instances make for an additional economy not recorded here.

The English Super-Block

The joint development of the automobile and of expensive street-pavements inspired the idea of differentiated dwelling-

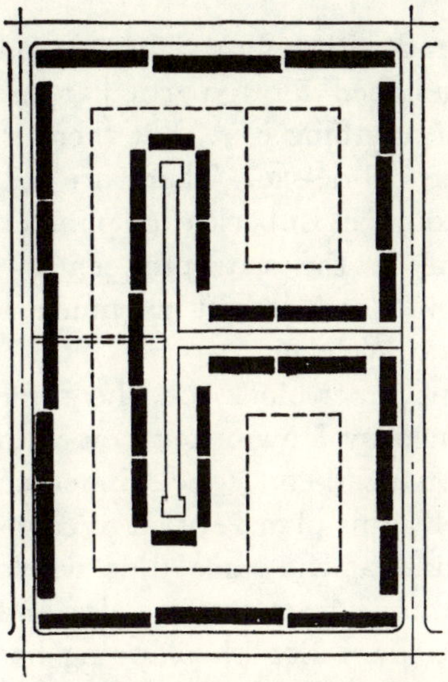

12 HOUSES PER ACRE

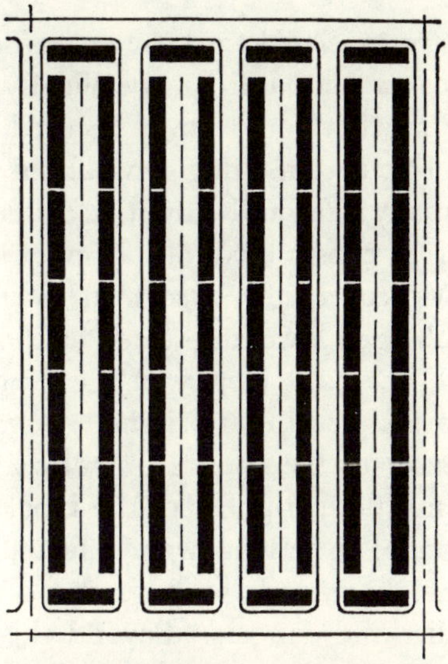

20 HOUSES PER ACRE

DEVELOPMENT OF 20 ACRES

	12 to acre	20 to acre
Average frontage per house	21 feet	21 feet
C. of raw land per acre	$1000	$1000
C. of 40 ft. roads per yd.	$51.25	$51.25
C. of 30 ft. roads per yd.	41.25	
NUMBER OF HOUSES	240	400
Gross area	20 acres	20 acres
Area of Roads	2.46 acres	4.76 acres
Net area	17.54 acres	15.24 acres
AVERAGE SIZE OF PLOT	353 sq. yds.	184 sq. yds.
Road frontage:		
40 ft. road	3,732 feet	10,370 feet
30 ft. road	2,162 feet	
AVERAGE ROAD FRONTAGE PER HOUSE	24.54 feet	25.9 feet
Total C. of land	$20,000	$20,000
Total C. of roads	$46,740	$88,575
Av. C. of land per house	$83	$50
Av. C. of roads per house	$195	$221
Av. C. of roads and land per house	$278	$271
C. per square yard of plot	$.79	$1.47
GROUND RENT PER PLOT PER WEEK, at 6%	$.32	$.31

(From: NOTHING GAINED BY OVERCROWDING, by Sir Raymond Unwin, a pamphlet published by the Garden Cities and Town Planning Association, 3 Gray's Inn Place, London.)

streets, closed to through traffic and with only a light, narrow pavement, and so specifically designed for a particular use that they could never be used for anything else. But there is, of course, nothing new about the cul-de-sac. There are still many small and attractive closed courts in Lübeck, each planned and constructed all at one time in the sixteenth century. Moreover, the mediæval English 'close' is just as much a planned 'dwelling-street' as those at Welwyn.

The next step was the English super-block, on the same principle as that originally suggested by Unwin, but now with most of the dwellings fronting on dead-end streets indented into the periphery of the block. By this plan very large economies in paving were effected, and at the same time whole neighborhoods were rendered immune from traffic noise and dirt and dangers. Beyond this, modern English planning has not gone, but there is hardly a single mechanical old-fashioned gridiron in the entire body of post-war English housing developments. The common in the center of the block is often quite large, allowing for tennis, allotment-gardens, playground, and occasionally even schools. The pro rata cost of land and land development rarely comes to more than fifteen per cent of the total cost of a new English house, and often is down as low as ten per cent.

A further step in the English super-block principle may be seen at Radburn, New Jersey, planned by Mr. Henry Wright and Mr. Clarence Stein. Here there are huge blocks indented with culs-de-sac, as in England, but the houses face inward on the central open space, and footways run across the interior of the block, underpassing the occasional traffic streets.

The German Super-Block: 'Zeilenbau'

What the English achieved by experiment and common sense, the Germans developed further into a science. The English plan does not, for one thing, permit of any very thorough orientation of dwellings for maximum sunlight. Also, unless it is very carefully and well designed, it tends toward an informality which can easily become mere spottiness. And the great desiderata of the German planners were sunlight

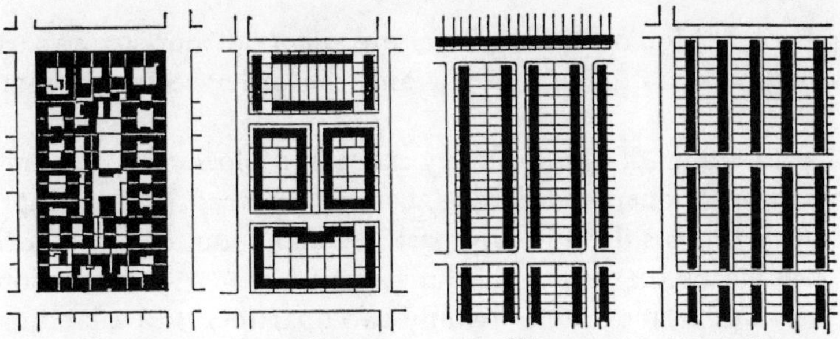

FOUR STAGES IN GERMAN BLOCK–PLANNING

I. is the typical 19th-century block, with rear buildings. II. shows smaller blocks with buildings all around the perimeter. III. has open-ended rows facing each other across traffic streets. IV. is a diagram of *Zeilenbau*, with the rows endward to the street and all facing in the same direction. From *Das Neue Frankfurt.*

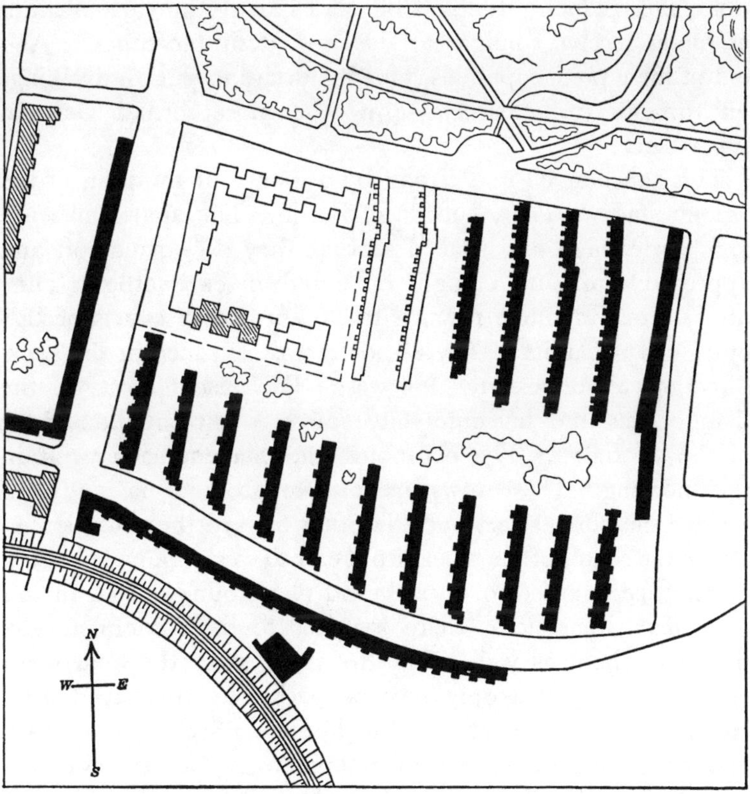

THE GERMAN SUPER–BLOCK IN PRACTICE

A plan of the Siemensstadt development, near Berlin, which includes a large central park, a school and a central heating plant and laundry.

From *Berliner Wohnbauten.*

and order. Moreover, the greater prevalence of four-story apartments made both the sunlight and the order relatively more urgent.

A maximum of *light* for every room in a block of apartments means single open-ended rows, carefully spaced, and no more than two rooms deep in any part. A maximum of air in such a row means that every dwelling must have cross-ventilation, which also means ordinarily only two apartments to a landing. A maximum of direct sunlight, per day and per year, means that the rows must be geographically oriented.

At first, the streets were put through as usual, one between each pair of rows, with cross-streets at the ends. But this was expensive and also made the buildings front in opposite directions, thus reducing the possibility of having the various kinds of rooms receive sunlight at the most desirable times. And out of these preoccupations, plus the desire to put all dwellings off through traffic streets, grew the more formal German super-block.

This can best be understood by a glance at the plan of the Siemensstadt *Siedlung*, outside of Berlin. The apartments are four stories high and spaced so that they do not cut off any appreciable amount of light or sun from each other. They are laid out in single rows, with no corners or courts or 'L'- or 'T'-shaped units. They all, or almost all, face in the same direction, almost exactly due west. The vast majority of the living-rooms and balconies have direct sun throughout most of the afternoon. The bedrooms and bathrooms have it in the morning. These rows are in two groups, one endward toward the north street and the other toward the south street. Down the center of the block, from east to west, is a wide central open space, planted for a park and playground. And, in this particular super-block, there happens to be a complete elementary school as well. For direct access to the apartment entrances there are only narrow paths, lightly paved with either gravel or concrete, and to be used only by pedestrians and hand-carts or in case of emergency by a fire-engine or ambulance. If such a block were planned to include garages, they would be located at the street end of the apartment rows.

What is the general effect? No closed courtyards, no traffic, no wasted pavement, and an open vista in two directions for every window and balcony. The open space 'flows' around the buildings, and yet the whole is urbane and orderly. Different architects have been employed to design different rows or groups of rows, and the variations in the use of more or less standard parts — in the shape of windows and balconies and the design of the stair-well — is enough to relieve any possible monotony, without spoiling the underlying unity. There is nothing 'pretty' or 'picturesque' about it, but it can be very handsome — in a way which has seldom been achieved since those two words became terms of architectural approbation. And the opportunities for broad, unfussy landscaping are tremendous.

This general scheme, known as *Zeilenbau*, was used in almost all the later housing developments in Germany, and has been adopted in various instances in almost every Continental country which is building modern housing. The idea of open-ended rows, with ample space between to permit of light and air and usable open space, and with only narrow streets within the development, is of course not new by any means. The sixteenth-century Fuggerei in Augsburg embodies it. Before the war Theodor Fischer in Munich built a colony whose general scheme is almost exactly like that of Siemensstadt. And many early post-war Danish developments were designed on the same general principle. At present there is almost no European country where perimeter building (around four sides of a block) is still considered 'standard.'

The actual economies involved vary, of course, according to the conditions and the details of the method. Gas and water mains are usually laid under the street pavements, while the connecting pipes to the apartments are carried through the cellars, a method which considerably facilitates repairs. With the same density of two-story buildings, the Frankfurt housing department figured that fifteen per cent of land-development costs (water, sewers, gas, pavement) were saved by the super-block method. Not to mention the fact that the houses are quieter and cleaner and that most of the land which would have gone into streets is now open park space. The disadvantage, obviously, is the fact that the dwellings are not directly accessible to a street. And in the case of developments not centrally heated, where the coal has to be carried to the dwelling itself, this can be a real inconvenience. The matter of garbage collection is usually facilitated by the use of specially designed carts and standardized receptacles.

A modification of *Zeilenbau* (designed, as a matter of fact, before that term became systematized) more akin to English planning can be seen in several German developments, notably in Nuremberg. Narrow dead-end streets which give access to all the apartments have been used and the dwellings face in opposite directions. The use of connecting open space and parks, through this and the surrounding neighborhoods, is particularly notable.

'Heliotropic Housing'

It is highly characteristic of the German planner that, once it was decided that dwellings should not face on through traffic streets, he developed a scientific method by which *every* house can face inward and not, as with the English, just the majority. The same applies to the German principle of orientation for sun. The Frankfurt housing officials worked out an elaborate set of diagrams early in their housing work, and their conclusions have been widely adopted throughout the country. The basis of calculations was a first-floor dwelling in an open-ended four-story row parallel on both long sides with other similar rows one hundred and fifty feet away. The purpose was to find the orientation of the rows which would provide the maximum of sunlight within all the rooms in *winter and spring* (sun being no great desideratum in the summer). The resulting scientific optimum for Frankfurt's geographical position was a row-direction of north-north-west to south-south-east. The living-rooms and kitchens are then put on the west side and the bedrooms and bathrooms, in so far as possible, on the east.

But this is no rule which can be applied too rigorously (and one feels that it is occasionally so applied in Germany). Some balance should certainly be permissible between maximum sunlight and some of the other things which are affected by orientation in any given situation. If the site happens to provide a possible view, it is certainly important to make the most of it, even with some slight modification of possible sunlight. And finally, in extreme climates like our own, one must also consider the possibility that a maximum of summer sun in all rooms might well be decidedly undesirable (particularly if this did not happen also to mean a maximum of breeze). Recent studies by Mr. Henry Wright tend to show that if living-rooms are toward the south, they receive more sun in winter and less in summer than if they face west. But the fact that the bedrooms in such a plan would rarely receive any sun at all would, of course, have to be taken into consideration. Probably, when all is said and done, the most important sun-and-light standard adopted in Europe is the rule that the space between buildings must be increased in direct proportion to the height of the buildings. And also that every dwelling must face in two opposite directions.

Can a Plan be Too 'Open'?

The old notion, often put forward by speculators, that dense building was necessary merely because there were so many people in a metropolitan area, can be demolished by a little simple arithmetic. Sir Raymond Unwin has shown that within the present area of Greater London it would be possible to house all of England and Wales at ten houses per acre, leaving the central district for business only, and putting a wide green belt around it. Sir Raymond was not obviously suggesting that anything like this should be done. But still, one is left with the question as to whether one would like to have even all the *present* population of London housed at ten families per acre.

A very challenging if somewhat perverse book was published in England last year, called *Town and Countryside.* Its author, Mr. Thomas Sharp, condemned most of the post-war English housing because it was done on open 'garden-city lines' (a term which in practice means little more than that there should be only twelve houses per acre). Now Mr. Sharp is neither a real-estate speculator lamenting the once-profitable congestion

TYPICAL BLOCK-PLANS

All of these plans are sections of larger state-aided community developments, and are presented at the same scale for purposes of comparison. Corresponding dwelling-plans are illustrated on page 196.

SCALE THROUGHOUT = Scale In Feet 0 16 32 64 128

ROW HOUSES

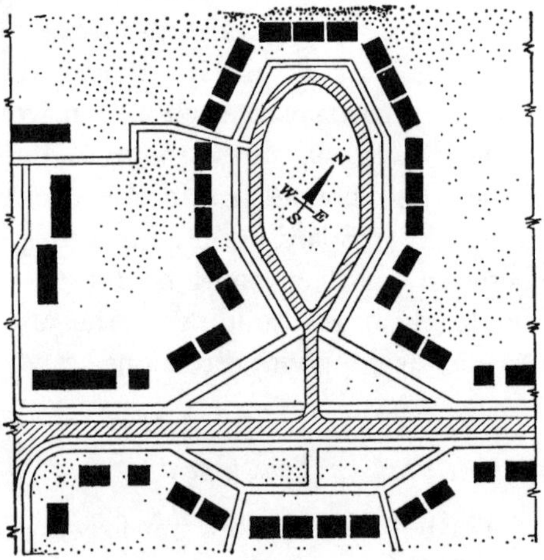

WELWYN, ENGLAND

A typical cul-de-sac in a development of 200 small houses, put up by the local government.

Stories: 2

Dwellings per acre: 12

See Plates 1 and 6

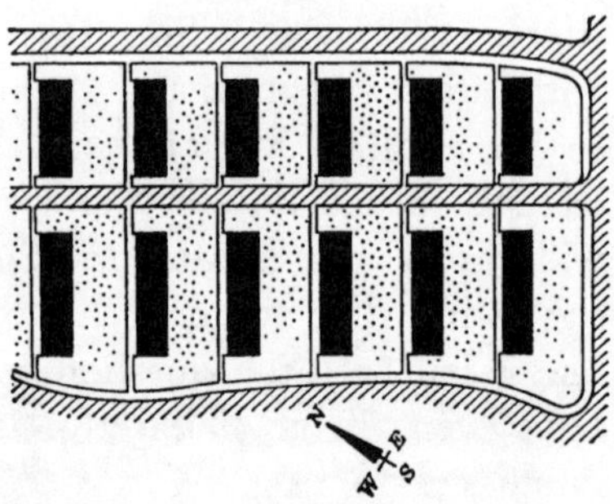

ZÜRICH: NEUBÜHL

Open-row houses in a super-block, part of a community of 195 dwellings put up by a co-operative society.

Stories: 2 (3 in other sections)

Dwellings per acre: 16

See Plate 39

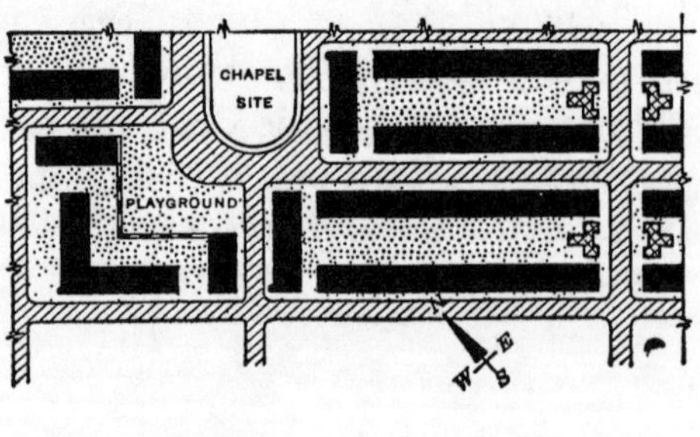

ROTTERDAM: KIEFHOEK

Slum rehabilitation within the old street-plan, in a development of 300 minimum houses put up by the city.

Stories: 2

Dwellings per acre: 30

See Plate 13

TYPICAL BLOCK–PLANS

APARTMENTS

BERLIN: SIEMENSSTADT

Oriented single-row planning in a super-block with central open space, in a development of 1800 dwellings, by a municipal housing society.

Stories: 4

Dwellings per acre: 32

See Plates 1 and 27, and p. 179

VIENNA:
KARL MARX HOF

Part of a large apartment complex, which includes complete community equipment, erected by the city government. It has 1400 dwellings.

Stories: 4 (5 in some other sections)

Dwellings per acre: 29

See Plate 41

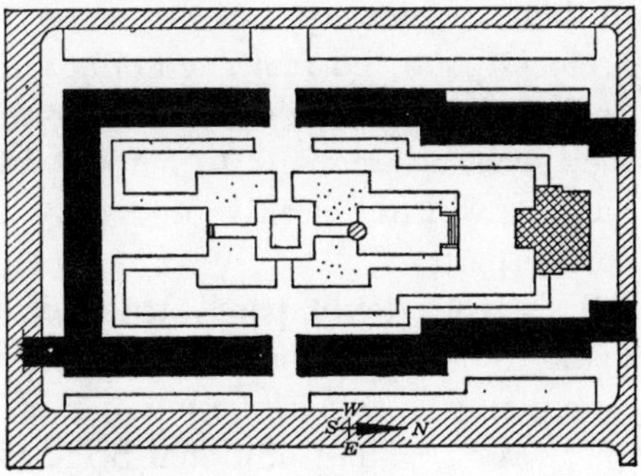

LONDON:
OSSULSTON ESTATE

Part of a central slum-clearance project, erected by the County Council, and containing 480 dwellings in all.

Stories: 5

Dwellings per acre: 52

See Plate 5

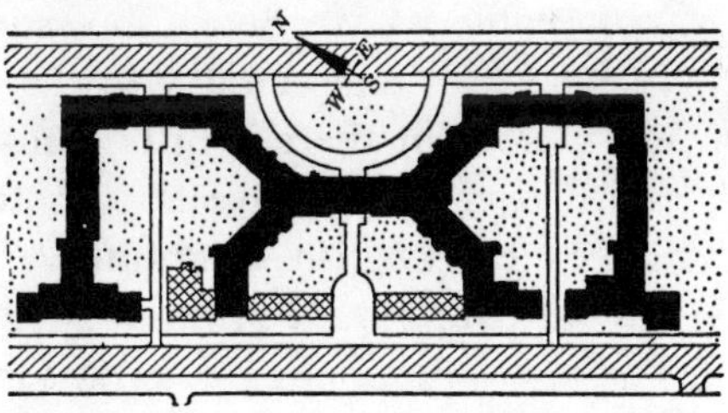

PARIS:
PLESSIS–ROBINSON

Part of a complete satellite town of 5600 dwellings, put up by the Housing Office of the Seine Department. Each apartment has an allotment garden.

Stories: 4

Dwellings per acre: 29

See Plate 21

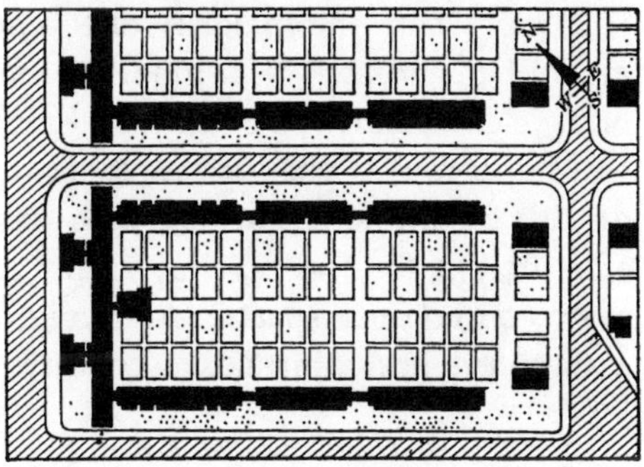

nor a radical objecting to the essentially quite middle-class atmosphere of most English housing. He is just simply a man who likes town to be town and country to be country, and does not think that there is anything to be gained by trying to mix the two. The rural atmosphere is spoiled, but no real urbanity results.

This is certainly true of the average American suburb, where all the houses stand jealously in the middle of their yards and are of raucously different sizes and styles. But even some of the new English housing developments seem to sprawl somewhat, though they were laid out and put up according to a unified design and are always built in attached groups of two to four houses or more. I do not think that this is necessarily due to their low density, but rather to the fact that there is often no focal point, no real beginning and end. There are schools and shops, but, instead of binding the neighborhood together, they seem occasionally to get lost in it. And never are they handled with the positive integral clarity of their best German counterparts.

This is no doubt partly true because no attempt has been made to develop a modern architectural vernacular to fit the new planning and construction methods. But that is not the only reason. The traditional brick-cottage style still employed was once able, as Mr. Sharp shows in his photographs, to create market-squares and country towns as urbanely positive as one could wish. But there is little comparable to them among the perhaps over-curved streets and too-dispersed houses of the average new English community, infinitely better though it is than anything built in the nineteenth century.

The most illuminating comparison here is not with Germany, where the whole conception of form is different, but with Holland, where the majority of the new housing developments are still constructed in a modified but nevertheless traditional brick vernacular. On any mathematical basis, the Dutch housing is not as good as the English. There is much greater density on the site, gardens and dwellings are both smaller, and there is far less ingenuity and spaciousness in the layout of streets and open spaces. And yet most of the Dutch work has a dignified and affirmative quality, perhaps inherent in its close economical neatness and admirable craftsmanship, which is lacking in all but the very best English housing. A school or a café or a public bath-house or two shops or a playground always seem to be really a central point, giving communal form to the whole neighborhood. Moreover, even in Vienna, where coverage and density are definitely too high in many developments, there is sometimes an integral neighborhood quality which is lacking in many new English suburbs.

V. BUILDING TYPES AND DWELLING PLANS

The One-Family House

The argument as to the relative merits of low houses and high or medium apartment-buildings has been going on ever since the middle of the last century. However, as very few decent flats were constructed before 1920 or later, the odds were almost always against them. Every housing-reformer believed that the ideal home was a small house with attached garden: anything else could be nothing more than an unfortunate compromise due to uncontrollable circumstances. To a great extent and with fundamental justice this belief still prevails. At least eighty-five per cent of the new English dwellings are small one-family houses or possibly two-story flats. The percentage is just as high in Belgium, and, outside of the central districts of the larger towns, in Holland and the Scandinavian countries as well. In the early years of post-war housing activity a good half of the new German dwellings were two-story one-family houses, and probably even a larger proportion of the French ones. At an exceedingly rough estimate in the eleven localities with which we are most directly concerned, I should say that very nearly half of the four and a half million government-assisted dwellings are of the one-family type.

But the one-family houses of Europe are not like those of America. The individual, free-standing house, except for an occasional open-country farmer or someone of exceptional means, has always been, and still is, practically unknown in most of Europe. The reasons are not merely traditional, and have nothing whatsoever to do with that mythical 'lower standard of living.' They are entirely realistic and thoroughly up-to-date. Why should money be spent for extra outside walls, extra land which always lies useless in the shadow of one house or the other, dead windows (or windows looking directly into other people's rooms), extra feet of pipe-line and street-pavement, and extra interior heat? Such money can be much more efficiently spent on better construction and more and better-lighted space within the house, or it can be saved outright. As Mr. Henry Wright has often pointed out, if many of our deep, narrow-fronted individual bungalows were merely turned around so that their short sides adjoined, and if all the windows were then concentrated front and back, a much more economical and very much more livable dwelling-type would result. Not to mention the fact that it would lend itself much better to positive architectural treatment.

The English houses, therefore, even when the general space-standards are very high, are invariably built in attached groups of two, four, six, or more. As a rear entrance is ordinarily considered indispensable (because of the coal fires), there are often through passages between each pair of interior houses. Wherever there is enough money, brick curtain walls connect the various groups, giving privacy to rear yards and enhancing a unified street-front. Small front lawns, usually unfenced, are provided. In Welwyn there is sometimes also a wide trough of grass between the sidewalk and the street-pavement, serving instead of a curb or gutter.

On the Continent one-family houses are usually built in longer rows and at a somewhat higher density. Outside of Holland, they are almost always oriented with care and rarely built solid around the perimeter of the block. The most satisfactory results of the *Zeilenbau* method of layout, from both an economical and a social point of view, according to several German authorities, have been obtained with rows of small one- or two-story houses. For one thing, in such a plan every living-room and kitchen can face west and also open directly onto the garden — a very desirable factor in a country where half the population eats out-of-doors throughout most of the summer. Moreover, the greater economy in streets and utilities by the super-block system have made it possible in some instances to increase the width of the houses and decrease their depth. Some of the new houses are less than twenty feet through from east windows to west windows, and have of course proportionately more frontage. Very few are deeper than twenty-eight feet. And finally, when the house fronts on a path and the next row is separated from it by the full width of its rear gardens, front lawns can be dispensed with or reduced to a minimum and all the garden space concentrated in the rear, where it is much more useful.

Private gardens are often quite small on the Continent (in Holland the whole site of a small house and yard is sometimes only eight hundred and fifty square feet), but as the houses are two stories high at the most (and often flat-roofed), there is usually ample space in so far as light and air are concerned. In many cases, there are larger allotments near-by for those who really want to indulge in productive vegetable-raising. And, whether it is due to this fact or not, one cannot help noticing that the smaller gardens of Holland and Germany are usually much better kept up and more attractive than the larger ones of England. In Frankfurt, the small street-front lawns of the Römerstadt houses are landscaped and cared for by the city. The rear gardens have been laid out in two sections, the one nearer the house planted in grass for a small children's play-space and a drying-yard, and the outer half for vegetable- and flower-beds. The result provides not 'dull uniformity' by any means, but the most harmonious and attractive rear-alley view that I have ever seen.

Multiple Dwellings

Two-story flats, whose outer aspect is very much the same as that of the usual houses, are occasionally constructed in England. Frankfurt put up a certain number of one-family houses with a small apartment on the third floor to be sublet by the tenant of the lower floors. The stairs are common, and the top floor has a sizable open terrace to make up for the garden, which belongs to the bottom floors. This type has not been used to any great extent, however.

In England the higher apartment-house, of four to six stories, is confined to the central metropolitan districts, usually in connection with slum-clearance projects. The standards of light, air, and outlook are much lower than typical apartment-standards on the Continent, but almost all the dwellings have direct cross-ventilation. In order to facilitate renting the top story, some of the London apartments provide duplexes, or 'maisonettes' for the top two floors.

On the Continent, however, and particularly in Germany, the apartment-house has undergone such a complete change from the nineteenth-century *Mietkaserne* that the blanket distinction between a good one-family house and a less good flat does not really hold any longer. For many types of family, the better services provided by a good modern apartment-building may make it more desirable. (There is, of course, little 'service' in the American sense in these apartments: no elevators, no incinerators, no doorman, and no electric ice-boxes.) But at three stories there is, I think, little to be said against a walk-up except for families with very small children (who probably should not have to live in apartment-houses in any case). Five-story walk-ups are still occasionally to be found in Germany, and even six once in a while in the Scandinavian towns, but everyone, including the architects who built them, would probably agree that they are too high.

Cross-ventilation and open-row planning mean ordinarily that there can be only two dwellings per stair-landing. Partly in order to eliminate some of these stairways, and partly to enable the front doors of apartments to open directly to the outer air, several countries have experimented with the outside balcony-corridor, running from end to end at each floor. This has been used for metropolitan flat-buildings in England for a generation, and indeed it was a typical mediæval contraption which survives to this day in many old rookeries. Perhaps the most interesting experimental modern use of such a corridor is that in Rotterdam, in connection with what are in effect super-imposed two-story houses built around a large central court. The corridor goes all around at the third story, and is wide enough to provide a sort of public esplanade for the upper tenants. Moreover, it is paved with translucent glass bricks, which cut off somewhat less light than a solid floor would do. Wide public stairs, and also a lift large enough to accommodate the delivery hand-carts prevalent in Holland, are located in the corners.

In Germany, where it is known as a *Laubengang*, it has been widely used on long row apartments, with a stairway at each end. Scattered inquiries, however, would not seem to indicate that it represents any net saving in construction cost. The stairs themselves must ordinarily be inside the building, or at least in a closed shaft. It is recognized that windows on such corridors must be above eye-level, and that living-rooms and bedrooms should not front on it. It is ordinarily only for the very smallest dwellings — particularly those for old couples or single people — that its advantages overweigh its disadvantages. If elevators were provided, it would of course facilitate a much greater relative saving.

'*Vom Wolkenkratzer zum Blockhaus*'

Ten or more years ago, Continental architects began to travel to America to see our skyscrapers. (If they did not travel, they looked at other architects' photographs.) All of them deplored the way we crowded our tall buildings on the land, and most of them were politely unenthusiastic about our habit of blowing up Greek temples to make a fifty-story façade. But a great many of them developed a burning desire to build really good skyscrapers, tall buildings which should use the finest modern engineering to produce a really modern environment. Wijdeveld and Le Corbusier were among the first. Gropius and other German architects have been equally insistent about the advantages of a single tall building in the middle of a large piece of land, as against a much larger coverage by low buildings housing the same number of people. Any number of drawings, even plans for whole cities (sometimes including that American ideal from the Age of Engineering Romance, triple-deckered streets), were enthusiastically published, but none of them was ever constructed. For one thing, there were a certain number of real advantages for most average families in living near the ground. And for another, techniques have not progressed to a point where a skyscraper is even temporarily 'economic,' except under the very special luxury-congestion conditions of the twenties in New York (and what a short period and what a long time ago that was!). And, having resulted not nearly so much from new economies in structural technique as from unregulated congestion and resultant speculation, a very tall skyscraper in the middle of a really adequate piece of land is still fundamentally an economic anachronism.

The more interesting of these *gratte-ciel* and *Wolkenkratzer* projects were those which included both high and low buildings, thus providing not merely a new mechanically standardized shell, almost as arbitrary as the old ones, but a recognition that different kinds of people require different things of their living environment. Many of the best housing developments which were actually constructed did recognize this on a smaller scale, and the combination of low houses with three- or four-story flats (as particularly at Neubühl) gives a good architect new elements which can be used to real effect in designing a community group. (It might be parenthetically remarked here that the rigid and mechanical application of zoning laws in America, which grade people only on the one hand according to income and on the other according to the height of building they happen to prefer, will be a great hindrance if and when we get around to neighborhood-unit design.)

And now the first concrete experiment in 'skyscraper' community housing does mingle high buildings with low ones. It is under construction at Drancy, near Paris, by the Public Housing Office of the Seine Department. Four sixteen-story towers, each containing four dwellings to the floor, are widely spaced to the south of a large central common. Grouped around the outside of the common are rows of three-story buildings. Steel skeletons are used throughout, with a covering of concrete slabs. Flats in the towers will rent for from $59 to $110 per *year* (at 1927 par), and those in the low buildings between $35 and $82. If this can really be done with no more than the usual State subsidy for workers' housing, the French have again quietly stolen a technological lead (in one department at least) from the Americans and the Germans, in much the same way that they did with reinforced concrete construction in the last century.

Meanwhile, the trend in Germany has all been in the opposite direction. Many of the same architects who once would have nothing but skyscrapers are now convinced (and often convincing) that the one-story dwelling presents an almost untried field of real possibility and potential merit. The general principle is that the saving of stairs and of almost all waste space, plus the possibility of using much lighter construction and eliminating cellars and attics, more than makes up for additional land and land-development costs. (At least it does in several different sets of paper calculations.) And in a country like Germany, where buildings are spaced according to height in any case, the added land-cost is not very great. Such houses would, of course, be built in oriented rows, with ends to the street. Architect Häring of Berlin probably has the best ideas on this subject, and three rows were constructed according to his design in the recent Vienna Exhibition Colony. The houses have a very wide frontage and are very narrow from front to back. All the living- and sleeping-rooms are on the front, toward their own garden, with a curtain wall of square-unit slab construction which permits as much glass as desired. In the rear are only bathrooms, kitchens, storerooms, and the like, with all the windows above eye-level, which permits a maximum of privacy for the row just behind. A simple system of roof-ducts provides adequate cross-ventilation whether the rear windows are opened or not. The fact that all dwellings have outside entrances and no stairs makes interior planning much freer than in any apartment- or even two-story house.

Oberbaurat Heinicke of Berlin wrote a whole book to show that merely the greater cubic efficiency of a one-story row (that is, with net dwelling area, construction cost per cubic unit, and open space per dwelling remaining the same, and road widths increasing somewhat in relation to their greater use) made its final unit dwelling cost cheaper than that of a five-story row, on raw land at any price up to seventy-seven cents a square foot. (Which would be an unthinkable figure in any outlying German district.)

Both Mr. Häring's and Mr. Heinicke's ideas, it might be added, are much more interesting than the actual small houses which are being erected in the new semi-rural colonies for the unemployed in Germany.

Dwelling Plans and Dwelling Equipment

A glance at the typical plans from various countries will probably be more enlightening than any detailed description.

Standards of interior dwelling-space and number of rooms per family are somewhat higher in England, taking the accomplishment as a whole, than anywhere on the Continent. The regulation English Government-assisted house has a superficial area of around seven hundred and fifty square feet (often larger), and consists of a living-room, a kitchen with laundry arrangements, three bedrooms, a bathroom, built-in cupboards or closets in most of the rooms, a special closet for coal storage, and a larder. There is often a garden-shed in addition. Heating is still ordinarily provided only by open fireplaces, in the living-rooms and in one or two of the bedrooms. The kitchens are small and eating is done in the living-room. Occasionally there is an extra sitting-room or 'parlour.' In many plans the houses are only about eighteen feet through from front to rear windows, and the living-room and sometimes one of the bedrooms extends all the way through. Both electricity and gas are usually provided, although occasionally only one or the other. In Welwyn particularly, a large number of houses have electric stoves and also small electric heating appliances. (This is possible because of the low rates at which the communally owned plant can supply electricity.) English houses usually have no cellar and no usable attic.

A minimum London County Council flat in a central area, with a living-room, a toilet, one bedroom, and a kitchen and bath combined, has a dwelling-area of at least five hundred and forty-five square feet, flats with more rooms being proportionally larger.

In Germany, the spatial standards of dwellings put up before 1930 were just about as high. Two-story one-family houses often had seven hundred and fifty square feet of superficial area even where there were only two bedrooms. With three bedrooms, they occasionally reached one thousand square feet. In general, the German plans tend to make the living-rooms as large as possible and the bedrooms of a minimum size, sometimes only large enough conveniently to fit a bed and a table and chair (shelves and drawers are often built in). The dwelling-area of flats was formerly about six hundred square feet on the average, including a bath and two bedrooms besides the living-room, small kitchen, and entry. Of recent

TYPICAL DWELLING–PLANS

These are in most cases the actual dwelling-plans used in the typical block layouts ***shown on*** *page* 184. *They are here presented at the same scale for purposes of comparison.*

ROW HOUSES

WELWYN, ENGLAND. This house (like most English houses) has no cellar, no usable attic, and no central heating, but low rates make it possible to use electricity for cooking and individual heating units. It receives an annual State subsidy, and an average worker could probably afford it if regularly employed.

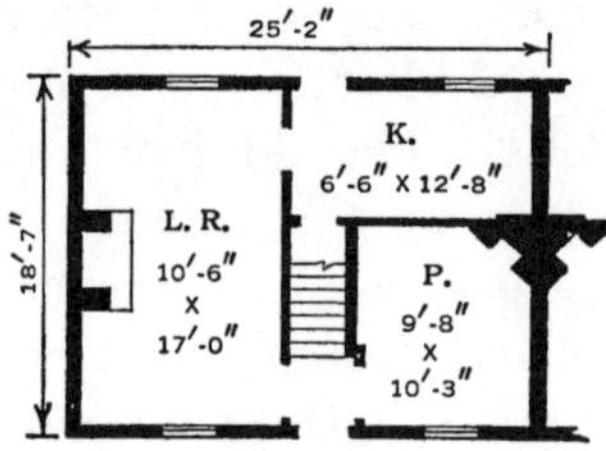

FIRST FLOOR

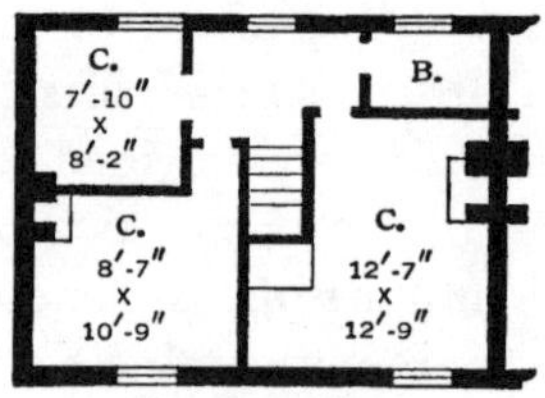

SECOND FLOOR

ZÜRICH: NEUBÜHL. This house is electrically equipped throughout, and is heated from a central community plant. Only middle-class or professional families can afford it. It receives a Municipal loan but no subsidy.

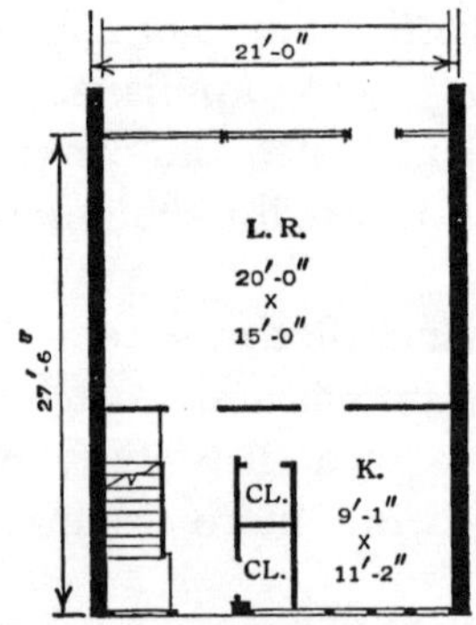

FIRST FLOOR

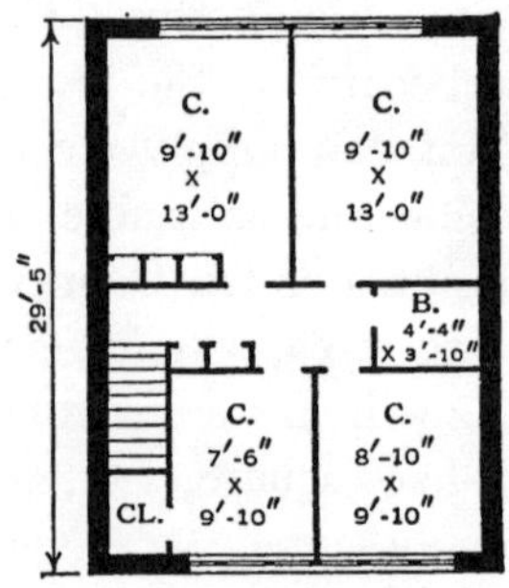

SECOND FLOOR

ROTTERDAM: KIEFHOEK. A Dutch house of absolutely minimum design, for the poorest workers, with large families. No bath within the dwelling. It receives a State and municipal subsidy.

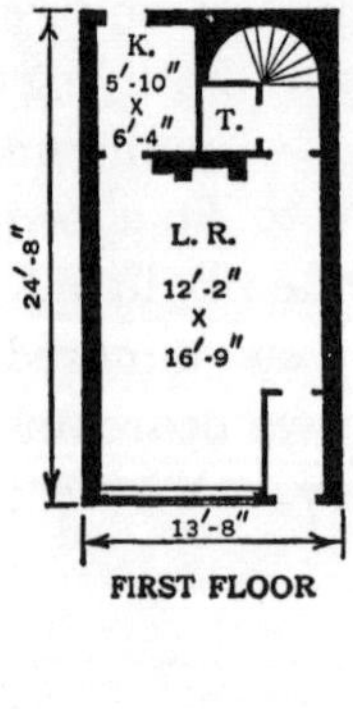

FIRST FLOOR

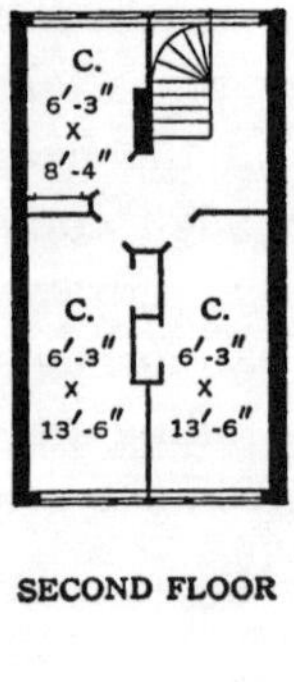

SECOND FLOOR

SCALE
THROUGHOUT =

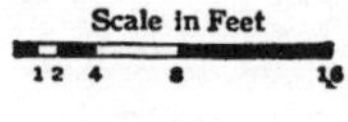

TYPICAL DWELLING–PLANS

APARTMENTS

LONDON: OSSULSTON ESTATE

A minimum London County Council flat, in a slum-reconstruction project. It has an open outside corridor to save stairs, and the bath-tub is in the kitchen. A very large proportion of subsidy is necessary.

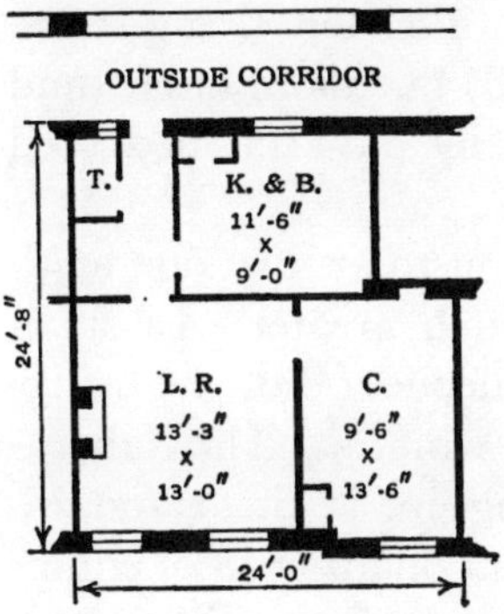

PARIS: PLESSIS–ROBINSON

A state-subsidized apartment in a new satellite suburb, which only a lower middle-class or skilled worker could afford. It has two balconies and a special alcove for clothes-drying.

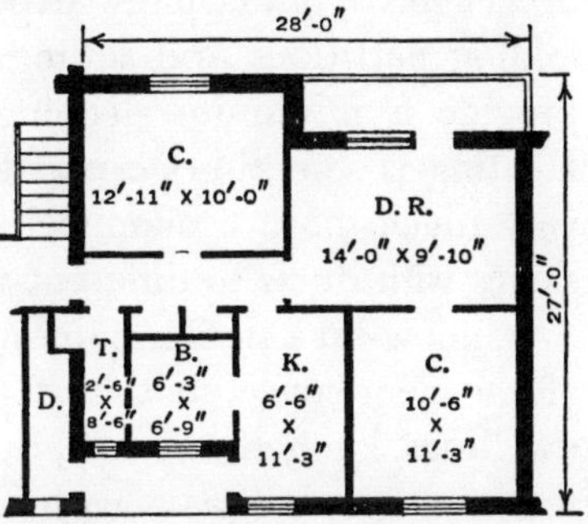

VIENNA: KARL MARXHOF

Typical municipal flat, which lowest paid worker could afford, because rent covers only upkeep. Lavish community equipment to some extent makes up for the lack of a private bath and the small rooms.

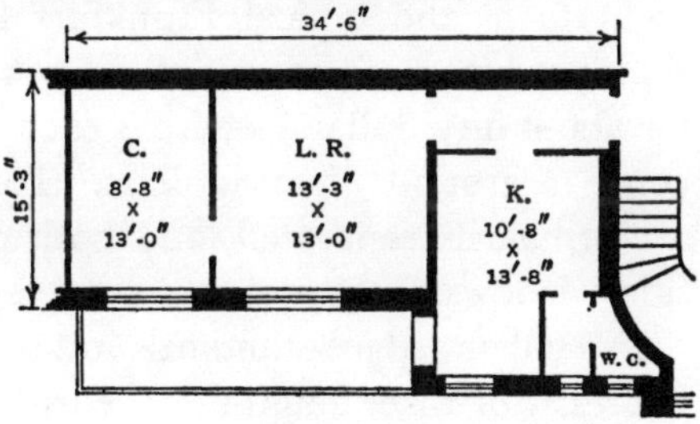

BERLIN: SIEMENSSTADT

Typical state-aided German apartment with bath and balcony. Better-paid workers could probably afford it if regularly employed.

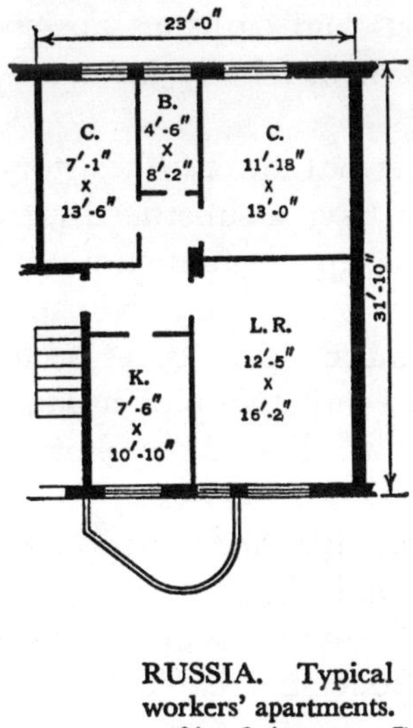

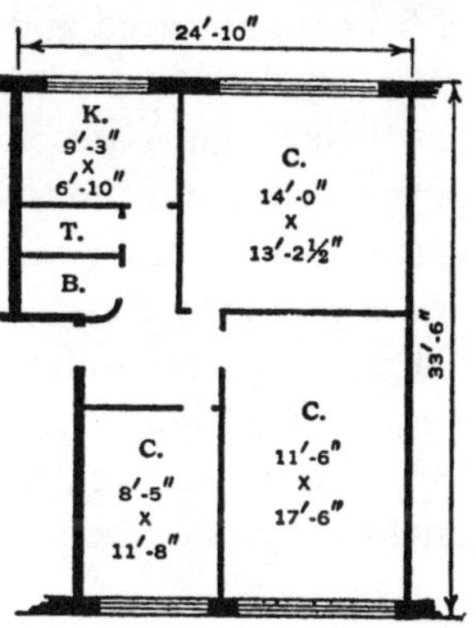

RUSSIA. Typical plan for new workers' apartments. Rent is fixed at 10% of income. Central heating.

years this area has been somewhat reduced, except for families with several children. Half-baths and showers are often provided instead of full tubs. The average flat has a balcony, usually adjoining the living-room: these are often used for eating on in the summer-time. Built-in cupboards and closets are frequent. Sometimes children's bedrooms are fitted with double-decker beds, and many experiments have been made with folding partitions and sliding screens or curtains, in order to provide a minimum sleeping-alcove off of the living-room. Heating is sometimes centrally supplied, but more often (and very much more economically) merely by old-fashioned tiled stoves with ducts to different rooms.

Window-area in Germany must amount to at least one tenth of the floor-space, but it is usually much greater. In small dwellings, kitchens are sometimes only alcoves off of the living-room, although always with an outside window. The 'laboratory' kitchen, not to be used for eating in, is the standard. Much work has been done toward the rationalization of equipment and furniture, although the new designs are still too expensive for ordinary workers in more cases than not. In Frankfurt, however, a complete set of standard kitchen equipment to fit the typical Frankfurt kitchen was designed and mass-produced. The entire *Frankfurter Norm* can be bought for about fifty dollars, whereas each piece bought singly would come to around ninety dollars. Toilets and baths or showers are ordinarily separated, and both of them usually have outside windows.

In Holland space-standards are somewhat lower. Two-story houses with three minimum bedrooms have a superficial area of from six hundred and fifty square feet up. A minimum two-bedroom flat is four hundred and fifty square feet. Kitchens and living-rooms are often combined. Individual baths occur only seldom, and the toilet can have a ventilating pipe in some localities instead of an outside window. Built-in cupboards are always provided.

French space-standards vary considerably. At Plessis-Robinson they are high, with seven hundred and fifty or more square feet of dwelling-area for a flat with a living-room, separate kitchen, two bedrooms, a bath, and front and rear balconies, one of them connected with a 'drying closet.' Recently in the Seine Department housing, an innovation in the shape of a 'water room' has been featured: a room adjoining the kitchen which includes a sink, a hot-water heater, a washtub, and a bath or shower. (The tub and shower are sometimes ingeniously, although I do not know how efficiently or economically, combined.) Balconies are usual for the new French apartments. There is often also a food-storage compartment built into the wall in such a way that there is a circulation of air through it. Another recent trick is a window which both opens outward on a side hinge and has a sliding sash.

Conditions as to space and number of rooms in the other countries are much the same in general, except that both standards tend to be somewhat lower in central flats in the Scandinavian countries, and also in Vienna. A few separate co-operative developments in Switzerland (which are, however, tenanted for the most part by middle-class people) have the highest standards of space and equipment and rooms in Europe. A two-story house in Neubühl, with four bedrooms, has a superficial area of eleven hundred square feet, and a wide partially covered terrace besides.

The size and extent of windows is not directly proportionate to the degree of consciously 'modern' architectural design. Many of the traditional brick cottages in England and Holland have wider windows than some of the dwellings in Frankfurt or Berlin. This is probably due in part to the fact that the climate is somewhat more severe in Germany. However, in many of the developments of distinctly modern design, notably in the work of Messrs. Gropius, Oud, Van der Rohe, and several Swiss architects, almost the entire outer walls are of glass.

New Influences on the Dwelling Plan

The attitude of the more progressive Continental architects toward the interior layout of a minimum dwelling has taken a great many different directions. And it must be admitted that the various points of this new architectural compass — social, hygienic, economic, technological, and æsthetic — have so far rarely if ever been integrated into any one 'solution.' Perhaps one difficulty was an occasional tendency to think that there could be any final or complete solution. Perhaps on the other hand there has been a certain weakness for *expertise:* sun-and-air specialists, standardization specialists, experts in modern spatial æsthetic, and so on.

However, these new influences are real and positive enough, and every one of them must play an essential part in the further development of modern housing technique. The broad psychological element in the new *Gestaltung* of dwelling layout springs more or less from the work and ideas of Le Corbusier and Frank Lloyd Wright. These two architects, working quite independently (although Mr. Wright's early houses precede those of M. Le Corbusier by almost thirty years), reacted against the notion of a dwelling as a series of little box-like rooms. They also discarded the conception of a window as a hole punched into a solid wall. A wall became merely a curtain, a definition of interior space, which could be hung with glass or some light synthetic material or metal, or poured in concrete, instead of being piled up in masonry fashion, by laying one brick on top of another. And the interior space itself became something which was directed rather than confined. Parlors, sitting-rooms, halls, dining-rooms, dens, all of them disappeared as such and were merged into one large living-space, carefully designed so that many different functions could be carried on in it at once.

Space really 'flows' in the best of these houses. And the use of large sheets of glass brings the exterior world — garden, view, sun — into a far closer relation with the interior than can ever be achieved with spotted tiny-paned windows. The lawn became an extension of the living-room. Better light, better ventilation, and a new breadth of freedom were built into these modern houses.

But there is nothing 'minimum,' in cost or any other way, about the luxurious houses of Le Corbusier and Wright. And when their followers endeavored to apply the new principles to low-cost housing, they found their opportunities somewhat limited, even in spite of the greater freedom of design made possible by the simple open planning. Sleeping-places, bathing-

STANDARD PARTS AND FLEXIBLE PLANS

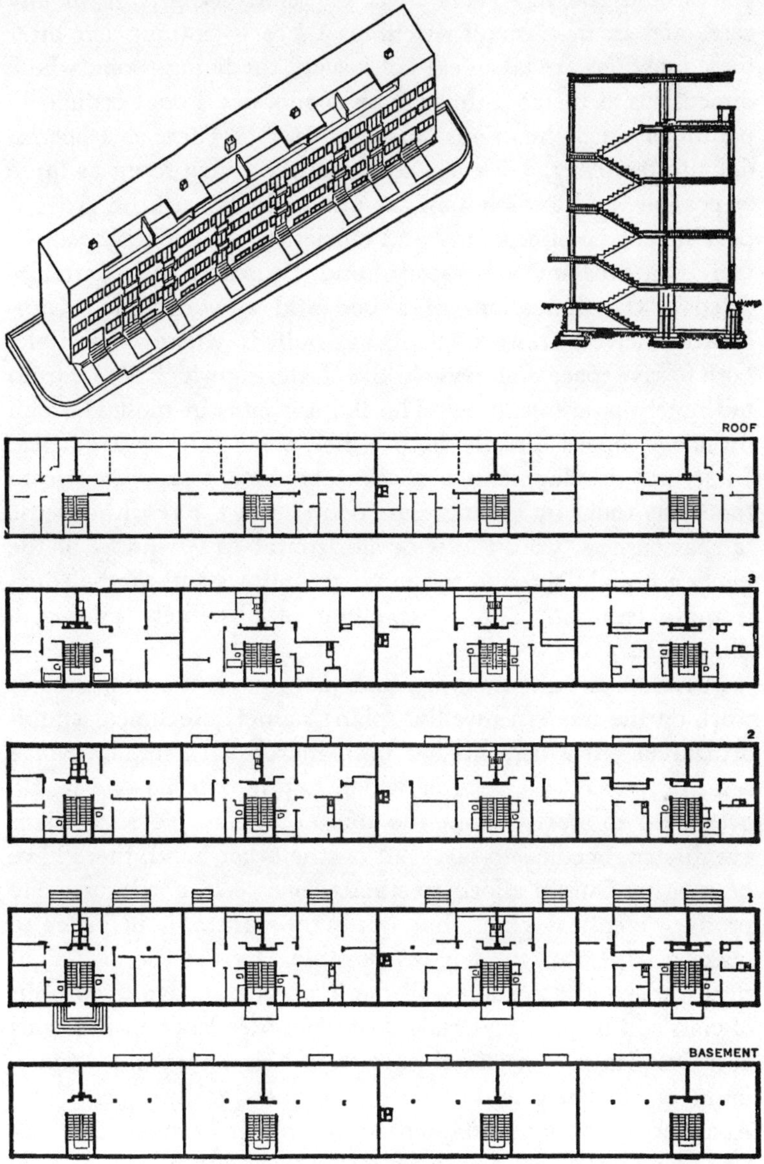

This apartment-house was designed by Miës Van der Rohe and built at Weissenhof, the Stuttgart exhibition housing development, in 1927. With a light steel frame, prefabricated partitions and standardized wall and window-units, there is a maximum of flexibility in interior plans. The basement shows the construction plan throughout, and the three living floors show flats designed for every size family but that statistical one of exactly 4.5 persons. On the top floor there are storage rooms, communal laundries and roof-gardens. (Drawings from *L'Architecture Vivante*, Summer, 1928.)

places, and cooking-places must be relatively private in any case, and in most small dwellings there is nothing left after these functions are taken care of, except the living-room, whose dimensions as dictated thus far by economics do not ordinarily permit of much luxurious 'space-flowing.' There has been a definite tendency, however, to make the living-room as large as possible, and to design all the other rooms with the greatest possible degree of economy and efficiency. A kitchen becomes merely a working laboratory, and bedrooms are carefully fitted to the dimensions of a bed and a work-table. Cupboards, shelves, drawers, closets are built in wherever possible, both to save space and to avoid the cluttering which comes from too much loose furniture. The living-room, in most German dwellings, opens directly onto either a balcony or a garden. In several developments a shallow kitchen is separated from the living-room by folding glass doors, and the resulting sense of spaciousness, from the wide horizontal east window of the kitchen straight through to the west windows and the balcony, is quite remarkable for a dwelling of absolutely minimum dimensions.

But there is quite another, and more concrete, influence at work on the modern dwelling plan: namely, technical standardization. At worst, this has been merely an effort to evolve a set of 'perfect' plans, after which happy date no one would ever need to worry about the matter again. No such plans eventuated, needless to say. But on the other hand, there have been many fruitful efforts to standardize *parts*, not in order to produce identical plans, but quite the contrary, in order to make a large variety of plans possible. By the use of a light steel frame and a curtain wall made up of standard-sized units of glass and opaque materials, Miës Van der Rohe at Stuttgart and Otto Haesler at Kassel have been able to provide a maximum of efficiency and variation in interior dwelling plans. Apartments specially adapted to the needs of small families, large families, families with many small children, and couples without children, are to be found in one building. There are even apartments which can be rearranged with comparatively little trouble and expense. The various national research agencies, particularly the State Society for Housing Research

FUNCTIONAL HOUSING FOR FRICTIONLESS LIVING

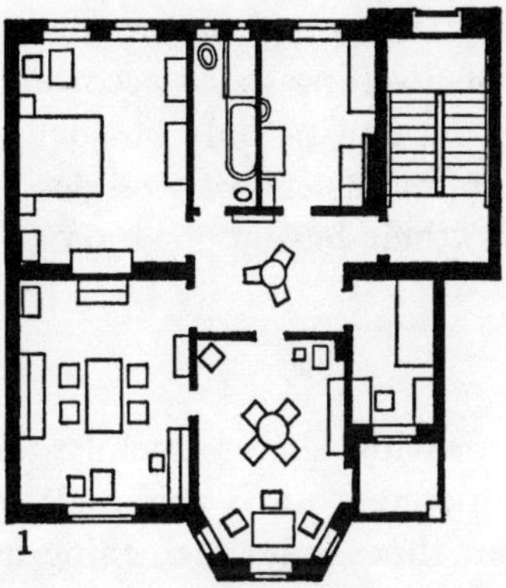

1

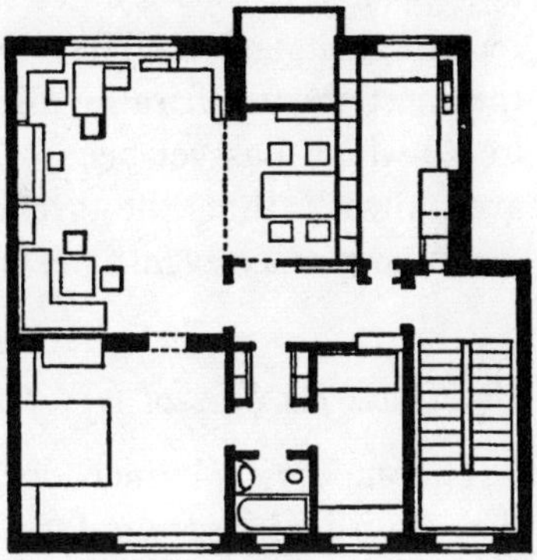

2

A. Bad Example

B.˙ Good Example

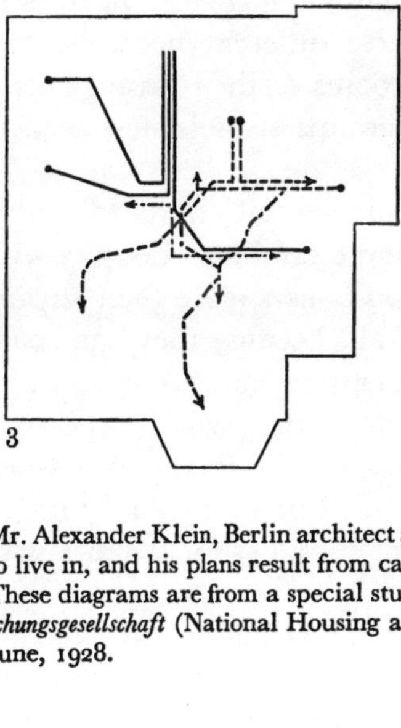

3

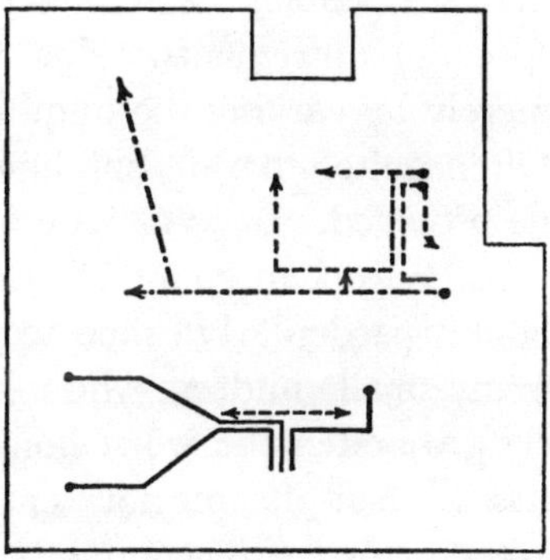

4

Mr. Alexander Klein, Berlin architect and planner, designs dwellings for real people to live in, and his plans result from careful study of people's necessary movements. These diagrams are from a special study which he made for the German *Reichsforschungsgesellschaft* (National Housing and Building Research Society), published in June, 1928.

in Berlin, have been very influential in promoting the efficient standardization of parts.

Finally, one must mention the work of Alexander Klein, whose interest has not been primarily either æsthetic or technological. He has studied the actual movements and daily requirements of families, and his plans probably represent the most thorough rationalization of dwelling-space according to *use* which has yet been achieved. It can be only on such a groundwork that the great developments now possible in technology may eventually be put to their best application.

Provisions for Special Groups

The modern planner does not provide shelter merely for that statistical 'average family' composed (so it is rumored) of exactly 4.5 persons. He realizes that there is no such thing as an average person, and that even a small housing development will include old couples, families with many small children, unmarried people, and families and individuals with all sorts of special requirements. Nor can these different needs be met merely by varying the number of rooms or their arrangement. Often quite separate buildings, or groups of buildings, need to be provided.

All European countries have made special efforts to supply houses particularly suited to very large families. Couples with many small children, who need good houses more than anyone else, are often the worst housed of all, because they can spare less of their income for rent. Sometimes entire communities are designed to accommodate them, with special play-spaces and kindergartens and day nurseries, on the theory that when all contribute to the hubbub, none will be bothered by it. In many countries, there are extra rent subsidies for families with three or more children.

Another group who receive special attention are the old people. There is not enough space in most small dwellings to accommodate grandfathers and grandmothers and great-aunts, who in any case are likely to prefer peace and quiet and privacy to boarding with their children. In England and Holland there are many groups of tiny cottages, often around a small green common, built in connection with larger housing developments. In Germany homes for old people are more likely to be built on the apartment-hotel principle: small apartments, often with private balconies, and with a central dining-hall and social rooms under the same roof. Mart Stam's *Altersheim* in Frankfurt and Haesler's in Kassel are two of the handsomest and most complete modern buildings in Europe, and to describe them one would have to invent some phrase with a different connotation from 'Old Folks' Home.'

Another admirably designed building in Frankfurt is the apartment-house for single women, whose one-room suites, simple and 'minimum' as could be, are as neat and well equipped as anything of the kind this author has ever seen at any price. And they probably rent for about six dollars a month. There is also in Frankfurt a colony for intensive gardeners, complete with green-houses.

And in many German cities, Frankfurt included, there are 'youth hostels' (*Jugendherberge*). These are for those thousands of young people who spend their vacations hiking, bicycling, and paddling across the country, usually with little if any cash. The towns provide hostels, with dormitories, and also with public kitchens in which the hikers can cook their own food if they cannot afford to pay for regular meals. Nor are they used merely by vacation trippers. During the school year, whole classes accompanied by their teachers may spend two or three weeks in the hostel of another city, learning history and geography at first hand. Special cheap railroad fares are provided for such excursions.

Studios for artists and craftsmen are part of the original equipment of housing developments by the Seine Department, and also by the city of Nuremberg. And the proof that London slum-clearance projects re-house the same people lies in the fact that neat brick sheds are attached to one of the best of these new complexes, to accommodate the coster-carts.

Amsterdam and The Hague meet the problem of that special group, the degraded slum-dweller who needs education before he can live freely and happily in a good new house. The system, although orderly to the last degree and apparently successful, would probably not be feasible in a less paternal country. 'Controlled dwellings' are built to serve as temporary accommodation for the people removed from a slum. The houses are just as good as the usual new Dutch house, but they are grouped around a central overseer's building, and are even closed in with a wall and a gate. In The Hague complex, the houses which radiate from the 'control' are for the latest arrivals and have no gardens at all. People graduate from these to the outer circle, where small plots are provided. And from thence, of course, to the ordinary housing colonies. If such a scheme is really necessary, whether one likes it or not, it provides solid food for thought on the nature of the nineteenth-century environment, and the importance of environment in general.

VI. CONSTRUCTION

Tradition and Experiment

The stage of post-war Europe was ready set for a positive advance in the technology and rationalization of house-production. Whole neighborhoods, even whole towns, were to be planned as a unit and constructed all at once. Large-scale methods were to be applied throughout. Costs had to be reduced. Many governments, in order to safeguard their enormous housing investments, set up impressive agencies for the sole purpose of making investigations and experiments in new materials and new methods. Hundreds of architects were convinced that the old building ways were obsolete, and that new forms must be devised to facilitate a modern solution.

In addition, in the years immediately following 1918, there was a grave shortage of all the traditional materials, particularly brick, and also a shortage of building labor skilled in the old trades. It is therefore no surprise that volumes could be filled with descriptions of structural experiments which have been carried out during the past fifteen years.

And yet, in so far as the general run of housing construction is concerned, one could hardly say that any very revolutionary change had been made. During the emergency, England tried any number of methods of using steel and concrete. But for the past ten years almost every new house has been made of ordinary old-fashioned bricks, laid in traditional hollow masonry walls, and has had a roof of either tile or slate. There are plenty of figures to show that these are still the cheapest houses they are able to build.

The public authorities of Amsterdam, around 1924, erected an entire village out of concrete. Forty different systems were tested, and about ten tried out on a large scale — including poured concrete, prefabricated concrete walls or parts of walls, and concrete blocks made on the job. Small houses for thousands of families, and also schools, shops, public buildings, and clubs, were put up. An enthusiastic report was published, to describe the economies thus effected. And yet all the recent housing in Amsterdam has been built of brick, by the usual and traditional methods.

Probably the most complete experiment was made in Frankfurt. There a government institute with the aid of the University conducted an exhaustive research into the possibilities of concrete. At length the local authorities decided to use large precast concrete units, measuring approximately 10 feet by 3.5 feet by 6.5 inches. The aggregate was slightly vulcanized lava — or pumice stone — found in the neighboring Rhine Valley, a very porous light rock with strong insulating qualities. Two factories were set up to make these units. A special small derrick was designed and manufactured to set the plates in place on the job. Houses were designed on the basis of these units, and several thousands of them were soon constructed. There were many obvious advantages. Much of the production was done in the factories, thus reducing the weather gamble. And eighteen men could put up the shell of a two-story house, including cellar and floors, in a day and a half, or two hundred and thirty hours of labor all together. The insulation, after the outside was stuccoed, was one hundred per cent better than in a brick house. It was officially estimated that the cost per unit of wall area was about ten per cent less by the new concrete method than by the old brick one. And yet, again, of recent years most of the new dwellings have been made of brick.

Poured concrete has been tried on a large scale in many places in Germany. At Dessau, Mr. Gropius' Törten development has concrete party walls and floors, the front and back walls being filled in with brick or hollow tile. Many new covering materials were used over wood or steel frames by the different architects of Weissenhof, the exhibition housing-development built at Stuttgart in 1927. And the general use of light steel frames for apartment-buildings, occasionally for small houses as well, made considerable headway in Germany up to 1932. Haesler's Rothenberg development at Kassel is probably one of the most interesting new housing-constructions in Europe, structurally as well as in exterior and interior plan.

But today in Germany they are no longer advancing the use of steel or concrete or new insulating materials or prefabricated parts.

At the Stockholm Exhibition of 1930, there were dozens of full-size houses and apartments, all of experimental design and construction. A hundred different new materials were exhibited and tried out. But the only kind of building which has so far really been rationalized in general practice in Scandinavia is wood construction for small suburban or country cottages.

In France a more or less traditional use of concrete (since the eighties, that is) has been considerably extended and developed in connection with post-war housing. And this, not only by M. Le Corbusier, but by the far more conservative Housing Office of the Department of the Seine. The latter makes a wide use of slag concrete, which is cast on the site into standardized forms suitable for walls, floors, and partitions. The slag comes from near-by plants, and the cost of transportation of materials, excessive in France since the war, is thereby greatly reduced. The new development at Drancy, with steel framing throughout and several sixteen-story apartments, has been briefly described in another section.

Rationalization of Method

By and large, no revolutionary accomplishment in structural technology has yet been evidenced. But in every country, and above all in Germany, there has been considerable real advance in economy and efficiency of method. Systematic and detailed time and production charts, of the type used in the erection of American skyscrapers, have been widely adopted. Large-scale construction has brought a vast increase in building machinery. Narrow-gauge tracks for hauling materials are used even in the primitive, semi-rural, new unemployed colonies in Germany. They are also extensively used in England, in order to save the wear and tear of trucking on light roads.

Work-processes and parts have both been increasingly standardized. In Germany the State Bureau for Housing and Building Research (*Reichsforschungsgesellschaft*) published innumerable studies, and itself supervised the construction of several large experimental developments. Doors, windows, hardware, fixtures, etc., have all been more or less standardized with official guidance. A Berlin official estimated that rationalization of method had alone cut housing construction cost by fifteen per cent.

The Present Impasse

Although the early results of technological experiment were not overwhelming, they were definitely full of promise. The quality of building, of insulation, of fireproofing, of mass-production design, was steadily growing better. Directive foresight was becoming more efficient, and the cost in physical labor was decreasing. Great possibilities were in the air, almost in the hand — until about 1931. From that time onward (particularly in Germany, the very place where the most fruitful experiments had been carried out) there was no more enthusiasm for 'rationalization.' Instead of taking the next step ahead, building technique either stood still or took several steps backward. Instead of better steel skeletons, lighter and better insulated walls, more efficient plumbing and heating, there were tiny wooden cottages without any conveniences at all, put up laboriously by the most antiquated methods. The German unemployed colonies are, it is true, the most extreme example of this tendency, but the same general direction may be remarked almost everywhere.

Why was it? There is just one answer. Human labor became so cheap, so nearly valueless, that it was no longer 'economic' to 'save' it by mechanical or scientific means, even if the product could thereby be improved. An army of men could be bought more cheaply than a few hours of electric power. By 1932, the average weekly income of a building-trade worker in Germany was just about *one quarter* of what it was in 1928, and even in the latter year it was only thirteen dollars per week. Moreover, an idle machine consumes no fuel, and one prevented from being built does not even bear a financial charge. But the *mores* allow that men must have a miserable minimum of food and money even when they are forced to be totally unproductive. Therefore, from 1931 on, such housing as was done in most countries — again above all in Germany — had as its primary aim unemployment relief and not good housing.

These facts are nothing which can be dismissed as merely a temporary setback due to a brief period of emergency. There is every reason to believe (and again Germany is only the most extreme example so far) that capitalism, in order to save itself at all, must resort to ever more desperate and compulsory measures to turn back the hands of the clock of science and technology. The question is likely to become only clearer as time goes on. Which do we prefer (even apart from broader matters): capitalism or the free use of our brains and our physical resources to make a better world to live in?

VII. ARCHITECTURE

THE canon of beauty requires expression of the generic. The 'novelty' due to the demands of conspicuous waste traverses this canon of beauty, in that it results in making the physiognomy of our objects of taste a congeries of idiosyncrasies. . . .

This process of selective adaptation of designs to the end of conspicuous waste, and the substitution of pecuniary beauty for æsthetic beauty, has been especially effective in the development of architecture. It would be extremely difficult to find a modern civilized residence or public building which can claim anything better than relative inoffensiveness in the eyes of anyone who will dissociate the elements of beauty from those of honorific waste. The endless variety of fronts presented by the better class of tenements and apartment-houses in our cities is an endless variety of architectural distress and of suggestions of expensive discomfort. Considered as objects of beauty, the dead walls of the sides and back of these structures, left untouched by the hands of the artist, are commonly the best feature of the building. . . .

The underlying norms of taste are of very ancient growth, probably far antedating the advent of the pecuniary institutions that are here under discussion. Consequently, by force of the past selective adaptation of men's habits of thought, it happens that the requirements of beauty, simply, are for the most part best satisfied by inexpensive contrivances and structures which in a straightforward manner suggest both the office which they are to perform and the method of serving their end.

— Thorstein Veblen: THE THEORY OF THE LEISURE CLASS.

In those crabbed and somewhat academic paragraphs, published in 1899, Veblen stated the philosophy of modern architecture, in its relation to the architecture of the nineteenth century, as well as it has ever been stated. And one of the most hopeful facts about both modern housing and modern architecture is that they are not two separate subjects. I have had to touch on architecture in every chapter on housing; conversely, it would be quite impossible to write a book about modern 'form' without dealing with the social, biological, and technical realities which underlie the housing movement.

Architecture is the Social Art

Every age of architecture is the direct expression of a social pattern: that of the nineteenth century equally with that of the thirteenth. And the degree to which an age achieves an integral 'style' in the matter of its buildings and their arrangement is very likely to be relative to the degree of order and integration in the society itself.

A great age of architecture cannot exist without the common acceptance, conscious or unconscious, willful or instinctive, of a basic norm of design. There must be common beliefs and common purposes in a large number of contemporary people. For architecture, first and last, is the social art, the expression of those forces which keep people together and not of those which separate and individualize. Buildings, and above all urban buildings, are not a medium for lyric, personal expression.

At best individualist buildings are prophetic experiments. At worst they are a particularly obnoxious form of exhibitionist advertising. And at dull middle they are merely the empty 'taste' of refined eclecticism.

Apparently, then, if we would have style, if we want good cities, we must give up something of individual freedom: the right of the artist to invent expression in public stone or steel for his private fantasies, inhibitions, personality; the right of the owner to exercise his instinct for competition and self-assertion as if his building existed all alone, battling with other buildings for the chance to survive.

But actually, how much of such 'freedom' does anyone really possess? What building in this urban age can be *seen* by itself, let alone divorced from its dependence on the underlying system of utilities, construction methods, materials, interrelating uses? And what artist has ever really been able to achieve a satisfactory personal fantasy with the refractory elements of a building — rooms, roof, windows, plumbing, available materials, labor, finance — however he may have distorted them from their most efficient forms?

Rampant individualism in architecture creates, not a sum of individual expressions which one may accept or discard according to one's own individual taste, but a single amorphous chaos. A single building is not a painting hung in a gallery — it is rather an arm or a leg or a spinal column of a larger organism which, if it is healthy, we may call architecture. If buildings do not express an integrated society (or at least a desire for such a society) they merely state the fact that society is discordant — and little more.

Monument and Vernacular

This was not, needless to say, the attitude toward buildings and cities entertained in the past century. The 'history of architecture' was the history of separate public monuments, with occasional apologetic digressions to include the larger and richer and more isolated private houses. Apparently few people, least of all the more successful architects, ever paid any attention or indeed even looked at the ordinary run of buildings. 'Art' implied 'luxury,' something unnecessary, an extravagance to be applied afterwards if the situation and the builder's pocket-book warranted the extra trouble. (In much the same way, science had to be 'pure'; that is, unrelated to direct human needs, in order to be valid or important.) From this point of view very little modern housing is architecture at all. But in the other sense, that of creating ordinary human environment, the whole movement belongs to architecture.

An age of building cannot be judged by its biggest and most expensive monuments alone. For the monuments have no real existence, and cannot even be explained, apart from the surrounding streets and houses, shops and gardens and factories. The spires and towers and gables of a mediæval town make one indivisible outline. The Renaissance palace is meaningless without the park and the avenue. The gas-tank, the smokestack, the tenement, and the ambiguous neo-Grecque façade make just as significant an ensemble. The monument may symbolize or intensify the whole, but reality lies in the vernacular. The side-streets of Lübeck or Florence, built by nobody knows whom, are just as important as an indication of the quality of the civilization which once reigned there, as the Marienkirche or the Cathedral.

And it has been the opportunity, and often the conscious purpose, of modern housing in Europe to establish a new vernacular to replace the chaotic and ugly old one. It was a movement toward a new kind of order in human environment. The fact that it has proceeded by instinct rather than by volition, from the small things up rather than from the big things down, has been the mark both of its vitality and its precariousness. For, at least in the countries immediately under discussion, there was no change in the larger framework of society corresponding in any degree to the revolutionary change in form and method of house-production. The planners and architects could build houses and neighborhoods which abolished the distinction between cheap and expensive, between my better and your worse. They could premise leisure and sun and air, and forms suited to materials and techniques and functions. And the people who lived in the new housing could find all this exactly to their taste. But, to provide only one partial example of the contradiction, what the architect was planning for as fruitful leisure in his world within a world descended finally in the shape of miserable unemployment. From another aspect, while the architect and the engineer were setting up methods and designing forms to accommodate great technological advances, governments were fast being pushed into the position of combating any further progress in machine production. But it would be difficult to dispose of several million houses as mere visionary Utopianism. There they are: perhaps the new vernacular is right and the monuments wrong! On the other hand, the fact that the movement was not imposed from above as a conscious policy, and did not follow in the wake of a vast political revolution, meant that there was no danger of a too sudden or dictatorial crystallization of this new vernacular. There was ample room for experiment and, since the break with the nineteenth century was so complete, there was great need for such experiment. The national housing policies provided the means and the opportunity, usually they also provided certain minimum standards, but they did not often provide any predigested picture of what the real nature of the new housing vernacular might be.

There is no need for detailed description of the typical forms and architectural treatment practiced in various sections of Europe since the war: they are illustrated at the back of this book. Here merely the general distinctions in point of view, which resulted in great differences of form, may be suggested.

Reworking an Old Tradition

With the exception of some of the early work in France and Belgium, there is no new housing in Europe which bears even a superficial resemblance to the general run of urban construction in the nineteenth century. There are few gimcracks, no false fronts, no cast-iron entablatures, very little suburban fancy business. Materials are ordinarily used with a degree of honesty, and ornament is reduced to a degree of simplicity.

But in many countries the new houses are not 'modern' in the sense of being innovations in form or material. Throughout England, and very widely in Holland and Scandinavia, the old cottage vernacular, lost since a hundred years ago except in remote rural regions, was revived and simplified for its new purpose. And in Holland and Denmark particularly, whether one personally happens to prefer the consciously modern work or not, one must admit that the traditionalists have been extraordinarily successful. At best, with their fine brick craftsmanship, their lack of all spurious ornament, and their clean, mpersonal lines, they are far more 'functional' and really modern than much of the surface modernism in France and Austria. In The Hague, and in some of the Danish apartment-blocks, this process of simplification has proceeded even farther. Large window-areas (traditional in Holland in any case) with large panes of glass, and a disdain for 'breaking up' good horizontal lines in the interests of quaintness or prettiness, characterize the best work. One great reason for the Dutch success is the fact that the ideal is a close and dignified urban neighborhood, of much the same general character as the compact village in which the cottage type originated. Streets as well as houses are often of brick, and the planting is formal rather than picturesque.

The English cottages, on the other hand, in their looser and more scattered arrangement (although representing a higher standard of space per family), are not nearly as effective. The houses themselves are more 'individualized,' with varying gables and broken roof-lines, and, such is the irony of these matters, the result is far more monotonous. A short straight street with well-designed and undifferentiated row houses is an architectural unit, but the moment you try to mass-produce 'individual' houses, no matter how you vary the units, there is something repetitious and fake about the result. This criticism does not wholly apply, however, to the best English work — particularly to certain sections of Welwyn, Nottingham, Winchester, and several other towns. It is when one comes to the very large developments, particularly that of the London Council at Becontree, that one is most conscious that the two-story brick cottage of traditional design is not an adequate all-purpose form for modern housing. There will be twenty-five thousand houses in Becontree, and that is just too great a strain on the capacity for informal charm of a semi-rural cottage.

Another tradition has been revived, however, in some of the work in Sweden and Norway and also in Germany and Austria: a much simplified version of what may be called late Baroque, although its only concession to the classic, ornamental or otherwise, is little more than an emphasis on symmetry.

The Romantic Moderns

There was a strong tendency among the various groups of early experimenters, from Art Nouveau to Expressionism, to treat a building as if it were a plastic mass, to be modeled like a piece of sculpture. The possibilities offered by concrete construction tempted them to fantasy and *tours de force* rather than rationalization or simplification of the building process. Fortunately, however, there was not a great deal of leeway for the plastic imagination in the design of low-cost housing. Only in Holland, where not concrete but less fluent brick was used, and where the movement was tempered by other influences, did the exuberant romantics leave any noteworthy mark on the new housing. The Arts and Crafts Movement, derived from Morris, but carried into much fresher fields by the Dutchmen Cuypers and Berlage, prepared the way. And Frank Lloyd Wright, a romantic through and through, but with a profound sense of the nature and use of materials and of the fact that a house is a house and not a solid piece of clay, had a very wide influence in Holland from about 1910 onward. The result was the Amsterdam School, whose many blocks of workers' houses and other buildings have a certain positive charm and occasionally a quality even better than that, in spite of the curved and waving bricks. There is a kind of good-natured and exaggerated humor about the work of De Klerk, as authentically Dutch as a Brouwer, which is not to be found in the neurotic meanderings of Art Nouveau. But their leader Berlage, like the initiator of Art Nouveau, Van de Velde, soon progressed to better things, and left the more extreme romantics well behind them.

Some of the Viennese apartments can also be put in the romantic category, largely because their modernism seems occasionally to have been applied afterward, to create a monumental effect, instead of being derived from any fundamentally fresh attitude toward the building itself. The assured light touch of the Josef Hoffmann School can still occasionally be discerned, even if the straightforward clarity of that other early Viennese modernist, Adolph Loos, is usually absent.

'Functionalism': A Positive Statement

In spite of their not infrequent dogmatism, the highly diverse group of architects who may be thus lumped together produced most of what is positive and fruitful, either actually or potentially, in the field of contemporary architecture. In the first place, they not merely accept the contemporary world and the conditions of modern building and living, but they *affirm* them. If we are to use the machine, if we are to have planned houses and cities, designed primarily for use and not for conspicuous waste, if we are to take advantage of new materials, then we must first get rid of all our preconceptions as to what a building *should* look like: for the new conditions (and, more subtly, our own turn of mind which resulted in the machines and the desire to 'plan') determine entirely new forms. No one would any longer endeavor to make an automobile look like a gilded royal coach, nor a steamship like a schooner: it is just as great an anachronism to attempt to make a modern house imitate a Tudor cottage or a Renaissance pavilion.

If we use the machine to simulate a handicraft product, all we get is a vulgar travesty. And it is because we did that for so long that the 'machine' fell into disrepute as a tool in the making of environment. But the machine can create its own kind of æsthetic and formal satisfaction. Economy of means is the very soul of art, and the machine, used on its own terms, can dramatize that economy as can no other tool. And indeed, as Mumford has said, that is just what the functionalists have done with regard to the whole matter of modern housing: they have made a positive virtue out of the necessity for economy.

But this is no petty, penny-scraping economy practiced by the modern architects, nor is the result a rigid and mechanical standardization. For the 'functions' which they recognize and plan for are far more complex than the mere matter of shelter. All those items of a 'minimum housing standard' which we sketched out in a preceding chapter, and in addition all the special needs of special groups, are the essential materials of their designs. And it is because they are *all* essential, and require land-planning and administrative control and non-speculative enterprise quite as much — even more — than they need the machine itself, that the 'prefabricated house,' now causing a certain amount of excitement in America, is no solution. For the individual house is not the right unit: it is too large and complex for a unit of standardization and it is too small and incomplete for a unit of planning. A good modern house cannot be designed, planned, built, or judged apart from its natural environment and also its neighborhood. There is no use in building wide windows if the only outlook is a back alley or someone else's wide window. There is no use in creating an impersonal idiom, suited to the construction and design of a large group, if the house will have to compete, as merely one more 'Style,' with a street full of Tudor and Italian villas.

In an age of architectural experiment like the past ten years, however, one must admit that it is *not* always possible so to judge a new building. And yet, whether it is complete or incomplete, consciously revolutionary or merely accidental, one cannot help looking at it from the point of view of the possibilities it presents for a real vernacular, for a civilized 'norm' of building. This fact often makes a building which happens to be good or better than average in *itself* not nearly as interesting or important as some other building, part of which may be downright bad. This is why the Empire State Building and Radio City, although both are handled with rather better 'taste' than the average skyscraper, are not half as important, in the development of modern architecture, as the Starrett Lehigh Building, although the latter has one of the worst 'architected' façades of recent years. For the latter, with its cantilevered floors and solid bank of windows, not to mention its ingenious facilities for the loading and distribution of goods, presents what is essentially a new architectural idiom and a new technical possibility.

There were many signs of the new movement well before the war. Architects were beginning to realize that the engineers had got ahead of them, and that some of the factories and bridges and grain elevators had more integral beauty than almost anything else built in the nineteenth century. Architecture, instead of being the 'master' art, had declined to the rank of pastry-cook luxury. At the Cologne Exhibition of 1914, several of the younger German architects had already pretty well clarified their point of view. The De Stijl group in Holland, including Van Doesburg and Oud, went somewhat farther in the same direction, with perhaps more direct influence from the cubist painters. But it was not until Le Corbusier's house was built for the *Esprit Nouveau* group at the Paris Exposition of 1925 that the movement really got under way.

Le Corbusier himself, although he coined the phrase, 'The house is a machine for living in,' has remained one of the more romantic and 'æsthetic' functionalists. In Germany, and recently in almost every other country on the Continent, there has been a whole school of architects devoted to *Die Neue Sachlichkeit* ('the new objectivity,' or 'the new realism'). And as many of these men have had the opportunity to apply their ideas to large-scale housing projects, their influence has been very great. The Bauhaus School, established in Dessau by Gropius, and lately the International Housing Congress with headquarters in Frankfurt and Zürich, have provided centers of education and information. At their most dogmatic, these architects believe only in 'pure engineering,' in using the best technical means available to provide suitable facilities for all the various human functions. A satisfactory architecture would result merely from technical forthrightness and scientific, orderly planning. And as a matter of fact, the general acceptance of orientation as a planning factor, and the development of the German *Zeilenbau* super-block, may be credited to the work of the *sachlich* architects.

But their best work is more than good engineering, nevertheless. And can there be, after all, any such thing as 'pure engineering' in architecture? There is always a choice, no matter how rigid the economies or how close the demands of use. There are a hundred ways to turn a balcony, many of them equally good structurally and functionally. But some are satisfactory to the eye and some are not. If we do not apply any surface ornament to a modern building, it is not because of any theological adherence to pure engineering, but because we happen *directly* to enjoy the more dynamic idiom of intersecting planes and smooth impersonal surfaces. Obviously such an idiom is based on structural technique, and must never deny either the construction or the use, but there is an art to it nevertheless.

Professor Schumacher, long the head of all the housing and city-planning in Hamburg, wrote:

'If today we conform to the exciting vibrations which run through our time, perceive dynamic suspense in architecture to be more in harmony with ourselves than static, soothing qualities; if we are influenced accordingly to express ourselves more easily in counterplay of rectilinear masses; if we are inclined to emphasize whatever the subjugation of statics brings out — then there flows through the medium of creation into architecture something which has not evolved from function and construction, but from the spiritual rhythms of the creator.'

Perhaps there have always been two essentially different kinds of attitude toward a building. To one group of people a house is a necessary evil, which should be designed in so far as possible to melt into its background. Broken lines and surfaces, 'textures,' the avoidance of everything rectilinear, are the means employed. But the other group likes a house *as such*, and makes it bold and positive, a statement of house-ness. The demarcation between the man-made world and the world of nature is sharply drawn. And if the more urbane and orderly modern housing belongs to the latter class, so do the white-painted New England villages.

Internationalism versus 'Heimatarchitektur': the Politics of Style

The modern architects have been working on a set of first principles — human requirements, materials, techniques — which traverse national boundaries. The results would, of course, vary to a considerable degree due to local conditions and special needs, but the basis was as international as that of thirteenth-century church architecture.

From the beginning, particularly in Germany, there were tremendous battles between the more radical architects and the old school, battles over minute points which yet appeared to implicate the entire social and political world. This in spite of the fact that there has been very little strictly traditional architecture in Germany since the war; for the work of such conservatives as Schmitthenner, Tessenow, and Bestelmeyer would be called 'modern' in America or England. But the battle was a real one, even though it seemed for a time to rage over little more than the matter of flat roofs versus peaked ones, and even though there is little visible difference other than the roofs between the neat white rows of 'conservative' Nuremberg and the neat white rows of 'radical' Frankfurt.

Finally the whole argument was carried over into politics. The National Socialists early fulminated against the 'internationalism,' the 'betrayal of Teutonic culture,' the *Kulturbolschewismus* of the modern architects. No decent German, they said, would live under a flat roof. And so the moderns are now entirely out of favor (if not out of the country), and what a Swiss critic calls the *Fingerspitzengefühl* architects are designing the few houses now being built.

But the politics of architecture are not quite so simple as this might make them appear. For, having already greatly influenced the new work in Scandinavia and France and Switzerland, the German functionalists' ideas are now beginning to make themselves felt even in Italy, with the direct encouragement of Mussolini.

And, on the other hand, this *Kulturbolschewismus* has not been faring so well, on the whole, in Russia. Many German architects have worked in the Soviet Union (particularly Ernst May, responsible for the major part of the work at Frankfurt, and Hannes Meyer, one of the left-wing engineering architects), but officially, there is considerable disapproval of what they call 'corbusierism.' In part this is an entirely healthy reaction against the dogmas of those German theorists who tended to reduce modern housing technique to a single 'perfect' solution, applicable in all cases. Mechanical diagrams are a mere travesty of real 'functionalism,' and it is all to the good if the Russians are choosing to make their own experiments and their own mistakes. But if Rome and Napoleon (as threatened) are to provide the only approved models for Soviet workers' cities, that will be quite a different matter, and one which will supply curious food for thought among the radicals, architects and otherwise, in other countries. At present, however, American architects who have worked in Russia report that the classicists have little influence in practice, and that all signs point toward great future achievements in modern planning and modern architecture. Indeed, there seems on the whole to be more leeway for free architectural experiment in Russia today than in any other country.

VIII. ECONOMICS AND ECONOMIES

IT WOULD be quite fruitless, even if it were possible, to make any exhaustive or detailed cost analysis in a survey like the present one. Conditions and methods of accounting vary from one country to another, and the abnormal monetary situation since the war makes it impossible in many cases to compare figures from one year to the next even in the same locality. Moreover, the transition of housing from a speculative business, operated solely for a maximum of immediate private profit, to a long-time public investment undertaking, recognized as of essential public utility and planned and controlled as such — all of this within thoroughly capitalist States — has naturally been accompanied by many complications and contradictions.

The most obvious *impasse* is the fact that, with the new planning method set up on terms of efficient production, maintenance, and use, and with minimum standards of quality decided upon from the point of view of public health, convenience, and long-time *real* economy, it is invariably found that the lower-income groups cannot pay an 'economic' rent for such a dwelling even when State funds are supplied at cost. This is an axiom of the capitalist world, true in 1929 and doubly true in 1934 with an enormous section of the population without any income at all. It is true of fairly stable countries with low interest rates, like Holland and Switzerland. It is true of countries with relatively high wage-levels, like Switzerland and the United States and Sweden. It is true of Germany, where the cost of raw land for housing has been reduced to an almost negligible quantity. And it would still be true even if technological progress suddenly halved the cost of producing the structural shell. For the first effect of factory fabrication could hardly be anything but increased unemployment; and the long effect under present conditions would almost certainly be a general lowering of wages. Every nation, then, has had but a single choice, if it intended to make any decent dwellings available to the average working-class family: raise real wages or grant some sort of outright subsidy to cover the spread. The latter was chosen, not by any means because it was the better way, but because it appeared to be the only feasible one at the moment. Forms of subsidy employed are described elsewhere. Not all subsidies, however, are wage-subsidies. In slum-clearance schemes, such as those in Holland and England and the various projects now pending in America, the enormous gap between an 'economic' rent and the rent which people can pay is almost entirely due to the exorbitant cost of the land. Most of the subsidy in such cases, therefore, is a direct grant in aid of the owners of slum property and should be honestly chalked up as such, and not as a cost of 'modern housing.'

There is another and subtler form of subsidy which should not be considered as primarily a *housing* cost. In Vienna, and to a certain extent in many other countries, rent-levels in public housing were kept very low not in order to raise real wages, but in order to make it possible for export industries to pay lower money wages than they could otherwise have done. In such cases the subsidy is largely a grant in aid of industry, and not of workers. Dr. Meyer Schapiro finds this policy nothing more nor less than governmental 'company housing' and, on economic grounds at least, there is considerable truth in the analogy.

In any case subsidies are expedients, resorted to only because of the inefficacy of our distributive systems. There are, however, two essential features of the economy of modern housing, as contrasted with a typical nineteenth-century or post-war American set-up, about which something more definite can be indicated. Without *cheap land* and *cheap money*, the entire planning method and the new housing standards are quite impossible of achievement. And vice versa, the possibility of reducing the cost of land and money rests on the new method. Primarily, it is a matter of taking the whole housing operation out of the speculative market, and thereby not only improving the long-time quality of the product, but puncturing inflated speculation land-prices and the prohibitive costs of speculative financial methods. For the unit cost of developed land is the most important single factor of original cost in determining the amenity of a housing project. And the cost of money is the most substantial item among the variables which determine the rental scale.

Briefly, one may show what the new approach has meant to post-war housing economy in Europe by two items. In America the cost of developed land ordinarily comes to at least twenty-five per cent of the total cost. In Europe, with far greater amenity and, in the case of apartments, much less density, site costs per dwelling unit are almost invariably under fifteen per cent of the whole and in England and Germany are usually nearer ten per cent. Moreover, various hidden factors widen this breach. High density in America often means expensive building types without any proportionate increase in interior amenity. And in most European countries the entire cost of pavement and sewers is included in the original figure, instead of being partly levied later in the form of taxes.

The difference between post-war European and post-war American methods of finance may be stated even more briefly. Presuming the same total initial cost per dwelling unit, the 'economic' rent (that is, before any subsidies are subtracted) throughout most of Europe would be just about *half* what it would be in an average speculative set-up in America. That is, a dwelling which cost four thousand dollars, let us say, to build, would have to rent for at least fifty dollars a month in ordinary practice in America merely to repay its obligations and provide for upkeep, while in Europe the same unit cost would usually be covered by a twenty-five- to thirty-dollar rent. In the next pages, figures to this effect will be presented in more detail.

Why Land Costs are Low

Outside of the very important economies in street and utility layout, which have been mentioned in other sections, the planned large-scale community housing method obviously makes it possible to reduce the cost of raw land itself. Land can be taken straight from agricultural use and devoted immediately to its fullest use as residential development, eliminating all the wasteful intervening operations of subdivision of lots, sale and resale, mounting taxes for unused services, and inflated hopes of high density.

But how can the new method actually be established in place of the old wasteful one? How can the speculative interim be cut out of the housing operation?

Obviously, the simplest way is the revolutionary one: forcible public confiscation of all private property and thus the total elimination of the 'real-estate interest.' But the experience of Europe shows that many of the worst features of land speculation can be prevented by less direct means and without confiscation. Two things are absolutely essential. Municipal governments must be imbued with intelligent, far-seeing, and really 'enlightened' self-interest, and they must have the power to regulate location and standards of new construction and to purchase large areas of land as they see fit.

The experience of the city of Berlin, while in no way exceptional, provides one of the most interesting examples of the place of a strong municipal land policy in the economy of modern housing. Straight up to 1914, land-speculation around Berlin was more extreme than in any other large continental city, and almost as bad as in an American boom town. A survey made just before the war showed that in eight surrounding districts more or less 'ripe' for small dwellings, the average cost of developed land ranged from $1.80 to $3.25 per square foot: a price which made the erection of tall, congested, 'rent-barracks' absolutely unavoidable. But the State and city-aided housing developments which have been constructed since 1926, all of them very open and spacious, figure site costs at from $.25 to $.30 a square foot! Nine tenths of the potential speculative 'value' was wiped out, and thus good housing and modern planning were made possible. Much the same contrast is true of all the other German cities. And it was accomplished without direct confiscation. How?

Berlin had been preparing, gradually, for a generation, for a frontal attack on the problem of inflated land-prices. The city had bought large areas of land surrounding the town, for sewage farms, for municipal forests, for recreation, and for potential housing-sites. Preparations were under way for enforcing a much more liberal standard of amenity and space in new housing, and for a new zoning plan. Then came the opportunity. There was no building during the war, and almost none, either private or public, until after the inflation. Land-prices had therefore taken a tremendous drop. And, in effect, what the municipal government did was to freeze them at the low level. A new building plan was put into effect, making it forever impossible to build congested dwellings of the old type even in the old districts, and enforcing completely 'open' planning in all outlying areas. And the city itself bought up ten thousand acres of raw agricultural land at about two thousand dollars an acre, much of which was destined to be used directly for new housing. At present, Berlin owns one third of its interior area (about seventy-eight thousand acres) and seventy thousand more acres outside, which form a partial green belt. Almost none of the land for new housing was obtained by condemnation, and, indeed, expropriation laws are rather conservative and difficult to work in Berlin. Where municipal land is used for co-operative or other semi-private limited-dividend housing, it is rarely if ever sold outright, but is leased cheaply for a long term. This in itself gives the city considerable control over standards of development.

The general policies of most German, Dutch, and Scandinavian towns are much the same. And the similar achievements of many English local authorities, although not by any means on such a large scale, are perhaps even more remarkable. They had even less tradition of land-purchase or control than most American cities, and yet ever since the war many of them have been buying up large estates as they became available, in the case of London and Manchester and Liverpool, large enough for complete satellite towns.

Why Rents are Low in Relation to Costs

As will be seen later in typical set-ups, the principal reason for the fact that the 'economic' return necessary on a given

GOOD HOUSES ARE CHEAPER THAN BAD ONES

ONLY 1 OUT OF 3 FAMILIES CAN AFFORD THIS MINIMUM HOUSE

the cost of this house can be reduced by:

1 LARGE-SCALE PLANNING.................... 5%*
Reduces cost of streets, utilities, financing. Increases amount of open green space. Improves quality of architectural design by adapting lot size to house and block size to terrain.

2 MASS-PRODUCTION..... .... 10%*
Reduces cost of materials and labor by simplification of manufacturing processes and unitization of parts.

3 REDUCTION OF FINANCIAL CHARGES........... 15%*
By:
(a) LIMITED DIVIDENDS. Voluntary investment at lower rates than those for speculative housing.
(b) STATE LOANS on approved housing at low rate of interest with long-term amortization.
"A 1% reduction in interest would mean an 8% reduction in rental."†

4 COMMUNITY CONTROL OF LAND USE........... 5%*
Prevents future speculation in land-values thereby guarding against high taxes, congestion and blighted areas.

RESULTING REDUCTION IN COST....... 35%*

CORRESPONDINGLY – SOCIAL, ECONOMIC AND AESTHETIC VALUE IS RAISED........... ?%

Note – Source; Report of the Committee on Large Scale Operations, the President's Conference on Home Ownership, 1931.

* Percentages are approximate adaptations by Mr. Henry Wright of those printed in the Report.

† Page 25 of the Report.

Experiments in America with each of these factors separately prove...that all four must be used together

THEN GOOD HOUSES COULD BE AFFORDED BY 2 OUT OF 3 FAMILIES

New houses in America during the past decades have reached only the upper third income-group. With adequate planning and modern non-speculative methods of finance, most of the middle third might be reached. For the under-paid and those with no income at all there must be either higher, regular wages, or a direct housing subsidy. (This chart was prepared by the author for the traveling exhibition of Modern Architecture of the Museum of Modern Art, New York.)

investment in European housing, and therefore the rent, is so much lower than in the case of American private enterprise, is a matter of cheap money. Most of this money has come from official or semi-official agencies. And here again the close and necessitous relationship between the new housing methods and the new means is obvious. The Public Works Loan Board of England, for instance, could not lend money at four and one-half per cent on the type of housing which, due to obvious speculative risks, has to pay six per cent in the open market plus very heavy discounts. The high cost of financing in ordinary speculative developments is not due to exploitation on the part of the lender half as much as to the essential risk of the enterprise. In the same way, the Board could not make its loans repayable by a sixty-year sinking fund, amounting to three tenths per cent per year, instead of the usual two or three per cent amortization rate in the private market, unless there were fair assurance that the houses would still be habitable and 'standard' in all important respects after half a century. Therefore, sound planning and construction, permanent amenities, and the insurance against blight which only large-scale operations can give, were imperative. In post-inflation Germany, where money was exceedingly scarce and expensive and where most of the public housing funds had to be raised by taxation, the low rate on these loans was even more vital.

Other items in the rent schedule, which are relatively lower in European housing than in ordinary American practice, may be explained partly by the new method and partly by different habits. The small vacancy item is made possible, of course, because these dwellings are ordinarily for people who have never before been able to afford new housing and because of the great shortage of any kind of dwelling in low rental categories. The lower cost of maintenance and administration is largely because there are fewer expensive services — no elevators, no doormen, and only occasional central heating and hot water. (Where the latter are supplied, they usually mean a small separate charge, as do most other communal facilities.)

Outside of England, the tax item is ordinarily much lower in proportion to rent than it is in America. This is occasionally due to remission of building-taxes on new low-cost dwellings, but not always; for most Continental cities derive a far greater share of their resources from income, luxury, and business taxes than from real estate. This is, as a matter of fact, of paramount importance in a much wider connection. Most German cities, when they took the necessary measures to deflate existing and potential speculative land-prices, were able to do so without seriously deranging their own financial structures. Municipal governments in America, on the other hand, at present so inextricably dependent on those inflated 'values' which are the very cause of their ruin, will probably have to undergo complete economic revision before they can even begin to deal adequately with their 'blighted areas.' The traditional English practice of taxing rents and not assessed land-values, which has always been condemned by liberals as a reactionary system, has as a matter of fact worked out rather well in so far as post-war housing is concerned. For large pieces of land in single ownership were still available quite near the towns, at low prices, their owners never having been forced into speculative subdivision by high taxes.

Typical Cost and Rent Schedules

A SMALL HOUSE IN ENGLAND

This is an average set-up for a minimum new house, put up by a local government with State and municipal aid at the end of 1932, as estimated by the Ministry of Health. It would be one of a group or row of four to six houses, in a community development similar to those illustrated at the end of this book, and planned at a density of not more than twelve dwellings per gross acre. Developed land is here figured at less than ten cents a square foot. The house is two-storied and has a living-room, kitchen, bath, and three bedrooms, and a net dwelling area of seven hundred and sixty square feet. There is no central heat, and no basement, due rather to local habits in all houses except those of the wealthiest, rather than to direct paring of standards. An 'unskilled' worker can pay for it, if he is regularly employed, but not if he is on a dole. The development is administered directly by the local government.

FIRST COST

Raw land	$73	4%
Land development:		
Roads	145	8%
Sewers	73	4%
Construction	1503	84%
Per house, total	$1794	100%

FINANCE

National loan, from Public Works Loan Board, at 4½% for 60 years, with sinking fund to pay. Covers whole cost. Annual subsidy from both State and local authority.

ANNUAL RENT
(and in percentage of initial cost)

Interest	$81	4.5%
Upkeep (management, repairs, insurance, and rent loss)	20	1.1%
Sinking fund	5	.3%
Taxes (at about 40% of actual rent)	23	1.3%
Annual costs	$129	7.2%
Subsidies:		
State, $36 per year, and local, $18 per year, for 40 years		
Equated to 60 years	49	2.7%
Annual rent	$80	4.5%

A SMALL HOUSE IN AMERICA

In the *Architectural Forum* for March, 1932, Mr. Henry Wright presented a factual cost analysis of a typical American detached frame house, built by a speculator for sale, and financed rather more conservatively than the average. Actual figures do not offer any real basis of comparison, as the house is somewhat larger than the English one, and the scale of costs very much higher. Annual charges in per cent of first cost do, however, offer a real indication. Obviously, it is impossible really to compare rentals with charges which include purchase price. However, it should be borne in mind that depreciation is so fast and certain on such a house that no builder would consider trying to rent it on an investment basis: in other words, the purchaser is left holding the bag.

FIRST COST

Developed lot	$1680	22%
Construction	4503	60%
Carrying charges, financing and sale	1317	18%
Total cost	$7500	100%

FINANCE

1st mortgage of $4000 and 10% equity, each at 6%. 2nd mortgage of $2750, amortized in 10 years.

ANNUAL CHARGES
(and in percentage of initial costs)

Interest, 1st mortgage	$240	3.2%
Interest and amortization 2nd mortgage	360	4.8%
Taxes and insurance	170	2.3%
Repairs	130	1.7%
Interest on investment and depreciation	220	2.9%
Total annual charges	$1120	14.9%
Minus amortization	275	
Net charges	$845	11.3%

Moreover, if annual charges are reckoned in proportion to initial *real* costs — that is, the actual cost of land and construction, omitting the price of mortgage discounts and sales promotion, which do not exist in the English set-up — total annual expenses come to about *eighteen per cent* of costs, and net charges to *thirteen per cent.*

AN APARTMENT IN GERMANY

FIRST COST

Raw land	$115	4%
Development	135	5%
Construction	2500	91%
Total	$2750	100%

FINANCE

1st mortgage from social insurance funds, $1100 at 7% plus ½% amortization.
Municipal mortgage, $330 at 2% plus 2%.
State mortgage out of the House Rent Tax at 1%, plus 1% after 5 years.
Equity, $80 at 5%.

ANNUAL RENT

(and in percentage of initial costs)

Interest	$100	3.6%
Amortization	12	.4%
(Plus $12 after 5 yrs.)		
Maintenance	36	1.3%
(Upkeep, water, administration, insurance, etc.)		
Ground tax	9	.3%
(Bldg. exempt)		
Rent-loss	5	.2%
Annual rental	$162	5.8%

Minimum-rental apartment in Berlin, built in 1930 by a semi-official housing society with a maximum of public aid. If the first mortgage were found in the open market instead of from a public savings bank or social insurance funds, it would be about eight and one half per cent instead of seven and one half per cent. It would be difficult to figure the actual amount of outright subsidy represented here, as its form is the loan of public funds at a rate less than that the government would have to pay if it borrowed them. Moreover, the State loans (which supplied the major part of housing aid in Germany) were not borrowed, but raised by a special direct tax on old houses, and therefore constitute the nucleus of a revolving fund even at a very low return. The dwelling itself has around six hundred and fifty square feet net dwelling-area, and includes a living-room, kitchen, two bedrooms, and a bath. It would probably be in a four-story building, part of a large community development similar to those illustrated, at a density of between thirty and forty-five families per gross acre (including streets). Developed land would figure at twenty to thirty cents a square foot. An average worker might have been able to pay for it in 1930 if he was regularly employed, but he could not do so today. If there is central heat, it would be paid for separately.

APARTMENTS IN AMERICA

The following table presents typical rental set-ups necessary to give the expected minimum return on initial investment, figured in percentage of capital cost of land and buildings.

(1) refers to a typical speculative development in New York City, built before 1929 and financed in the open market. Its coverage would be seventy per cent or more, and the building would be a five-story walk-up. When new, it could be afforded only by the upper-third income group.

(2) would be typical for a limited-dividend housing development, built under the New York State Housing Law of 1926, with tax-exemption for twenty years on the buildings and a loan from an insurance company on two thirds of the cost, at five per cent. Interest on one third equity, six per cent. It would be a four- or five-story walk-up, covering at least fifty per cent of its site. A few members of the lower-middle income group might have paid for it in 1928, but probably not at present.

(3) is representative of contemplated large-scale projects in New York City, planned to be erected by a public authority and receiving a maximum of aid and subsidy under the present regulations (March, 1934): that is, a government loan to cover the whole cost, at four per cent with amortization at one and one-half per cent; an outright grant of thirty per cent of the construction cost; and tax-exemption on the buildings. This is figured at an average height of four and one half stories, a gross coverage (including central recreation space and streets) of thirty per cent, and a land cost of one dollar per square foot. If the site-cost were increased to five dollars a square foot, which would probably be a minimum for slum-clearance projects, the necessary rental per cent of cost would be only slightly increased, but the initial cost per identical room would rise from \$1135 to \$1580, and therefore the *actual* rent would be \$9.36 per month per room instead of \$6.42 as in the present case.

SPECULATIVE VERSUS PUBLIC UTILITY HOUSING

A diagram showing the minimum annual costs and the actual rentals on an original investment of $1000, in various typical instances of post-war construction and two types of project now possible with government aid in America. An indication of why the speculative real estate business in America has served only the wealthiest third of the population, and that inadequately. (The figures are as nearly comparable as possible, the cost of heat being eliminated in every case.)

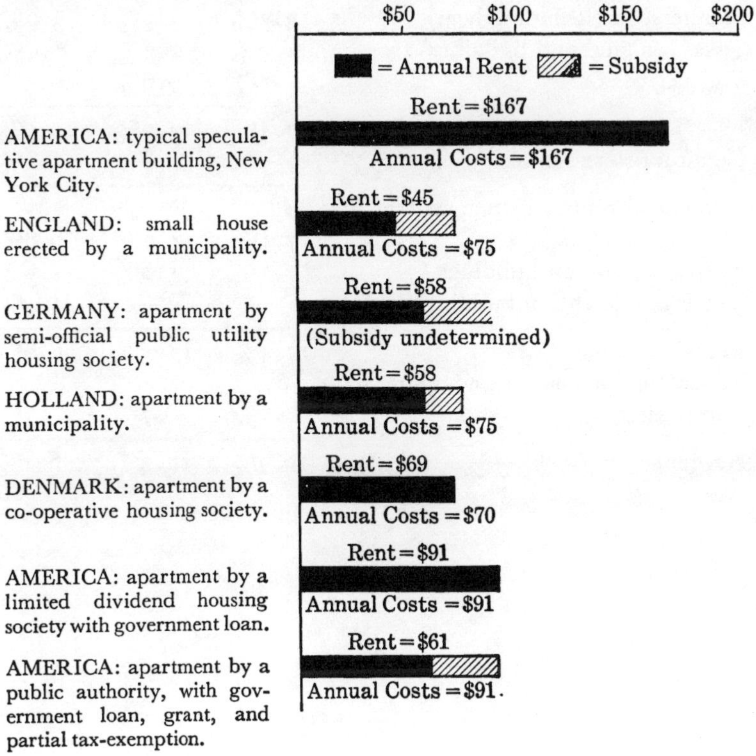

Only people in the middle-income group could afford the former rent, while the latter would probably fall at just about the border-line between the middle and lowest income thirds, with some of the last able to pay for it if they were regularly employed and did not have large families. The development would be large enough so that the increment on store rentals might be preserved to the benefit of the community, as was not the case in (1) or (2). Data from a study by Mr. C. S. Stein.

	(1)	(2)	(3)
Interest	6.0%	5.3%	4.0%
Discounts	2.3%	0.2%	—
Amortization	2.0%	3.0%	1.5%
Maintenance (including heat)	3.3%	3.3%	3.0%
Taxes (on land and buildings)	2.3%	2.3%	1.9%
Vacancies	1.5%	0.6%	0.5%
	17.4%	14.7%	10.9%
Credit for store rentals	—	—	1.1%
'Economic' rental, in per cent of first costs	17.4%	14.7%	9.8%
Tax-exemption on buildings (—)	—	1.6%	1.6%
30 per cent grant on buildings (—)	—	—	1.4%
Actual rent	17.4%	13.1%	6.8%
Minus cost of heat, to compare with European set-ups	.7%	.7%	.7%
Net rent	16.7%	12.4%	6.1%

IX. MODERN HOUSING FOR AMERICA?

The Past: a Handful of Experiments

As has been shown in another section, there are in this country almost no dwellings which can be said to measure up to the minimum working standard of modern housing as it has been accepted in European practice. We have had our frustrated slum-reformers, thousands of them, and our liberal or sentimental enthusiasts for improving 'the home.' But we lacked both the tradition of civic responsibility and those inner movements of collective revolt which paralleled the property individualism of the nineteenth century in Europe, and which finally united (in a somewhat unstable combination, it is true) to form the productive post-war housing policies. Moreover, the ideal of individual home-ownership, our strongest heritage from the frontier, has been exploited so intensively that a very large proportion of the population still tends (in spite of foreclosures, evictions, and the collapse of paper 'values') to approach the housing problem in the rôle of petty capitalists rather than as workers and consumers. Even to many of those who have lost or never achieved their 'own' houses, the idea of holding title to a piece of land and a building remains, in spite of all the contrary facts, the vague symbol of both respectable security and sudden riches.

Nevertheless, we have had our experiments in modern community housing, and a scattered few of them were on a par with European practice in quality if not in rental scales. The Government housing for war workers, particularly that at Bridgeport, Connecticut, and at Camden, New Jersey, created an almost sensational precedent in quality of community planning as well as in public responsibility. If it had been carried forward, this movement might well have served to mitigate the present contrast between post-war housing in Europe and that in America. But these houses (which would undoubtedly have been ordinary barracks if it had not been for the example of English war-workers' housing) were allowed to lapse into unrestricted private ownership. And, in spite of the acute shortage which was to mount for several years and result finally in disastrous 'emergency' measures and a period of feverish jerry-building, most of the large Government program was hastily scrapped immediately after the Armistice.

While Europe was providing Government aid designed specifically to produce better houses at lower rents, New York City was subsidizing the speculative building industry. Every dwelling begun between the beginning of 1921 and April, 1924, was tax-exempt in part or in whole until 1931. According to the calculations of Dr. Edith Elmer Wood, these dwellings (almost all sub-standard, many of them flimsy frame houses closely covering whole square miles in the outlying districts, and every one of them probably too expensive for any but the top-third income group) cost the taxpayers very nearly $200,000,000. This is *direct* subsidy: what they will cost eventually, in terms of foreclosure, bankruptcy, tax-delinquency, and all the other extravagances of expensive blight, no one can begin to estimate at present. Needless to say, there is no city in Europe whose outright subsidies for planned low-cost housing or slum-clearance come anywhere near $200,000,000.

In 1926, however, the much-compromised efforts of those scattered few individuals who understood the situation finally resulted in a New York State Housing Board, and a law under which the Board is authorized to grant tax-exemption for twenty years on limited-dividend housing which reaches a certain standard and falls below a certain rental. No means of providing cheap credit were set up, however, and the result to date is only around ten thousand apartments. Moreover, due to exorbitant land-costs and expensive money, it cannot be said that *any* of them approach the ordinary accepted European standard of light, air, and space, and very few were within reach of the lower paid half of the population even in 1928. As a precedent for large-scale co-operative action on the part of a trade-union group, however, the two developments of the Amalgamated Clothing Workers are worthy of particular mention.

Also in the region of New York City, the City Housing Corporation, a limited-dividend society, conducted two important experiments in community planning which, although they did not reach below the top income third, have had great influence on subsequent housing and planning ideas (if not on much visible accomplishment) throughout the country. Sunnyside in Queens shows what comprehensive planning can achieve by way of increased living amenity even within an old-fashioned gridiron street layout. And Radburn, New Jersey, is the first American attempt to build a complete preplanned community on English Garden City principles. Here the idea of the super-block, with indented dead-end streets, as used in ordinary practice in English housing, was carried one step farther to accommodate that particular American condition, the automobile. All the houses face inward on continuous parks, traversed by footways entirely separated from the streets. Underpasses link one super-block to the other, and it is possible to go from any house to school or shops without crossing a street.

There have been other scattered experiments by foundations and limited-dividend societies, notably the Rosenwald and Marshall Field apartments in Chicago and the work of the Society of Phipps Houses in New York. Chatham Village, the recent development in Pittsburgh by the Buhl Foundation, is probably the best example of modern planned housing in the country. There are, of course, quite a number of middle-class suburbs which are 'restricted' in one way or another and more or less planned at the start — Mariemont, outside of Cincinnati, is the most famous of these — but none of them constitutes a complete experiment in modern housing. The State of California has assisted several thousand veterans and a few others to purchase homes or farms on comparatively easy terms, but the results, in so far as form and planning quality are concerned, are just like any individual or speculative construction. Among several more or less abortive experiments in public and semi-public housing, dating from the days of post-war shortage, that of the city of Milwaukee is one of the more interesting. But the houses (which were laid out in groups around a common) were eventually sold off without restrictions, and the enabling law laid on the shelf until very recently.

Throughout the country, then, there are not more than twenty thousand dwellings erected since the war on a permanently non-speculative basis, and with any pretensions to large-scale planning or fundamental change in the quality of house-production and neighborhood environment. Twenty thousand to set against 4,500,000 in a section of Europe with only slightly more population than that of the United States. Moreover, not more than half of the twenty thousand really achieve a degree of permanent amenity and freedom from congestion which is the minimum working standard for 'modern housing' in Europe. And of the remaining ten thousand few or none were available to the lower-paid half of the population who need good houses the most. All in all, this is not a very grand achievement.

'Housing' Becomes a Public Issue

But suddenly today, instead of being one of those vague words which always appear as a subhead in any set of liberal reform measures, 'housing' has universally become matter for front-page news and editorial controversy. Simultaneously, it appears that the reasons for doing or not doing housing are almost exactly equal to the number of special 'interests' in the country. And the mere worker-consumer, who merely for better or worse lives in houses and works in cities (when extraneous conditions permit him to do either), still stands on the side-lines, not knowing in which direction he should throw his weight.

For not very many of these new reasons for doing 'housing' seem to have much to do with actually setting up a method of constructing better and cheaper houses and putting a stop to the rising tide of urban blight. Economists, both liberal and otherwise, urge 'housing' as a means of providing emergency employment and as one of the few potentially self-liquidating forms of public works. Cities and various sections of the financial interest see in it a chance to rehabilitate economically blighted areas. Social workers, politicians, and a few of the more pessimistic slum-owners think that housing can mean only the spectacular, immediate clearance of the most noisome slum districts, at any cost. Architects and engineers are inclined to feel that housing, however dull by comparison with skyscrapers or

Norman villas, is their one glimmer of hope in a drab future. A group of industrialists and technicians is fascinated with the notion that the prefabricated dwelling might, like the automobile industry after the war, provide an entirely new boom market to exploit. Romantic reactionaries hail it as a means of putting restless urban unemployed safely 'back on the land' in handmade homesteads with vegetable gardens. A few of the more forward-looking see in government-assisted community housing a real tool for regional planning and industrial recentralization. Others see only new sources for municipal graft. Labor is apparently more worried about the dangers of prefabrication than about either immediate employment or better houses to live in. And the radicals firmly believe, with considerable logic, that this is just one more thing which can never be accomplished within the framework of a capitalist society.

This chaos is accurately mirrored in the recent history of official housing policy in Washington. Introduced in the first place primarily as an emergency measure to provide employment and not as a housing policy *per se* at all, it has got steadily more and more involved with various side-issues until it looks as if the whole thing might result in little more than a deadlock. The avowed purpose, originally fairly constructive and ambitious, has been pared down and compromised until now it appears to be only a half-hearted desire to tear down a few of the more spectacular central slums — but only if this can be done without hurting anyone's feelings or really changing anything important. Another branch of the Administration is dabbling in homesteads. That is where the matter rests at present, and if the delays and progressive limitations of policy continue to mount in the future as they have in the past, all the talk will eventuate in not even a modicum of temporary employment, let alone a fundamental change in the method by which we provide shelter and construct our cities. And a great opportunity will have been lost.

For the simple fact which underlay even the most special agitation still stands. Namely, that all the old methods of providing houses for people of average income or less have utterly and miserably failed. There is a whole shelf of recent literature for proof, and a whole gallery of exhibitions and charted surveys for evidence. Briefly stated, it all amounts to the same thing. The average new dwelling has been growing steadily more expensive, more wasteful, and less adequate to the real needs of the individual, the family, the city, and the nation. The combined efforts of speculative builders, building and loan associations, and individuals building for themselves, cannot supply a new dwelling at a price which even half the population can pay. And the buildings which they do construct are for the most part either built-in slums, or so badly laid out and constructed as to constitute incipient 'blighted areas' from the start. The net result is that the American Standard of Living today, even in times of 'prosperity,' is one of the lowest in the western world with respect to light, air, facilities for group living, and even basic sanitation.

Moreover, quite a large number of people have begun to realize that there is a better way to do things. That the justling small builders and the front-foot lots and the miserable straggling suburbs and the ideology of individual Home Ownership must go. And in their place must come a technique for building complete communities designed and administered as functional units and constructed by large-scale methods. And finally, that only governments can make the decisive step and set up the new method of house-production as a long-time social investment, to replace the wasteful and obsolete chaos still prevailing.

Why, then, this deadlock? Is it just simply impossible to inaugurate an efficient and realistic housing procedure within our present social-economic framework? Perhaps it *is* impossible. And if it is, that is certainly one of the most cogent arguments against the institutions of capitalism and private property that could possibly be found. Nevertheless, there is still the fact that good low-cost modern housing has been done (however temporarily or incompletely, and whatever else may have been left undone) in any number of European countries with governments more or less similar to our own. A new housing method has been set up, so visibly effective and fruitful that, in all its essentials, it must be accepted as *the* way to build a modern environment until some better method shall have been devised. Most of this book has been devoted to describing this method, its background and its achievements. But perhaps, in conclusion, we should consider some of the more pressing questions now being posed in America, in the light of this European experience.

The Matter of Slum-Clearance

The main purpose of all European housing policies has been to provide a large number of modern dwellings, in planned neighborhoods, as quickly and cheaply as possible. These were the essentials. To clear out and rebuild insanitary areas at the same time would obviously have been desirable: but without exception it was found that a housing program in a capitalist democracy which *began* with slum-clearance would inevitably compromise every one of the essentials — and result in very few new dwellings to boot. So far only two countries, Great Britain and Holland, have undertaken any important rehabilitation of old districts, and in both cases these efforts were of much lower quality than the rest of the housing program, and represented anywhere from two to four times the outright cost to the government.

It was not careful reasoning in the light of known facts, but the sudden sweep to power of a Conservative Government in Great Britain, which at the end of 1932 brought the astonishingly productive housing program to a stop, 'in order to concentrate on slum-clearance.' Great Britain has slowly but steadily been cleaning out and rebuilding slum areas ever since 1890, and had indeed somewhat accelerated the pace during the decade after the war. And the great uproar about the 'terrible slums' raised by the Tories during the past year and a half, together with the sacrifice of the normal building program, have resulted in not one more foot of insanitary area being cleared than would reasonably have been achieved in any case. And in spite of the fact that England has slum expropriation laws which would be considered wildly radical and confiscatory in this country, and in spite of the fact that land-prices in England are never anything like what they are here, it still costs just about twice as much to re-house a slum-dweller in a tenement on the site of his former dwelling as in a small house on outlying land. According to a survey made in 1931, in Liverpool, the municipal subsidy would have to be four times as high in the former case as in the latter.

The great stumbling-block to large-scale slum-clearance in a society based on private property is of course the high cost of assembling the site. And the cost of land is the most significant single factor in determining the quality of new housing. (In New York City it is so all-important that if the government were to buy up the cheapest conceivable slum-district at present prices, and were to erect very mediocre housing thereon — four- or five-story flats with a high density and inadequate recreation space — and if it were further, as proposed, to write off one third of the cost of the construction by outright grant, the rentals would still be considerably higher than those for a really good project on undeveloped land, at half the coverage, and with no subsidy.)

There are in fact three distinct economic types of 'slum,' each with an entirely different bearing on the problem of clearance. There is first the traditional type of central insanitary area which is high-priced because of the actual profits which the landlords reap from present congestion. In most European cities, because there is still not a quantitative sufficiency of low-cost dwellings of any kind, this type prevails. Central slum-areas tend to remain overcrowded and therefore profitable and expensive. This may be called the *exploitation-slum.*

Then there is the insanitary, rundown area which may or may not be overcrowded, but whose land-prices are based, not on present profits, but on speculation as to more intensive future use. Large areas in many American cities, half-empty and dilapidated but still scaled to skyscraper hopes, belong to this type, which can be classified as the *speculation-slum* par excellence.

And finally there is the *blighted area,* a later growth of either of the other types, or merely the result of population movements away from the center to the outskirts. That is, a dejected area which has lost a large part of its population and is therefore not on a paying basis (either to the owners or to the city which provides the utilities and services in return for inadequate taxes), and which offers no near hope of being turned to more intensive use.

If the purpose of a national housing policy is to build good dwellings quickly and cheaply, then the only kind of site which should be considered for immediate action, other than new cheap land, is the last-mentioned type of completely deflated area. To deal directly with any other type of slum (under any conceivable present policy of condemnation or compensation) is not to promote good housing, but to subsidize the most exploitive and speculative branches of the real-estate interest. The only effective mode of attack on the exploitation and speculation slums is the indirect one. By building an ample supply of low-cost houses in other districts, by condemning insanitary dwellings as unfit for human habitation, and by thus raising the standard of demand and lowering the pressure on sub-standard areas, exploitive profits, and their accompanying land-prices, can be deflated. And by legally limiting the height, coverage, and density of new building in a given district to that required by good standard housing, speculative hopes and prices can be curbed in the same way.

But there will have to be adequate additional controls even if large-scale clearance is to be effected only on properties at present almost completely deflated. The mere fact that the Government has bought one blighted district will raise speculative hopes on other areas, equally blighted. Here is what Mr. John J. Clarke, Liverpool authority on public administration and housing, wrote about slum-clearance policies.

In addition to prohibitive costs, he says, and the fact that no matter how it is worked the same people are never re-housed on the same spot, 'another objection to such clearances is the high value which they indirectly set upon other insanitary areas. As we have seen, most of the displaced slum-dwellers remove to other slums, thus forcing the already too high rents up to a higher figure still. These fresh accessions to already overcrowded districts increase the value of this property to the owners, and the purchase price (especially the compensation price, in the case of compulsory purchase) rises in proportion. This method of dealing with the slums has encouraged the development of a new industry, viz., the buying up of property in insanitary areas in order to reap a rich harvest of compensation from the municipal pocket.' (Obviously, much the same problem would arise in connection with large-scale housing on new land, unless the municipality has a strong, long-time policy of purchase and use-control.)

Any logical person may well inquire: Why should public authorities have to pay the asking price to owners of property which must be torn down because it constitutes a public menace? Why should such owners not rather be prosecuted under the laws designed to protect consumers from inferior or spoiled goods? Obviously, there is no logical reason: but we are not discussing a logical economic system.

England, as a matter of fact, has a law which in *theory* permits expropriation of insanitary areas with compensation (which can be arbitrated afterward if no quick agreement is forthcoming) based only on the value of the land as a cleared site for good-standard low-cost housing. Nevertheless, it very apparently does not work out that way. Delays are long and costly. Final prices are always high. And, even after a large part of the site-cost has been written off as sheer loss, high tenements covering a very large portion of the site are put up, in marked contrast to the spacious and economically constructed small-house groups on the outskirts. And still the rents are almost never low enough for any of the former inhabitants of the district, although again, the project is legally supposed to re-house the same people. The 'intensive' attack of the past year and a half has done nothing to remedy any of these conditions.

In many cases, the high prices of central American slum-areas are already without any foundation whatsoever. People have been moving out of the worst districts for the past decade, even though what they moved to may already be well on the way toward a new slum. Our cities are not going to grow much larger, and there will be little if any further demand for skyscrapers. Most cities are overbuilt with expensive upper-class apartment-houses as it is. Owners of decayed properties and the banks and insurance companies which hold them in mortgage or foreclosure are just beginning to realize what this situation may mean. And as it becomes clearer, there is sure to be more and more pressure for 'slum-clearance,' on the chance of unloading land on the government while prices are still high.

The danger is much greater than the mere question of wasting taxpayers' money in order to reimburse slum-owners for having gambled wrong or for maintaining a public nuisance. The real danger (and that it is a concrete one is shown by the English experience) is that, once the government has paid a high price for the land, sub-standard dwellings will almost certainly be erected on it — that is, buildings covering too much of the site, too high, with inadequate recreation facilities, and using the old obsolete street-plan. In the present state of flux and uncertainty and opportunity, even one such reconstruction in a district would be a major disaster. For it might well crystallize land-prices, housing standards, building forms, for a generation to come. (Even revolutions cannot immediately overcome the weight of past habits, as witness some of the recent tenements in Moscow.) A whole new era of 'reform' slums might be inaugurated, quite comparable to the one initiated by the philanthropic reformers of the eighties and nineties. And the great danger, then as now, comes not so much from the obvious 'interests' (for anyone can recognize and allow for the desire of a man to sell his property as high as possible) as from that earnest, hard-working, righteous, indignant group of people who, by refusing to see beyond the immediate situation, always seem to end up by supporting the very thing which they think they are fighting.

Modern housing, if it is to be done at all, cannot be patchwork. It is not 'reform' within the old pattern. It is either an entirely new method of providing an entirely new standard of urban environment, or it is nothing. Once this point of view is accepted, exclusive emphasis on slum-clearance becomes as illogical as if the early automobile manufacturers had directed all their efforts to buying out the still prosperous carriage-makers and razing their factories, instead of building automobiles.

The first point to be settled in the American slum problem is really a very simple one. It is merely: *Shall we stop building new slums?* All the rest must come after. Instead of trying vainly to salvage the past, we must first safeguard the future.

'Subsistence Homesteads' are not Modern Housing

The search for an easy short-cut to individual security has received a tremendous boost during the past few years, on both sides of the Atlantic. Hundreds of schemes have been devised and enthusiastically urged, many of them as ingenious as those of alchemists seeking the secret for transmutation of metals, most of them as romantic as the search for the Northwest Passage.

Almost all of these schemes boil down to just one thing: a small piece of arable land for each family (not large enough to produce anything for sale), with some sort of a house on it. And, just as with slum-clearance, on the surface this is obviously a 'good' idea. Unemployed paupers, owning nothing whatsoever, are to find themselves not only with permanent shelter but with the means of providing some portion of their own food. Instead of canned rations in a tenement, or soup in a flop-house, fresh vegetables and healthy outdoor work amid pleasant surroundings. Moreover, relief could be cut down. What could be neater? And, as a matter of fact, 'subsistence homesteads' have been taken up with considerable concrete enthusiasm in Washington, with several projects already under way and many more to come. Indeed, the idea has received official attention much less divided and procrastinating than has the cause of 'housing' itself.

But there are many ramifications to the homestead question, and before we endorse any really large-scale program, perhaps we should inquire once more into the experience of Europe.

The idea of rendering the individual less dependent for his life and living on the erratic extremes of urban employment conditions, by providing him with a garden, is as old as the factory system. Older, in fact; for the whole system of cottage industries depended on it. As a working principle, it has served dozens of social and political philosophies at one time or another, from the anarchism of Prudhon and Kropotkin to the feudalism of Ruskin. At present it is one of the keystones of Hitler's Nationalism.

Many of the most thorough social-economic theories have rested on the notion of planned communities combining within their limits a balance of variegated industry and intensive agriculture. In the working philosophy of Kropotkin and Patrick Geddes, this included the possibility of balanced work for all individuals. The entire Garden City Movement sprang from such an ideal. The demand for allotment gardens by workers living in urban tenements, very strong in central Europe ever since the period of starvation during the war, is of course merely the other end of the scale.

But 'unemployed colonies,' as they have been developed in Germany and as they seem likely to be projected in this country, are quite another thing from fundamental regional planning on the one hand, and small allotments on the outskirts of large cities on the other. The truth of the matter is that if even a very small part of the current talk about 'homesteads,' 'subsistence gardens,' 'decentralization,' and 'putting people back on the land' had been put into practice in the manner suggested, we should already have succeeded in transforming not only a large number of our present city-dwellers but most of our farmers as well, into a new American peasantry with a standard of living and an outlook for the future probably about equal to that obtainable in the Balkan rural regions.

Perhaps I should not be so vehement had I not seen the results of the emergency homesteading movement in Germany. There, since 1931, when reactionary forces began to tip the scales, no public money has been lent for new housing unless each dwelling was accompanied by a sizable allotment garden tract and the houses built for themselves by groups of unemployed workers whose labor became their 'capital' investment. On the surface some of these colonies are picturesque enough, and at worst the fact that they are likely to be built in arranged groups, and with some benefit of the admirable technique of community planning lately developed in Germany, makes them rather better than the average American equivalent would probably be.

But what is the net result? The 'dole' of such people is cut down to almost nothing. Shelter and some food they most certainly have, but what of the future? If work opportunities return to the cities, they have no means to go and look for them. If jobs are handed to them on a silver platter, they are miles and marks and hours away from them. Considerations of soil and scientific agriculture have played little or no part in their location; rather, they have been set out on the cheapest piece of land that a city happened to have available. Nor have they been located with any regard to future industrial sites; on the contrary, cheap land means that they are usually far from highways, railroads, and power sources. In addition, they have few or none of the social, cultural, or educational facilities which are so dearly prized in even the poorest old German villages. Families are tied to a sub-standard house and a miserable 'subsistence-level' existence for themselves and their children, for thirty years. In short, the *Randsiedlungen*, taken by and large, are nothing more nor less than poor-farms, and the only people who really benefit from them are likely to be the people who pay the taxes which support the dole. The cycle of 'modern housing' has turned back on itself, back to the pauper hand-outs of the mid-nineteenth century. It is worth noting that the subsistence-homestead movement in Germany was first urged by the Liberals, but that now, when the Liberals have vanished, the movement fits perfectly into Hitler's conscious and energetic policy of turning potentially dangerous urban workers into a helpless pauper peasantry.

Even so, there was more excuse for such a movement in Germany than there ever could be in America. Germany does not produce enough food for her own population, and, with little prospect for betterment in either trade or international relations for a long time to come, Rights and Socialists alike felt that it was necessary for her to 'dig herself in.' But in America we are busily engaged in destroying our produce and reducing our productivity, even as it is. And every new group of homesteads for urban workers will contribute just that much toward reducing professional farmers to a subsistence standard of living as well.

Ardent American homesteaders might respond to all this in one of several ways. They might say that what they mean is something quite different from a German *Randsiedlung*: they intend to raise people's standard of living, to provide power and labor-saving machinery and the means for a rich and varied creative life. Or they might say, well and good: pauper peasants are better off, and better for the political stability of the country, than starving proletarians.

The latter position seems to the author a perfectly honest one, provided that is the kind of stability we are looking for. But do we really want it? Quite aside from considerations of social justice, what does it imply? It implies admitting that science and power and the machine are too much for us, and that the only thing we can do to save whatever we want to save is to crawl back two or three hundred years and try to forget the whole nightmare. This, in substance, is what Germany has apparently decided, and what most of central Europe seems in process of deciding.

But as for the first proposition, this author believes that it just can't be done — or not until a great many other things have been done first. A small homesteader who uses electric power, who enjoys a balanced and varied diet, who demands good schools, roads and means of transportation, who clothes his family decently and occasionally patronizes doctors and dentists, requires an absolute minimum of fifty dollars in hard cash per month (even in the most nearly 'self-sufficient' plans yet offered), no matter how energetic and resourceful his family may be. Where will it come from?

One of the offered answers is that 'some member of the family will work in town.' But this, first of all, limits the range of possible location. More important, it immediately involves efficient transportation and the existence of a regular job not requiring too much waiting around, hunting down, or personal availability on the part of the applicant. It is also necessary that the job provide a very decent wage for short hours, and that the worker be tractable to the idea of giving up all or most of his wages for the privilege of living far away from his work and probably doing chores in his off hours as well. Moreover, the worker can hardly be the head of the family, for even three-acre homesteads require considerable and constant tending.

Another answer, this time from the President of the United States Chamber of Commerce, is that a factory or two will be 'decentralized' along with a group of homesteads. And here we come to one of the most ironic dilemmas that the present economic system can provide. Modern science and technology and the principles of regional planning point straight to the decentralization of industry, to smaller plants, motor trucking, and the wider network of electricity instead of coal and steam. And yet, under the wage-and-profit system, and without complete replanning and recentralization, how is a small electric plant surrounded by homesteads different from an ordinary old-fashioned 'company town,' one of the abominations of the nineteenth-century heritage? Only in this, that with the workers tied to their farms and committed to vegetable-raising, wages are very likely to be even lower than heretofore. Indeed, lower wages are the principal bait in almost all present decentralization of industry.

It would seem to this writer that most unemployed urban families would be quite justified in being willing to sacrifice something in the quality of their food and surroundings rather than be quite as hopelessly 'secure' as they might find themselves on even the most ingenious subsistence homestead. For, when all is said, what used to be true is still true now. A homesteader must either be able to raise cash crops on which he can make a reliable profit, or he must have a regular and safe cash income for short work-hours from a source which cannot exploit his lack of bargaining freedom — or he must be satisfied to be a hand-to-mouth peasant, with a shack on a stony hillside, a wooden plow, a potato patch, and a level of existence somewhat lower than that of the city slum-dweller.

No, subsistence farms are not modern housing. On the other hand, no new planned housing, urban or otherwise, has a right to be called 'modern' if it does not provide adequate gardens conveniently, for all who may desire to work them. But let us not put the amateur family garden on an 'economic,' compulsory basis.

Where is the Demand?

'Housing' is a public issue, if one is to judge from the press, the surveys, the speeches, the enthusiasm of architects, technicians and social workers, and the organized indignation of those representing property interests. But is there really anything in America as yet which could properly be called a 'housing movement'?

The answer is no. And the answer explains why all the earnest activity of various individuals has so far been largely frustrated, and why the issue itself has been clouded and sidetracked. Movements are not made, when all is said and done, by a handful of specialists — however admirable their intentions may be, however rational their proposals. And above all, no housing movement can be launched that way. For 'housing' is no simple little matter to be solved in purely technical or bureaucratic terms. It is deeply involved with every department of our social and economic framework, and the smallest change in current methods is bound to have enormous reverberations. What is done or left undone today must sooner or later affect the life and living of every individual and group in the country. To effect any such change, it is axiomatic that there must be a motivating force stronger than the powers which are resisting it. And unemployed architects and scattered idealists just do not supply that force.

There are two lines in the history of modern housing, as the early sections of this book attempted to show. One is the line of rational investigation, of scientific and technical research, of individual imagination and experiment. To this line belong the Utopians and the Fabians, the co-operators and the early modern architects, and also most of the more sincere promoters of housing today in America. At their best they were all trying to clarify in terms of human environment what Montesquieu called 'the necessary relations derived from the nature of things.' At their weakest they were mere fugitives from reality.

The other line is the whole broad history of mass emotion and popular desire. Often it had little or no direct connection with 'housing' *per se:* the revolutionists of 1848 were not primarily revolting against the slums, but they were nevertheless responsible for the epidemic of 'model tenements' and worried reformers which followed on their defeat.

The two lines were of course closely interrelated. The possibility of mass action inspired all that was most valid in the experiments and Utopias. Conversely, the images and suggestions of a different world inspired discontent with the old one. And, if it had not been for the earlier experiments, the workers and consumers would probably not have known what they wanted in that period after the war when their voices became temporarily and partially effective. Certainly, without the handful of architects and planners who had given thought to the matter before their opportunity arose, the quality of post-war housing would never have been as high as it was.

But the touchstone, after all, of the post-war housing movement in Europe was the organized and well-informed demand: the German trade-unions who were prepared to carry out a large-scale housing program with governmental aid on their own initiative; the townspeople of England who elected Councillors on a housing platform; and everywhere, the workers who wanted not merely housing but revolution and a whole new social framework. The various Labour and Social-Democratic governments, muddled and cowardly though they were in almost every other respect, were clear on one point: they represented a body of citizens who demanded a positive program of good housing — not merely for some vague, hypothetical 'slum-dwellers,' but for themselves and their families, because they were thoroughly dissatisfied with the nineteenth century way of doing things and believed that there was a new way.

The lack of such a demand is the principal reason for all the obstacles which have piled up in the path of housing in America. If the demand were there, most of the obstacles, now seemingly insurmountable, would melt away. But instead of fostering such a demand, many of the most earnest housing promoters seem conscientiously to evade the fact that the issue is essentially a political one, in the broadest scope of the term. Their faces are turned, fruitlessly, in the opposite direction. They either pull the ears of the 'real estate interest,' or else endeavor to wheedle those same interests into the belief that housing would somehow work out to their pecuniary advantage after all.

The lack of an effective articulate demand is also largely responsible for a certain air of unreality which hangs over the matter. That distant, miracle-working image, 'Washington,' is the center of all eyes and all hopes, all praise and all criticism. Washington alone, apparently, can let loose the benevolent flood which will put everybody to work, clear up all the slums and dot the country with model developments duly stamped with the accolade of Federal approval. And yet there is something more impossibly 'un-American' about this vision than there would be in the reddest of red revolutions.

Benevolent paternalism, *Kathedersocialismus*, has absolutely no roots here at all. We got things for ourselves, because we knew what we wanted, or we did without. In all Europe there has never been any such centralization or *specialization* of housing responsibility as that contemplated today in America, whether in paternal Germany or Communist Russia or London-ruled England. And it is the firm opinion of this author that there will never be any realistic housing movement in this country until the workers and the consumers — and the unemployed — themselves take a hand in the solution.

We have a much vaunted tradition of individual initiative and 'self-sufficiency,' above all in housing matters. Can this force be transformed into effective *group initiative*, the only form of action which can supplant the environment of the nineteenth century with really modern houses and workable cities? There are a few signs of promise. The single housing project now under construction which emanated from a group of people who wanted good houses to live in — that of the Hosiery workers union in Philadelphia — is a very special case, not applicable in detail to many other situations. But it has already resulted in a considerable quickening of interest on the part of other organized workers in the region.

There was a time — and it was not so long ago — when the vast majority of Americans had one active ideal in common whatever the differences in their condition: to own a house and a lot. Many of them achieved it (particularly, as a matter of fact, in the Philadelphia region). Today most of them are being gradually forced to realize what a mockery that great symbol of security and progress and respectability has become. Sooner or later, all of them must face it.

If only a small part of the vast energy which was once directed toward individual home-ownership were now organized to demand a realistic program of modern housing — the best dwellings that planners can plan and that labor and materials can build (and we have an abundance of all three) — then there would be an American housing movement indeed.

THE END

APPENDIX TO PART THREE

NATIONAL HOUSING MEASURES

1850–1934

NOTE

This appendix comprises brief histories of the housing measures and resulting quantitative achievements in various European countries, both before and since the war. The housing policies of England, Germany, Holland, Belgium, France, and Austria are presented in some detail. Norway, Sweden, Denmark, and Switzerland are treated less fully, not because their work is less important but because the measures adopted are not essentially very different from those in other countries.

Considerable public utility housing has also been built since the war in Italy, Czecho-Slovakia, Finland, Poland, and Hungary. It has not been described in this book, either because it seemed on the whole less significant, or because the author has not had the opportunity to judge for herself, or has not found adequate data available.

Housing in Soviet Russia is omitted (with the exception of a few photographs and scattered notes) partly because the author has not been in Russia, and partly because the movement there is only just beginning, while in most countries under discussion it has been active for at least fifteen years. In many of them, indeed, the era of 'post-war housing' is already a closed chapter. After another five years Russian housing will undoubtedly be worth a book all to itself. However different the basic conditions of housing in Russia may be, though, the actual methods are not at present very sharply to be distinguished from those employed in other countries. Government funds and a certain amount of central control, with actual construction and administration delegated to local co-operative groups or local governments, is equally true of Russia, England, and Germany (even though the rents are more likely to be related directly to paying-power in the former than in either of the latter).

Aside from laws and policies and statistical achievements, the *technique* of modern housing is a subject which transcends national boundaries. Critical analysis of standards, planning and construction methods, and architecture, has therefore been presented by subjects in Part Four of the main body of this book.

I. ENGLAND

Before the War

Mid-nineteenth century Britain could already claim distinction in several not wholly unrelated fields. She was farthest advanced in the process of industrialization; she was the wealthiest and most powerful nation on earth; she had the largest areas of downright slum dwellings and the greatest proportion of pauper population residing in them; she had collected a terrifying array of figures and reports on death-rates, epidemics, and 'social unrest' and their correlation with the black environment of her cities; she had the busiest group of worried Tory philanthropists and reformers with their uplift societies and grim model tenements; she had a Public Health Act (1848); and she already had on the books the first piece of legislation (1851) which, although fruitless at the time, admitted and permitted public responsibility in the matter of building and renting low-cost dwellings.

The next thirty years saw the enactment of a whole series of laws which form the basis of English housing policy to this day. The Shaftesbury Act of 1851 enabled towns of over ten thousand to erect and rent cheap houses, to buy or use their own land for housing purposes, and to borrow from the Public Works Loan Fund in order to finance housing. The Terrens Acts of 1866–1868 gave local authorities the power to condemn or repair at the expense of the owner any house adjudged insanitary. The Cross Acts of 1875–1882 gave the larger towns complete powers of condemnation, compulsory purchase, and re-housing, either on the same site or in outlying districts. The three directions of attack on the housing problem were consolidated and made more workable finally in the Act of 1890. The only major additions which have been made since this Act were in the shape of various town-planning measures (of which the first was John Burns' Housing and Town Planning Act of 1909), the post-war provisions for public subsidy in addition to loans, and the imposition of a statutory obligation with regard to housing and slum-clearance. By 1914, the London County Council alone had put up about ten thousand small houses in outlying areas, in addition to providing for some eighteen thousand persons within clearance schemes, and itself directly administered and rented these properties.

But the real history of pre-war housing in England cannot be found either in the statute books or in figures of accomplishment. The change in effective policy from 1850 to 1910 is, on the one hand, well indicated by the difference between Shaftesbury's Society for Improving the Condition of the Labouring Classes, patronized by Prince Albert, and the National Housing and Town Planning Council, founded in 1900 almost entirely on the initiative of labor and consumer organizations. Politically, the period marks the shift of initiative in matters of housing policy from the Tory philanthropists to the Labour Party, the Fabians, and that new race of architects and planners who were beginning to see that the problem of human environment had to be attacked somewhere near its roots. Physically, the distinction is that between the Peabody Foundation tenements of the sixties and the various co-operative community experiments of which Letchworth Garden City, started in 1902, was the most significant. In short, the 'housing problem' had progressed from the mere matter of shelter for paupers to the whole question of how to build decent, workable cities for everybody. Quantitatively, not much had been done. But qualitatively, some of the London County Council's early suburban schemes and almost all of the war-workers' housing had reached a point which has not been greatly improved upon in England in all the vast body of post-war housing.

Post-War Housing

With returning soldiers looking for the 'Homes for Heroes' which they had been promised by Lloyd George, with prices sky-high, rent restrictions, and unaided private enterprise out of the running as far as average housing was concerned, and with a cool shortage of a million dwellings, plus an additional need of one hundred thousand per year, something had to be done. The first thing established by the Act of 1919 was a definite statutory obligation on the part of local governments 'to consider the needs of their area with respect to the provision of houses for the working classes... and, as often as occasion arises... to prepare and submit to the Minister of Health a scheme for the exercise of their powers.'

The only fundamental innovation in post-war housing legislation was the *subsidy*. And the principal thing which differentiates one law from another is the amount of the subsidy, who shall pay it, and which building agency should be most favored. The reason for the subsidy, of course, was the spread between an 'economic' rent and the rent which those who needed houses could afford to pay. The principal variations between the different laws are as follows.

ADDISON ACT OF 1919: It was necessary to dynamite the general economic apathy with regard to building. Three forms of State Subsidy were offered, in addition to the usual provisions with regards to loans. To local governments constructing their own housing, who would themselves contribute a certain subsidy in fixed proportion to their tax valuation, the State offered to cover any additional annual loss — in effect, a blank check. (The Ministry of Health, of course, retained the right to audit both plans, costs, and rents.) To public-utility societies, the State undertook to cover thirty per cent (later fifty per cent, then forty per cent) of the interest and redemption charges on approved schemes. To private enterprise non-repayable lump-sum payments were made, fixed first at $650 to $800 per house and later increased, specifications as to cost and type being supplied by the Government. Under this Act, within two years, about 170,000 dwellings were started by the local governments, and some 44,000 by private enterprise, including a minor proportion by housing societies. It is not surprising that building costs rose to inordinate and exploitive heights (the ratio of materials to labor in a pre-war house was about half and half; by 1921 it was two to one), and that the cost to the State was very great. But it should be noted that the Labour Minister of Health, Christopher Addison, had originally included in his scheme a real plan for providing materials through an official agency, the only way in which it could have been worked economically. In any case, the entire system of subsidies was repealed in 1921, and presently the $5000 house declined to a $2500 house. The ensuing two-year stoppage was not only a great disaster in itself, but brought to an untimely end the successful new Building Guilds (part of the Guild Socialism Movement), a first attempt to weld the English building trades into comprehensive units on a rationalized and co-operative basis.

CHAMBERLAIN ACT OF 1923: Mr. Baldwin's Conservative Government granted to local authorities thirty dollars per year for twenty years and lump-sum grants to private builders in various forms. Also, in order to encourage private enterprise, one of the very few English experiments in tax-exemption was initiated. Under this law 75,000 houses were erected by local authorities, 351,000 by private enterprise, and about 12,000 by public-utility societies.

WHEATLEY ACT OF 1924: The Labour Government of this year liberalized the 1923 measures, providing a subsidy to local authorities of forty-five dollars per house per year for forty years, raised somewhat in rural districts to allow for the greater costs of building and the lower wage-scales. Any loss over and above these subsidies must be borne directly by the local governments. This loss varies greatly, but in general the largest cities, where land-values are highest, have had to sustain the greatest additional expense. In Welwyn Garden City, where the cost of sites has not been inflated between the purchase of raw land and its ultimate use, and where the best English standards of planning and architecture are utilized, houses that reach the lowest-paid workers in the district actually bring in a slight profit to the Council. The additional local subsidy under this and the 1930 Act was normally about eighteen dollars per year for forty years.

1930: The cost of building having declined somewhat, the subsidies were revised downward once more, to thirty-seven dollars for towns and fifty-four dollars for rural districts. It was intended that this Act should guarantee a greater degree of future stability in housing matters, unfortunately not realized. Under the 1924 and 1930 Acts, up to the present, some 750,000 houses have been erected by local authorities and 423,000 by private enterprise, the latter including a few thousand by public-utility societies.

1932: TOWN AND COUNTRY PLANNING ACT. This very important law, although not directly concerned with the housing shortage, may be termed a further outgrowth of that three-cornered fusion of Fabian Socialism, the Garden City, and Regional Planning, which has already been noticeable to some extent in the housing policies. Its general purpose, considerably mangled in passing Parliament, was stated by Sir Raymond Unwin to be nothing less than a fundamental change in the conception of land. Instead of every field and plot being considered a potential building-site, land should now be accepted as permanent open space until it has been decided right and proper that it should be built upon. The Act as passed can hardly be said to live up to this principle, and its complicated provisions cannot be described in this space, but some of the main features may be noted. The planning authority of Regional or Joint Town Planning Committees is furthered; 'amenity,' 'natural interest,' 'beauty,' and 'historic' or 'architectural value' are recognized as proper statutory considerations in planning or prohibiting streets or buildings; it is theoretically possible to prohibit most forms of chaotic 'ribbon development' and of 'spotted building fever';

it is possible to zone and replan built-up areas; it greatly facilitates the procedure of a local authority desiring to set up a satellite town outside its limits with State funds; it makes easier the acquisition of land by local authorities; and it forces local authorities to prepare and submit town-planning schemes.

ACT OF 1933: The Conservative Government suddenly put a stop to all subsidies for small-house construction, except in the case of slum-clearance. The theory was that costs had dropped far enough to permit private enterprise to re-enter the field. Building and loan societies were to be encouraged, and public-utility societies which had received State assistance were to be compelled to use their funds only for low-cost construction. On the other hand, the local authorities were supposed to 'concentrate on slum-clearance.' The result, however, has been almost exactly nothing. No more houses were put up by private enterprise than would have been built in any case, and these were all for the middle class. The demolition of slums proceeded no faster than usual. And there is still a great shortage of dwellings for the low-income groups. The indignation has been so great and so wide-spread, however, that it is more than likely that some form of subsidy for house construction by local authorities will soon be reinstated.

Slum Clearance

As we have already seen, the three principal modes of attack on the problem of inadequate housing were well formulated before the war in England. *Repair*, embracing all the passionate platitude of those reformers who, like Octavia Hill, have a taste or talent for nursing, came in with the Torrens Acts of 1868. *Demolition*, implying if used as a single weapon more hatred for the houses than interest in the inmates, was the main feature of Mr. Cross's Acts of 1875. And *construction*, the backbone of the English post-war housing movement up to 1933, curiously enough came first of all via Lord Shaftesbury.

But demolition and reconstruction of insanitary areas were also carried on after the war, and with special measures. By the Act of 1919, the Government theoretically stood the whole loss over the fixed rate of municipal contribution, for slum-clearance as well as for new housing. Moreover, compensation for compulsory sale, before the war always exorbitant, was established on a new basis. Payment was required only for the value of the land as a *cleared site* — and this was further reduced if the land were to be used for re-housing or for an open space. Also, the land could be taken over upon approval of the scheme, and the price arranged by arbitration later. However, very few clearances schemes were approved by the Ministry under this Act.

THE ACT OF 1925 was primarily designed to promote slum-clearance. An unhealthy area was defined as one 'in which (*a*) there are any houses, courts, or alleys unfit for human habitation, (*b*) the narrowness, closeness, and bad arrangement, or the bad condition of the streets and houses or groups of houses, or the want of light, air, ventilation, or proper convenience, or any sanitary defects are dangerous or injurious to the health of the inhabitants either in the buildings in the area or in the neighboring buildings.' Properties not adjudged unhealthy may be included in the scheme to render it more efficient or economical. Fifty per cent of the loss was donated outright by the State. Something, but not very much, was accomplished under this law.

The most effective Act to promote slum re-housing was that of 1930, which changed the method of providing financial assistance. The State grant toward clearance and re-housing takes the form of a fixed annual subsidy on a unit basis of eleven to seventeen dollars per year for forty years for each person displaced and re-housed. Local authorities must contribute an annual subsidy of eighteen dollars per dwelling, and ordinarily must contribute much more besides, particularly if the same people are to be re-housed on the same spot at suitably low rentals. (A recent Liverpool report estimates that it would cost them just about four times as much in municipal subsidies to re-house the slum tenant on the spot as it would to do so in an outlying district.) The Act also permits the towns to grant rent rebates when necessary, to enable the slum inhabitants to pay for the new dwellings. All local authorities were required to submit five-year programs of slum demolition and improvement.

Altogether, by the middle of 1932, 11,687 dwellings had been demolished and most of their 78,798 inhabitants re-housed either in new dwellings on the same site or in entirely new developments. About half of this was done in London.

As has been noted, the intention of the 1933 Act to force the local authorities to 'concentrate on slum-clearance' has, in spite of a tremendous amount of speech-making and publicity, resulted in no more demolition and re-housing of slum-dwellers than could ordinarily have been expected.

Municipal Housing and Municipal Finances

Although Greater London authorities, including the London County Council, the Metropolitan Borough Councils, etc., now own and let more than one hundred thousand houses and flats, and provide, therefore, the most spectacular example of municipal housing in Europe, the actual set-up in a smaller city may be more illuminating because more typical. Below are a few figures from a recent report by the Liverpool Corporation:

Number of houses, etc., provided by Corporation	26,427
Number of private enterprise houses subsidized	4,294
Area of city	24,195 acres
Acreage of principal housing estates	2,543 acres
Population of city, 1931	855,539 persons
Population of subsidized houses (estimated)	135,000 persons
Percentage of population in State- and rate-aided houses (approximate)	15¾ per cent
Net housing debt	£15,090,743
Gross annual rental, including rates at 14*s.* in the pound	785,000
Exchequer subsidies, 1930–31	430,398
Net cost of housing to city, 1930–31	116,558
Equaling a rate in the pound of	5*d.*
Product of penny rate	23,620

(*Note:* The last item means the product of a penny tax on every pound of rental income in the city, and is the English system of judging the assessed value of a city.)

The number of cottages per thousand of population erected by the authorities in twelve of the largest cities is as follows:

Nottingham	49	Leeds	19
Birmingham	37.5	Southampton	18.5
Liverpool	29.2	Cardiff	18.3
Leicester	25	Stoke	12.2
Newcastle	23.2	Plymouth	11.9
Manchester	21.5		

England and Wales: National Summary

In the period 1919–1933, some 2,112,000 new dwellings were put up in England by the following agencies:

Construction agencies	*Number of dwellings*		*Per cent*	
Government assisted:				
(of these about 40,000 in rural parishes)				
Public authorities	758,000		36	
Public-utility societies	22,000		1	
Private enterprise	400,000		19	
Total assisted		1,180,000		56
Unassisted private enterprise		932,000		44
Total dwellings constructed		2,112,000		100

According to the 1919 estimates of the shortage and of normal requirements, about 2,400,000 new dwellings would have been needed. In addition, the 1931 census showed a much greater increase in family units than had been allowed for. If all the new houses were economically available to the people who needed them, there was still a shortage. As, generally speaking, only housing put up by public authorities is let at rentals which the average worker can pay, and as probably half of even these houses can hardly be paid for by unskilled workers, it will be seen that the claims of various English authorities against the present Government, for discontinuing the constructive housing program, are probably well founded.

The fact that unassisted private enterprise was able to build such a large number of houses in this period is ample proof that the activities of the Government were in a field not in any way touched by normal real-estate practice. Indeed, it is more than probable that the rise in the standard of demand set up by the Government — in matters of planning amenity — may well have stimulated ordinary building trade for the upper-income groups as well.

Housing and the National Budget

The Government's annual contribution to the nearly one million and a quarter State-assisted houses built since 1919 now amounts to about $75,000,000. There is, of course, a further charge on the local authorities, although much less than this sum. And it is after all a rather minor item, when considered in conjunction with the accomplishment and with other items of the budget. The subsidies were only about 1.7 per cent of the national budget in 1932 (scarcely the cost of three first-class battleships, and many millions less than the amount spent on the Royal Air Force alone). In the year 1929–1930 the local authorities paid out about $180,000,000 solely for poor-relief. Moreover, it should not be forgotten that, during a period of mounting unemployment and depression, a very large share of the more than two and a half billion dollars' worth of Government-aided house-construction would have had to be paid out in any case in the form of relief or a dole.

Scotland

In Scotland, much the same legal apparatus has applied as in England and Wales. But the situation itself is very different. While

England, straight through the nineteenth century up to this day, has remained primarily a country of two-story one-family houses, the Scottish cities from the early years of the Industrial Revolution onward (and even earlier in Glasgow) produced what is probably the world's worst norm of high tenement-house construction—with the possible exception of New York. While the typical slum in England is an occasional back-to-back or alley house, that of Scotland is a one-room dwelling in a six- to eight-story massive stone structure. Therefore, while the English overcrowding problem is largely a matter of 'surplus' families and dwelling-shortage, the Scottish one is more the question of room-overcrowding and of totally inadequate dwellings to begin with. Measured in 'dwellings' and families, there was hardly any shortage at all in Scotland. Measured in rooms and population, two million people lived more than two per room and one million more than three per room.

Government-aided housing in Scotland in the period 1919–1933 is slightly more in proportion to the number of families than it was in England. The total assisted houses were 176,000 with a far greater proportion put up by local authorities, and more also involved slum-clearance.

Construction Agency	*Number of houses*		*Proportion*
Local authorities:			
New land	102,100	133,000	75%
Slum-clearance	31,500		
Public-utility societies	600		1% (−)
Private enterprise	41,800		24%
Total	176,000		100%

Slum-clearance in Glasgow goes back to 1866, when eighty acres were cleared and thirty thousand persons displaced — but not re-housed by the city. Philanthropic housing started in 1870, and public housing was done before even London had made the venture.

Ireland

The problem of Ireland is similar to that of England, with perhaps more emphasis on the rundown rural slum. There are, however, plenty of tenements in the cities.

Before the war, Ireland made relatively far greater use of the British Housing Acts than did England. By 1892, local authorities with Government loans had put up some fourteen thousand cottages. By 1917, there were forty-eight thousand such cottages, which

Sydney Webb calls 'healthy, but unfortunately very ugly.' As a matter of fact, the local authorities had, since the Irish Labourers' Act of 1883, a statutory obligation to provide housing, whether it involved subsidy or not (which it ordinarily did). The rents were extraordinarily low and lead one perhaps to consider the bitter meagerness of Irish wages rather than the virtue of the authorities. Dublin first built houses in 1907, and has built some every year since, except during the war.

Since the war, about fourteen thousand houses have been erected with contributions from the Government. Nine thousand of these were put up either by public-utility societies or by private enterprise (the latter being usually small farmers). The remaining five thousand were built by the local authorities. The total contribution of the State, two thirds of which went toward municipal construction, has been around $10,000,000. Most of this has been in the form of outright lump-sum subsidies.

II. GERMANY

Early Background

In Germany, as in England, the general character of post-war housing policy was well established long before 1914. Contrary to England, it is very difficult to establish a few important dates in legislative history in order to describe the early achievements. There was in fact no national housing law on the books before the war, but this was merely because the far greater statutory powers of the cities and the States did not require such special legislation in order to undertake responsibility for low-cost housing. It is possible, however, to distinguish two periods in the pre-war history of German housing, approximately before and after the late eighties, when the social-insurance legislation was passed and also the law which recognized co-operative and limited-dividend housing societies.

Public opinion on the housing question in Germany has never been confined, as it was in most other European countries before the war and in America up to this day, to the comparatively small question of cleaning up a few of the most insanitary slums. This was partly due to the fact that the German cities, whose major industrial growth came later, were not as chaotically constructed and did not as a rule have the flimsy shacks and alley slums common in other countries. On the other hand, they had a period of urban land-speculation comparable to none (land-values around Berlin before the war were often eight or ten times what they were in London) and all rents were relatively very high and dwellings small and crowded. In the middle of the century, inflated land-prices were encouraged rather than remedied by the activities of municipal governments, who laid out wide paved streets in big blocks and permitted high buildings and excessive coverage. The co-ordination and extension plan for Berlin and Charlottenburg in 1858, in the words of Dr. Hegemann, prescribed tenements ('rent-barracks') for four million future Berliners. Therefore, the typical German nineteenth-century slum — indeed the typical residential construction — was a six- or seven-story tenement with two or three 'back-buildings,' firmly constructed and usually supplied with water, but of a grimness only surpassed in the worst Glasgow flats and in the New York Old Law tenement.

Before the War

There has been a recognized 'housing problem' in Germany ever since the late forties, but there, as in other countries, the model tenements put up by worried aristocrats and the Liberal efforts to promote home-ownership were on the whole either ineffectual or worse. It was not until the bitter shortage of 1870–1875 that the forces which were to shape later policies really began to take form.

The Marxian Socialists were agitating against any partial reforms whatsoever; and they were, incidentally, educating all German workers, whether revolutionary or not, to a much more concrete understanding of their power and their real interests. Workers' organizations demanded municipal land measures, municipal housing, and aid for co-operative societies. On the other hand, there was the newly founded *Verein für Socialpolitik*, fountain-head of the strong movement in favor of what is usually called 'socialism of the chair' or *Kathedersocialismus*, but which is in actuality State and Municipal Capitalism. The cities, in many cases merely reviving mediæval powers and responsibilities, began to purchase large areas of land, to exercise considerable control over land-use, and to engage in a variety of public-utility businesses, among them low-cost housing. And finally, the more advanced architects and technicians began to take an interest in housing and city-planning, and therefore to ally themselves either with workers' organizations or the Burgher 'socialists.'

In 1889 a law was passed which granted certain favors to co-operative housing societies, and by 1914 there were no less than fourteen hundred such organizations doing active work. Most of them were formed by the prospective tenants themselves, who supplied little or no equity, and most of the dwellings remained in collective ownership. Community equipment, such as kindergartens, laundries, social rooms, libraries, etc., was a feature from the start, and the standards of design, layout, and amenity were almost invariably much higher than those prevailing in speculative developments. The influence of this work on the high standard of demand after the war is probably incalculable.

But the large volume of co-operative housing would not have been possible without the cheap money supplied by the social-insurance funds, which were officially encouraged to make loans on public-utility housing. By the end of 1913, the insurance foundations had invested some $114,000,000 in housing, a sum which probably produced a good 150,000 dwellings.

The various States and local authorities were meanwhile increasingly active in housing matters on their own account. Official housing funds were set up for Prussia in 1895, for the Empire in 1901, and later for most of the other States. At first this money was largely used to construct dwellings for public employees, but the field was gradually extended to include all forms of public-utility or co-operative housing society. The Prussian Decree of 1901, issued jointly by the Ministers of Trade and Commerce, Interior, Religion, and Agriculture, advised that the cities should accept full responsibility, not merely for housing their own employees, but also for housing conditions in general — by building themselves, by supporting and subsidizing public-utility societies, and by purchasing large tracts of land and renting them below cost for housing purposes. Several provincial governments complied by imposing most of the recommendations as statutory obligations. By 1909 at least half of the larger German cities had directly assisted in the construction of low-cost public-utility housing. In addition to the insurance funds and those especially set up by States, money was provided out of the proceeds of the land-value increment tax (a national law of 1911) and by the semi-official savings banks.

The Situation After the War

The foregoing paragraphs should have served to indicate that post-war activities, in housing as in other matters, represented nothing revolutionary in Germany. The Socialists (after their left wing had dropped off to form the Communist Party, which the Social Democracy regarded as its worst enemy straight through to the bitter end) were little more 'socialist,' either practically or theoretically, than the more progressive burghers of the nineties. Which is to say that they were not socialists at all, in the Marxian sense. They merely carried some steps farther the policy, already clearly defined, of governmental responsibility for a certain minimum standard of security and health and civic amenity, and of regulating private enterprise in certain basic fields by governmental competition or monopoly. If they had not been confronted on the one hand by a critical housing shortage, and on the other by an insistent demand for *better* housing from workers who already knew very clearly the difference between good houses and bad ones, it is highly unlikely that they would have accomplished what they did.

The quantitative shortage, based on 'extra' families, was estimated at a million dwellings in 1920. In addition, several hundred thousand dwellings per year were needed to take care of the normal increase in population, and obsolescence. This need has by no means been met.

The great stumbling-block in house-production, either by the Government or by private enterprise, was the scarcity and high cost of money. A first mortgage which would have been four per cent before the war was ten per cent or higher afterwards, if obtainable at all, and was still eight and one half per cent in 1929. The post-war rent for a privately financed new house in 1927 would have been four hundred per cent of the pre-war rent for the same construction. Meanwhile, wages had increased by only fifty per cent. Rent restrictions were stringently enforced, and vacant dwellings were temporarily commandeered. Unassisted private enterprise was therefore quite out of the question in so far as the great mass of housing was concerned: it is merely remarkable that it produced as many dwellings as it did.

At first, on the basis that the rise in building costs was only temporary, the various governments undertook to cover the difference between the actual cost price and what was considered a 'normal' cost. This they did either by constructing themselves and writing off part of the investment, or by granting outright subsidies to public-utility societies. The House Rent Tax, described later, was first instituted in 1921, and part of its proceeds went into these subsidies. Most of the 700,000 dwellings erected from 1919 through 1925 received some sort of public aid. But, as it became evident that pre-war conceptions of 'normal' were lost forever, it was necessary to set up a long-time policy to replace the temporary measures. And the next period, from 1926 through 1931, marks the most fruitful epoch of modern housing which the world has yet to show.

From 1926 *through* 1931

A source of building capital was the first essential. And the primary fact of German housing policy from 1925 on is the Hauszinssteuer, or *House Rent Tax*. It is levied on all buildings built before the war, and takes advantage of the fact that mortgages were to all practical purposes wiped out during the inflation and the owners thereby presented with a large part of the capital value of their buildings. ('House-owners were the only war-victors' was a slogan of the period.) The tax amounts to from ten to fifty per cent of pre-war rents, varying with the amount of depreciation. About $2,680,000,000 was raised in this way in the seven years from 1926 through 1932 (more than twice the income-tax yield), of which $1,251,600,000 was loaned out on second mortgages for low-cost housing. The rest was used for general budget expenditures. In 1929 this tax amounted to $420,000,000 and was some 12.6 per cent of the total tax and tariff income.

These second mortgages constitute both Government investment and Government subsidy, for they were loaned at a rate of interest considerably lower than the price paid for other money by the Government, usually at about one per cent, with one per cent amortization to start after five years. A typical financial set-up for a unit dwelling costing three thousand dollars in 1930 would be about as follows:

First mortgage in the open market, at about 8½ per cent (includes amortization)	$1200
Second mortgage House Rent Tax, at 1 per cent (amortized at 1 per cent after five years)	1200
Equity (sometimes partly in the form of land made available by the city) at 7 per cent	600

In the case of the very lowest-cost dwellings, the first mortgage would probably be provided by one of the official or semi-official agencies (such as the social-insurance funds) at a rate about one per cent lower. Or the first mortgage might be very small and a third mortgage provided by the city itself, at a rate somewhat lower than cost.

The House Rent Tax funds are administered directly by the cities, who receive back a fixed proportion of the actual tax which was raised within their limits. The municipal housing authorities act very closely with the city-planning and engineering offices (they are usually all in one department) and exercise much influence over the architecture and planning not merely of their own constructions but of all State-assisted housing.

During the five years of greatest activity, 1927 through 1931, the astounding number of 1,436,000 new dwellings were erected in Germany — or twenty-two dwellings per thousand inhabitants, or very nearly one dwelling for every ten families. Of this number about a million, or seventy per cent, were directly aided by some form of Government financing. And most of the rest probably profited by municipal land policies, semi-official loans, tax-exemptions, or other indirect means of assistance.

Ten per cent of these million and a half dwellings were put up directly by public authorities; thirty-four per cent by public utility building societies (many of them allied with the trade unions); and the remainder by private enterprise (although such private enterprise as received government aid was set up as a rule on a public utility, limited dividend basis).

During these same five years the total dwelling construction investment may be divided as follows:

I. Private capital for first mortgages		$1,529,000,000	46%	
Of which:				
Mostly semi-official	Savings banks			18%
	Insurance bodies			9%
	Public credit organizations			7%
	Private mortgage banks			12%
II. Public funds		$1,440,000,000	43%	
Of which:				
House rent tax				28%
Other public loans				11%
'Employers' payments'				4%
III. Equity from building societies, builders, and 'dwelling-awaiters'		$378,000,000	11%	11%
TOTAL		$3,347,000,000	100%	100%

The average cost of these 1,436,000 dwellings was therefore around $2330 complete. Of the total public outlay for housing, about three per cent was distributed directly by the State, twenty-seven per cent by the 'Länder' (rural housing), and the remaining seventy per cent by the cities.

The net housing outlay (minus income and interest) amounted in 1929–1930 to:

0.1 per cent of the total State budget
7.9 per cent of the total provincial budgets
12.5 per cent of the total municipal budgets

The net housing outlay compares with various other items on the budgets thus, in 1929–1930:

MUNICIPAL GOVERNMENTS	
Total expenditure	$1,349,000,000
Housing	157,000,000
Police	54,000,000
Education	254,000,000
Health	55,000,000

ENTIRE NATIONAL BUDGET, ALL GOVERNMENTS	
Total	$4,182,000,000
Housing	240,000,000
Education	554,000,000
Science and Art	101,000,000
Welfare (Health, Relief, etc.)	752,000,000
War charges	1,004,000,000

In addition to direct expenditure for housing, municipalities have guaranteed large numbers of loans issued by private agencies. From 1924 through 1929 these amounted to one half (or about $250,000,000) of the sum of their direct loans, not counting the House Rent Tax.

Land Policy

As important as the governmental policy of direct financial assistance, and more important than the form which this may happen to take at any given period, is the traditionally grounded and to all appearances permanent policy of German municipalities with regard to the acquisition of land. Most German cities have always owned large sections of their territory (twenty-five per cent or so on the average and all the way up to Ulm with eighty-five per cent). And all of them acquired great tracts during the period after the war when prices were often as low as one fifth of pre-war prices. Berlin, for instance, bought nearly ten thousand acres of land within its boundaries, at an average price of about five cents a square foot. Berlin now owns more than one third of its area, or seventy-eight thousand acres, plus another seventy thousand acres outside of its boundaries.

The effect of such a policy on housing is obvious. From 1919 through 1926, two fifths to four fifths of all the land used for new dwellings was from the municipal domain. From 1927 through 1929, seventy towns contributed or leased cheaply for housing purposes some six thousand acres of their property.

In 1920, for the first time, municipalities were authorized to expropriate unbuilt land for housing purposes. The compensation was to be 'reasonable,' without allowing for any increases in nominal value arising from war conditions.

From 1931 *to the Present*

In November, 1931, the German housing policy underwent a fundamental change. The shortage of urban dwellings had not been made up in spite of the tremendous activity of the preceding years, but as the crisis deepened, the proportion of the population which could pay for the new houses and apartments grew smaller and smaller. 'All houses are too expensive for the unemployed,' and there were six million of them by 1931. Moreover, it began to look as if the problem of unemployment were a permanent one, and thousands of workers left the cities for the country, thus enhancing the rural housing difficulties which were already bad enough. And finally, political considerations made it seem not only desirable but necessary that Germany should be put on a more nearly self-sufficient basis as far as food at least was concerned.

The State had already contributed somewhat to agricultural colonization, and by 1932 about sixty thousand dwellings in farm settlements — mostly in East Prussia — had been established with official aid. Allotment gardens on the outskirts of the city, either separate from the dwellings or planned in connection with new *Siedlungen*, have been extremely popular ever since the war. They number about 1,700,000 and cover at least 250,000 acres. But, taken as a whole, housing had been largely of an urban nature, for urban workers.

Therefore, the Reich decreed that no national funds would be available for housing except for very small absolutely minimum dwellings attached to gardens large enough to provide at least partial support for the tenant. The holdings were to be between 6000 and 30,000 square feet (they average around 10,000 or a little less) and the total cost of land and dwelling, including a certain amount of capital equipment such as implements, beasts, etc., must not be over $750. As $2000 to $2500 was the average cost of Government-assisted dwellings up to 1930, it will be seen that standards had to be enormously lowered all around. The State grants a loan not above $625 for each holding, guaranteed by means of a mortgage, with interest at four per cent and one per cent amortization (interest for the first three years at three per cent or less). The remainder of the cost is supplied partly by the actual labor of the tenant, who provides no other capital, and is paid only his unemployment allowance throughout, and partly by the city or by another loan. The State loan gives precedence to any other mortgages that are registered. The colonist is supposed to be a free owner of his property within thirty years.

At the time of the first decree, the State allotted $12,000,000 for this purpose. Other funds were earmarked later, and up to the present some $45,000,000 have been allotted for about 60,000 such dwellings. The whole movement seems to have been given at least a strong rhetorical backing by the Hitler régime.

German materials must be used throughout, and the methods of construction have been necessarily of the simplest.

It must not be thought, however, that an individual unemployed goes out and builds his own shack all by himself as he may. The ordinary procedure is for the city to lay out a *Siedlung* on a piece of city-owned land — usually quite far from the town — and then either directly or by means of a housing society to select a hundred or more unemployed workers who, under trained supervision, build as a unit the hundred houses needed for their use. In selecting the workers, care is taken that all the building trades are represented and that totally unskilled labor is not more than a half or a third of the whole number.

Of the planning and general philosophy of these unemployed colonies something has been said in another section. It may be mentioned here that they are ordinarily very inaccessible, and that they have seldom been set out with any larger agricultural, industrial, or land-economic plan in mind.

The Outlook

The House Rent Tax, very little of which has been earmarked for housing during the past few years in any case, is due to be gradually reduced beginning in 1935 and will be no longer levied at all by 1940. Therefore, unless the financial situation should ease up or new sources of money be found, no housing on the 1928 scale can be expected. Whatever is done under Hitler's leadership is almost certain to be in the nature of rural or semi-rural colonization, for political as well as economic reasons. There are many indications among the sporadic activities of the various cities during the past year that all future emphasis will be placed on individual initiative and home-ownership. The day of the co-operatives (which were often of a trade-union or political character) is definitely over.

As for the future of that long and close and on the whole very happy relation between the city governments and the form and location of new housing-construction, it is difficult to predict at this time. If one is to judge by a manifesto published last spring in the *Baugilde*, official organ of the German Architectural Society, much pressure is being exerted to stop all planning and regulation and 'bureaucratic interference,' not to mention actual construction by public bodies. If such a change can be effected, in the light of the past fifty years, it will have been a reactionary revolution indeed.

Summary of Accomplishment

Just about three million new dwellings have been made available in Germany since 1919, at least eighty per cent of them with direct public aid. Large though this figure seems, at an annual need of two hundred thousand merely to take care of the increase in population, it will be seen that the original quantitative shortage, let alone the qualitative one, has hardly been touched. There are still hundreds of thousands of families without any separate dwelling. Moreover, with the decrease in wages and the increase in unemployment, the number of the new dwellings available for the lower-income groups has grown steadily smaller. Also, the price of food and clothing has been excessively high all through the post-war period and, although rents have been kept down by regulation to about twenty-five per cent above their pre-war level, the proportion of income available for rent has not been large enough to pay for even a minimum new subsidized dwelling in many cases. Therefore, while the slums remain badly overcrowded, there are even a few of the more luxurious new houses (chiefly those built before 1929 during the period of optimism) which stand empty.

As for slum-clearance, it can be readily understood that very little if anything has been attempted. Moreover, German slums are not like the more obvious English ones — comparatively small and well-defined areas cluttered with ramshackle cottages. They are more like those in New York: entire districts covered with tall, standardized, and unfortunately very firm tenements which no mere patching can alleviate.

The real significance of German housing from 1925 to 1931 is not that it was cheap, which it was not, but that it could have been done at all under the economic and financial circumstances then prevailing. And, much more, that it constituted technically and often æsthetically an entirely new method of approach to the whole question, a method and a body of ideas and experiments which no later housing can afford to ignore. What Germany added to the science of social and environmental planning has been described in other sections.

Who Paid for German Housing?

A note must here be added in response to the often-heard rumor that all the German housing was perfidiously paid for 'out of American money.' This idea was first embroidered, I believe, by Garet Garrett in the *Saturday Evening Post* in an article which was later circulated as a pamphlet under the title 'Other People's Money' and over, it might be added, 'the compliments of the Chemical Foundation, Inc.' This is no place in which to consider the interesting ramifications thus presented, but the claims of Mr. Garrett should be briefly compared with the facts.

Germany, it seems, had been loaned a great deal of money by America in order to rehabilitate her industries in order to make profits with which to pay reparations, which in turn should have paid off the war-debts which were owed to America. But Germany, according to Mr. Garrett, chose rather the primrose path of spending the money on parks and swimming-pools and especially on monstrous and luxurious housing developments which were not at all needed. A perfect orgy of criminal extravagance, in short. Only it just does not happen to be true.

To take the 'unproductive' items — the swimming-pools and stadiums — first. According to Mr. Bruening, the total sum spent by German cities on 'luxuries' from 1924 through 1930 was only about $57,500,000, although nothing had been done for ten years before. This covers all outlay for art and science, physical culture and athletics, swimming-pools, child welfare, recreation, public gardens, parks and forests. It represents just 2.5 per cent of the total municipal indebtedness, and if it had all been loaned from abroad it would have amounted to almost exactly 1 per cent of the outstanding foreign credits in Germany in July, 1931. So it could not have been the stadiums which were snatching the war-debt payments out of our mouth.

As for the housing, an observer who had merely seen the financial set-ups for the new dwellings might well remark that as investments they are a good many times as sound as the real-estate developments of the same period in America turned out to be, and that it might well have been fortunate if some of our money had gone into them. Looking at them in 1934, from the vantage-point of one of our newly blighted suburban areas, one might be glad that Germany at least had something to show for our period of prosperity. But as a matter of fact, relatively few of the houses have any foreign money under them.

Bruno Schwan, Burgomeister of Berlin and director of the German Society for Housing Reform, collected the available figures in a response to Mr. Garrett's attack. In July of 1931, according to the Baseler Gutachten, the total foreign loans outstanding in Germany amounted to $5,750,000,000. Of this amount only $2,250,000,000 were in long-term loans, the only important type of credit as far as housing is concerned. The total capital value of the residential construction between 1924 and 1931 was about $4,500,000,000. And, by eliminating the House Rent Tax loans, the owners' equity, the insurance and savings bank loans, etc. (all official figures), Herr Schwan shows very clearly that the absolute maximum possible of foreign investment in German housing could not have been more than 13 per cent of the capital cost, or under $600,000,000 or 10 per cent of the total foreign loans, which included a large proportion of Swiss and Scandinavian mortgages. Moreover, the shortage has by no means been made up, and every cent that has gone into housing was a necessary expenditure.

But the psychological reality of Mr. Garrett's impression of German city-development remains, and it is much more illuminating than his over-patriotic statistics. What honest American reporter, seeing a well-laid-out residential district or a good modern building for the first time, would not naturally suppose it to be something extraordinary, and therefore doubtless extravagant?

III. HOLLAND

Of all the countries in the world, Holland is perhaps the clearest example of the effect of a particular regional environment on the activities and general character of a population. By nature and industrial history just as individualistic as the French or the English, and with the same proud and jealous burgher heritage as that of the German cities, the circumstances of their land and living yet developed in them a degree of co-operative realism not to be found in the other three countries. 'Neo-technic' planning probably begins with the Dutch dikes and the systematic reclamation of the polders, just as the draining and development of the bottom of the Zuider Zee is one of its most interesting manifestations today. And the public housing policy of Holland, although it did not really begin until after the *Act of* 1901, has so far been the most effective — both in houses per population and in lowness of rental in proportion to wages — of any national effort. Relatively more slum-areas have been demolished as well. Moreover, this has been accomplished at an outright cost to the Government relatively lower than in most of the other countries.

Before the War

In the eighteen-fifties, the Netherlands had the same flurry of 'model' housing and still-born legislation, directly inspired by the activities of Prince Albert, but nevertheless quite traceable to the fear of revolution, as had most Continental countries. Then in the seventies a State Commission issued a very black report on housing conditions, and the city of Amsterdam started to provide land and funds for public-utility housing. Nothing much was accomplished, however, until the *Act of* 1901, which was a model piece of comprehensive housing legislation in its day, and is still the basic law of Holland.

This Act, first of all, obliged all local authorities to set up minimum standards of light, space, ventilation, sanitation, and occupancy. It provided machinery for surveying conditions, for condemnation of insanitary dwellings, and for expropriating slum properties or unbuilt areas for housing purposes (urging that only the 'use-value' be paid on such land). It required all towns of over ten thousand population and any fast-growing smaller ones to make detailed extension-plans, including parks, building-lines, etc. And finally, it set up a whole system of public aid for the financing of public-utility housing. State loans are provided through the agency of the local authorities (who were responsible for payments). These loans can cover up to one hundred per cent of the cost, and run for fifty years (later fifty years on the building and seventy-five on the land), repayable in equal annual installments, with interest at the rate currently quoted on State debentures. After the war this rate was usually four and three-fourths per cent. Ordinarily, the society's equity amounts to very little, as the share capital of members bears no relation to the cost and is usually only about ten dollars or less per family. Loans are also available for direct municipal housing. Subsidies could be provided by lowering the loan charges, half the loss being borne by the State and half by the local authority. Public-utility societies (much more stringently defined in Holland than elsewhere) must be authorized by the Government, must engage only in low-cost housing, and must limit their dividends to four per cent (later six per cent). *Members are not allowed to buy their houses.* A central Housing Commission passes on the projects.

Under this Act about 16,000 dwellings were constructed from 1905 to 1914, in addition to a certain number put up with municipal aid alone. During the war, the activity was greatly intensified, additional subsidies were provided to cover the rising building costs, and from 1915 through 1918 more than 31,000 State-aided houses were constructed. In 1918, an Emergency Act made it possible for local authorities to be compelled to furnish and assist new housing. Rent-control was in force, and a temporary system of outright grants to private builders was initiated which produced 8500 houses in two years.

Since 1919

The immediate shortage was estimated at 100,000 dwellings in 1920, with an added annual need of 37,000. Special measures were devised, and the next few years saw the greatest period of Dutch housing activity. From 1919 through 1922, one family out of every thirteen was housed in a new dwelling. From 1919 through 1924, the emergency subsidy legislation begun in 1914 (consisting of annual grants by the State toward rent deficits) had provided about $5,100,000 in fresh annual grants (about two thirds out of the State exchequer and one third out of the local authorities). These affected about 65,000 dwellings and reached as high as $57 per dwelling per year for the 40,000 dwellings aided thereby in 1920 and 1921. This is not a constantly accumulating figure, however, as it has occasionally been possible to raise the rents and reduce the national obligation. In 1929 the entire State expenditure on this item had dropped to under $3,000,000. (If, on the other hand, the rents had to be lowered, the local authorities stood the full additional burden.)

The grants to private builders were also increased in 1920. Subsidies were fixed at a definite sum per unit of dwelling-area, varying only in accordance with the index of building costs. From 1921 to 1923, when this was stopped, about 104,000 dwellings with an average grant of $500 were put up. Many of them also received official loans.

The worst of the shortage having been met and building costs reduced, most of the emergency legislation was withdrawn in 1924. Loans continued to be granted to public-utility societies, more by the cities than by the national Government. Subsidies were restricted to twenty dollars per dwelling per year, the State and the city each contributing half. Of late years this has usually been granted only for slum-clearance purposes.

Summary of Accomplishment

From 1919 through 1928, about 450,000 new dwellings were constructed in all, of which at least 200,000 received some form of direct State aid and probably 50,000 more either received aid from municipalities or the Postal Savings Bank or were put up by unaided public-utility societies. As a remarkably large proportion of these houses were directly within reach of those who needed them most, the emergency shortage may be said to have been met (a claim which cannot be made by many other countries).

This fact, coupled with the even more important one that the new standards and economical housing methods seem to have been firmly established, even in so far as ordinary private enterprise is concerned, has enabled the cities to turn to *slum-clearance*. Amsterdam has condemned around five thousand dwellings since the war, cleared most of them away, and provided about three thousand new ones expressly designed for the former slum-dwellers. The Hague is well started on a complete reconstruction of the various insanitary neighborhoods, including the old portion of the fishing village at Scheveningen. The new quarters for the fishermen's families are for the most part already constructed near-by.

Agencies: Of the 450,000 dwellings:

about 110,000 were put up by public-utility societies (almost all assisted);

about 40,000 were put up by local authorities (almost all assisted by the State);

and 300,000 were put up by private enterprise (about 65,000 assisted by the State).

To keep the management of housing out of politics, municipal developments — particularly those of The Hague — are turned over to semi-official societies operated quite independently of the city government. Housing societies in Holland are almost invariably founded and administered by the tenants or would-be tenants themselves. Groups usually center around some common interest, either religious, political, or even sometimes, according to Dr. Wood, vegetarianism or the single tax. The present writer stumbled on a Rotterdam community which seemed to be full of enthusiastic Esperantists.

Housing and the Budget: In 1928:

National Budget	$360,000,000
Annual subsidies on about 65,000 houses	3,000,000
Education	47,000,000
Outstanding housing loans (all being repaid without loss to State). (affecting about 200,000 dwellings)	253,000,000

The cost of housing looms considerably less in municipal budgets. It is not a great price, one would say, for the most outstanding housing achievement, quantitatively speaking, in the modern world.

Present Outlook

There is no country in which the new method of housing — community-unit planning, large-scale construction, supervised standards, and long-time investment financing — has so completely superseded the old speculative piecemeal method. There is much private construction, at fairly low rentals, which has just as high a standard as the official housing. One can confidently expect, therefore, that modern housing is a permanent institution in Holland. The most interesting present work is the construction of entire new villages, by an authority created for the purpose, on the reclaimed bottom of the Zuider Zee — an area which will eventually add some ten per cent to the area of the country.

IV. BELGIUM

Before the War

Wages have always been very low in Belgium, and, although Brussels at the end of the century was one of the most advanced cities in Europe in the matter of water-supply and sanitation, overcrowded slum conditions in Belgian cities were among the worst. Official inquiries began as early as 1837, and a 'Technical Exhibition' on housing was organized by the Government in 1848. In the sixties and seventies various laws offered a few minor favors to housing societies, which were also granted limited liability at that time.

The Act of 1889, however, was the first real housing law. It was more or less copied in the French Law of 1894 and had some influence likewise in Germany. Its entire purpose was to promote home-ownership among Belgian workers. There were three main sections in the law: one to further housing surveys, education, etc., by means of *Comités de patronage* set up in each administrative district; the second, to provide cheap funds by authorizing the General Savings Bank, an official institution, to loan to various types of building society; and third, a curious feature whereby the building society could insure its payments by taking out an endowment life insurance policy, through the General Savings Bank, on the life of the house-purchaser. All the houses had to be sold to strictly industrial workers (although only the better-paid could take advantage of it). The Bank made loans at slightly lower rates to the societies who insured their clients, the average being around three per cent. Various tax-exemptions were allowed on all workers' housing.

Up to 1914, about 60,000 houses had been built and sold in this way, and the bank had loaned some $20,000,000. Of the 213 housing societies existing in 1912, 150 merely made loans (like any American building and loan association) and 63 put up houses themselves. Only 18 of these societies were co-operative. Obviously, there was nothing in such measures — however much they may have benefited the individuals who were able to purchase the houses —

which could effect any great change in general methods of planning, layout, or construction of dwellings. And the owners were, I believe, quite free to speculate in their property at a later date if the opportunity presented itself. These housing efforts were allied with another movement which is often reflected in early housing literature in America. 'Cheap trains,' to enable workers to live far out in the country, were often thought to be the great cure-all. And in Belgium, where the very low wages maintained by a largely export industry made gardening on the side almost a necessity, cheap 'workmen's tickets' were supported by the Government.

After the War

The situation in 1919 was a very acute one. Eighty thousand dwellings had been ruined by the war, and in addition there was a shortage variously estimated at from 100,000 to 200,000. Of the war reconstructions nothing need be said here, as they were carried on through special agencies. One should mention, perhaps, that in the reconstructed Belgian villages a certain amount of replanning of residential quarters was done, which was not the case in most of the French rebuilding.

The Act of 1919, prepared before the war, set up a National Housing Society to combat the housing problem of districts devastated by the nineteenth century rather than by the war. Shareholders in the Society are the State and the provinces, and the seven positions on the administrative council are carefully allotted to two Liberals, three Catholics, and two Socialists. This society does not build, but encourages the establishment of local housing societies whose own capital, amounting to one fifth of the cost, is subscribed in mixed amounts by the State, the towns, the provinces, charitable institutions, employers, and private citizens. The remaining four fifths is loaned by the Government for sixty-five years, at a rate varying from two to four per cent, but always less than the cost of the money to the State. Since 1927, the National Society has been authorized to issue Housing Bonds at about six per cent, the State making up the difference. During the early years aided houses were not allowed to be sold, but since 1922 conservative politics and the desire of the State to get back some of its investment has somewhat changed this policy. All the new developments, however, are planned and constructed as units under the careful supervision of the central society, which maintains various testing and research bureaus.

The Patronage Committees have continued to operate with the

National Savings Bank and the building and loan societies (some of which actually construct developments themselves), much as they did before the war. And in addition there are several large private organizations and foundations, such as the League of Large Families, the League against Slums, etc., which provide housing funds at low rates.

Accomplishment

The total dwellings thus constructed up to the middle of 1933 is approximately as follows:

Through the National Society	63,000
Other houses built with subsidies	35,000
Houses built with loans which do not involve subsidy	100,000
Total	198,000

No housing is done directly by the local authorities. Slum-clearance has recently received more encouragement, but has not so far been very fruitful.

V. FRANCE

Before and since the war, France has done relatively much less work in the field of public aid and promotion of housing than either England or Germany — from the point of view both of quantity and of planning or architectural significance. Due to her almost stable population during the past decades, her quantitative housing problem has been confined to the cities, whose population has continued to increase. The Seine Department, which includes Paris and its suburbs, grew by about twelve per cent in the fifteen years after 1911. Moreover, the primary purpose of most French housing legislation, from 1889 to the present date, has been to increase the birth-rate. That is, State-aided housing is bestowed particularly on 'large families,' not so much on the theory that every family is entitled to a decent, separate abode, but as a reward for virtue and encouragement to more virtue. Until the establishment of the Public Offices for Low-Cost Housing, just before the war, every effort in aid of housing went to promote individual home-ownership and therefore reached only the better-paid workers.

Before the War

The period 1831 to 1848, between two cholera epidemics and ending in a revolution, witnessed many surveys, protests, and for the most part quite fruitless sanitary efforts. In the fifties, Napoleon III, influenced by the example of Prince Albert, indulged in a brief, spectacular, and totally ineffective flurry of housing activity. The results were all too expensive for any but the comfortable middle class, and the tenements at least were among the worst 'model' dwellings ever constructed. The Mulhouse experiment, which Engels called the Parade-Horse of Europe, did display a certain technical ingenuity in plan and equipment, but speculation in the houses soon made it nothing more than an upper-middle-class suburb. In Paris, Haussmann's activities destroyed a certain number of slums, but did nothing to re-house the people displaced.

In the eighties a few more constructive critics began to appear, under the leadership of Le Play's *Société d'Economie Sociale*. Then in

1889 the first International Housing Congress was held in Paris, and the *Société Française des Habitations à bon Marché* was founded under the leadership of Jules Siegfried. And finally the *Act of* 1894 was passed, which was almost an exact copy of the Belgian legislation of 1889. Local patronage committees were established under a central council. The Government Bank of Deposits and the National Old Age Retirement Fund, as well as the savings banks, were authorized to make loans at low rates to various types of building and loan society. Certain tax-exemptions on cheap dwellings were allowed. With the Ribot Law of 1908, which merely extended these principles to include semi-rural and allotment-garden projects, French housing continued along conservative lines until 1912. Up to the war, the various loaning agencies had granted some fifteen million dollars, which probably aided in the erection of about thirty thousand dwellings. Most of this sum was distributed either through purely loan societies to individuals, or to 'co-operative' building societies in which the shareholders are the house-purchasers.

In 1912 was authorized the establishment of Public Housing Offices (*Offices Public d'Habitations à bon Marché*), which have been responsible for most of what is valuable or interesting in the post-war achievement. These are semi-official local organizations which administer the sanitary laws regarding dwellings, and also initiate and manage various welfare enterprises, including housing. They are responsible to the Ministry of Health, but enjoy considerable autonomy. Supported by the local authorities, they are directed by a board of eighteen members, one third of whom are appointed by the prefect, one third by the local council, and one third by various local welfare institutions. They are authorized to borrow directly from the governments and also from the special funds earmarked for housing purposes.

Also, in 1912, special subsidies to house large families were inaugurated, and a large program of direct public construction was planned for Paris, destined to be shelved until after the war.

After the War

In 1919 and the following years rent-control, exorbitant building costs, and a tremendous quantitative shortage of dwellings in the cities necessitated further measures. Quite apart from the devastated areas (which, as in Belgium, were speedily reconstructed by an entirely special arrangement), it was estimated by various persons including M. Georges Risler, head of the Musée Social, that the shortage of dwellings was about one million, in addition to 250,000 downright slums which should be demolished.

The system of subsidies authorized in 1912 was put into operation and liberalized in 1919 (also the year of the compulsory town-planning act). A large number of Public Housing Offices were set up. But nothing much was accomplished until after the Act of 1922. From 1920 to 1927, the State and official agencies loaned 1416 million francs (at the stabilized value of 1927, about $57,000,000) for housing, at rates of 2 to 3.5 per cent, covering up to 75 per cent of the cost. It was estimated that the loss of the State as between given and accepted interest was in 1926 about $9,000,000. In addition, direct subsidies amounted to about $10,000,000 a year. About 43 per cent of the loans and most of the subsidies went for direct *building* purposes, mostly to the Public Housing Offices. The rest went to credit agencies, which usually reloaned to individuals to put up their own houses. These funds resulted in about 58,000 new dwellings between 1920 and 1927. Which was by no means enough.

The Loucheur Act of 1928 was designed to facilitate a five-year program of 200,000 minimum-cost dwellings and 60,000 'moderate' ones. It encourages home-ownership somewhat and reserves in theory three-fifths of the funds to assist private individuals to build houses for their own use, and provides for the co-operative construction of flats. The financial support for the minimum houses is more liberal, loans being granted at two per cent up to ninety per cent of the cost. Lump-sum subsidies are granted for special groups: war invalids, victims of industrial accidents, or families with two or more young children, who need little or no capital in order to purchase.

Government losses of interest (figured at about $37 per dwelling per year for twenty-five years) were estimated at $2,920,000 for 1930, rising to $9,600,000 in 1943, which will remain in force until 1969 for the 260,000 houses thereby assisted. M. Risler has, however, pointed out that the very high taxes on materials, etc., bring in considerably more income to the Government per unit of outlay for construction purposes, than it loses in interest.

Net Accomplishment to Date

Under the Loucheur Act, the allotted 200,000 minimum dwellings and a certain number of the 'moderate' ones have been constructed. And at the beginning of 1933, a further allowance of $40,000,000 for housing purposes was made, bringing the total loans since 1927 to more than $500,000,000. The total assisted dwellings since the war amount to about 300,000, of which around forty-five per cent were erected by the Public Housing offices and the local authorities. Forty-five per cent of the housing advances have gone to the Paris district, but, as some 25,000 dwellings have in the mean time been demolished there (very few of them by official agencies), the net numerical shortage has not been greatly relieved. The most interesting work, although little of it is up to the German or English technical standard, has been done by the Public Housing Office of the Seine Department, whose zone of activity lies in a belt around the outside of Paris.

VI. AUSTRIA

Before the War

The heritage of bad housing conditions and bankrupt cities left by the Empire was one of the worst in Europe. In a survey of ninety-two towns in 1912, more than fifty per cent of the dwellings consisted of only one room, with a kitchen. Meanwhile, the average persons per dwellings was over four. Moreover, the actual form of the tenements in the larger cities was worse than almost anything on the Continent in so far as coverage, ventilation, light, etc., were concerned. Also, as is always the case in such speculation-tenements, rents were exceedingly high. It was calculated that a Viennese worker paid more for one room and kitchen than did a Londoner for a living-room, three bedrooms, kitchen, and bath in relatively pleasant surroundings.

The Government went through a few gestures, patterned on the German measures, and there were the usual imperial showcase 'models.' A Central Association for Housing Reform was organized in 1907, and a housing department was even set up in the new Ministry of Public Works in 1908. A small State housing fund was established in 1911, for the purpose of making loans to public-utility societies. The official Accident Insurance Institute constructed some low-cost housing on its own account. A few cities, particularly Vienna, started buying land for housing purposes. But the total output of public-utility housing before the war was not more than twelve thousand dwellings, located chiefly in Vienna and Prague, and absolutely nothing had been done to raise general standards or improve ordinary methods.

Austria as a Whole

A fund to aid public-utility housing societies had been set up by the National Government in 1921, which was the only form of Federal assistance until 1929. Its effect was negligible, however, as only some 8800 houses were put up with its assistance in the whole country. Since 1929, a small Federal tax has been levied in order to provide more funds for housing. In general, it can facilitate only middle-class construction, but about 2600 dwellings in Vienna have so far been thus assisted.

Outside of Vienna, a certain amount of municipal housing was carried on by a few of the larger towns, notably Linz.

Post-War Vienna

The history of Austrian housing and of Viennese housing are two different matters, and the latter is by far the more important. The situation of Vienna after the war was a very special one all the way around. Once the wealthy center of an empire of fifty-four millions, it is now a congested city of two millions with an impoverished and mountainous hinterland of only five million more. Which is much as if New York City were suddenly forced to depend for both its market and its ordinary supplies on New York State alone. In addition, Vienna was a semi-Socialist city in a conservative State and the National Government could not be relied on for any concrete assistance. There could be little attention, therefore, to 'normal' economics: the entire situation was fundamentally an uneconomic one from the start. Both the virtues and the compromises in what they have done must be considered in this light, and their accomplishment is in any case a remarkable one.

The inflation had wiped out all private building capital. Rent restrictions and the very low wages made it impossible to do any sort of building for an 'economic' rent. Moreover, wages had to be kept low on account of tariff boundaries and because seventy per cent of Austrian industry must necessarily be for export trade, the country being by no means self-sufficient even in the barest necessities. There could, therefore, be no question of either unaided private enterprise or even of Government loans at a reduced figure. If houses were to be built, they would have to be let at a figure to cover only the upkeep; the capital cost must be written off at the start. No government could borrow money very long for such an undertaking, and the funds had necessarily to come out of ordinary income. The solution was much the same as the German House Rent Tax, but carried some steps farther.

In 1923 a system of rent taxes was put into operation, whose income amounts to some five million dollars a year, or about 6 per cent of the total value of rents in 1914. However, it is sharply graded so that the 86 per cent of total buildings represented by small dwellings and small shops pay only 24 per cent of the tax, while the most luxurious half per cent pay 41.7 per cent of the tax. In conjunction with this, rents are restricted to a figure which covers merely upkeep, taxes, and a management fee, with no return on capital investment. (The inflation had already, of course, wiped out all mortgages.) With this money, as well as with other tax-income, the city of Vienna built its houses. The investment is written off the books when the buildings are constructed, and the rents cover only upkeep. What it really amounts to is not socialism by any means, except in so far as the housing is designed for those poorest people who actually need new dwellings the most, but rather an indirect subsidy to industry in the assurance of low wages. Profits are regulated to a certain extent on the other end by the municipal industrial investments. Vienna in 1928 had an interest in some sixty-six different industries, outside of the numerous utilities owned and operated directly by the city, and her profits on utilities were another source of revenue for house-construction.

The buildings were put up and administered directly by the municipal government, and materials were bought through a central purchasing agency which itself conducted enough productive enterprise to maintain a control over prices. The city claims to have cut costs thirty per cent by control, experiment, and rationalization.

In order to cut down costs of development and to make use of existing roads and utilities, most of the Viennese housing has been in the form of large apartment-blocks located wherever sites could be secured within the city. Coverage is considerably higher than in Germany and England, and dwelling areas are smaller. But this is made up for to a certain extent by admirable communal facilities, which we shall describe in a later section.

In addition to the flats, however, about six thousand one-family houses with gardens in sixteen suburban communities have been provided, for the most part through the agency of co-operative societies. For a time, the members of the society were allowed to provide their capital in the form of labor on the job. But the difficulties and waste involved caused the scheme to be abandoned. Conditions had enabled the city to purchase cheaply a great deal of land both in and outside of its boundaries, and by 1927 about 3300 acres of this domain had been used for garden colonies.

Accomplishment and Outlook

From 1924 through 1928, $60,000,000 were spent by the city in constructing 33,000 dwellings, together with community facilities to go with them such as schools, laundries, etc. Building expenditures in 1928 amounted to about one fourth of total tax-income. The total number of city-aided dwellings constructed since the war is now about 62,000 — all but about 3000 of them directly by the municipal government. Only a few thousand houses were put up by unaided private enterprise.

Socialist housing in Vienna is of course a completely closed chapter, and the outlook for any sort of effective future housing policy is exceedingly dim. The triumphant Fascists went a step farther in reaction than even their National Socialist neighbors: for they actually destroyed by bombardment a large part of the housing achievement of their predecessors.

VII. THE SCANDINAVIAN COUNTRIES

Before the War

In Copenhagen there are groups of houses built for Government employees in the sixteenth and seventeenth centuries, renovated and still in use. And what may be called the first co-operative housing society (opinions vary, for there is no clear line of demarcation) was established there in 1851. The cholera year of 1853 saw the initiation of a Physicians' Society which erected many dwellings with the aid of the Government, owning 727 by 1900. In 1887 a State housing fund was established which, with few variations, still continues to make loans on second mortgages at five per cent interest plus one per cent amortization. In 1896 an English doctor making a survey of public health wrote that Copenhagen had provided more and better workers' housing than any other Continental capital. He also commented on the community equipment included in these colonies — day nurseries, steam laundries, etc.

In Stockholm, from 1880 on, the city had a policy of buying up large tracts of rural land outside its limits, amounting in 1912 to more than twice the total inner area of the town. This land was laid out in garden suburbs and industrial zones as it was needed, the lots being either sold with a guaranty against speculative resale or let on long leases. Stockholm also started to lend money at low rates to housing societies in 1879, and had already started to build dwellings for its own employees in 1875. By 1910, thirteen per cent of the dwellings in the town were owned either by the city, the State, or co-operative societies. In Oslo, the city started to build housing around 1896 and set up a separate housing bureau in 1911.

In all the Scandinavian countries from the eighties and nineties onward, but particularly in Denmark in connection with the co-operative movement, there was very effective legislation and financial assistance for agricultural homesteads.

After the War: Denmark

A temporary system of subsidies to cover the rising cost of building operated between 1917 and 1922. The second mortgage loans out of the State Fund were continued and the sum available increased. From 1917 through 1921, at least thirty-three thousand dwellings were put up with State aid, or two thirds of the total constructed during the period. In addition, the local authorities erected many dwellings on their own account and provided credit and land for co-operative societies. Such aid as was given to private enterprise was ordinarily confined to persons building for themselves, usually in rural districts, and with some sort of control over resale in order to prevent speculation. Copenhagen sells its land for low-cost housing purposes at ten per cent of the nominal value, but with a condition enabling it to repurchase at the end of ninety years.

In Copenhagen from :920 through 1929, 45,800 dwellings were erected, of which:

9,300 by the city itself
18,700 by public utility societies, usually co-operative
17,800 by private enterprise, many of them receiving State or municipal aid and therefore controlled against speculation.

Every fifth person in Copenhagen now lives in a dwelling put up either by the town or by a public-utility society, and therefore out of the speculative market.

Sweden

Subsidies were provided from 1917 through 1921, and a system of official credits operated after 1920, finally resulting in a permanent Housing Loan Fund in 1929. Of the 130,000 dwellings put up from 1917 through 1929, almost half were erected with some sort of assistance. The construction agencies were as follows:

The State	2,200	
Local authorities	10,000	
Housing societies	16,000	(aided for the most part by the National Insurance Fund)
Private enterprise	29,200	(for the most part, houses constructed for themselves by the owners, usually in rural districts)
Total assisted	57,400	

Standardized mass-produced wooden houses, to be put up by the owner, are given with loans up to ninety per cent of total cost, the remaining ten per cent being supplied by the builder in the form of his own labor.

In Stockholm, more than one tenth of the population now lives in co-operative developments, which remain in collective ownership.

Norway

Temporary subsidies and permanent loan-funds have been in operation. In the five largest towns (population 478,000), from 1914 through 1928, almost all the dwellings erected received some sort of official aid (14,900 out of 16,600). Of the assisted dwellings, the agencies of construction were:

Local authorities	7,800
Public utility societies	4,800
Private enterprise	2,300
Total	14,900

That is, housing for about one person out of seven.

The city of Oslo has probably the most comprehensive system of municipal housing-construction developed by any town other than Vienna. From 1912, just after its housing office was established, through 1931, it had itself erected 7240 dwellings (which remain in municipal ownership) and it aided in the provision of 6300 co-operative or public-utility houses. This makes a total of 13,500 dwellings accommodating some 54,000 persons — or more than one fifth of the population of the city.

VIII. SWITZERLAND

Switzerland has long been rated one of the most nearly successful bourgeois capitalist democracies. Her economic stability and the lack of great extremes of wealth are reflected in the fact that private enterprise has been more nearly able to solve the problem of low-cost housing than it has in any other country. Moreover, dwelling standards are on the whole fairly high. Even in rural districts, most of the homes have adequate plumbing and heating, and have had electricity for a generation. (This is due largely to the fact that the Swiss villages are compactly planned, and are not 'open country farms' such as we have in America.) Moreover, the cost of money for housing in the ordinary open market — an indication not only of stability but of sound methods of layout and construction — is relatively low. At the end of 1930 the interest rate on a first mortgage was under 5 per cent, on a second 5 to 5½ per cent, and the official discount-rate 2.89 per cent.

Even so, however, there is a more or less acute housing problem which, as in the other countries, reached its high point just after the war, but is always present. And, also as in the other countries, long-time measures have been adopted with which to meet it.

Subsidies were provided by both the federal, canton, and city governments during the period 1919 to 1926, and since that time occasionally for special purposes such as families with a large number of children. The total official housing expenditure during this period was about $18,000,000, almost all of which went in aid of public-utility housing. From 1926 through 1930, 60,000 dwellings were built in all in some 350 towns representing fifty-six per cent of the population. Of this number 10,000 were co-operative dwellings with official assistance (usually merely loans without loss to the Government) and about 1000 were put up directly by the towns.

The canton and city of Zürich are outstanding in housing matters. Of the above-mentioned 10,000 co-operative dwellings, more than 7000 are in Zürich Canton. And the city of Zürich, between 1910 when it set up its housing organization and the end of 1931, had aided 10,000 co-operative dwellings and constructed about 2100 itself. Very few, if any, of these houses can be sold to individuals, which means that almost a quarter of the population of the city lives in dwellings removed from the speculative market.

A measure worth noting is a fund granted to the Swiss Housing Association by the State for the purpose of encouraging experiments in technique, etc. The money is loaned to co-operative societies who desire to make such an experiment, and is paid back by them without interest after the houses have been constructed.

A SELECTIVE BIBLIOGRAPHY

A SELECTIVE BIBLIOGRAPHY

MATERIAL significant in the history of 'housing' comes necessarily from a wide variety of sources, many of them only indirectly concerned with housing itself. The author has here attempted to bring together all the primary sources which she found most valuable or interesting, and also some suggestion of the many other fields which are worth exploring in this connection. Much of this material is today of only historical value, and many of the items included have no more intrinsic importance than hundreds which have been omitted. It is hoped, however, that this list will provide a fair indication of the type and variety of information available to the housing student. The most important items are marked with an asterisk (*). The categories are necessarily somewhat arbitrary, but will serve to indicate the particular emphasis of publications listed under them.

I. BACKGROUND MATERIAL

A. Slums and Nineteenth-Century Cities

**Engels, Friedrich*, THE CONDITION OF THE WORKING-CLASS IN ENGLAND IN 1844. London, 1892. A classic work on the environment of the 19th century.

**Hammond, J. L. and Barbara*, THE TOWN LABOURER, 1760–1832. London, 1917 (reprinted 1932).

Seeley, Robert B., THE PERILS OF THE NATION: An Appeal to the Legislature, the Clergy, and the Higher and Middle Classes. London, 1843. The title is self-explanatory.

Beames, Thomas, THE ROOKERIES OF LONDON: Past, Present and Prospective. London, 1852 (2d ed.). One of many diatribes by English preachers of the period.

BACK-TO-BACK HOUSES, A Report by the Medical Officer of Health. City of Manchester, 1893. Typical of early housing surveys.

**Barnes, Harry*, THE SLUM: Its Story and Solution. London, 1931. A long book on English housing whose early sections are full of material otherwise difficult to track down.

HOUSING PROBLEMS IN LIVERPOOL, Liverpool University Settlement, 1931. A brief pamphlet summarizing an exhaustive survey of central slum districts.

Darby and Hamilton, ENGLAND, UGLINESS AND NOISE. London, 1930. Typical of many indignant English pamphlets of a non-professional nature.

Bolitho, William, CANCER OF EMPIRE. London, 1924. Hair-raising but superficial journalism on Glasgow slums.

Royal Commissions on Housing. Reports. Some of the best and fullest source material on English housing conditions are contained in these lengthy hearings.

Hamp, Pierre, LE TAUDIS. Article in La Grande Revue, March, 1918, Paris.

Huber, Victor Aimé, DIE WOHNUNGSNOT DER KLEINEN LEUTE. Leipzig, 1865. Survey by the first important German housing reformer.

**Hegemann, Werner*, DAS STEINERNE BERLIN. Berlin, 1930. A thorough and critical history of the physical condition of a metropolis and the forces which shaped it.

Schwan, Bruno, DIE WOHNUNGSNOT UND DAS WOHNUNGSELEND IN DEUTSCHLAND. Berlin, 1929. Published by the Deutsche Verein für Wohnungsreform, no. 7.

Schwan, Bruno, DIE WOHNUNGSVERHÄLTNISSE DER BERLINER ALTSTADT. A pamphlet by the Deutsche Verein für Wohnungsreform, no. 10.

**De Forest, R. and Veiller, Lawrence*, THE TENEMENT HOUSE PROBLEM. Including the Report of the New York State Tenement House Commission of 1900. 2 vols. New York, 1903. The classic document on housing conditions and 'reform' measures in early 20th century America.

B. Ideas Utopian, Revolutionary and Technical

**Owen, Robert*, NEW VIEW OF SOCIETY: Tracts Relative to this Subject. London, 1818. Owen's justly famous Plan, as it was presented to the Association for the Relief of the Manufacturing and Labouring Poor. Includes a drawing. A most important document, in the history of both Socialism and Housing.

Cabet, Etienne, VOYAGE EN ICARIE. Paris, 1848. The starting-point for many colonial experiments.

Fourier, Charles, CITES OUVRIERES. Paris, 1849. Des Modifications à Introduire dans l'Architecture des Villes. A curious compound of practical common sense and mystical abstractions.

Wakefield, Edward Gibbon, A VIEW OF THE ART OF COLONIZATION. London, 1849. Influenced Ebenezer Howard in his development of the Garden City idea.

Buckingham, James Silk, NATIONAL EVILS AND PRACTICAL REMEDIES, with the Plan of a Model Town. London, 1849. A practical and highly bourgeois Victorian Utopia, complete with drawings.

Marx, Karl, and Friedrich Engels, THE COMMUNIST MANIFESTO. London, 1848. The first clear declaration of revolutionary Communism and its opposition to partial reform, including housing.

Engels, Friedrich, SOCIALISM UTOPIAN AND SCIENTIFIC.

**Engels, Friedrich*, ZUR WOHNUNGSFRAGE. First published in 1872 in a Leipzig newspaper. Reprinted with a modern Communist commentary, Berlin, 1930. A keen revolutionary analysis of the purposes and achievements of mid-nineteenth century housing reformers, it exerted a wide influence among early German Social Democrats.

Bebel, August, DIE FRAU UND DER SOCIALISMUS. Translated as 'Woman under Socialism.' The revolutionists' Utopia, extremely popular in Germany in the nineties.

Ruskin, John, MUNERA PULVERIS. New York, 1891. UNTO THIS LAST. New York, 1869. Political ideas of a Utopian Tory. Influenced Octavia Hill and many other reformers.

Booth, Charles, LIFE AND LABOUR IN LONDON. London, 1892. Included in this list because it is the prototype of the modern, detailed, scientific survey.

Morris, William, NEWS FROM NOWHERE. London. A Communist Utopia which turned its back on the Machine.

Morris, William, ARCHITECTURE, INDUSTRY AND WEALTH: Collected Papers. London, 1902. Including many remarkably sound ideas on modern architecture and other matters which were not, unfortunately, realized in Morris's own work.

Clutton Brock, A., SOCIALISM AND THE ARTS OF LIFE. Fabian Tract no. 177, London, 1915. One of the best early critiques on industrial design.

Bellamy, Edward, LOOKING BACKWARD. Boston ca. 1888. An American vision of the Planned Society, still interesting in spite of its occasionally Fascist flavor.

**Kropotkin, Peter*, FIELDS, FACTORIES AND WORKSHOPS. First published in London, 1898, revised in 1913. A plea for balanced industry and agriculture in small autonomous communities, backed up with much interesting scientific data, by an anarchist geographer.

**Howard, Ebenezer*, GARDEN CITIES OF TOMORROW. London, 1902. First published as TOMORROW, 1898. The blue-print for Letchworth, Welwyn, and the whole international Garden City movement.

Wells, H. G., ANTICIPATIONS OF THE REACTION OF MECHANICAL AND SCIENTIFIC PROGRESS UPON HUMAN LIFE AND THOUGHT. New York and London, 1902. Ingenious and stimulating, if by no means profound.

Wells, H. G., A MODERN UTOPIA. New York, 1905. Somewhat thin, but amusing. More interesting in its mechanical details than in its social philosophy.

Unwin, Raymond, COTTAGE PLANS AND COMMON SENSE. Fabian Tract no. 109, London, 1902. One of the best early studies of modern housing technique, by a leader in the housing movement.

* *Unwin, Raymond*, NOTHING GAINED BY OVERCROWDING. A pamphlet issued by the Garden Cities and Town Planning Association, London, 1918. Showing how senseless much land-crowding is, even from the profit viewpoint.

* *Geddes, Patrick*, CITIES IN EVOLUTION. London, 1915. A series of admirable papers on various aspects of planning in England and on the continent, by the father of regional planning.

Branford, Victor, and Patrick Geddes, OUR SOCIAL INHERITANCE. London, 1919. Papers of uneven value containing much significant data on the need for understanding our cultural and physical resources before we can begin to plan.

Unwin, Raymond, TOWN PLANNING IN PRACTICE. London, 1909. Still one of the best treatises on the technique of town planning.

* *Webb, Sydney*, SOCIAL MOVEMENTS. Cambridge Modern History, Volume XII. Includes an excellent analysis of the many branches of our social life which have been gradually 'socialized' within the capitalist framework.

* *Mumford, Lewis*, THE STORY OF UTOPIAS. New York, 1922. An admirable study of the various historic Utopias and a criticism of the two contemporary 'half-worlds,' Coketown and the Country House.

Mumford, Lewis, THEORY AND PRACTICE OF REGIONALISM. Sociological Review, London, January and April, 1928. How we are exploiting our physical resources to our own eventual ruin, and what must be done about it.

* *Mumford, Lewis*, TECHNICS AND CIVILIZATION. New York, 1934. A thorough history of the relations between men and machines,

which illuminates many aspects of both nineteenth-century cities and modern housing.

C. Pre-War Housing: Great Britain

Elsam, Richard, HINTS FOR IMPROVING THE CONDITION OF THE PEASANTRY IN ALL PARTS OF THE UNITED KINGDOM, by Promoting Comfort in their Habitations. London, 1816. One of the first books on 'model housing,' illustrated by the architect.

Roberts, Henry, THE DWELLINGS OF THE LABOURING CLASSES. London, 1850. With reference to the Model Houses of the Society for Improving the Condition of the Labouring Classes, etc.

Hill, Octavia, HOMES OF THE LONDON POOR. London, 1875, revised 1883. The effect of the Cross Acts, which promoted 'rehabilitation and repair.'

Hill, Octavia, HOUSE PROPERTY AND ITS MANAGEMENT. Collected papers from the sixties to the nineties. New York, 1921.

Glasgow Workmen's Dwellings Company Ltd., SOME EXPERIMENTS IN HOUSING: 1891–1901. Descriptive pamphlet.

Meakin, Budgett, MODEL FACTORIES AND VILLAGES: Ideal Conditions of Labour and Housing. London, 1905. Eulogy of company housing and paternalism in general. Illustrated.

Co-Partnership Tenants Housing Council, THE GROWTH OF AN IDEA: the Book of the Garden Suburb. London.

**Dewsnup, E. R.,* THE HOUSING PROBLEM IN ENGLAND. Manchester, 1907. A good summary of pre-war housing measures in England.

**Berlepsch-Valendàs,* DIE GARTENSTADTBEWEGUNG IN ENGLAND, IHRE ENTWICKLUNG UND IHR JETZIGER STAND. Munich, 1912. A very good description, illustrated.

D. Pre-War Housing: Germany

Weidenbacher, Josef, DIE FUGGEREI IN AUGSBURG: die Erste Deutsche Kleinhaus-stiftung. Augsburg, 1926. Description of a 16th century model housing development. Illustrated.

Hoffmann, C. W., DIE WOHNUNGEN DER ARBEITER UND ARMEN. Berlin, 1852. The work of the first German housing society. Illustrated.

**Jäger, Dr. Eugen,* DIE WOHNUNGSFRAGE. Berlin, 1902. 2 vols. Includes a very good analysis of all the various political forces and viewpoints on the housing problem in Germany at the time, and much solid economic data.

Adickes and Beutler, DIE SOZIALEN AUFGABEN DER DEUTSCHEN STAEDTE. 1903. The case for municipal socialism. Adickes was the famous liberal-Socialist Mayor of Frankfurt.

Voigt, Andreas and Paul Geldner, KLEINHAUS UND MIETKASERNE: Eine Untersuchung der Intensität der Bebauung vom Wirtschaftlichen und Hygienischen Standpunkte. A defense of exploitive land-sweating, of curiosity value only. Berlin, 1905. Illustrated by one 'model' experiment.

**Horsfall, T. C.*, IMPROVEMENT OF DWELLINGS AND SURROUNDINGS OF THE PEOPLE. Manchester, 1905. Contrast of English local administrative methods and achievements with German, to the overwhelming advantage of the latter. More than historically interesting.

Berlepsch-Valendàs, BODENPOLITIK UND WOHNUNGSFURSORGE EINER DEUTSCHE MITTELSTADT. Munich. Municipal land-ownership and other social measures in Ulm.

Jacobi, Dorothea, DIE GEMEINNÜTZIGE BAUTÄTIGKEIT IN DEUTSCHLAND. Staats. und Socialwissenschaftliche Forschungen no. 167. 1913. A complete analysis of co-operative housing in Germany before the war, and its political implications. Not illustrated.

Howe, Frederick C., SOCIALIZED GERMANY. New York, 1915. Somewhat indiscriminate enthusiasm for the merits of municipal control in Germany.

DIE GESCHICHTE DER BERLINISCHEN BODENGESELLSCHAFT: Ein Überblick über ihre 30 Jährige Tätigkeit. Berlin, 1921. Illustrated history of the work of one of the large-scale private real estate companies of pre-war Germany. Interesting for contrast with modern Germany housing.

**Eberstadt, Rudolph*, HANDBUCH DES WOHNUNSWESENS UND DER WOHNUNGSFRAGE. Jena, 1910. Revised edition, 1920. Illustrated treatise by the best German critic of housing and city-planning before the war.

E. Pre-War Housing: General and Miscellaneous

Müller, Emile, HABITATIONS OUVRIERES ET AGRICOLES: CITES, BAINS ET LAVOIRS. Paris, 1855. Model housing in Europe before 1855, handsomely illustrated. Shows the development at Mulhouse.

**Müller, Emile and Emile Cacheux*, LES HABITATIONS OUVRIERES EN TOUS PAYS: Situation en 1878. Paris, 1879. A monumental atlas, with plans and measured drawings, which received a gold medal at the Exposition Universelle of 1878. Work from several countries included.

Cacheux, Emile, ARCHITECTURE: L'Architecture à l'Exposition; Etudes sur les Habitations Ouvrières Exposées en 1889. Paris ca. 1890. Description of the international group of model dwellings shown at the Exhibition.

**Cacheux, Emile,* LES HABITATIONS OUVRIERES EN TOUS PAYS. Paris, after 1900. A large atlas, with exhibits from many countries, showing all the most interesting work of the period.

Cheysson, Emile, LA QUESTION DES HABITATIONS OUVRIERES EN FRANCE ET A L'ETRANGER. From the Revue d'Hygiène, August, 1886. A good analysis, by a follower of Le Play, the sociologist.

Hale, Edward E., WORKINGMEN'S HOMES: Essays and Stories. Boston, 1874. Typical and sentimental journalism from the early days of the 'own your own home' movement.

Raffalovich, Arthur, LE LOGEMENT DE L'OUVRIER ET DU PAUVRE. Paris, 1887. Great Britain, France, Germany, Belgium and the U.S. Not illustrated.

Legge, Thomas Morison, PUBLIC HEALTH IN THE EUROPEAN CAPITALS. London, 1896. A very good summary of sanitary measures and housing at the end of the 19th century.

Gould, E. R. L., THE ECONOMICS OF IMPROVED HOUSING. Yale Review, May, 1896. Summary of the remarkably prosperous economic condition of model housing societies in Europe and America.

Howe, Frederic C., EUROPEAN CITIES AT WORK. New York, 1913. Municipal socialism, including housing and the ownership of utilities, in Germany and England.

*GOVERNMENT AID TO HOME OWNING AND HOUSING OF WORKING PEOPLE IN FOREIGN COUNTRIES. U.S. Department of Labor: Bureau of Labor Statistics. Washington, 1915. A complete statistical summary of governmental housing measures in Europe before the war.

L'AMELIORATION DU LOGEMENT A AMSTERDAM, a pamphlet prepared by the Housing Authorities of Amsterdam for the International Housing Congress of 1913.

Werkner, Albert, DER KLEINWOHNUNGSBAU IN BUDAPEST. Germany, 1913.

LA CITE LINEAIRE: Nouvelle Architecture des Villes. Report by the Compañia Madrileña for the International Housing Congress of 1913 (?). Translated by G. Benoit-Levy. Description of the Spanish 'linear city' experiment.

International Housing Congress. Held at various intervals and in different cities from 1880 onward. Reports are valuable.

II. COMPREHENSIVE SOURCES ON POST-WAR HOUSING

A. History, Laws, Statistics of Achievement

International Housing Congress, later International Housing and Town Planning Congress. Held at intervals of two or more years. Published reports are full of every sort of information on housing.

* *Wohnen und Bauen,* published in German, French and English by the Internationaler Verband für Wohnungswesen, Frankfurt am Main. See complete files, particularly the seven *Congress Publications* brought out for the International Housing Congress in Berlin, 1931. Congress Publication II, THE SOCIAL IMPORTANCE OF HOUSING NOW AND IN THE FUTURE, with expert reports on every aspect of housing from a dozen different countries, is probably the most important.

International Housing and Town Planning Bulletin, published by the International Federation for Housing and Town Planning, London. See complete files. Published in English, French and German.

* *International Labour Office,* HOUSING POLICY IN EUROPE: Cheap Home Building. Geneva, 1930. A very valuable summary of laws and numerical achievements in the field of government-aided housing in Europe since the war. By countries.

Méquet, G., HOUSING PROBLEMS AND THE DEPRESSION. International Labour Review, Geneva, February, 1933. A survey of the achievements and present status of the housing movement, with some proposals.

Unwin, Sir Raymond, THE INFLUENCE OF HOUSING CONDITIONS ON LEISURE. International Labour Review, Geneva, June, 1824.

Wood, Dr. Edith Elmer, THE HOUSING OF THE UNSKILLED WAGE EARNER. New York, 1919. A brief survey of the housing problem, and the measures designed to cope with it, in America and Europe.

Wood, Dr. Edith Elmer, HOUSING PROGRESS IN WESTERN EUROPE. New York, 1923. A detailed account of early post-war housing measures in England, Holland, France and Belgium.

Pribram, Karl, HOUSING, in the *Encyclopedia of Social Sciences*, Volume VII. New York.

Unwin, Sir Raymond, HOUSING, in the *Encyclopedia Britannica*. A very useful survey of European post-war housing measures and achievements.

Kampffmeyer, Hans, LES COOPERATIVES DE CONSTRUCTION SUR LE CONTINENT. In the *Revue des Etudes Cooperatives*, July–Sept., 1928, and October–December, 1928.

Alfred, Helen L., MUNICIPAL HOUSING. Pamphlet published by the L.I.D., New York, 1932.

INTERNATIONAL GLOSSARY OF TECHNICAL TERMS USED IN HOUSING AND TOWN PLANNING, in English, French, German and Italian. Published by the International Federation for Housing and Town Planning, London, 1934.

B. Technique and Architecture

*DIE WOHNUNG FÜR DAS EXISTENZMINIMUM, published by the Internationale Kongresse fur Neues Bauen, Frankfurt, 1930. Valuable comparative analysis of typical dwelling plans from various countries, with articles by various authorities.

*RATIONELLE BEBAUUNGSWEISEN, published by the Internationale Kongresse fur Neues Bauen, Frankfurt, 1931. Typical layout plans from various countries, uniformly presented for comparison as to orientation, coverage, building heights, etc.

Schuster, Prof. Franz, THE BUILDING OF SMALL DWELLINGS WITH REASONABLE RENTS, Congress Publication IV, by the Internationaler Verband fur Wohnungswesen, Frankfurt, 1931. German, French and English throughout. Comparative data for different countries.

*THE PLANNED COMMUNITY, with Analytical Charts of American and European Housing. Compiled for the Housing Exhibition of the Subcommittee on Housing of the A.I.A., 1933. Reprinted from the *Architectural Forum*, April, 1933. Photographs and uniform technical comparison of typical housing developments in America and Europe.

Kampffmeyer, Dr. Hans, WOHNUNGEN, SIEDLUNGEN UND GARTENSTAEDTE IN HOLLAND UND ENGLAND. Berlin, 1926.

Gropius, Dr. Walter, INTERNATIONALE ARCHITEKTUR. Bauhausbücher no. 1, Munich, 1927. A small book including examples of some of the best modern housing.

Yerbury, F. R., MODERN EUROPEAN BUILDINGS. New York. A picture-book, catholic in taste.

Taut, Bruno, DIE NEUE BAUKUNST. Stuttgart, 1929.

Hitchcock, Henry Russell, Jr., MODERN ARCHITECTURE. New York, 1929. Historical background of the 'international style.' Dogmatic but scholarly presentation of the 'functional' viewpoint in modern architecture.

Behrendt, Dr. Walter Curt, DER SIEG DES NEUEN BAUSTIL. Berlin. The achievements of modern architecture, by one of the ablest European architectural critics.

**Adler, Dr. Leo*, NEUZEITLICHE MIETHÄUSER UND SIEDLUNGEN. Berlin, 1931. A handsome book of photographs of modern housing, mostly German.

Platz, Gustav Adolf, DIE BAUKUNST DER NEUESTEN ZEIT, 2nd ed. Berlin, 1931. A monumental study of modern architecture, in the series brought out by the Propylaean Verlag.

Hitchcock, H. R., and Philip Johnson, THE INTERNATIONAL STYLE: Architecture Since 1922. New York, 1932. A well-selected picture-book, including many examples of modern housing.

*MODERN ARCHITECTURE: International Exhibition. Museum of Modern Art, New York, 1932. The well illustrated catalog of a fine exhibition, including an article on Housing by Lewis Mumford.

III. GREAT BRITAIN: POST-WAR HOUSING

A. Comprehensive Sources

Clarke, J. J., THE HOUSING PROBLEM: Its Growth, Legislation and Procedure. London, 1920. A good summary of the situation at the end of the war.

**Aldridge, Henry R.*, THE NATIONAL HOUSING MANUAL. Published by the National Housing and Town Planning Council. London, 1923. A complete history of the dwelling house, leading up to post-war housing in England.

**Barnes, Harry*, HOUSING: The Facts and the Future. London, 1923.

Clark, G. W., THE HOUSING OF THE WORKING CLASSES IN SCOTLAND. Glasgow, 1930. A comprehensive survey.

B. Political and Social Aspects

Addison, Christopher, THE BETRAYAL OF THE SLUMS. London, 1922. The complete political and economic history of the Housing Act passed by England's first Labour Government, by the former Minister of Health.

Cole, G. D. H., and Margaret, RENTS, RINGS, AND HOUSES. London, 1923. How Labor housing measures were exploited by the building trusts.

Simon, Sir Ernest Darwin, HOW TO ABOLISH THE SLUMS. London, 1929.

Simon, Sir Ernest Darwin, THE ANTI-SLUM CAMPAIGN, London, 1933. How the Conservative Government obstructed the housing movement by 'concentrating on slum clearance.'

C. Technical and Descriptive Data

**Purdom, C. B.,* THE BUILDING OF SATELLITE TOWNS. London, 1925. The history, description and workings of Letchworth and Welwyn Garden Cities.

de Soissons, Louis, and Arthur Kenyon, SITE PLANNING IN PRACTICE AT WELWYN GARDEN CITY. London, 1927. Photographs and plans of super-blocks and culs-de-sac.

**London County Council,* HOUSING (1927) and HOUSING (1928–1930). Published by the Council. Complete descriptions, with plans and photographs, of London County Council housing.

**Howitt, T. Cecil,* NOTTINGHAM HOUSING SCHEMES, 1919–1928. Published by the City of Nottingham. Plans, photographs and descriptions of some of the best housing in England.

Adams, Thomas, ECONOMIC DENSITY OF LOW-COST HOUSING IN ENGLAND. In the volume by Whitten and Adams, NEIGHBORHOODS OF SMALL HOMES. Cambridge, Mass., 1931.

McDonald, J. R. H., MODERN HOUSING, London, 1931. Assorted arguments for flat roofs, reinforced concrete and modern architecture, by a Scotch contractor.

Sharp, Thomas, TOWN AND COUNTRYSIDE: Some Aspects of Urban and Rural Development. London, 1932 and New York, 1933. Strong criticism of English housing technique by a man who believes that towns should be towns.

Abercrombie, Patrick, TOWN AND COUNTRY PLANNING. Home University Library, 1933. A brief popular history of city and regional planning.

Chapman, Henry, THE TOWN AND COUNTY PLANNING ACT. London, 1933. Analysis of England's new planning legislation, by the Secretary of the International Federation for Housing and Town Planning.

BRISTOL AND BATH, REGIONAL PLANNING SCHEME, 1930, 2 vols. Typical of the best of the many recent British regional surveys. Complete list obtainable from the Garden Cities and Town Planning Association, London.

THE NEW SURVEY OF LONDON LIFE AND LABOUR. Eight volumes to date. London. Charles Booth's survey brought up to date.

*SLUM CLEARANCE AND REHOUSING, the first Report of the Council for Research on Housing Construction. London, 1934. A very complete technical analysis.

D. Reports and Publications

National Housing and Town Planning Council: *Reports.* London.

Ministry of Health: *Reports, Manuals,* Copies of Legislation.

London County Council: *Reports.*

*Garden Cities and Town Planning Association: *Town and Country Planning, a Quarterly Review* (formerly *Garden Cities and Town Planning*). Miscellaneous pamphlets also. London.

Architect and Building News, a periodical. London.

IV. GERMANY: POST-WAR HOUSING

A. General and Political Aspects

*DREISSIG JAHRE WOHNUNGSREFORM: 1898–1928, by the Deutsche Verein für Wohnungsreform. Berlin, 1928. A generation of housing reform.

*HANDWÖRTERBUCH DES WOHNUNGSWESENS, by the Deutsche Verein für Wohnungsreform. Jena, 1930. An exhaustive encyclopedia, sparsely illustrated, covering the entire political and technical field of housing in Germany. Complete bibliographies for each subject treated.

Bruck, Dr. W. F., editor, DIE DEUTSCHE SIEDLUNG, 1932. Münster, 1932. Papers on various phases of planning and financing, with emphasis on the semi-agricultural colonies.

Wagner, Martin, DIE SOCIALISIERUNG DER BAUBETRIEBE. Berlin, 1919. Beginning of the movement by the building trades unions to eliminate the contractor.

Elsas, Fritz and Erwin Stein, DIE DEUTSCHE STÄDTE, IHRE ARBEIT VON: 1918 BIS 1928. Berlin, 1928. Duties and achievements of the strong municipal governments in Germany.

DIE ENTWICKLUNG DER DEUTSCHEN BAUWIRTSCHAFT. Semi-annual statements published by the Deutsche Bau- und Bodenbank Aktiengesellschaft, which include much valuable statistical data on housing.

Mulert, Dr., DIE FINANZIERUNG DES WOHNUNGSBAUES. ca., 1928. A pamphlet which explains, among other things, the House Rent Tax.

**Kahn, Ernst*, MÖGLICHKEIT UND GRENZEN DER MIETSENKUNG IN DEN NEUBAUWOHNUNG. Frankfurt, 1932. A valuable pamphlet showing the great importance of amortization rates in housing finance.

Schwan, Bruno, OTHER PEOPLE'S MONEY? Reprint from *Die Wohnung*, no. 3, 1932. An answer to the charge that German housing was built with American money.

B. General Descriptive and Technical Data

**Block, Dr. Fritz*, ed., PROBLEME DES BAUENS. Vol. 1: WOHNBAU. Potsdam, 1928. Illustrated articles by most of the advanced housing theorists on all phases of planning, economics and construction.

Müller-Wulckow, Walter, WOHNBAUTEN UND SIEDLUNGEN AUS DEUTSCHEN GEGENWART. Leipzig, 1929. Assorted photographs and plans of new German housing and communities, in the inexpensive Blue Book Series.

Giedieon, Siegfried, BEFREITES WOHNEN. Zürich, 1929. A small book with many photographs, demonstrating the concept of a modern house.

**Völckers, Otto*, WOHNBAUFIBEL, Stuttgart, 1932. Baubücher Series, Volume 12. A very stimulating, critical and well-illustrated book on various aspects of German housing method.

**Reichsforschungsgesellschaft* für Wirtschaftlichkeit im Bau- und Wohnungswesen, Berlin. This State-subsidized research and experimental agency published numerous important documents and reports. The following are particularly recommended:

DIE KÜCHE DER KLEIN UND MITTELWOHNUNG, June, 1928.
GRUNDRISSGESTALTUNG UND HAUSWIRTSCHAFT, 1929.
STÄDTE UND STRASSENBAU, by Ernst May, etc., 1929.

VOLLVERSAMMLUNG BEI KROLL, April, 1929. Contains an analysis of building heights in relation to open space by Walter Gropius.

DIE WIRTSCHAFTLICHE BEDEUTUNG DER GRUNDRISSTYPISIERUNG, April, 1928.

HAUSFRAU, WOHNUNG UND WIRTSCHAFT, by Frau Dr. Luders, April, 1928.

DIE MECHANISIERUNG DER HOCHBAUSTELLEN, EIN MITTEL ZUR RATIONALISIERUNG DES WOHNUNGSBAUES, April, 1928.

ÜBERBLICK ÜBER DIE ARBEIT DER REICHSFORSCHUNGSGESELLSCHAFT, April, 1930.

BAULICHE EINZELHEITEN, April, 1929. A group of prominent architects outline a construction program.

ARBEITUNTERSUCHUNGEN IN BAUBETRIEBEN. Rationalization of labor.

BETONBAUBEWEISEN, April, 1928. Miscellaneous data on concrete construction.

*The *Reichsforschungsgesellschaft* also published complete technical and financial analyses of its experimental housing developments at Frankfurt-Praunheim, Dessau-Torten, Berlin-Haselhorst, etc.

Spiegel, Hans, DER STAHLHAUSBAU: WOHNBAUTEN AUS STAHL. Leipzig, 1929. Steel house construction, with plans, photographs and descriptions, from America and England as well as Germany.

**Haesler, Otto*, ZUM PROBLEM DES WOHNUNGSBAUES. A pamphlet of technical and economic analysis of the Rothenberg development in Kassel, by one of the best pre-Nazi housing architects.

Heinicke, E., DIE FLACHBAUWOHNUNG FÜR DAS EXISTENZMINIMUM. Berlin, 1931. An analysis, with itemized costs, showing the advantages of one-storied row-house construction.

Lotz, Dr. Wilhelm, WIE RICHTE ICH MEINE WOHNUNG EIN? Berlin, 1930. Photographs, usually with prices, of well-designed interior furnishings available in Germany in 1930.

Schuster, Franz, EINE EINGERICHTETE KLEINSTWOHNUNG and EIN EINGERICHTETES SIEDLUNGSHAUS. Frankfurt about 1930. Booklets illustrating simple and inexpensive furniture designs, by one of the best German architects.

Schuster, Franz, EIN MÖBELBUCH. Frankfurt ca., 1930. More furniture designs, many of them ready-made in German factories.

C. Housing in Particular Localities

**Schumacher, Fritz and Wilhelm Arntz,* KÖLN: ENTWICKLUNGSFRAGEN EINER GROSZSTADT. Munich, 1923. One of the best and most thorough German city-plans.

BAU UND WOHNUNG, published by the Deutsche Werkbund. Stuttgart, 1927. Description of the Werkbund's exhibition housing development at Weissenhof, Stuttgart.

**Architecture Vivante,* Spring and Summer, 1928, Paris. Complete plans, structural details and photographs of the Weissenhof Siedlung at Stuttgart.

*DAS WOHNUNGSWESEN DER STADT FRANKFURT AM MAIN. Frankfurt, 1930. A good brief history of housing conditions and housing measures in a city whose modern housing achievement is outstanding in Europe.

**Das Neue Frankfurt,* Frankfurt on the Main. See particularly the numbers for February-March and April-May, 1930, which provide thorough, detailed descriptions of Frankfurt's remarkable housing achievement from 1925 through 1930, under the leadership of Ernst May.

40 JAHRE AKTIENBAUGESELLCHAFT FÜR KLEINE WOHNUNGEN, Frankfurt am Main 1890–1930. Brief history of the work of one of the largest and most progressive German housing societies.

Bauer, Catherine, ART IN INDUSTRY. article in *Fortune,* May, 1931. Summary of Frankfurt's post-war housing achievement.

DIE TÄTIGKEIT DES SIEDLUNGSVERBANDES RUHRKOHLENBEZIRK. Report of the Administrative Committee of the Ruhr Regional Planning Association before the Prussian Landtag, 20th of July, 1926. Summary of the activities and purposes of the most famous regional planning experiment.

Ehgötz, Hermann, DER GENERALSIEDLUNGSPLAN FÜR DEN RAUM ESSEN. 2 vols. Ca. 1928. Complete description of the plan for the Ruhr coal and iron region.

Klapheck, Richard, SIEDLUNGSWERK KRUPP, Berlin, 1930. The history of Krupp company housing.

**Gropius, Walter,* BAUHAUSBAUTEN IN DESSAU. Bauhausbücher no. 12. Munich, 1931. Descriptions and photographs of the Bauhaus School, the professors' houses, and the Törten housing development, Dessau.

*_Schallenberger, J. and E. Gutkind_, BERLINER WOHNBAUTEN DER LETZTEN JAHRE. Berlin, 1832. Photographs, plans and financial set-ups of post-war housing in Berlin.

*_Schumacher, Fritz_, DAS WERDEN EINER WOHNSTADT. Hamburg, 1932. Post-war housing and city-planning in Hamburg, by the man who was responsible. Fully illustrated.

D. Unemployed Colonization (pre-Nazi)

Muesmann, Prof. Adolf, ed., DIE UMSTELLUNG IN SIEDLUNGSWESEN. Stuttgart, 1932. Theory and practice of the 'Stadtrandsiedlung' or subsistence homestead.

DIE ZUKUNFT DER DEUTSCHEN SIEDLUNG. Published by the Freie Deutsche Akademie des Städtebaues. Berlin, 1932. Pamphlet on the technique and requirements of the suburban garden colony.

Migge, Leberecht, DIE WACHSENDE SIEDLUNG NACH BIOLOGISCHEN GESETZEN. Stuttgart, 1932. A small scientific book on intensive gardening, by one of the best German landscape architects. Closer to Kropotkin than to Nazi colonization methods.

Wagner, Dr. Martin, DAS WACHSENDE HAUS. Berlin, 1932. Illustrated catalog, with critical articles, for the Berlin Exposition, Sonne Licht und Luft für Alle, 1932. From week-end cottages to subsistence homesteads.

E. Publications Whose Files are Worth Looking Through

*_Die Form_, Berlin. Organ of the Deutsche Werkbund.

Baugilde, Berlin. Organ of the German Architects' Association (BDA).

Bauwelt, Berlin.

Die Wohnung, Berlin.

Wohnungswirtschaft, Stuttgart.

Moderne Bauformen, Stuttgart.

V. HOLLAND: POST-WAR HOUSING

Berlage, Keppler, Kromhout and Wils, ARBEIDERSWONINGEN IN NEDERLAND. Rotterdam, 1921. Photographs, plans and costs of Dutch housing — much of it from the romantic 'Amsterdam' period.

*AMSTERDAM: DEVELOPMENT OF THE TOWN HOUSING IMPROVEMENT. Published by the city of Amsterdam, 1924. Includes descriptions of the experimental 'concrete village.' English translation.

SLUM CLEARANCE IN AMSTERDAM. Published by the municipal housing department, Amsterdam, 1930. Plans and photographs.

Nederlandsch Instituut voor Volkshuisvesting en Stedebouw, Amsterdam. Publishes many reports on Dutch housing, particularly the monthly magazine, *Tijdschrift voor Volkshuisvesting en Stedebouw*. Also published by the Institute:

*DE WONINGWET, 1902–1929. A large book which illustrates all the best Dutch housing achievement. Amsterdam, 1930.

HET NIEUWE LAND: DE OPBOUW VAN DE WIERINGERMEER. Amsterdam, 1932. Community housing projects for the land reclaimed from the Zuider Zee.

**Oud, J.J.P.*, HOLLANDISCHE ARCHITEKTUR. Bauhausbücher no. 10. Munich, 1926. (Enlarged edition, 1929.) Modern 'functional' architecture in Holland, by one of the best modern architects in Europe.

Hitchcock, H. R., Jr., J. J. P. OUD. In the series 'Les Maîtres de L'Architecture d'Aujourd'hui.' Paris, 1931. Monograph on Oud's work.

Van Loghem, J. B., BOUWEN: HOLLAND. Amsterdam, 1932. Modern architecture in Holland, with sub-titles in four languages, including English.

VI. FRANCE: POST-WAR HOUSING

Sellier, Henri, LA CRISE DU LOGEMENT ET L'INTERVENTION PUBLIQUE. 4 vols. Paris, 1921. The shortage, physical conditions, and governmental measures. Not illustrated.

Sellier, Henri, and A. Bruggeman, LE PROBLEME DU LOGEMENT. Published by the Carnegie Foundation for International Peace. Ca. 1930. Further history of French housing measures and the crisis.

Office Public d'Habitations à Bon Marche du Departement de la Seine. Paris. Reports and Publications.

Garnier, Tony, UNE CITE INDUSTRIELLE: Etude Pour la Construction des Villes. Lyons. Early ideas on modern housing and architecture by one of the vanguard.

**Le Corbusier*, VERS UNE ARCHITECTURE. Paris, 1923. Published in London and New York, 1928, as TOWARDS A NEW ARCHITECTURE. One of the classics of modern architecture.

Le Corbusier, URBANISME. Paris, 1925. Published in London and New York, 1929, as THE CITY OF TOMORROW. The sky-scraper Utopia.

**Stonorov and Boesiger*, LE CORBUSIER UND PIERRE JEANNERET: Ihr Gesamtes Werk von 1910 bis 1929. Zürich, 1930. Monograph on the work of Le Corbusier.

Giedieon, Siegfried, BAUEN IN FRANKREICH, EISEN UND EISENBETON. Leipzig. Modern construction methods and architecture in France.

Lurçat, André, ARCHITECTURE, Paris, 1929. A book on modern architecture by one of the best modern architects.

Publications:

L'Esprit Nouveau, Paris. (1920–1925.) Le Corbusier's theories of modern architecture first expounded.

Plans, Paris. (1931–1932.) Includes much later Le Corbusier material.

Urbanisme, Paris. See particularly Sept.–Oct., 1932, for descriptions and illustrations of housing by the Seine department, and also Paris slum-clearance.

**L'Architecture Vivante*, Paris.

L'Architecture d'Aujourd'hui, Paris.

VII. OTHER COUNTRIES: POST-WAR HOUSING

Société Nationale des Habitations et Logements a Bon Marché. Brussels. *Reports* of the Conseil d'Administration. Government-aided housing in Belgium.

**Byggmästeren*, Stockholm. Monthly architectural and technical magazine, largely devoted to modern architecture and housing.

*HSB, Stockholm. One of the largest and most successful co-operative housing societies in the world. Publishes many reports and illustrated pamphlets.

Swedish Exposition of 1930, Stockholm. Catalogues. Much experimental modern housing was shown at this Exposition.

**Arkitekten*, Copenhagen. An architectural magazine whose files would show most of the best of Danish housing and modern architecture.

*BOLIGARBEIDET GJENNEN TYVE ÅR, 1911–1931. Published by the Oslo Kommunale Boligråd. Oslo, 1932. A complete illustrated history of Oslo's remarkable municipal housing achievement.

*_Ruf, Dr. Walter,_ DIE GEMEINNÜTZIGEN BAUGENOSSENSCHAFTEN DER SCHWEIZ. Schriften des Schweizerisches Verbands für Wohnungswesen und Wohnungsreform no. 5. Zürich ca. 1929. Illustrated history of co-operative housing in Switzerland.

*_Das Werk,_ Zürich. One of the best architectural magazines in Europe. See particularly the housing number, May, 1933.

Schweitzerische Bauzeitung, Zürich. A technical architectural magazine, with much material on housing.

*_Danneberg, Robert,_ VIENNA UNDER SOCIALIST RULE. Vienna, 1928. English translation. Detailed account of municipal housing and other activities under the Socialist government.

*DIE WOHNUNGSPOLITIK DER GEMEINDE WIEN. Vienna, 1929. Brief illustrated history of post-war housing in Vienna.

DAS NEUE WIEN, 1926–1928. 4 volumes. Vienna ca. 1929.

KOOPERATION IM SYSTEM DER WOHNUNGSWIRTSCHAFT IN DER SOWJETUNION. Moscow, 1929. A pamphlet describing how co-operative methods have been introduced into Soviet housing practice.

Kaganovich, L. M., THE SOCIALIST RECONSTRUCTION OF MOSCOW AND OTHER CITIES IN THE U.S.S.R. New York, 1931. Present state of municipal services in Moscow and other towns, with plans for their future extension.

Rodin, A., MOSCOW, OF TOMORROW. Moscow, 1932. English pamphlet describing the plans for the Moscow region, including housing. Megalopolis is still the ideal.

Kholodny, T., MOSCOW OLD AND NEW. Moscow and Leningrad, 1933. Illustrated pamphlet.

VIII. AMERICA: THE HOUSING PROBLEM

Report of the U. S. Housing Corporation, Henry V. Hubbard, Ed., 2 vols. Washington, 1919. Illustrated history of the first large-scale governmental experiment in housing.

Whitaker, C. H., THE JOKE ABOUT HOUSING. Boston, 1920.

Aronovici, Carol, HOUSING AND THE HOUSING PROBLEM. National Social Science Series, 1920.

Magnussen, Leifur, HOUSING BY EMPLOYERS IN THE UNITED STATES. Washington, 1920. 'Model' company housing.

Magnussen, Leifur, THE HOUSING SITUATION IN THE UNITED STATES. Geneva: International Labour Office, 1925.

*Regional Planning Number, *Survey Graphic,* May, 1925. An attempt to relate the new needs in housing, community planning, city planning, and regional planning, by various members of the Regional Planning Association of America.

Final Report of the *New York State Housing and Regional Planning Commission,* 1926. Basis for a realistic State plan.

New York State Housing Board. Reports from 1929 to date. Housing by limited dividend societies in New York city. See particularly material on Amalgamated Clothing Workers' developments.

Holden, Arthur C., with *Clarence Stein and Henry Wright,* A PRIMER OF HOUSING. New York, 1927. A good graphic analysis, as far as it goes.

**Wood, Dr. Edith Elmer,* RECENT TRENDS IN AMERICAN HOUSING. New York, 1931. A comprehensive and sound statement of the problem, and a history of the experiments. Emphasis on social and economic aspects rather than political or architectural. With a good American bibliography.

Editors of *Fortune,* HOUSING AMERICA. New York, 1932. A dramatic statement of the problem peters out into a weak and limited solution.

President's Conference on Home Building and Home Ownership. 10 Vols. Washington, 1932. Reports are very uneven. The best is that of the Committee on Large Scale Operations, in Volume II.

Stein, Clarence S., HOUSING. Article in the Encyclopedia Britannica under the heading Social Architecture. A useful summary.

Wright, Henry, THE AUTOBIOGRAPHY OF ANOTHER IDEA. *Western Architect,* September, 1930. Description of the plan for Radburn, New Jersey.

Mumford, Lewis, MASS-PRODUCTION AND THE MODERN HOUSE. *Architectural Record,* January and February, 1930. Why technology and big business can never 'solve' the housing problem.

Stein, Clarence S., OUTLINE OF COMMUNITY HOUSING PROCEDURE. *Architectural Forum,* 3 issues, winter, 1932–1933.

Wright, Henry, WHAT DOES THE ARCHITECT KNOW ABOUT SMALL HOUSE COSTS? *Architectural Record,* December, 1931 and February, 1932.

Wright, Henry, THE SAD STORY OF AMERICAN HOUSING, and A MANUAL OF HOUSING, I and II, in *Architecture,* March, July and August, 1933. Illuminating technical analysis.

Corey, Lewis C., LAND SPECULATION. Article in the Encyclopedia of Social Sciences, Volume IX. A good general analysis.

Laidler, Harry W., PUBLIC OWNERSHIP HERE AND ABROAD. L.I.D. New York, 1933.

Bemis, A. F., and J. Burchard, THE EVOLVING HOUSE: A HISTORY OF THE HOME. Cambridge, Mass., 1933. A lengthy history of the dwelling house greatly weakened by the American habit of treating a house as a completely self-sufficient object, existing in a void.

Bemis, Albert Farwell, THE ECONOMICS OF SHELTER. Cambridge, 1934. Statistical analysis of present housing methods, not leading anywhere in particular except to the 'mass-produced house.'

*NEW HOMES FOR A NEW DEAL: A complete program for slum clearance and housing relief. A pamphlet reprinted from articles in the *New Republic* by Albert Mayer, Henry Wright and Lewis Mumford. New York, Spring, 1934. A good statement which does not quite come to grips with the political problems involved.

LAW AND CONTEMPORARY PROBLEMS: LOW-COST HOUSING AND SLUM CLEARANCE. Duke University, March, 1934. Studies of varying value.

Jeanes, W. W., HOUSING OF UNION HOSIERY WORKERS IN PHILADELPHIA. Philadelphia, 1933. A concrete, detailed survey of housing conditions among members of the American Federation of Full-Fashioned Hosiery Workers, preparatory to designing their housing project.

IT IS impossible at this complex initial stage of the housing movement in America to present anything like an adequate selective bibliography of current reports, surveys, releases, articles, programs, pamphlets, etc. The history of this period in American housing will have to be written later on. For news and lists of the latest reading-matter on the subject, however, consult the *Monthly Letter* of the *Housing Information Bureau of* the *Welfare Council of New York City*, and also *Millar's Housing Letter*, published in Washington. For critical and technical analysis, see the *Housing Study Bulletin* of the *Housing Study Guild*, New York. Most of the projects now being built or considered have been illustrated at one time or another in the *Architectural Record* or the *Architectural Forum*, both published in New York. National organizations whose releases or publications should be of general interest to anyone concerned with American housing problems are the *National Association of Housing Officials*, with headquarters in Chicago, the *National Public Housing Conference*, centered in New York, and the *Labor Housing Conference*, located in Philadelphia.

INDEX

INDEX

INDEX

CATHERINE BAUER (1905–1964) was an influential lobbyist for federally sponsored public housing and helped draft the Housing Act of 1937. She held key roles in organizations such as the Regional Planning Association of America and served as architecture consultant for the Museum of Modern Art. She taught at Harvard University and the University of California Berkeley.

BARBARA PENNER is professor in architectural humanities at the Bartlett School of Architecture, University College London. She is author of *Bathroom* and has coedited many books on gender, space, and architecture. She is a contributing editor to *Places Journal.*

A

B

C

'HOUSING': GERMANY, ENGLAND, HOLLAND

A. A row of apartments by Walter Gropius in the Siemensstadt development, Berlin. B. Houses grouped around a cul-de-sac at Welwyn Garden City, by C. M. Hennell and C. H. James. C. Flats at the Hook of Holland, by J. J. P. Oud.

A

B, C

D

EARLY ANTECEDENTS OF MODERN HOUSING

A. Naarden, typical late-mediæval Dutch town-planning. B. The Fuggerei, built in Augsburg in 1519. C. One of several planned cul-de-sac streets from seventeenth-century Lübeck. D. Nyboder, a Copenhagen housing scheme from 1630. (*Photos:* A, *KLM;* B, *Staatliche Bildstelle.*)

A

B

C

ENGLAND: BLACK, GRAY, AND GREEN

A. Industrial slum at Preston, late nineteenth century. B. Speculative 'By-Law' slum in London, around 1900; this type sometimes reached a density of 50 houses per acre. C. Post-war municipal housing at Nottingham, 12 per acre. (*Photos:* A *and* C, *Aerofilms;* B, *Ewing Galloway.*)

3

A

B

C

THREE KINDS OF METROPOLITAN SLUM

A. Central chaos. (This particular 'insanitary area' has been cleared by the London County Council.) B. Philanthropic 'model tenements' from the seventies, a built-in slum. C. The chaos of uncontrolled expansion; comprehensive planning is the only cure.

A

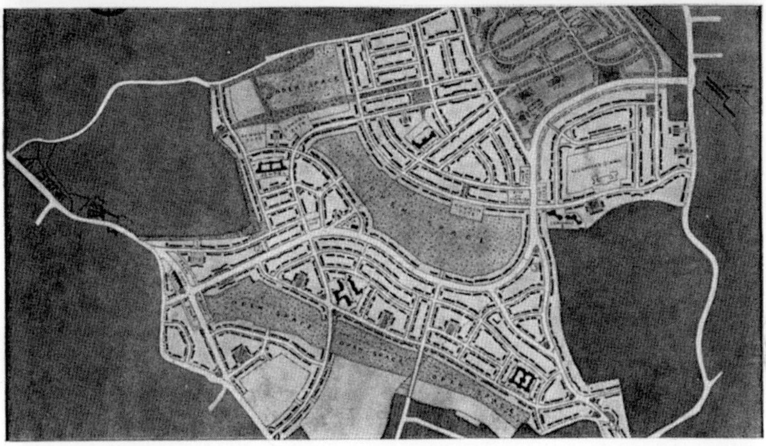

B

C

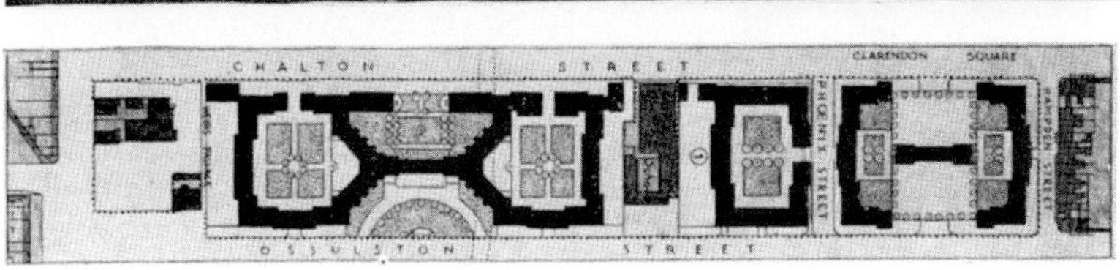

D

LONDON: PREVENTION AND CLEARANCE

A. London County Council housing at Roehampton. B. Council housing at Downham; unbuilt areas are permanent open space. C and D. The Ossulston Estate, a slum-clearance scheme. Costs twice as much per unit as good housing on new land. (*Photos: London County Council.*)

A

B

C

HOUSES DO NOT FACE ON TRAFFIC STREETS

A. A cul-de-sac in a Council housing development at Ruislip-Northwood, by A. S. Soutar. B and C. Typical groups of small houses at Welwyn Garden City. C was designed by L. de Soissons and A. Kenyon.

A

B

'NOTHING GAINED BY OVERCROWDING'

A. A housing scheme by Percy Houfton for the Bolsover Colliery, in 1895. The houses face inward on the walks and common. Large blocks with interior open space were also used at Port Sunlight. B. A typical post-war housing development from Nottingham, showing the large blocks with indented culs-de-sac. All the schools are here grouped in the center. (*Photos:* A, *Arthur Hobart;* B, *Aerofilms.*)

A

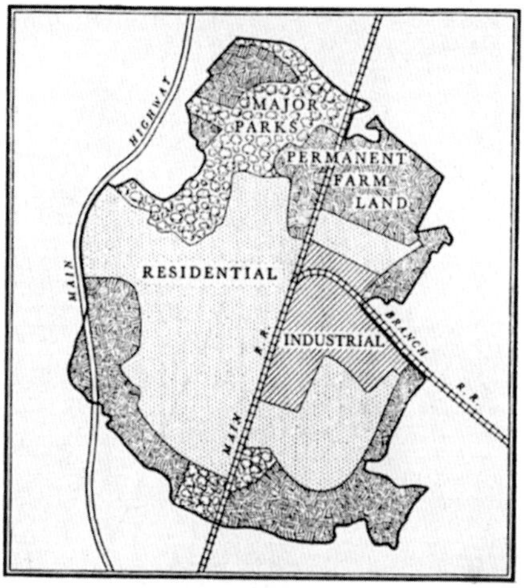

B, C

D

PLANNED TOWNS PRESERVE THE COUNTRY

A. Houses overlooking the common at Bournville, founded by George Cadbury. B. An open-air school at Welwyn. C. Use-plan of Welwyn Garden City. D. Part of Norton Common, Letchworth, Garden City. (*Photos:* A, *Harold Baker Ltd.*; B, *F. R. Yerbury;* D, *Julian Taylor.*)

A

B

C

D

PLANNED TOWNS REVIVE URBANITY

A. A group of flats around a closed court at Welwyn. B. Council houses at Welwyn, by L. de Soissons. C. Typical speculators' road-rash, neither town nor country. D. Traditional urbanity in England: the old village of Blanchland. (*Photos:* C, *Aerofilms;* D, *Mr. Thomas Sharpe.*)

A

B

C

HOLLAND: THREE VIEWPOINTS ON 'STYLE'

A. Co-operative housing in Amsterdam, 1923, by one of the romantic moderns, P. Kramer. B. Reworking a good vernacular tradition: municipal housing in The Hague. C. Shops in a Rotterdam municipal development by J. J. P. Oud, 1922. (*Photo:* C, *Museum of Modern Art.*)

A

B, C

D

AMSTERDAM HAS A NEW TRADITION

A. A group of middle-class apartments by H. P. Berlage, who was influenced by Frank Lloyd Wright. B. Slum-clearance in the oldest section. C. Co-operative housing by de Klerk, leader of the romantics. D. 'The concrete village,' Watergraafsmeer, a large-scale municipal experiment.

A

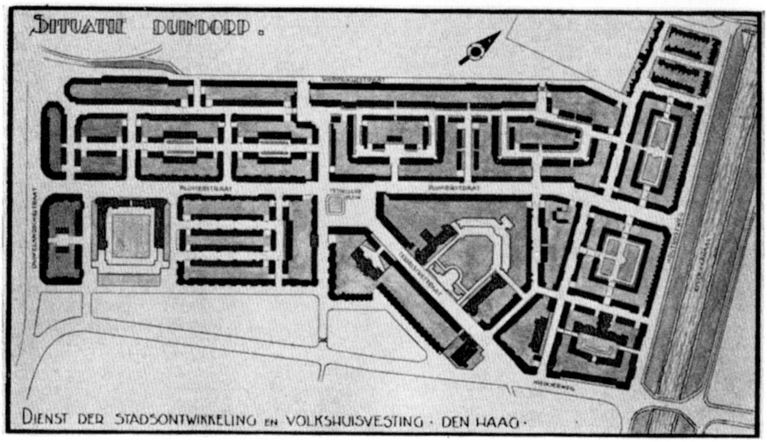

B

C

THE HAGUE: A GOOD BRICK VERNACULAR

A and B. A municipal housing development, Duindorp. The central buildings on the plan are schools. Although much denser than English housing, its simplicity and directness give it more character than have most of the latter. C. Court in a co-operative block of apartments.

A

B

C

CITY HOUSING IN ROTTERDAM: KIEFHOEK

A slum-clearance development for lowest-income workers with large families, designed by the city architect J. J. P. Oud. Two playgrounds, shops, an administrative building and a chapel (c) are part of the community. (*Photos:* A, *KLM;* B *and* C, *Van Ojen.*)

A

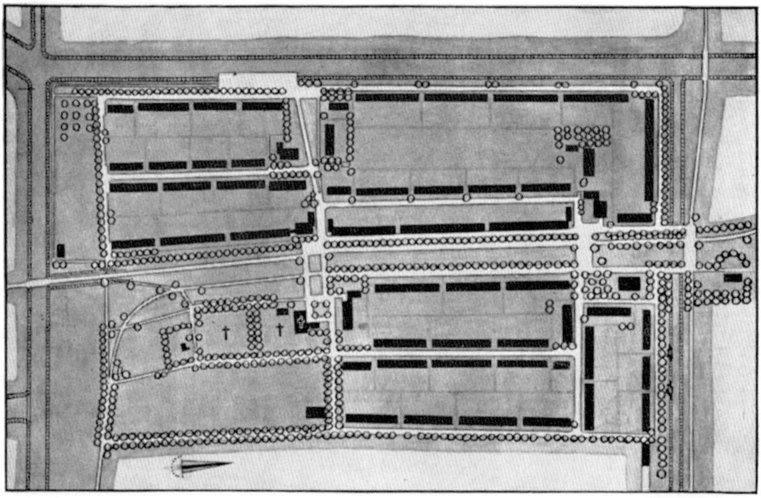

B

C

FOR THE BOTTOM OF THE ZUIDER ZEE

This enormous reclaimed area is being completely planned from the start. A. The first houses built on the new land. B. Typical plan for a new village. C. Houses at Vreewijk near Rotterdam, by Granpré-Molière, who will build many of the Zuider Zee villages. (*Photo:* A, *KLM.*)

A 

B 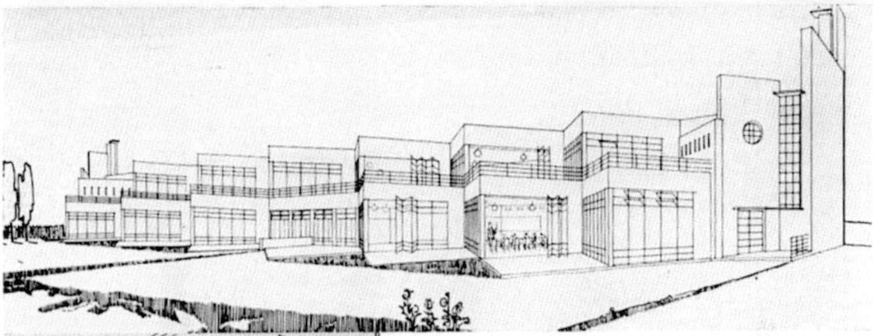

C, D 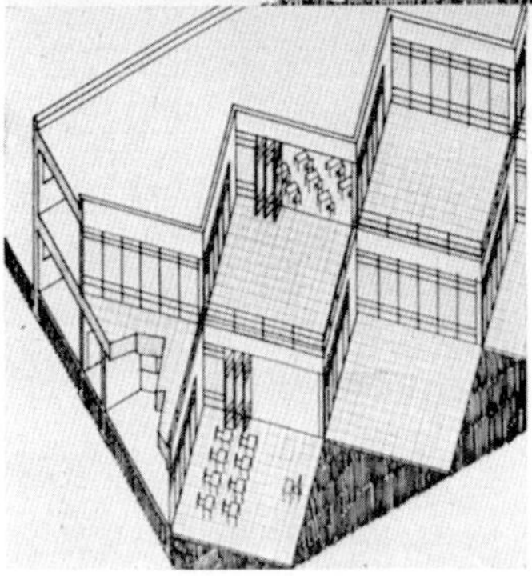 

E 

MODERN SCHOOLS IN HOLLAND

A. Open-air municipal school in Amsterdam. B and C. Project for a new Amsterdam school from the city architect's office. D. A glass and concrete Amsterdam school by the architect Duiker. E. One of the numerous modern schools in Hilversum by the town architect, Dudok.

A

B

C

HOUSING IN BELGIUM

Most Belgian housing is conservative, and presents few innovations in plan or architecture. Much of it, however, maintains a good cottage tradition. The illustrations are from a development at Boitsfort by the society 'Le Logis.' C shows a rear 'alley.'

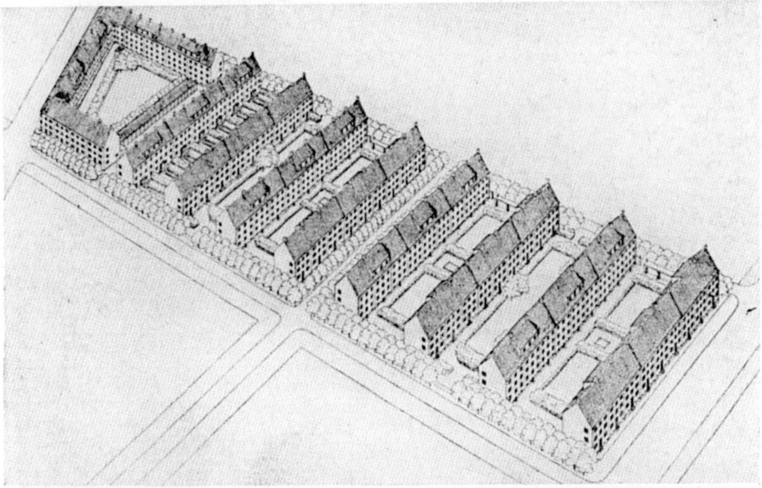

A

B

C

DENMARK IS AN ORDERLY COUNTRY

A. A co-operative housing development in Copenhagen, planned by Paul Baumann, with apartments in open rows. B shows typical rear gardens. C. Community housing for a religious society, centering around the uncompleted Grundtvig's Church. (*Photo:* C, *Flyverkorpset.*)

A

B

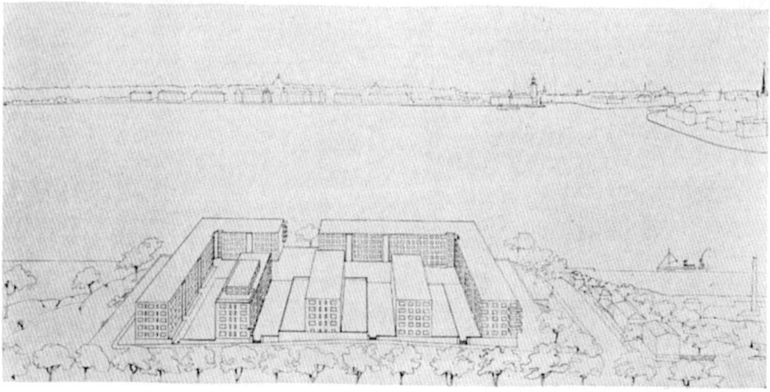

C

OSLO AND STOCKHOLM

A. One of the very large number of municipal apartment houses in Oslo.

B and C. A block of apartments in Stockholm by the H.S.B., one of the largest co-operative housing societies in the world. (The H.S.B. also maintains summer resorts at the seashore for its members.)

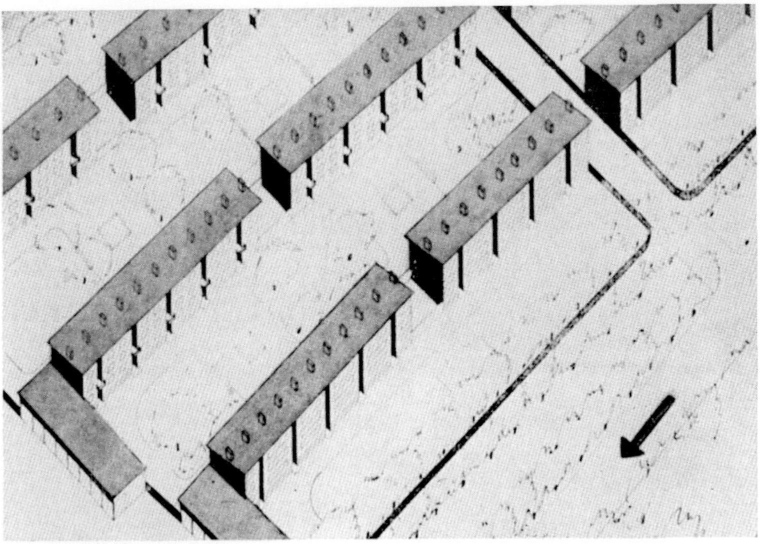

A

B

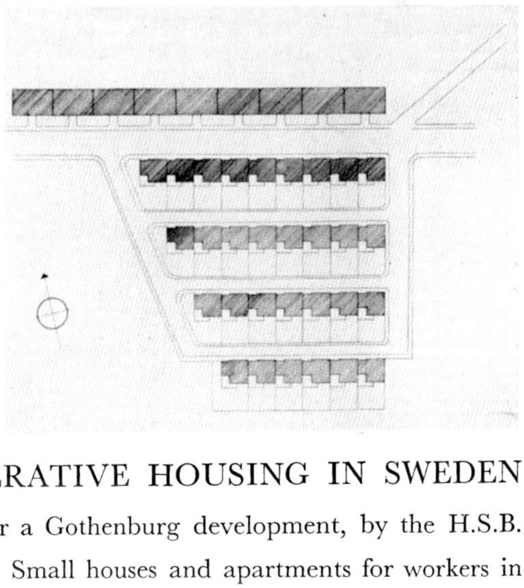

C, D

MODERN CO-OPERATIVE HOUSING IN SWEDEN

A. Open-row planning for a Gothenburg development, by the H.S.B. housing society. B and D. Small houses and apartments for workers in the Co-operative Society's flour-mill (C) at Hästholmen, on a rocky promontory near Stockholm. The architect is Eskil Sundahl.

A

B

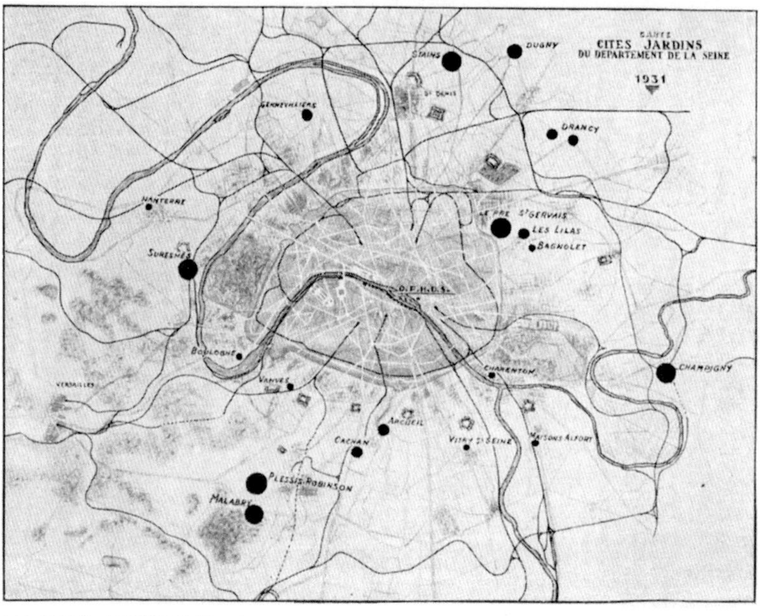

C

PARIS: THREE CHAPTERS IN CITY-BUILDING

A. Costly window-dressing: the Boulevard Haussmann. B. Meanwhile congested upper-class apartments straggle off into 'the zone,' Paris slum belt. C. But the Seine Department's housing developments make the new move toward re-centralization. (*Photos: Cie. Aér. Française.*)

A

B, C

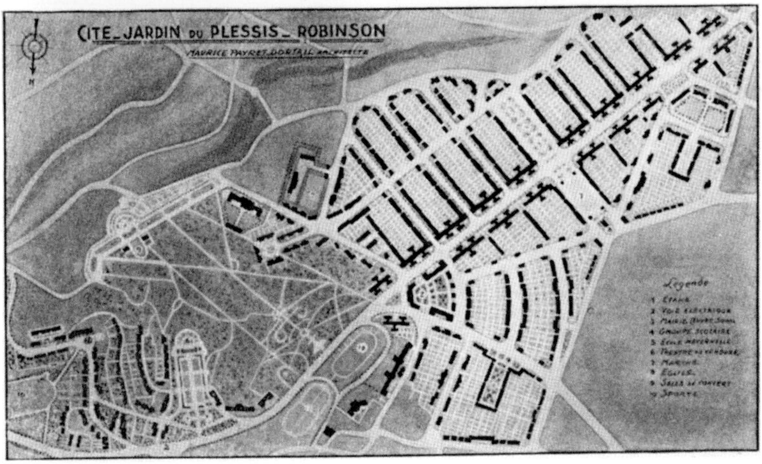

D

PARIS: PLESSIS-ROBINSON

A complete residential town for 25,000 people, built by the Housing Office of the Seine Department. It includes schools, markets, churches, an open-air theater, social halls, parks and individual gardens. Note the studios for artists in C. (*Photo:* A, *Cie. Aérienne Française.*)

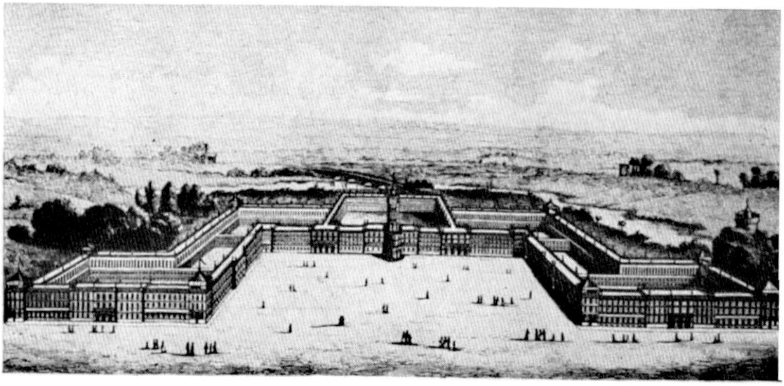

A

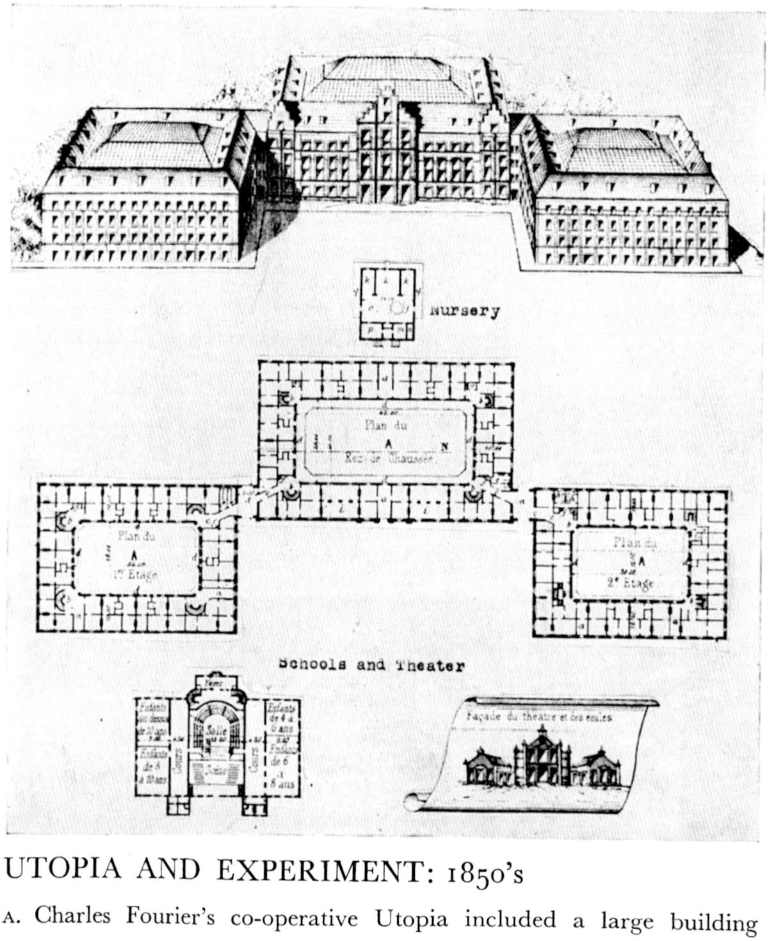

B

UTOPIA AND EXPERIMENT: 1850's

A. Charles Fourier's co-operative Utopia included a large building complex (*Phalanstère*) to provide living, working and recreation space for 2000 persons, all parts connected by covered galleries. Of the many experiments inspired by this dogmatic social planner, the one at Guise was the most enduring. B. One unit of the *Familistère* at Guise, erected by Charles Godin in connection with his co-operative heating apparatus plant. Each flat has cross-ventilation and opens onto an outside corridor much like those in modern Germany.

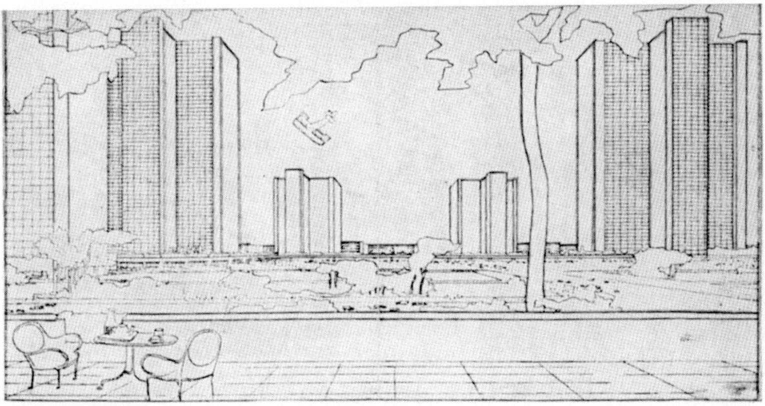

A

B

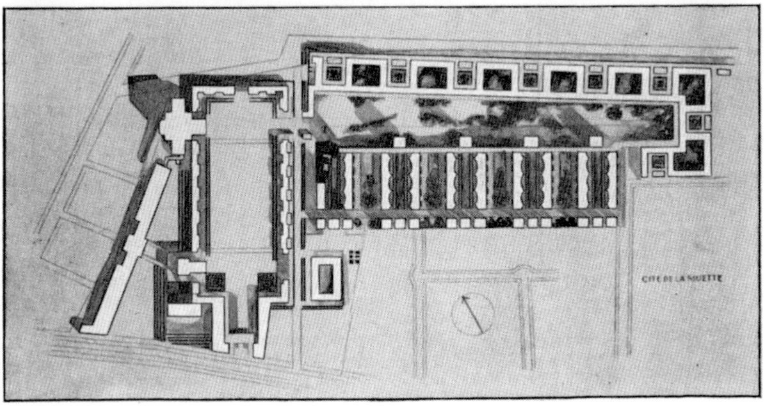

C

UTOPIA AND EXPERIMENT: 1930's

A. Le Corbusier would use modern technology to replace the chaotic congestion of nineteenth-century Paris with majestic, widely spaced skyscrapers. This ideal, whether it is a valid 'modern' Utopia or not, has influenced many paper projects and several experiments. B and C. Progress photograph and plan of the Cité La Muette, erected by the Department of the Seine near Paris, with four sixteen-story towers flanking the central open space, to the north of the three-story rows.

A

B

FROM 'UTILITARIAN' TO 'FUNCTIONAL'

A. Philanthropic co-operative community at Mulhouse, *ca.* 1860, famous early 'model housing.' Planned by Müller and Cacheux, it included schools, public baths and laundry, etc. Its honest utilitarian character is closer to the best 'modern' housing than much of the later gingerbread-romantic. B. The Rothenberg *Siedlung* at Kassel, 1930–32, planned by Otto Haesler. Oriented rows in a super-block; balconies; variety of dwelling-plans; school and playground in the center; service buildings and shops on the periphery; steel construction. (*Photo:* B, *Museum of Modern Art.*)

A

B

C

BERLIN, 1930, 1914, 1900

A. Part of the 'Ideal Britz' development, built by Gehag, one of the great pre-Nazi trade-union housing societies. B. A speculative development built just before the war. C. Bayrischer Platz, the best there was at any price in Berlin, 1900. (*Photos:* B, *Hegemann;* C, *A.K.I.*)

A

B

C

TYPICAL MODERN BERLIN HOUSING

A. Apartments by Hans Scharoun in the Siemensstadt development, built by a municipal housing society. (For plan see page 179.) B. The *Siedlung* Zehlendorf, bordered by the municipal forest. C. Apartments by Paul Mebes. (*Photos:* A, *Museum of Modern Art;* B *and* C, *Köster.*)

A

B

C

LANDMARKS OF MODERNISM

A. The Bauhaus school at Dessau, by Walter Gropius, 1925: primary source of 'modernism' until its demise in 1933. B. Two houses by Le Corbusier in the Werkbund Exhibition, Weissenhof Siedlung, Stuttgart, 1927. C. Apartment by Miës Van der Rohe in the same Exhibition.

A

B

C

FRANKFURT ON THE MAIN

A. The Römerstadt development, separated from the city by a permanent park, reclaimed from marshland by the municipality. B. The nineteenth century, 'down by the railroad station.' C. The mediæval nucleus.

A

B

C

FRANKFURT-RÖMERSTADT

One of many developments directed by Ernst May as housing chief, put up by the city, and turned over to a semi-official society for management A. Looking from Frankfurt proper across the Nidda River. B, C. Rear gardens and front view. (*Photos: Collischonn.*)

A

B

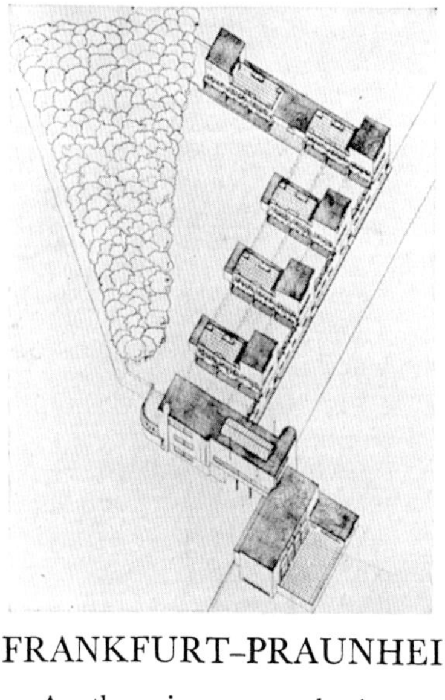 

C, D

FRANKFURT–PRAUNHEIM

A. Another view across the 'green belt.' B. One-family houses with a separate apartment above. C. The Praunheim 'pavilion school,' each classroom with a terrace. D. Frau Grete Lihotsky designed the *Frankfurter Küche*, whose equipment is sold complete, to fit Frankfurt kitchens.

A

B

C

SACHLICHKEIT VERSUS *ART NOUVEAU*

A. Römerstadt apartments from the rear, and a modern school. B. The Friedrich Ebert *Siedlung*, whose engineering-modernism is so 'pure' as to seem perhaps a trifle mechanical. C. 1910 co-operative housing in Frankfurt, with *Art Nouveau* façaderie. (*Photo:* A, *Wolff.*)

A

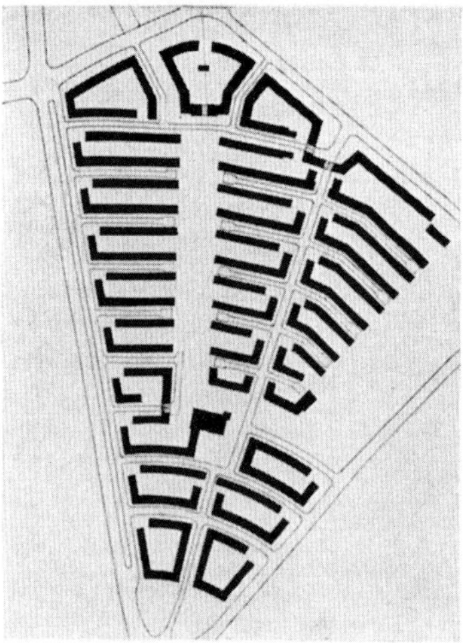

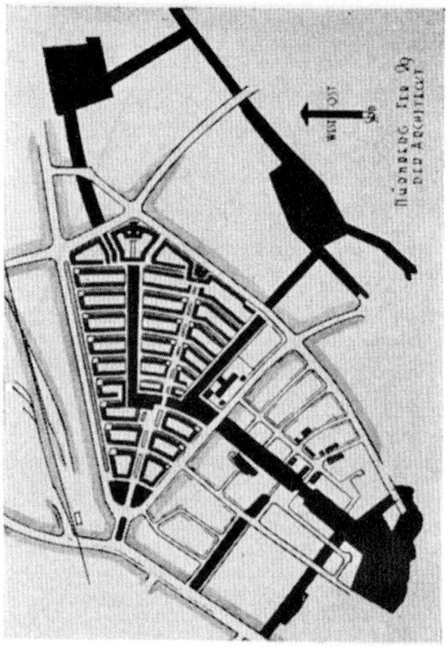

B, C

D

NUREMBERG PLANS CONTINUOUS PARKS

A and B. Municipal housing on a super-block plan, with dead-end streets and a broad central park, laid out by Oberbaurat Sorg. C. Showing how the park connects with other permanent green open spaces in the neighborhood. D. Using the end of an open row for artists' studios.

A

B, C

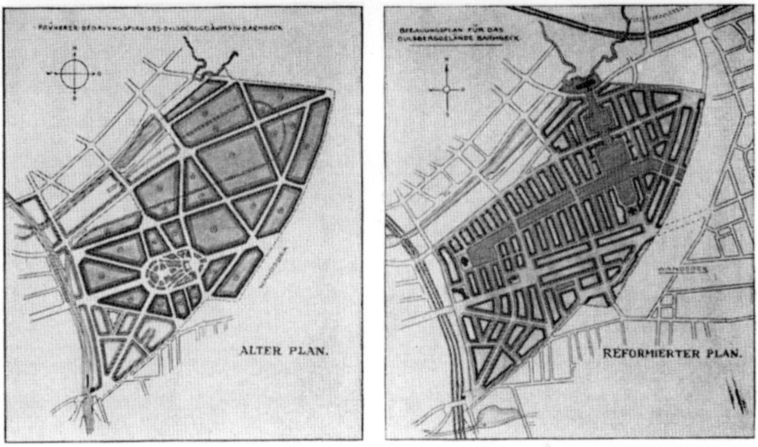

D

HAMBURG MODERNIZED HER CITY–PLAN

A and D. Municipal housing in Barmbeck, around a continuous central open space. B. The pre-war plan for this area, with a muddled street-layout. C. The new plan, by Hamburg's former planning chief, Dr. Fritz Schumacher. (*Photos:* A, *Baubehörde Hamburg;* D, *Dransfeld.*)

A

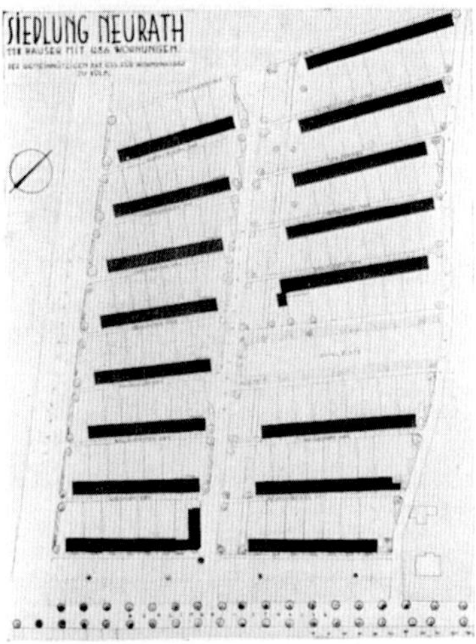

B, C

D

COLOGNE: SIEDLUNG NEURATH

A minimal housing development built by a public corporation in 1930. It has two-story flats, with extra bedrooms available in the attic story. A and D. The kindergarten, adjoining the playground. B. The plan, with oriented rows. C. View from the main street. (*Photos: Mantz.*)

A

B

C

COLOGNE: SIEDLUNG KALKERFELD

This development, more expensive than Neurath, was built in 1929, and designed by Riphahn and Grod. A. It includes apartments with roof terraces, and one-family houses. B. Model of the entire development. C. Interior of an apartment. (*Photos: Mantz.*)

A

B

C

MERSEBURG: RATIONAL DWELLING PLANS

A. Part of the large Bad Dürrenberg development (for plan see page 163), designed by Alexander Klein. On the right is an outside corridor in an apartment-house. B. View from kitchen to living-room. C. Study by Mr. Klein for one of the dwelling-plans. (*Photos: Krajewsky.*)

A

B

C

'VON WOLKENKRATZER ZUM BLOCKHAUS'

A. A German skyscraper project from the 1920's, by Walter Gropius. B. Ingenious one-story houses by Hugo Häring in the Vienna Werkbund Exposition of 1932. C. But the recent German 'subsistence homesteads' are *not* 'modern housing.' This is a Nuremberg *Randsiedlung*.

A

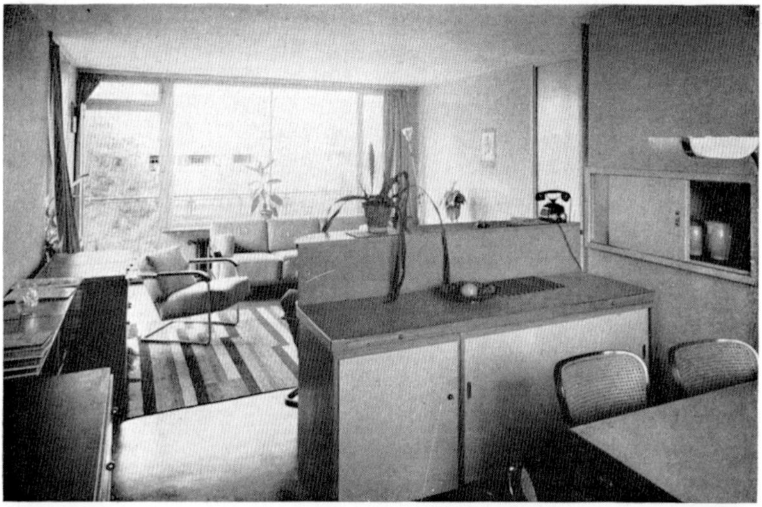

B

C

MODERN HOUSING IN SWITZERLAND

A. Eglisée, Basel, minimum housing built by 13 architects in collaboration, for the Swiss Housing Exhibition of 1930. B. Interior of a Neubühl apartment (see next plate). C. Utohof, housing by the city of Zürich, grouped around a cul-de-sac and a school. (*Photo:* A, *Aviatik Basel.*)

A

B

C

D
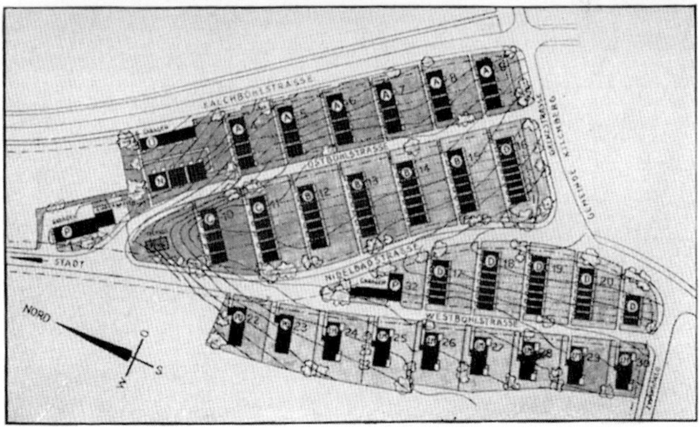

NEUBÜHL: A CO-OPERATIVE IN ZÜRICH

Planned by seven young architects, this development includes a maximum of choice in dwelling-types, a central plant for heat and hot water, a kindergarten, garages, and a restaurant. A. Apartments with balconies. B. One-family houses. C. Studio-houses for single people. D. Plan.

A

B, C

D

BUILT–IN SOCIAL FACILITIES: VIENNA

A. The Reumannhof, one of the large apartment complexes built by the socialist municipal government and rented to lowest-paid workers. B. Kindergarten in the Karl Marx Hof. C. Gymnasium in the Fuchsenfeld development. D. Wading pool at Fuchsenfeld.

A

B

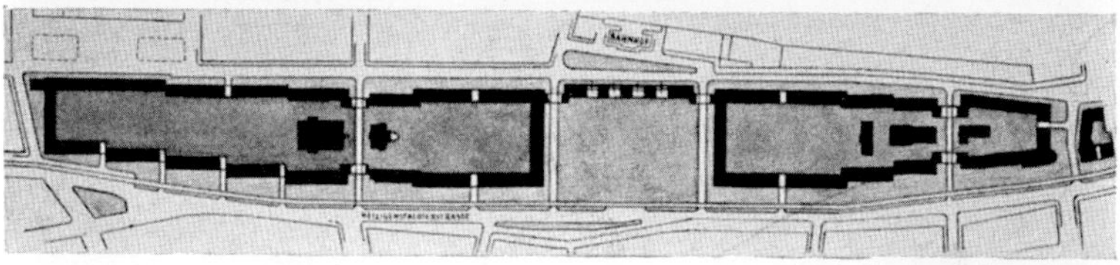

C

D

VIENNA: SOCIALIST AND IMPERIAL

A. The Karl Marx Hof, one of many municipal housing developments recently wrecked by the Fascists. B. Plan of the Karl Marx Hof, which housed 1500 families. C. Suburban housing by the municipality. D. Normal residential construction in Imperial days: will it return?

A

B

C

WORKERS' HOUSING IN THE U.S.S.R.

A. Part of the new city of Dnieprostroi under construction. Layout and architecture influenced by German housing technique. B. A Workers' Club in Moscow. C. Housing of a classical bent in Leningrad. (*Photos: Soviet Photo Agency.*)

A

B

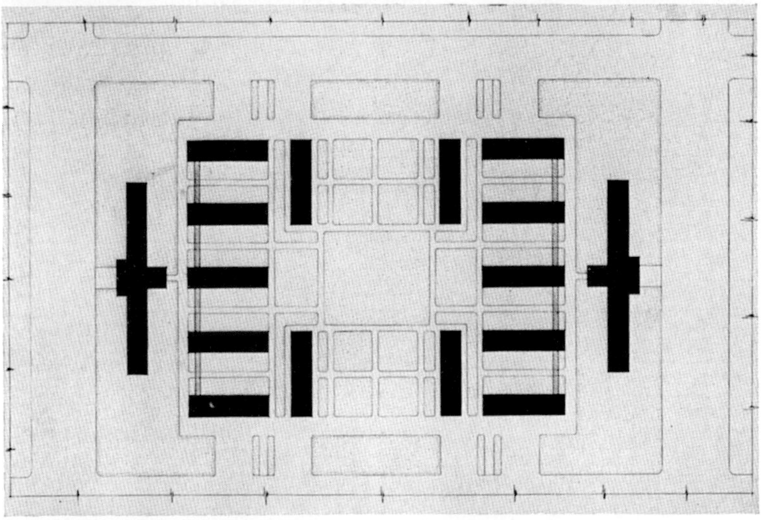

C

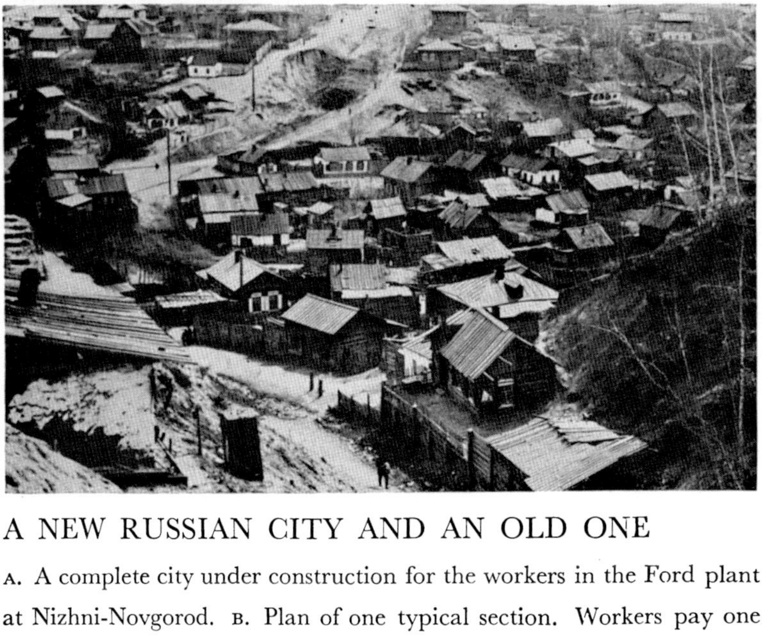

A NEW RUSSIAN CITY AND AN OLD ONE

A. A complete city under construction for the workers in the Ford plant at Nizhni-Novgorod. B. Plan of one typical section. Workers pay one tenth of their income for rent. C. Part of Novosibirsk before reconstruction. (*Photos: Soviet Photo Agency.*)

A

B

C

AMERICA: HERITAGE FROM THE PAST

A. *Outright slums.* This happens to be from a Pennsylvania mining town. B. *Blight, chaos, and dilapidation,* in any town that ever had a boom. This picture is typical of whole square miles of Chicago. C. *Megalopolitan congestion.* New York, homes of every income level.

A

B

C

TWENTIETH-CENTURY HOUSING IN AMERICA

A. 'Own Your Own Home.' (These particular houses in Queens were tax-exempt.) B. The façades may be Olde Englishe, Spanish-Type or variegated. C. New Law tenements in New York, the result of arduous 'reform.' *Only the luckiest third could pay for any of these.*

A

B

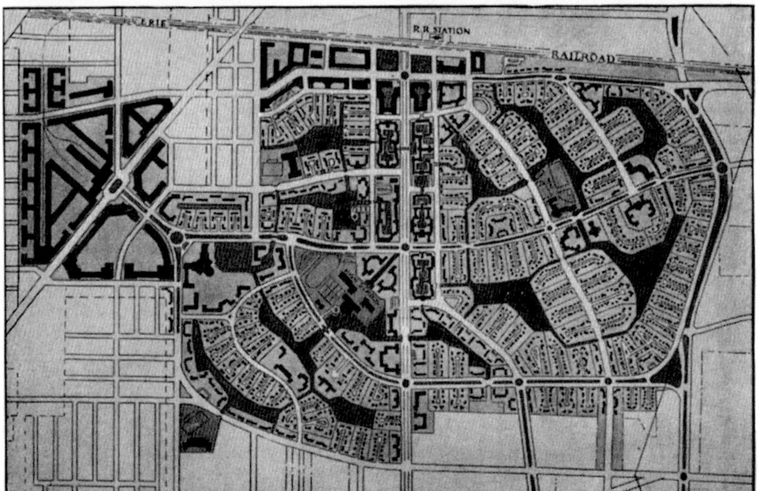

C

EXCEPTIONS TO THE AMERICAN NORM: I

Two developments by the City Housing Corporation, both planned by Clarence Stein, Henry Wright and associates. A and B. Sunnyside Gardens in Queens. C. Plan of Radburn, New Jersey. All houses face inward on connecting parks. (*Photos:* A, *Brown Bros.;* B, *Amemya.*)

A

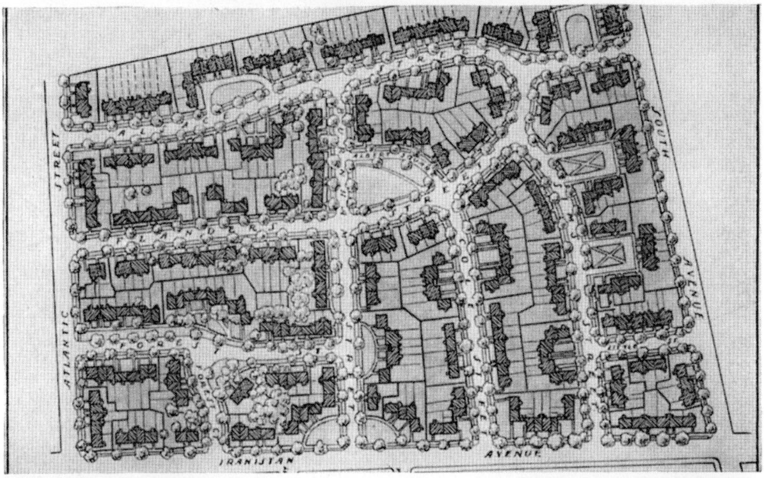

B

C

EXCEPTIONS TO THE AMERICAN NORM: II

A. Chatham Village, Pittsburgh, planned for the Buhl Foundation by Stein and Wright. B. Government war-housing in Bridgeport, Connecticut. C. The Phipps Garden Apartments in Long Island City, designed by Mr. Stein. (*Photos:* A, *Aerial Surveys;* C, *Wurts Bros.*)

A  PITTSBURGH

B  ROTTERDAM

C  THE BRONX

D  FRANKFURT

REAR YARDS: A SIMPLE PLANNING TEST

(*Photos:* A, *Rembrandt;* B, *Van Agtmaal;* D, *Ilse Bing.*)